MW01012586

FOUNDATIONS OF PLAY THERAPY

Second Edition

FOUNDATIONS OF PLAY THERAPY

Second Edition

EDITED BY
Charles E. Schaefer

WILEY
John Wiley & Sons, Inc.

Library of Congress Cataloging-in-Publication Data:

Foundations of play therapy / edited by Charles E. Schaefer.—2nd ed.
    p. cm.
  Includes bibliographical references and indexes.
    ISBNs 978-0-470-52752-8; 978-111-801324-3; 978-111-801325-0; 978-111-801326-7; 978-111-809478-5
    1. Play therapy. I. Schaefer, Charles E.
  [DNLM: 1. Play Therapy. WM 450.5.P7]
  RJ505.P6F68   2011
  618.92'891653—dc22
                                      2010039798

Printed in the United States of America
10 9 8 7 6 5 4 3 2 1

Contents

v

Preface

Play therapy has been the leading psychotherapeutic intervention with children since the beginning of the 20th century. The goal of *Foundations of Play Therapy, 2nd Edition* is to provide the reader with a comprehensive introduction to the field of play therapy.

The first part of the book, Fundamentals of Play Therapy Practice, is completely new. The chapters are designed to supply the basic information needed to understand and practice play therapy. Chapter 1 encompasses a number of the essential concepts and practices that all beginning play therapists need to master. Chapter 2 contains an overview of the therapeutic powers of play, that is, the change mechanisms that are the heart and soul of play therapy. The third chapter informs the reader about the clinical, professional, and ethical issues that are likely to arise in the practice of play therapy.

One of the strengths of Play Therapy is the diversity of theoretical approaches that are currently being applied in clinical practice with children and adolescents. These models offer a broad and firm foundation for the application of therapeutic play to the wide range of psychological problems experienced by youth.

Part II of the book contains a detailed description of the major theories of play therapy, including Psychodynamic Models, Humanistic Models, Systemic Models, as well as a number of Emerging Models. Each of the 18 chapters is written by a leading authority on the particular theoretical model. All of the chapters from the first edition have been revised and updated so as to present a state-of-the-art overview. In addition, four new theoretical chapters have been added to reflect the broad range of current models, namely, Narrative Play Therapy, Solution-Focused Play Therapy, Experiential Play Therapy, and Integrative Play Therapy.

Psychiatrists, psychologists, social workers, counselors, child life specialists, nurses, occupational therapists, and family therapists at all levels of training and experience will find *Foundations of Play Therapy, 2nd Edition* informative and clinically useful. Like the first edition, this book is likely to become an essential text for introductory courses and workshops on play therapy across the globe.

—Charles E. Schaefer

About the Editor

Charles E. Schaefer, PhD, RPT-S, is Professor Emeritus of Psychology at Fairleigh Dickinson University in Teaneck, New Jersey. He is cofounder and Director Emeritus of the Association for Play Therapy. He is also founder and codirector of the Play Therapy Training Institute in New Jersey. Dr. Schaefer coordinates an International Play Therapy Study Group held annually in Wroxton, England.

Among his books on play therapy are *Play Therapy for Preschool Children; Empirically-Based Play Interventions for Children; Contemporary Play Therapy; Short-Term Play Therapy for Children; The Playing Cure: Individualized Play Therapy for Specific Childhood Problems; Game Play; 101 Favorite Play Therapy Techniques; Adult Play Therapy, Adolescent Play Therapy; Play Therapy for Very Young Children;* and *Play Diagnosis and Assessment.* In 2006, he received the Lifetime Achievement Award from the Association for Play Therapy. Dr. Schaefer is a frequent presenter at national and international play therapy conferences. He has been a guest on the *Good Morning America, Today,* and *Oprah Winfrey* TV shows. His private practice in clinical child psychology is located in Hackensack, New Jersey.

Contributors

Athena A. Drewes, PsyD, RPT-S
Director of Clinical Training
Astor Services for Children and
*   Families*
Poughkeepsie, New York

Eliana Gil, PhD
Director of Clinical Services
Childhelp
Arlington, Virginia

Eric J. Green, PhD, LMFT, RPT-S
Assistant Professor, Dept. of Counseling
*   University of North Texas–Dallas*
Dallas, Texas

Heidi Gerard Kaduson, PhD, LLC
Private Practice
Monroe Township, New Jersey

Susan M. Knell, PhD
Clinical Psychologist
Spectrum Psychological Associates
Mayfield Village, Ohio

Terry Kottman, PhD, RPT-S
Director
The Encouragement Zone
Cedar Falls, Iowa

Garry L. Landreth, EdD, RPT-S
Regents Professor, Counselor
*   Education*
University of North Texas
Denton, Texas

Alan J. Levy, PhD, LCSW, DSNAP
Associate Professor
Loyola University, Chicago, School of
*   Social Work*
Chicago, Illinois

Evangeline Munns, PhD, RPT-S
Clinical Psychologist
Munns Psychological Consultant
*   Services*
King City, Canada

Julie Blundon Nash, PhD, RPT
On-Site Behavioral Health Director,
*   Foster Care*
Clinic Coordinator, Community Health
*   Center*
Middlesex County, Connecticut

Donald R. Nims, EdD, RPT-S
Professor of Counseling
Western Kentucky University
Bowling Green, Kentucky

Byron E. Norton, EdD, RPT-S
Family Psychological Services
Greeley, Colorado

Carol C. Norton, EdD, RPT-S
Family Psychological Services
Greeley, Colorado

Violet Oaklander, PhD
The Violet Solom Oaklander Foundation
Los Angeles, California

Kevin O'Connor, PhD, RPT-S
Distinguished Professor,
*   Director, Clinical PhD and PsyD*
*   Programs at Alliant International*
*   University*
Fresno, California

Cynthia A. Reynolds, PhD, RPT-S
Professor, Dept. of Counseling
University of Akron
Clinton, Ohio

Daniel S. Sweeney, PhD, RPT-S
George Fox University
Portland, Oregon

Aideen Taylor de Faoite, MA
Educational/School Psychologist
Tulla, Ireland

Laura J. Tejada, MS, RPT-S, LMFT, PCC, NCC
Doctoral Candidate in Marriage and
*   Family Therapy*
University of Akron
Akron, Ohio

Risë VanFleet, PhD, RPT-S
Director, Family Enhancement & Play
*   Therapy Center*
Boiling Springs, Pennsylvania

PART I

FUNDAMENTALS OF PLAY
THERAPY PRACTICE

Chapter 1

PLAY THERAPY
Basic Concepts and Practices
Julie Blundon Nash and Charles E. Schaefer

> *Oh, every child just once in their life should have this chance to spill themselves out all over without a "Don't you dare! Don't you dare! Don't you dare!"*
>
> *Jerry, age 7*

> *No. I don't have to break that window. I don't have to go on acting like I always have. I don't have to do everything just because I get the idea to do it. I don't have to hit people just because I feel like hittin' 'em. I guess it's because I didn't know before I could just feel mad and in a while it would go away—the bein' mad—and I would be happy again. I can change. I don't have to stay the same old way always because I can be different. Because now I can feel my feelings!*
>
> *Harold, age 8*

Jerry and Harold were clients of Virginia Axline, a leading figure in the world of play therapy (Axline, 1979, p. 520). These children entered therapy because of behavior problems and an inability to express their emotions in appropriate ways. Perhaps better than anyone, Jerry and Harold portray the true experience of play therapy as an opportunity to take control of the emotions that can sometimes run rampant. Their statements continue to ring true today, even as play therapy has evolved to include numerous theoretical orientations utilized around the world.

This chapter is intended to provide an overview of the basic concepts and practices of play therapy. Play therapy has a rich history dating back to Freud and the beginnings of psychoanalytic theory and is continually being developed and expanded. The following pages will define and describe play therapy, including the importance of using play in a therapeutic setting, the playroom and suggested materials, the stages of therapy, inclusion of caregivers, and the effectiveness of play interventions.

DEFINITION OF PLAY THERAPY

The Association for Play Therapy has defined *play therapy* as "the systematic use of a theoretical model to establish an interpersonal process wherein trained play therapists use the therapeutic powers of play to help clients prevent or resolve psychosocial difficulties and achieve optimal growth and development" (Association for Play Therapy, n.d.). This indicates that play therapy is a therapeutic modality firmly grounded in theoretical models. The major theories of play therapy will be described in detail later in this book. Some examples include psychoanalytic, child-centered, cognitive-behavioral, prescriptive, and family play therapy.

The definition of play therapy also indicates that play therapists strive to recognize, acknowledge, and utilize the therapeutic powers of play. These therapeutic powers, also known as change mechanisms, are the active forces within play that help clients overcome their psychosocial difficulties and achieve positive development.

IMPORTANCE OF PLAY THERAPY

The therapeutic powers of play can be classified into eight broad categories: communication, emotional regulation, relationship enhancement, moral judgment, stress management, ego boosting, preparation for life, and self-actualization. Chapter 2 contains a detailed description of the specific healing agents inherent in play. These change mechanisms form the foundation for the theoretical models and, thus are the heart and soul of play therapy.

Play has many benefits in life, regardless of age. Play is fun, educational, creative, and stress relieving and encourages positive social interactions and communication. When playing, children learn to tolerate frustration, regulate their emotions, and excel at a task that is innate. Children can practice new skills in a way that makes sense to them, without the structured confines of "the real world" or the need to use verbal language. There are no mistakes too big to overcome through play, and no challenges too tricky to attempt. Play gives children a chance to master their worlds as they create, develop, and maintain their own senses of self. Children use play to communicate when they do not have the words to share their needs and look to adults to understand their language. As Landreth (2002a) aptly pointed out, play is a child's language and toys are the words.

A BRIEF HISTORY OF PLAY THERAPY

Sigmund Freud, through his work with Little Hans, first brought the idea of therapeutic play into the practice of psychotherapy (Freud, 1909). Freud wrote that play serves three main functions: promotion of freer self-expression (especially of instincts considered taboo), wish fulfillment, and mastery of traumatic events. To master traumatic events through play, a child reenacts the event with a sense of power and control of the situation. This allows the child to bring repressed memories to consciousness and relive them while appropriately releasing affect. Termed abreaction, this process is different from catharsis because abreaction includes the reliving and mastering of the experience itself rather than the simple release of affect (Freud, 1892, as cited in Erwin, 2001). While some theorists have described catharsis in terms of a hydraulic theory of built-up negative energy that quickly discharges, more recent authors suggest that negative emotions are often brought out and released slowly as a child gradually assimilates the experience through repetitive play (Pulaski, 1974).

Melanie Klein continued the idea of using play for child therapy in a psychoanalytic framework. In particular, she believed that play allowed unconscious material to surface, and the therapist could then interpret the repressed wishes and conflicts to help the child understand his or her problems and needs. Klein agreed with the gradual approach to understanding and assimilating negative experiences as well as the need to relive and master such experiences through play (Klein, 1955). Klein worked with younger children than traditional psychoanalysts would see.

One technique that Klein (1955) pioneered involved the use of miniatures. When children play with miniature toys, they often feel a sense of control over these objects as the representation of real-world objects or people. Margaret Lowenfeld took this idea further and developed the World Technique. This technique involves a sand tray and access to water and miniature objects that represent larger scale items. Sandplay therapists typically have a wide selection of miniatures available, for example, people, animals, buildings, landscape items, methods of transportation, archetypes, and supernatural beings. In the World Technique, children are given the opportunity to create an imaginary world in which they can express whatever they desire. Children may develop realistic or fantastic worlds, peaceful or aggressive worlds, orderly or chaotic worlds (Lowenfeld, 1939). These sand trays are considered to be expressions of predominantly unconscious material and utilized as such in therapy.

Another psychoanalyst who used play therapeutically was Anna Freud (1946). She helped to bring child therapy, particularly child analysis, into a more widely used arena. She believed play was important because it enabled the therapist to establish a therapeutic alliance with the child. Similarly, recent research has suggested that a strong therapeutic relationship is necessary for effective therapy.

In the middle of the 20th century, Virginia Axline brought a more humanistic, person-centered approach to child and play therapy. In particular, Axline (1947) espoused the belief that the necessary conditions for therapeutic change were unconditional positive regard, empathic understanding, and authenticity. She also stated that children are better able to express their thoughts, feelings, and wishes through play than with words.

The following chapters will provide more details about these classical theories of play therapy, together with more recent models, including cognitive-behavioral, prescriptive, solution-focused, narrative, and integrative play therapies.

WAYS OF IMPLEMENTING PLAY THERAPY

Like traditional talk therapy, play therapy can be implemented in a variety of formats. For example, child-centered play therapists tend to utilize individual sessions with the child and allow the child the freedom to express himself or herself with little direction from the therapist. The role of the therapist is to encourage the child's appropriate expression of emotions and give the child a sense of control over the therapeutic relationship. Therapists who utilize other modalities, such as cognitive-behavioral play therapy, often structure the therapeutic process more, depending on the assessed needs of the child.

Filial therapists train parents to be cotherapists and implement the therapeutic process through parent–child interactions. Filial therapy sessions are similar to client-centered play therapy ones, but in the sessions the parents encourage positive interactions that will persevere beyond the constraints of the therapy room (Guerney, 2000). Family play therapy that utilizes other modalities (such as cognitive-behavioral or group approaches) to encourage involvement of caregivers has also been shown to be effective (Bratton, Ray, Rhine, & Jones, 2005).

Group play therapy has been applied to a number of presenting problems. Therapy groups may be either nondirective or directive in nature. In directive groups, sessions are typically psychosocial in nature and focus on a presenting issue that the children share in common, such as social skills deficits, acting out behaviors, or past trauma (e.g., Flahive & Ray, 2007; Spence, 2003; Sweeney & Homeyer, 1999).

APPLICATIONS OF PLAY THERAPY

Play therapy clients can be infants/toddlers (Schaefer, Kelly-Zion, McCormick, & Ohnogi, 2008), preschoolers (Schaefer, 2010), or elementary and high school students (Gallo-Lopez & Schaefer, 2005). Clients can come from many socioeconomic backgrounds, including those who are homeless (Baggerly & Jenkins, 2009). Play therapy can also be utilized with adult and elderly clients (Schaefer, 2003). While play therapy with adolescents and adults is continuing to gain popularity, most current therapeutic interactions are with children ages 3 to 12. Thus, *child* will be used throughout this chapter to designate the play therapy client.

Play therapy is a modality that can be truly flexible in its location. The space can be an outpatient clinic or office setting, a school (e.g., Ray, Henson, Schottelkorb, Brown, & Muro, 2008), a home, the scene of a disaster (e.g., Dripchak, 2007), a hospital bed (e.g., Li & Lopez, 2008), or a playground. Play therapy can take place in a fully stocked playroom or with materials pulled out of a suitcase. Play therapy is limited only by the extent of the therapist's flexibility and creativity.

THE PLAYROOM AND SUGGESTED MATERIALS

Playrooms vary greatly, depending on the setting of therapy and the therapist's needs and style. Theoretical orientation and type of therapy also contribute to the design of the play space. For example, therapists using Theraplay or group play therapy require a good amount of clear, open floor space. Landreth (2002a) has described ideal features of a playroom to be used for individual therapy sessions. He suggests 150 to 200 square feet of space; easily cleaned materials, furniture, and floors; shelves for toys and cabinets for extra supplies; a sink with running cold water; child- and adult-sized furniture; a desk or table for artwork; a marker or chalk board; and an attached bathroom.

In terms of play materials, the selection of toys and other items to be included certainly varies, depending on the therapist's theoretical orientation, personal ideas and values, and budget/space issues. There is a selection of basic items that are consistently useful. These include the following: animal families, baby doll (with bottle), dishes/plastic silverware, doll families, doll house or box with furniture, puppets, toy soldiers, blocks and other building materials, clay, art supplies (markers, crayons, large paper, tape, blunt scissors), small pounding hammer, two telephones or cell phones, doctor's kit, small soft ball, playing cards, small box with lid, and transportation toys (cars, airplane, ambulance, etc.). In addition to these items, such items as masks, mirrors, rope, dinosaurs, plastic tools, cardboard bricks, Lincoln logs, books, board games, a magic wand, dress-up clothes, and a sand tray and miniatures can also be beneficial.

Another useful feature of a playroom is separation of space. This might be achieved by variations in floor coverings, such as vinyl flooring near water or sand areas and carpets/area rugs in other spaces. Most play therapists like to separate materials by function to include a designated area for dollhouse play, another for sand trays, a third for puppets, and so on.

All other factors aside, predictability and consistency are perhaps the two most important features in a play space. Children should be able to know that the materials they need are available and easily located. If they keep encountering unfamiliar items, they will spend most of the therapy session exploring the items rather than playing with them (Kottman, 2001).

A general rule is that every item in the playroom should serve a therapeutic purpose. So, one should carefully select rather than haphazardly collect the play materials. Also, toys or games that are easily broken or expensive and games that are very complicated should be avoided (Kottman, 2001).

HOW TO BEGIN AND END A SESSION

While the process of play therapy is often intuitive to children, few parents know what to expect when they bring their child for individual play therapy. It is helpful to meet with parents without the child present to discuss presenting concerns as well as introduce parents to play therapy. An explanation to parents that children often cannot use words to express their feelings and problems and instead use play is usually well understood. Play therapy can then be described as a way to learn about the child's concerns and problems through play and to help the child find ways to overcome them.

For the child, initial sessions often include an introduction to the play space and therapeutic process. Both should be given at the child's developmental level and with appropriate amounts of information. Younger children are often happy to hear that the playroom is a space for them to play in many ways, while older children can understand more about the process. The amount of information given to a child is also dependent on the theoretical orientation of the therapist. For example, Theraplay therapists would likely provide very little introduction for the child, while other therapists might explain the reason the child is being brought for therapy, what is going to happen in session, and meeting times.

Children use the initial session to explore not only the play space but the therapist as well. Play therapists should generally allow the child to explore at his or her own pace and not give suggestions about which materials to use. During the first session, therapists should focus on developing rapport by creating a warm, comforting, safe environment for the child.

When ending a session, play therapists must decide whether a child will help pick up the toys or not. This is a personal and theoretically oriented decision. Nondirective therapists such as Virginia Axline would not encourage children to pick up the playroom. Instead, they gave a warning 5 minutes before the end of session so that the child can mentally prepare to leave.

For most children, announcing when 5 minutes remain is sufficient. Some children require more time to put themselves back together mentally and would benefit from a 10-minute warning followed by a 5-minute warning. This is something that is often dependent on the child's age and level of functioning.

LIMIT SETTING IN PLAY THERAPY

Although limits on a child's behavior in the playroom are generally kept to a minimum, they are needed on occasion for two main reasons: (1) to ensure the physical safety of the child and the therapist and (2) to prevent the destruction of the play materials and the playroom. Typically, play therapists do not state the limits in advance but only as the need arises. Thus, a play therapist might begin a session by saying to the child: "You can play with whatever you like in here! If there is anything you can't do, I'll let you know."

In stating a limit, the noted play therapist Haim Ginott (1959) recommended the following four-step procedure. First, help the child express his or her feelings or wishes underlying the misbehavior ("You're angry at me because you can't take the toy home").

Next, clearly and firmly state the limit (I'm not for hitting!"). Third, try to point out an acceptable alternative to the inappropriate behavior ("You can pound this clay to get your anger out"). Finally, enforce the limit as needed ("We have to end the play now because you still want to hit"). This procedure avoids the extremes of being too harsh or too soft in teaching children responsible behavior.

Limits are most often set on acts of physical aggression (either to therapist or materials), unsafe behaviors, and socially unacceptable behaviors (including inappropriate displays of affection; Landreth, 2002b). Limits should also be set when a child tries to take a toy from the playroom, as well as when engaging in disruptive behaviors such as continuing to play past the end of session or trying to leave early (Landreth, 2002b). Limits are often initially uncomfortable for play therapists to apply, but one can become skilled at it with practice and patience.

INCLUDING PARENTS AND CAREGIVERS

There is growing evidence that including parents in the therapeutic process is beneficial (Bratton et al., 2005). Therapists utilizing family play therapy models such as filial, parent–child interaction therapy, and Theraplay train caregivers to be directly involved as cotherapists to their children. In the beginning stages of these therapies, play therapists teach caregivers how to use play interactions with their children to foster a more positive relationship. Webster-Stratton and colleagues have published numerous studies on social skills training groups for children who have conduct problems and their parents. In these studies, children received social skills training while their parents learned parenting skills and ways to promote their children's new skills. The involvement of caregivers in these studies led to maintained improvements in both the children's behaviors and the parents' skills (Webster-Stratton & Hammond, 1997).

STAGES OF PLAY THERAPY

There are three main stages to the therapy process. The first, *rapport building,* involves the initial sessions wherein the child and therapist begin to build a working relationship. The therapist is still gathering information about the child and his or her experiences, and the child is learning about the play space and process of therapy. Depending on the therapeutic orientation, these play sessions are typically supportive in nature and allow the child time to feel safe and comfortable in the play sessions.

The second stage is *working through.* This is the lengthiest of the three stages and is where much of the therapeutic change occurs. In this stage the therapist selects and applies the most appropriate change agent(s) inherent in play (e.g., abreaction, storytelling, a therapeutic relationship).

During the working-through stage, play themes often becoming apparent and offer a window into the child's inner world. Play themes are those topics that reappear across play sessions. They may stem from unmet needs/desires, unresolved conflicts, or difficulties the child is trying to master or is struggling to understand. Some examples of common play themes are aggression, attachment, competition, control, cooperation, traumatic events, death/grief, fears, fixing something that is broken/damaged, gender, good versus evil, identity, limit testing, mastery of developmental tasks, need for approval or nurturance, power, problem solving, regression, replay of real-life situations, school, sexuality, social rules, transitions, vulnerability, and win/lose situations. The therapeutic use of these themes will depend on the theoretical orientation of the therapist.

The final stage of play therapy is *termination.* The therapist and child have used the therapeutic process to ameliorate or resolve the presenting problem(s). The termination stage is intended to allow the child and family to take ownership of the changes that have occurred and to prepare the way to ongoing improvements.

CHARACTERISTICS OF EFFECTIVE PLAY THERAPISTS

A review of the play therapy training literature suggests that there are personal characteristics such as patience, flexibility, and love of children that all therapists need to work with children. In regard to the characteristics of a "good" play therapist, Nalavany and colleagues (2005) found in a sample of 28 experienced play therapists that they rated the personal qualities of empathy, warmth, and genuineness as most essential, while they considered theoretical knowledge and technical skills to be less important but easier to acquire.

Harris and Landreth (2001) outlined eight of the most essential characteristics of child-centered play therapists. This list includes genuine interest, unconditional acceptance, and sensitivity to the child. Their list also includes the ability to create a sense of safety, to trust a child to lead the course of therapy in a gradual and natural manner, and to honestly believe that a child is capable of solving his or her problems while setting the few necessary limits needed to help a child in this process.

THE EFFECTIVENESS OF PLAY THERAPY: A REVIEW OF META-ANALYTIC OUTCOME RESEARCH

While the clinical utility of play therapy has long been reported anecdotally in the field, more studies using rigorous research methods are definitely needed to firmly establish the effectiveness of play therapy. A compilation of previous, well-designed play therapy research is presented in the book *Empirically Based Play Interventions for Children* (Reddy, Files-Hall, & Schaefer, 2005). In addition, there are several promising meta-analytic studies on the effectiveness of play interventions. In a review of 42 published and unpublished studies, including dissertations, LeBlanc and Ritchie (2001) found the average effect size of play therapy outcomes to be 0.66 using a meta-analytic approach. This is a medium to large effect size (Cohen, 1977) and indicates statistically significant improvement in the children (LeBlanc & Ritchie). Previous meta-analytic studies of non-play-based therapeutic interactions with adults and children reported mean effect sizes of 0.68 (Smith & Glass, 1977) and 0.71 (Casey & Berman, 1985), respectively. In Casey and Berman's study, when play-based interventions were examined separate from non-play-based therapies, a mean effect size of 0.65 was found. These results suggest that interventions utilizing play therapy are as effective as talk-based therapies.

Bratton and colleagues (2005) recently performed a more comprehensive meta-analysis of play therapy interventions. Like LeBlanc and Ritchie (2001), Bratton and her colleagues analyzed only studies that included play therapy interventions as opposed to previous analyses that included traditional talk-based psychotherapies. These researchers identified 93 studies of play therapy by using the definition of play therapy that was determined by the Association for Play Therapy. They found a large mean effect size of 0.80 (Bratton et al., 2005).

These meta-analytic investigations also shed light on specific treatment and participant characteristics that led to improvements noted in the children. In particular, these meta-analyses highlighted the importance of including parents in children's treatment. When parents were trained to act as cotherapists, higher effect sizes were seen across studies (Bratton et al., 2005; LeBlanc & Ritchie, 2001). Filial and parent–child interaction therapies often include parents in an effort to improve interactions between parents and children as well as teach parents skills that can be used after therapy has ended. Also, both studies suggested that having 30 to 35 sessions of play therapy was the optimal number for identifying positive changes on outcome measures (Bratton et al., 2005; LeBlanc & Ritchie, 2001).

SUMMARY

The goal of this chapter is to provide a basic introduction to the field of play therapy. From its psychoanalytic roots, the field of play therapy continues to expand its theoretical base and be applied to clients across the life cycle and throughout the world. The following chapters will introduce the reader to the diversity of theoretical approaches to play therapy, including psychoanalytic, child-centered, cognitive-behavioral, Gestalt, prescriptive, and integrative.

Play therapy is a powerful modality for working with children, adolescents, adults, groups, and families. Play therapists recognize the importance of play for normal development, as well as its many therapeutic powers or change mechanisms. The personal qualities of play therapists that facilitate a therapeutic relationship include empathy, warmth, genuineness, and unconditional acceptance of the child.

REFERENCES

Association for Play Therapy (n.d.). *About play therapy overview.* Retrieved April 1, 2010, from www.a4pt.org

Axline, V. M. (1947). *Play therapy.* New York, NY: Ballantine Books.

Axline, V. M. (1979). Play therapy as described by children. In C. E. Schaefer (Ed.), *The therapeutic use of child's play* (pp. 517–534). Northvale, NJ: Aronson.

Baggerly, J., & Jenkins, W. W. (2009). The effectiveness of child-centered play therapy on developmental and diagnostic factors in children who are homeless. *International Journal of Play Therapy, 18*(1), 45–55.

Bratton, S. C., Ray, D., Rhine, T., & Jones, L. (2005). The efficacy of play therapy with children: A meta-analytic review of treatment outcomes. *Professional Psychology: Research and Practice, 36*(4), 376–390.

Casey, R., & Berman, J. (1985). The outcome of psychotherapy with children. *Psychological Bulletin, 98*(2), 388–400.

Cohen, J. (1977). *Statistical power analysis for the behavioural sciences* (Rev. ed.). New York, NY: Academic Press.

Dripchak, V. L. (2007). Posttraumatic play: Towards acceptance and resolution. *Clinical Social Work Journal, 35,* 125–134.

Erwin, E. (Ed). (2001). *The Freud encyclopedia: Theory, therapy, and culture.* New York, NY: Routledge.

Flahive, M. W., & Ray, D. (2007). Effect of group sandtray therapy with preadolescents. *Journal for Specialists in Group Work, 32*(4), 362–382.

Freud, A. (1946). The role of transference in the analysis of children. In C. E. Schaefer (Ed.), *The therapeutic use of child's play* (pp. 141–150). Northvale, NJ: Aronson. (Reprinted from *The psycho-analytical treatment of children.* London, UK: Imago.)

Freud, S. (1909). *Analysis of a phobia in a five year old boy.* London, UK: Hogarth Press.

Gallo-Lopez, L., & Schaefer, C. E. (Eds.). (2005). *Play therapy with adolescents.* Lanham, MD: Rowman & Littlefield.

Ginott, H. (1959). The theory and practice of therapeutic intervention in child treatment. *Journal of Consulting Psychology, 23,* 160–166.

Guerney, L. (2000). Filial therapy into the 21st century. *International Journal of Play Therapy, 9*(2), 1–17.

Harris, T. E., & Landreth, G. L. (2001). Essential personality characteristics of effective play therapists. In G. Landreth (Ed.), *Innovations in play therapy: Issues, process, and special populations* (pp. 23–29). New York, NY: Brunner-Routledge.

Klein, M. (1955). The psychoanalytic play technique. In C. E. Schaefer (Ed.), *The therapeutic use of child's play* (pp. 125–140). Northvale, NJ: Aronson. (Reprinted from *American Journal of Orthopsychiatry, 25,* 223–237.)

Kottman, T. (2001). *Play therapy: Basics and beyond.* Alexandria, VA: American Counseling Association.

Landreth, G. L. (2002a). *Play therapy: The art of the relationship* (2nd ed.). New York, NY: Brunner-Routledge.

Landreth, G. L. (2002b). Therapeutic limit setting in the play therapy relationship. *Professional Psychology: Research and Practice, 33,* 529–535.

LeBlanc, M., & Ritchie, M. (2001). A meta-analysis of play therapy outcomes. *Counseling Psychology Quarterly, 14*(2), 149–163.

Li, H. C., & Lopez, V. (2008). Effectiveness and appropriateness of therapeutic play in preparing children for surgery: A randomized, controlled trial study. *Journal for Specialists in Pediatric Nursing, 23*(2), 63–73.

Lowenfeld, M. (1939). The world pictures of children: A method of recording and studying them. *British Journal of Medical Psychology, 18,* 65–101.

Nalavany, B. A., Ryan, S. D., Gomory, T., & Lacasse, J. R. (2005). Mapping the characteristics of a "good" play therapist. *International Journal of Play Therapy, 14*(1), 27–50.

Pulaski, M. A. (1974). The importance of ludic symbolism in cognitive development. In J. F. Magary, M. Poulson, & G. Lubin (Eds.), *Proceedings of the third annual UAP conference: Piagetian theory and the helping professions.* Los Angeles: University of Southern California Press.

Ray, D. C., Henson, R. K., Schottelkorb, A. A., Brown, A. G., & Muro, J. (2008). Effect of short- and long-term play therapy services on teacher–child relationship stress. *Psychology in the Schools, 45*(10), 994–1009.

Reddy, L., Files-Hall, T., & Schaefer, C. E. (Eds.). (2005). *Empirically based play interventions for children.* Washington, DC: American Psychological Association.

Schaefer, C. E. (Ed.). (2003). *Play therapy with adults.* Hoboken, NJ: Wiley.

Schaefer, C. E. (Ed.). (2010). *Play therapy for preschool children.* Washington, DC: American Psychological Association.

Schaefer, C. E., Kelly-Zion, S., McCormick, J., & Ohnogi, A. (Eds.). (2008). *Play therapy for very young children.* Lanham, MD: Rowman & Littlefield.

Smith, M., & Glass, G. (1977). Meta-analysis of psychotherapy outcome studies. *American Psychologist, 32,* 752–760.

Spence, S. H. (2003). Social skills training with children and young people: Theory, evidence, and practice. *Child and Adolescent Mental Health, 8*(2), 84–96.

Sweeney, D. S., & Homeyer, L. E. (1999). Group play therapy. In D. S. Sweeney & L. E. Homeyer (Eds.), *The handbook of group play therapy* (pp. 3–14). San Francisco, CA: Jossey-Bass.

Webster-Stratton, C., & Hammond, M. (1997). Treating children with early-onset conduct problems: A comparison of child and parent training interventions. *Journal of Consulting and Clinical Psychology, 65,* 93–109.

Chapter 2

THE THERAPEUTIC POWERS OF PLAY AND PLAY THERAPY

Charles E. Schaefer and Athena A. Drewes

Play is as natural to children as breathing. It is a universal expression of children, and it can transcend differences in ethnicity, language, or other aspects of culture (Drewes, 2006). Play has been observed in virtually every culture since the beginning of recorded history. It is inextricably linked to how the culture develops poetry, music, dance, philosophy, and social structures—all linked through the society's view of play (Huizinga, 1949). But how play looks and is valued differs across and within cultures (Sutton-Smith, 1974, 1999).

The use of fantasy, symbolic play, and make-believe is a developmentally natural activity in children's play (Russ, 2007). Play is not only central but critical to childhood development (Roopnarine & Johnson, 1994). For a variety of species, including humans, play can be nearly as important as food and sleep. The intense sensory and physical stimulation that comes with playing helps to form the brain's circuits and prevents loss of neurons (Perry, 1997). Play is so critical to a child's development that it is promoted by the United Nations 1989 Convention on the Rights of the Child, Article 31.1, which recognizes "the right of the child to rest and leisure, to engage in play and recreational activities appropriate to the age of the child and to participate freely in cultural life and the arts." Play is perhaps the most developmentally appropriate and powerful medium for young children to build adult–child relationships, develop cause–effect thinking critical to impulse control, process stressful experiences, and learn social skills (Chaloner, 2001). Play can provide a child the sense of power and control that comes from solving problems and mastering new experiences, ideas, and concerns. As a result, it can help build feelings of confidence and accomplishment (Drewes, 2005). Through play and play-based interventions, children can communicate nonverbally, symbolically, and in an action-oriented manner.

Play is not only essential for promoting normal child development but has many therapeutic powers as well. All therapies require, among other factors, the formation of a therapeutic relationship, along with the use of a medium of exchange (Drewes, 2001). The use of play helps establish a working relationship with children, especially those who lack verbal self-expression, and even with older children who show resistance or an inability to articulate their feelings and issues (Haworth, 1964). The presence of toys and play materials in the room sends a message to the child that this space and time is different from all others. It indicates to children that they are given permission to be children and to feel free to be fully themselves (Landreth, 1983).

Play is used in therapy by play therapists and child clinicians as a means of helping children deal with emotional and behavioral issues. Play therapy and the use of play-based interventions is by no means a new school of thought (Drewes, 2006). The use of play to treat children dates back to the 1930s to Hermione Hug-Hellmuth, Anna Freud, and Melanie Klein. Several adult therapies have since been adapted for use with children, such as child-centered play therapy adapted by Virginia Axline (1947), sandplay therapy evolving out of Jungian theory through Margaret Lowenfeld (1979) and Dora Kalff (1980), and cognitive-behavioral play therapy by Susan Knell (1993).

In the safe, emotionally supportive setting of a therapy room, the child can play out concerns and issues, which may be too horrific or anxiety-producing to directly confront or talk about, in the presence of a therapist who can help them feel heard and understood. The toys become the child's words and play their language (Landreth, 1991), which the therapist then reflects back to the child to foster greater understanding.

CURATIVE FACTORS OF PLAY

Therapists from differing theoretical orientations have long been interested in the healing or curative factors in psychotherapy. It is only over the past 25 years that child clinicians and researchers have looked more closely at the specific qualities inherent in play behavior that makes it a therapeutic agent for change (Russ, 2004). The goal is to understand what invisible but powerful forces resulting from the therapist–client play interactions are successful in helping the client overcome and heal psychosocial difficulties. A greater understanding of these change mechanisms enables the clinician to apply them more effectively to meet the particular needs of a client (Schaefer, 1999).

Freud wrote of insight, facilitated by the therapist's interpretations and analysis of transference (Schaefer, 1999) as the key component toward curing a client in psychoanalysis.

Yalom (1985) wrote about "therapeutic factors" or change mechanisms that he believed were inherent in group psychotherapy (Schaefer, 1999). They included acceptance, altruism, catharsis, instillation of hope, interpersonal learning, self-disclosure, self-understanding, universality, vicarious learning, and guidance (Schaefer, 1999). Bergin and Strupp (1972) offered critical factors that transcended theoretical schools of thought: counterconditioning, extinction, cognitive learning, reward and punishment, transfer and generalization, imitation and identification, persuasion, empathy, warmth, and interpretation (Schaefer, 1999).

Schaefer (1999) was the first to describe the therapeutic powers of play. Based on a review of the literature, he identified 25 therapeutic factors, which will be discussed later.

Self-Expression

Developmental limitations in expressive and receptive language skills, limited vocabulary repertoire, and limitations in abstract thinking ability contribute to young children's difficulty in communicating effectively. Perhaps the major therapeutic power of play that has been described in the literature (Schaefer, 1993, 1999) is its communication power. In play, children are able to express their conscious thoughts and feelings better through play activities than by words alone. Children are naturally comfortable with expression through concrete play activities and materials (Landreth, 1993). Use of symbolic representation and expression through dolls and puppets provides emotional distance from emotionally charged experiences, thoughts, and feelings. Through indirect expression in play, the child can gain awareness of troublesome affects and memories and begin the process of healing.

Access to the Unconscious

Through the specially chosen toys, games, and materials for their therapeutic and neutral stimulus qualities, the child can reveal unconscious conflicts via the defense mechanisms of projection, displacement, and symbolization (Klein, 1955). With the support of the play therapist, in a safe environment, the child can begin to transform and integrate unconscious wishes and impulses into conscious play and actions (Schaefer, 1999).

Direct and Indirect Teaching

Play allows you to overcome knowledge and skills deficits in clients by direct instruction. For example, when you teach social skills to children using dolls, puppets, and role-plays, the children are more likely to learn and remember the lessons. The use of fun and games captures children's attention and increases their motivation to learn.

Storytelling and the use of play narratives allow the child to join in interactive fantasy play with the therapist (Schaefer, 1999). This in turn can result in the child's learning a lesson or solution to his/her problem (Gardner, 1971). This is a gradually paced, indirect method with room for repetition that allows for less emotional arousal than direct confrontation (Frey, 1993). Play narratives enable clients to organize their fragmented memories and experiences into a cohesive, meaningful story (Pennebaker, 2002).

Abreaction

Through the use of play, children reenact and relieve stressful and traumatic experiences and thus gain a sense of power and control over them (Schaefer, 1999). Through repetitive play reenactments, the child is able to gradually mentally digest and gain mastery over horrific thoughts and feelings (Waelder, 1932). Children show a natural tendency to cope with external events and traumas through play. After the horror of 9/11, many children were observed building towers with blocks and crashing toy airplanes into them. "Post-traumatic play can be effectively used therapeutically. It is, in fact, the most potent way to effect internal change in young traumatized children" (Terr, 1990, p. 299).

Stress Inoculation

The anticipatory anxiety of upcoming stressful life events such as a family move, starting school, birth of a sibling, or visit to a doctor or dentist can be lessened by playing out the event in advance (Wohl & Hightower, 2001). By playing out with miniature toys exactly what to expect and using a doll to model coping skills, the strange can be made familiar and less scary to the child.

Counterconditioning of Negative Affect

Two mutually exclusive internal states are not able to simultaneously coexist, such as anxiety and relaxation or depression and playfulness (Schaefer, 1999). Thus, allowing a child to play hide-and-seek in a darkened room can help a child conquer the fear of the dark. Or dramatic play with hospital-related toys helps to significantly reduce hospital-specific fears. Rea, Worchel, Upchurch, Sanner, and Daniel (1989) found hospitalized children's adjustment was significantly improved (anxiety significantly reduced) for the randomly assigned group that was encouraged to engage in fantasy play with both medical and nonmedical materials.

Fantasy play allows the child to move from a passive to an active role; for example, the child can role-play giving an injection to a doll patient. Fantasy play also facilitates the expression of several defense mechanisms such as projection, displacement, repetition, and identification (Schaefer, 1999).

Catharsis

Catharsis allows for the release and completion of previously restrained or interrupted affective release via emotional expression (e.g., crying) or activity (e.g., bursting balloons, pounding clay, or punching an inflated bunching bag) (Schaefer, 1999). Emotional release is a critical element in psychotherapy (Ginsberg, 1993).

Positive Affect

While involved in play, children tend to feel less anxious or depressed. Enjoyable activities contribute to a greater sense of well-being and less distress (Aborn, 1993). In play, both children and adults are likely to elevate their mood and sense of well-being (Schaefer, 1999). Sustained high levels of the stress hormone cortisol can damage the hippocampus, an area of the brain responsible for learning and memory, which results in cognitive deficits that can continue into adulthood (Middlebrooks & Audage, 2008). Laughter and positive affects help to create the opposite effect, releasing mood-boosting hormones and endorphins, lowering serum cortisol levels, and stimulating the immune system (Berk, 1989). Play and playfulness and their potential for mirth and laughter become antidotes to negative affects such as anxiety and depression (Schaefer, 1999).

Sublimation

Sublimation allows the channeling of unacceptable impulses into substitute activities that are socially acceptable (Schaefer, 1999). The child who physically hits another may be redirected, helped to practice, and learn through repetition alternatives such as the expression in "warlike" board games (chess, checkers), card games (war), or competitive sports activities (Fine, 1956; in Schaefer, 1999).

Attachment and Relationship Enhancement

Play has been found to facilitate the positive emotional bond between parent and child. Studies of filial therapy (Ray, Bratton, Rhine, & Jones, 2001; VanFleet & Guerney, 2003), Theraplay, and parent–child interaction therapy (Brinkmeyer & Eyberg, 2003; Hood & Eyberg, 2003) have shown success in promoting parent–child attachment and relationship enhancement (Drewes, 2006). Through step-by-step, live-coached sessions, the parent/caregiver and child create positive affective experiences, such as playing together, which results in a secure, nurturing relationship. Gains are reflected, via research, in improvements in parental empathy, increased perception of positive changes in the family environment, self-esteem, perception of the child's adjustment, and perception of the child's behavioral problems, along with the child's self-concept and changes in the child's play behavior (Rennie & Landreth, 2000).

Moral Judgment

Piaget (1932) first asserted that children's spontaneous rule-making and rule-enforcing play in informal and unsupervised play situations was a critical experience for the development of mature moral judgment. Game play experiences help children move beyond the early stage of moral realism, in which rules are seen as external restrictions arbitrarily imposed by adults in authority, to the concept of morality that is based on the principles of cooperation and consent among equals (Schaefer, 1999).

Empathy

Through role-play, children are able to develop their capacity for empathy, the ability to see things from another's perspective. Role-playing different characters in social play has been found to increase altruism (Iannotti, 1978) and empathy (Strayer & Roberts, 1989), as well as social competence (Connolly & Doyle, 1984).

Power/Control

Children feel powerful and in control during their play. They can make the play world conform to their wishes and needs (Schaefer, 1999). In marked contrast to the sense of helplessness children experience during a disaster, play affords them a strong sense of power and control. The child towers over the play materials and determines what and how to play during the therapy session. Eventually, this competing response (power) helps overcome the child's feelings of insecurity and vulnerability.

Competence and Self-Control

Play provides children with unlimited opportunities to create, such as through stories, worlds constructed in a sand tray or drawings, whereby they can gain a sense of competence and self-efficacy that boosts their self-esteem (Schaefer, 1999). In addition, by engaging in activities, such as game playing or construction play, children can learn self-control through thought and behavior stopping, which can help them to stop and think and plan ahead. As a result, the child can anticipate the consequences of various potential behaviors and actions. These skills can be mastered through practice opportunities and positive reinforcement and can consequently then generalize into any number of settings (e.g., school, home, social settings).

Sense of Self

Through the play and child therapist's use of a child-led, child-centered approach (Axline, 1947), a child can begin to experience complete acceptance and permission to be himself without the fear of judgment, evaluation, or pressure to change. Through a commentary on the child's play, the therapist provides a mirror, figuratively speaking, by which the child can understand inner thoughts and feelings and develop an inner self-awareness (Schaefer, 1999). Play can also provide the opportunity for the child to realize the power within to be an individual in one's own right, to think for oneself, make one's own decisions, and discover oneself (Winnicott, 1971). Since this is often a unique experience, Meares (1993) noted that the field of play is where, to a large extent, a sense of self is generated. He concluded that play with an attuned adult present is where experiences are generated that become the core of what we mean by personal selves (Schaefer, 1999).

Accelerated Development

Preschool children's levels of development can advance in play beyond the ordinary accomplishments of their age period and function at a level of thinking that will only become characteristic later on (Schaefer, 1999). Vygotsky (1967) observed that children in play are always above their average age and above their daily behavior.

Creative Problem Solving

Numerous studies have demonstrated that play and playfulness are associated with increased creativity and divergent thinking in children (Feitelson & Ross, 1973; Ross, 1988; Schaefer, 1999). Since in play the process is more important than the end product, children can freely, without fear of consequences, come up with novel combinations and discoveries that can aid them in solving their own problems and social problems (Sawyers & Horn-Wingerd, 1993; Schaefer, 1999). Indeed, there is "something about play itself that acts as a vehicle for change" (Russ, 2007, p. 15). Divergent thinking has been thought to be a mediating link between pretend play and coping strategies (Russ, 1988) whereby children who are good at pretend play (use of affect and fantasy) are better divergent thinkers, have more coping strategies, and could more readily shift from one strategy to another (Christiano & Russ, 1996). Goldstein and Russ (2000–2001) found in a study with first-grade children that there was a positive and significant relationship between imagination in play and the frequency of coping responses and variety of strategies used, even when the sample was controlled for IQ. Russ (2007) and Singer (1995) speculate that it is divergent thinking that underlies children's pretend play, which has received empirical support. Being able to think up and find different uses for objects (e.g., clay, blocks), create different endings to stories, or devise scenarios of action can increase divergent thinking (Dansky, 1999).

Fantasy Compensation

In play, children can get immediate substitute gratification of their wishes. A fearful child can be courageous, or a weak child can be strong. Robinson (1970) saw play as essentially a compensatory mechanism, operating much like a daydream. Impulses and needs that cannot find expression in real life find an outlet through fantasy.

Reality Testing

Play experiences allow children to practice reading cues in social situations and can help differentiate fantasy from reality situations. In social pretend play, children often switch back and forth between the roles they are playing and their real selves (Schaefer, 1999). Frequent engagement in pretend play allows for better discrimination between reality and fantasy (D. G. Singer & Singer, 1990).

Behavioral Rehearsal

In the safe environment of play, socially acceptable behaviors, such as assertiveness versus aggressiveness, can be rehearsed and practiced. The play and child therapist can model in play new behaviors that are more adaptive for the child through use of puppets and role-play, which the child can then repeatedly practice to ensure skill development and mastery (Jones, Ollendick, & Shenskl, 1989; Schaefer, 1999).

Rapport Building

One of the most potent therapeutic powers of play is the relational component of rapport building. This occurs when the client responds positively to the playful and fun-loving therapist. Since most children do not come willingly to therapy, they need to be initially engaged in the process through therapist/child play interactions. Also, since "play is the language of the child," it provides a natural medium for communicating with and establishing a relationship with the child (Landreth, 1983, p. 202).

Prescriptive Play Therapy

Each of the well-known schools of play therapy (i.e., client-centered, cognitive-behavioral, and psychodynamic) emphasizes one or more of the curative powers of play. The prescriptive eclectic approach (Kaduson, Cangelosi, & Schaefer, 1997) advocates that play therapists become skilled in numerous therapeutic powers and differentially apply them to meet the individual needs of clients. The prescriptive approach is based on the individualized, differential, and focused matching of curative powers to the specific causative forces underlying the problem of a client (Kaduson et al., 1997). When therapists have a greater understanding of these change mechanisms, they can then become more effective in meeting the particular needs of the client.

Norcross (2002) also advocates a prescriptive approach to treatment whereby techniques are modified to match the client's diagnosis or presenting problem. Moreover, therapists should change their interpersonal style of interaction to match the client's style in order to improve treatment outcome.

Future Research

Although there are numerous outcome studies now attesting to the efficacy of play therapy with children, there are few, if any, process studies of play therapy. Process studies seek to identify the specific mediators, that is, therapeutic factors that produced the desired change in the clients' behavior. Play therapists also need to look at which change agents in play can be combined to optimize treatment effectiveness. A clearer knowledge of the array of therapeutic factors underlying play therapy will allow child clinicians to borrow flexibly from available theoretical positions to tailor their treatment to a particular child (Kaduson et al., 1997).

CONCLUSION

This chapter has briefly highlighted the various therapeutic change mechanisms within play that can help clients overcome their psychosocial difficulties. The therapeutic factors within play should not be viewed as mysterious but as capable of being understood, altered, and even fully controlled. The use of individualized treatment goals facilitates and guides the therapist in deciding which therapeutic powers to apply. Further research is needed to elucidate the specific therapeutic powers of play that are most effective with specific presenting problems of clients.

This prescriptive matching of change agents with underlying causes will result in the most cost-effective play interventions.

REFERENCES

Aborn, A. I. (1993). Play and positive emotion. In C. E. Schaefer (Ed.), *The therapeutic powers of play* (pp. 291–308). Northvale, NJ: Aronson.

Axline, V. M. (1947). *Play therapy: The inner dynamics of childhood.* Boston, MA: Houghton Mifflin.

Bergin, A. E., & Strupp, H. H. (1972). *Changing frontiers in the science of psychotherapy.* Chicago, IL: Aldine.

Berk, L. S. (1989). Eustress of mirthful laughter modified natural killer cell activity. *American Journal of Medical Science, 298,* 390–396.

Brinkmeyer, M. Y., & Eyberg, S. M. (2003). Parent–child interaction therapy for oppositional children. In A. E. Kazdin & J. R. Weisz (Eds.), *Evidence-based psychotherapies for children and adolescents* (pp. 204–223). New York, NY: Guilford Press.

Chaloner, W. B. (2001). Counselors coaching teachers to use play therapy in classrooms: The Play and Language to Succeed (PALS) early, school-based intervention for behaviorally at-risk children. In A. A. Drewes, L. Carey, & C. Schaefer (Eds.), *School-based play therapy* (pp. 368–390). New York, NY: Wiley.

Christiano, B., & Russ, S. (1996). Play as a predictor of coping and distress in children during an invasive dental procedure. *Journal of Clinical Child Psychology, 25,* 130–138.

Connolly, J. A., & Doyle, A. (1984). Relation of social fantasy play to social competence in preschoolers. *Developmental Psychology, 20,* 797–806.

Dansky, J. (1999). Play. In M. Runco & S. Pritzker (Eds.), *Encyclopedia of creativity* (pp. 393–408). San Diego, CA: Academic Press.

Drewes, A. A. (2001). The possibilities and challenges in using play therapy in schools. In A. A. Drewes, L. J. Carey, & C. E. Schaefer (Eds.), *School-based play therapy* (pp. 41–61). New York, NY: Wiley.

Drewes, A. A. (2005). Play in selected cultures. In E. Gil & A. A. Drewes (Eds.), *Cultural issues in play therapy* (pp. 26–71). New York, NY: Guilford Press.

Drewes, A. A. (2006). Play-based interventions. *Journal of Early Childhood and Infant Psychology, 2,* 139–156.

Feitelson, D., & Ross, G. (1973). The neglected factor—play. *Human Development, 16,* 202–223.

Fine, R. (1956). Psychoanalytic observations on chess and chess masters [Monograph]. *Psychoanalysis, 4,* 1.

Frey, D. (1993). Learning by metaphor. In C. E. Schaefer (Ed.), *The therapeutic powers of play* (pp. 223–237). Northvale, NJ: Aronson.

Gardner, R. (1971). *Therapeutic communication with children. The mutual storytelling technique.* New York: Science House.

Ginsberg, B. G. (1993). Catharsis. In C. E. Schaefer (Ed.), *The therapeutic powers of play* (pp. 107–141). Northvale, NJ: Aronson.

Goldstein, A. B., & Russ, S. W. (2000–2001). Understanding children's literature and its relationship to fantasy ability and coping. *Imagination, Cognition, and Personality, 20,* 105–126.

Haworth, M. R. (1964). *Child psychotherapy: Practice and theory.* Northvale, NJ: Aronson.

Hood, K. K., & Eyberg, S. M. (2003). Outcomes of parent–child interaction therapy: New directions in research. *Cognitive and Behavioral Practice, 9,* 9–16.

Huizinga, J. (1949). *Homo ludens.* London, UK: Routledge & Kegan Paul.

Iannotti, R. (1978). Effects of role-taking experiences on emotion, altruism and aggression. *Developmental Psychology, 14,* 119–124.

Jones, R. T., Ollendick, T. H., & Shenskl, F. (1989). The role of behavioral versus cognitive variables in skill acquisition. *Behavioral Therapy, 29,* 293–302.

Kaduson, H., Cangelosi, D., & Schaefer, C. (1997). *The playing cure: Individualized play therapy for specific childhood problems.* Northvale, NJ: Aronson.

Kalff, D. (1980). *Sandplay: A psychotherapeutic approach to the psyche.* Santa Monica, CA: Sigo Press.

Klein, M. (1955). The psychoanalytic play technique. *American Journal of Orthopsychiatry, 35,* 223–237.

Knell, S. M. (1993). *Cognitive-behavioral play therapy.* Northvale, NJ: Aronson.

Landreth, G. L. (1983). Play therapy in elementary school settings. In C. E. Schaefer & K. J. O'Connor (Eds.), *Handbook of play therapy* (pp. 202–212). New York, NY: Wiley.

Landreth, G. (1991). *The art of the relationship.* Muncie, IN: Accelerated Development.

Landreth, G. (1993). Self-expressive communication. In C. E. Schaefer (Ed.), *The therapeutic powers of play* (pp. 41–63). Northvale, NJ: Aronson.

Lowenfeld, M. (1979). *The world technique.* London, UK: Allen & Unwin.

Meares, R. (1993). *The metaphor of play.* Northvale, NJ: Aronson.

Middlebrooks, J. S., & Audage, N. C. (2008). *The effects of childhood stress on health across the lifespan.* Atlanta, GA: Centers for Disease Control and Prevention, National Center for Injury Prevention and Control.

Norcross, J. C. (Ed.). (2002). *Psychotherapy relationships that work.* New York, NY: Oxford University Press.

Pennebaker, J. W. (2002, January/February). What our words can say about us: Toward a broader language psychology. *APA Monitor,* 8–9.

Perry, B. D. (1997). Incubated in terror: Neurodevelopmental factors in the "cycle of violence." In J. Osofsky (Ed.), *Children in a violent society* (pp. 124–149). New York, NY: Guilford Press.

Piaget, J. (1932). *The moral judgment of the child.* New York, NY: Harcourt.

Rae, W., Worchel, R., Upchurch, J., Sanner, J., & Daniel, C. (1989). The psychosocial impact of play on hospitalized children. *Journal of Pediatric Psychology, 14,* 617–627.

Ray, D., Bratton, S., Rhine, T., & Jones, L. (2001). The effectiveness of play therapy: Responding to the critics. *International Journal of Play Therapy, 10,* 85–108.

Rennie, R., & Landreth, G. (2000). Effects of filial therapy on parent and child behaviors. *International Journal of Play Therapy, 9*(2), 19–37.

Robinson, E. S. (1970). The compensatory function of make-believe play. *Psychological Review, 27,* 429–439.

Roopnarine, J., & Johnson, J. (1994). A need to look at play in diverse cultural settings. In J. Roopnarine, J. Johnson, & F. Hooper (Eds.), *Children's play in diverse cultures* (pp. 1–8). Albany: State University of New York Press.

Russ, S. (1988). Primary process thinking on the Rorschach, divergent thinking, and coping in children. *Journal of Personality Assessment, 52,* 539–548.

Russ, S. (2004). *Play in child development and psychotherapy: Toward empirically supported practice.* Mahwah, NJ: Erlbaum.

Russ, S. W. (2007). Pretend play: A resource for children who are coping with stress and managing anxiety. *NYS Psychologist, XIX,* 5, 13–17.

Sawyers, J. K., & Horn-Wingerd, D. M. (1993). Creative problem-solving. In C. E. Schaefer (Ed.), *Therapeutic powers of play* (pp. 309–322). Northvale, NJ: Aronson.

Schaefer, C. E. (1993). *The therapeutic powers of play.* Northvale, NJ: Aronson.

Schaefer, C. E. (1999). Curative factors in play therapy. *Journal for the Professional Counselor, 14*(1), 7–16.

Singer, D. G., & Singer, J. L. (1990). *The house of make-believe: Play and the developing imagination.* Cambridge, MA: Harvard University Press.

Singer, J. L. (1995). Imaginative play in childhood. Precursor of subjunctive thoughts, day-dreaming, and adult pretending games. In A. Pellegrini (Ed.), *The future of play theory* (pp. 187–219). Albany: State University of New York Press.

Strayer, J., & Roberts, W. (1989). The association of empathy, ego resiliency, and prosocial behavior in children. *Journal of Applied Developmental Psychology, 10,* 227–239.

Sutton-Smith, B. (1974). The anthropology of play. *Association for the Anthropological Study of Play, 2,* 8–12.

Sutton-Smith, B. (1999). Evolving a consilience of play definitions: Playfully. In S. Reifel (Ed.), *Play and culture studies* (Vol. 2, pp. 239–256). Stamford, CT: Ablex.

Terr, L. (1990). *Too scared to cry: Psychic trauma in childhood.* New York, NY: HarperCollins.

United Nations Convention on the Rights of the Child. (1989). Article 31.1. Retrieved on April 20, 2008, from www2.ohchr.org/English/law/crc.htm

Van Fleet, R., & Guerney, L. (Eds.). (2003). *Casebook of filial therapy.* Boiling Springs, PA: Play Therapy Press.

Vygotsky, L. S. (1967). Play and its role in the mental development of the child. *Soviet Psychology, 17,* 66–72.

Waelder, R. (1932). The psychoanalytic theory of play. *Psychoanalytic Quarterly, 2,* 208–224.

Winnicott, D. W. (1971). *Playing and reality.* New York, NY: Basic Books.

Wohl, N., & Hightower, D. (2001). Primary Mental Health Project: A school-based prevention program. In A. A. Drewes, L. J. Carey, & C. E. Schaefer (Eds.), *School-based play therapy* (pp. 277–296). New York, NY: Wiley.

Yalom, I. D. (1985). *The theory and practice of group psychotherapy.* New York, NY: Basic Books.

Chapter 3

PLAYING IT SAFE
Ethical Issues in Play Therapy

Cynthia A. Reynolds and Laura J. Tejada

Ethics has been defined as standards of conduct or action in relation to others (Levy, 1972) and as acceptable or good practice according to agreed-upon rules or standards of practice established by a profession (G. Corey, Corey, & Callanan, 2007; Cottone & Tarvydas, 2007). Play therapists operate under the ethics of their specific profession such as counseling, marriage and family therapy, psychology, school counseling, and social work. There are also practice guidelines specific to best practices in play therapy available from the Association for Play Therapy at the following Web address: www.a4pt.org/download.crm?ID=28051.

In the field of ethics, there are three common ethical dichotomies, which have opposing viewpoints: ethical absolutism vs. ethical relativism, utilitarianism vs. deontology, and egoism vs. altruism (Remley & Herlihy, 2007). *Ethical absolutism* is founded on the idea that there are some ethical or moral standards that are universal, and they apply at all times in all situations to all people. For example, a play therapist might believe that the confidentiality of the relationship with the child should never be violated. Another play therapist might take a more relativistic approach and believe that confidentiality with a child is relative to the unique child, the situation, the family, the culture, and the context. Next, a play therapist operating from a *utilitarian approach* examines what the effect of an action will be and believes that the ends can justify the means. This could entail using a paradoxical intervention that produces a desirable outcome. In contrast, a play therapist with a *deontological approach* is focused on what is inherently right. From this stance, a play therapist may refuse to use the same paradoxical intervention because he/she believes it is never appropriate to use such a tactic, even if it does sometimes work. Finally, a play therapist practicing *egoism* may make decisions based on self-interest while the *altruistic* play therapist is most concerned with helping others.

Two perspectives that Remley and Herlihy (2007) find helpful in understanding how to link ethical ideals to professional practice are *principle ethics* and *virtue ethics*. Principle ethics examines "What should I do?" The most commonly discussed ethical principles include respect for autonomy, nonmaleficence, beneficence, justice, fidelity, and veracity (Kitchener, 1984). *Respect for autonomy* refers to client self-determination, specifically working toward decreasing client dependency and fostering independent decision making, which is a relatively Western society-based ethic that may not be valued in other cultures (Sue, Arrendondo, & McDavis, 1992).

Nonmaleficence means doing no harm to clients. *Beneficence* is doing good for clients by actively promoting their mental health and wellness. *Justice* carries with it the obligation to treat clients fairly and has implications for nondiscrimination and equitable treatment for all. *Fidelity* means fulfilling a responsibility of trust by being faithful to promises made to clients. *Veracity* refers to the obligation to deal honestly with clients and other professionals.

In contrast, virtue ethics is concerned with "Who should I be?" Virtue ethics looks at specific character traits of human beings such as integrity, discernment, acceptance of emotion, self-awareness, and interdependence with the community. A person with *integrity* does what he or she believes is right rather than be pressured by obligation or fear of consequences. A *discerning* person is able to tolerate ambiguity, maintain perspective, and understand the link between current behavior and future consequences. *Acceptance of emotion* is practiced by a virtuous person as he/she knows that emotion can inform reasoning. *Self-awareness* is of utmost importance, as assumptions, biases, and convictions affect the relationships with clients and others. A virtuous practitioner knows that values are context laden and understands the importance of *interdependence with the community*.

Codes of ethics have been developed for a variety of reasons (Herlihy & Corey, 1996; Mappes, Robb, & Engels, 1985; VanHoose & Kottler, 1985) including to protect the public; to educate members of the profession; to ensure accountability; to serve as a catalyst for improving practice; to protect the profession from government; to help control internal disagreement, thus promoting stability in the profession; and to protect practitioners in terms of malpractice suits or state licensing complaints (Fischer & Sorenson, 1996).

Welfel (2002) believes that professional ethics encompasses four dimensions. Mental health counselors must have sufficient knowledge, skill, and judgment to use efficacious interventions; have respect for the human dignity and freedom of the client; use the inherent power responsibly; and act in ways that promote public confidence in the mental health professions. The following 11 statements are offered as a way for mental health professionals to assess their own level of ethical readiness and fitness. Read each one and consider if it is true or false for you.

- *I understand the need for ethical codes and guidelines.* I know that the primary reason ethical codes and guidelines are needed is to protect the public from the misuses of power. Clients come to us in a vulnerable or needy state, viewing us as having power over them.

  Ethical codes are also instructive for members of the profession and their clients about acceptable behaviors of mental health professionals. Ethical codes and guidelines provide standards that mental health professionals are expected to follow and can be held accountable for practicing. When mental health professionals come to consensus about what is good practice and this practice is codified into ethical standards, the level of care provided is raised for all clients. Finally, when there are major violations, the government usually gets involved to provide oversight. Most mental health practitioners would prefer self-regulation over governmental regulation.

- *I have read the ethical codes and guidelines of my profession.* This is my most fundamental responsibility as a mental health practitioner. Otherwise, I have no clue if what I am doing is right or wrong. My ignorance of the ethics does not afford me any protection. I have found that each time I read the ethical codes, my understanding of them deepens.

- *I keep the latest copies of the ethical and legal codes and practice guidelines of my profession readily available in case I need to refer to them in a hurry.* Most ethical codes are updated on a regular basis, and state licensing boards often make several changes a year. With most organizations going "green," there are no longer paper copies distributed, so I download the latest copies once a year and keep them in a binder. I have found that the time when I have an ethical crisis is usually the time my computer is exceptionally slow, not able to get Internet, or unavailable. I also prefer to leaf through paper pages rather than trying to scroll back and forth between 40 pages of online codes or between two separate documents of legal guidelines and ethical codes.

- *I have a trusted colleague or peer that I can consult with when needed regarding ethical issues.* It is important to have an ethics buddy who has agreed to be there to consult any time day or night. You should have developed a high level of trust with this person and can count on him or her to set you straight if need be. Both parties document the consultations given and received (Gottleib, 2006).

- *I can recognize at least one ethical issue per day on the job.* It is normal to have at least one ethical issue per day on the job. If you cannot discern any, you may need to update your training with an ethical class or workshop. You may not be tuning in to what is occurring right in front of you at work.

- *I have a limited scope of practice and follow the guidelines of my profession.* As a school counselor, I do not do family counseling. I may consult with the family regarding the success of their child in school, but if I have not been trained in a systemic perspective, I limit what I do with families. If I attend one weekend workshop on Eye Movement Desensitization and Reprocessing (EMDR) or hypnosis, that does not qualify me to advertise those as areas of expertise. If I have never taken a class in play therapy or counseling children, I am operating outside my scope of practice to say I am qualified to work with children or do play therapy. Operating outside of one's scope of practice means risking a malpractice suit.

- *I belong to my professional organization(s) and their listservs and keep my license(s)/certificate(s) up to date with the appropriate continuing education units (CEUs).* If you are ever called to court to testify, one of the first questions from an attorney for either side will be, "To what professional organizations do you belong?" This is because one of the primary reasons professional organizations and their listservs exist is to keep practitioners updated regarding legal and ethical changes. Professional conferences and workshops are held, and CEUs are granted in areas of best practices, empirically validated treatments, ethics, cultural diversity, supervision, and so on. Some states have entities that monitor completion of the appropriate CEUs. Other states require licensees to attest that they have completed the appropriate CEUs, but only a small percentage are randomly selected to provide the actual documentation to the licensing board. In those states, a frequent violation is the lack of completion of the CEU requirements. Although some mental health practitioners choose not to join their professional organizations because of cost, it is even more financially risky not to be a member. Many organizations offer free ethical consults to members as well.

- *I have a high tolerance for ambiguity and appreciate the complexity of ethical dilemmas.* If you need an immediate answer to a problem, if you rush to judgment, if you are more comfortable with either/or thinking, it will be difficult for you to take differing perspectives and see issues from others' points of view. In order to fully be engaged in the ethical decision-making process, it is critical to have an open mind, a tolerance for ambiguity, and an appreciation of the complexity of ethical dilemmas. As a play therapist, you need to be able to view a dilemma from the perspective of not only the child but also the caregivers, institution, and so on.

- *I engage in self-care and assess my professional fitness so that I am able to make quality ethical decisions or get help if impaired.* Much of our time and energy is spent dedicated to caring for others, but our ability to share our talents rests with our ability to take care of ourselves. Just as the flight attendants tell us to put on our own oxygen masks before assisting our traveling companions, we must be able to prioritize our own well-being. We need to become aware of the signs of exhaustion, burnout, and overload and monitor ourselves in order to be the best for our clients.

- *I am aware of the most common ethical issues that emerge when working with children.* Three of the top issues regarding working with children are confidentiality/privileged communication, divorce/custody, and touch. Play therapists must be prepared to grapple with ethical issues in these areas as a typical part of practice. *Confidentiality* is an ethical term that refers to the idea that there is the expectation that what is discussed in the relationship is private, whereas *privileged communication* is a legal term. Exceptions to confidentiality may include harm to self, harm to others, abuse, and court order. Privileged communication laws protect clients from having confidential communications disclosed in a court of law without permission. Based on age and state statutes, parents are generally the holders of the privilege regarding their child's counseling. Note that some states may not extend privileged communications to the profession of school counseling. Often, doing play therapy with children involves walking a tightrope between the child's expectation and need for privacy and the parent's legal right to know.

With over 50% of marriages ending in divorce in the United States and the decades of research on the effects of divorce on children, it is inevitable that play therapists will be serving children of divorce. There are specific legal codes that exist in states that address parental consent for services, access to records, and the like. One frequent legal violation that occurs in the area of divorce/custody is when a mental health practitioner who is not a trained custody evaluator goes to court to testify regarding custody arrangements. Another frequent violation is providing counseling to the child without the custodial parent's permission. When working with children of divorce, it is critical to be up to date with your state's legal codes as well as the ethical standards of your profession in these areas.

Touch is an especially relevant topic in working with children, as many younger children naturally want to touch and be touched. Other children may have specific personal, familial, or cultural values or conditions such as attachment disorders, medical illnesses, sexual and/or physical abuse, autism, and so on, which would mediate touching. Touching that occurs between a female therapist and male/female child is often viewed differently than touch between a male therapist and male/female child. Because of the potential for harm to the child, and the power differential between child and therapist, touch is often frowned upon by professional mental health organizations. Some states even require documentation in case notes of any touch that occurs, and again, it is critical to be familiar with your state's requirements. The Association for Play Therapy has developed a paper on touch that can be downloaded from its Web site at a4pt.org/download.cfm?ID=28052.

- *I know how to use and apply at least one ethical decision-making model.* I know that ethical dilemma models provide frameworks for how to make difficult decisions. I also know that ethical and legal codes do not always coincide.

  Ethical decision-making models were created to help mental health practitioners deal with complex situations where there is no one clear answer (Kitchener, 1984; Pope & Vasquez, 1998). There are a variety of them from which to choose (Cottone & Claus, 2000), including feminist (Hill, Glaser, & Harden, 1995) and social constructivist (Cottone, 2001) models. Often, various ethical codes and standards conflict with each other. Although at times they appear to be very similar, each profession (counseling, psychology, social work, marriage and family therapy, school counseling) has slightly different ways of viewing ethical considerations. A well-trained mental health profession has at least one model committed to memory and knows how to apply it to specific ethical issues.

In reading the preceding ethical readiness and fitness section, you can assess yourself in terms of strengths and weaknesses and make a plan if you decide there are areas for improvement. The following section assumes you are ethically fit and ready to deal with ethical issues as a professional on the cognitive level. It explores some of the more common emotional and behavioral reactions of professionals to ethical issues.

PREDICTABLE CHARACTER POSTURES UNDER STRESS

When human beings are under stress, they tend to retreat to defensive postures in order to cope. An ethical dilemma can be seen as a threat to a counselor, as there is potential for harm to clients, legal ramifications, ethical violations, and loss of license or employment. There are certain predictable character postures that mental health professionals may assume during these stressful times. An understanding of the dynamics of these postures will assist professionals in appreciating the common reactions to ethical dilemmas, what lies behind these defensive postures, and what is needed to adequately address ethical dilemmas.

The following are fictional stereotypes, and any resemblance to actual animals or persons, living or dead, is purely coincidental. There is no conscious intention to denigrate either gender or species of animal in these fictional portrayals. It is also important to note that these postures may appear at some level in all of us.

The Puppy

The Puppy is a neophyte who makes rookie mistakes. The Puppy is trying to do the right thing but accidently makes a big mess right in the middle of things. Puppies typically are interns or new professionals who are still learning the basics on the job. They are generally good-hearted and care deeply. With some close mentoring, they generally mature and grow into the profession. The Puppy's motto is "Oops, I am sorry I messed up."

Jeff was hired on the spot after his internship, was eager to learn, and wanted to please all. His optimism and passion for the field of marriage and family therapy was contagious. During an interaction with an office assistant, he was told to "file it over there by the paper shredder." He shredded 10 pages of client insurance paperwork, thinking he was doing as told. All of the paperwork had to be reconstructed from scratch.

Have you ever made a "Puppy" mistake?

The Turtle

The Turtle avoids dealing with ethical issues by hiding in his shell. The Turtle's motto is "If I can't see it, it must not be unethical." The Turtle is easily overwhelmed by drama, is slow to process, and needs lots of time to deliberate and consider options. The refusal to come out of the shell is self-protection: "If I have to see this stuff, it means I have to recognize and deal with it. And that means I could mess it up and get into big trouble. Therefore, I am better off not to even be aware of it in the first place."

Juan was a competent therapist, but after being burned several times for bringing up ethical issues, he found himself coming to work and not interacting with anyone. By avoiding contact with others on the job, he avoided conflict.

Have there ever been times when you took on "Turtle"-like behavior when you just couldn't deal with an issue or a workplace environment?

The Hen

The Hen is almost the complete opposite of the Turtle. She overreacts to ethical concerns. Her anxiety is so strong that it keeps her in a state of frenzy, and she is unable to calm down and think the issues through logically. Although her intent is honorable, her frenzied state can leave a path of destruction in its wake. The Hen's motto is "The sky is falling, the sky is falling."

Sonya was a very dedicated and vigilant practicum instructor in the psychology department clinic. She often approached colleagues for help resolving ethical concerns with students, as she had no tolerance for ambiguity and little ability to think issues through on her own. At first, people were willing to assist, but over time, they treated Sonya with a cold shoulder. She appeared not to be able to distinguish levels of severity and acted as if every event were a major crisis. No one wanted to get involved, as her level of anxiety was overwhelming.

Have you ever let your anxiety get completely out of control in such a way that it hinders rational thought or scares others away?

The Snake

The Snake manages to slither past ethical concerns by minimizing issues and feelings, epitomizing the slippery slope phenomenon. The Snake's motto is "Calm down, no big deal, this is the real world here."

Beth, a graduate assistant in a counseling program, found a CD that was left overnight in the department computer lab by an internship student that contained a very detailed and clearly identified client history and treatment plan from a local agency. She immediately took it to the chair of the department. The chair suggested that Beth simply contact the internship student and return the CD: "No big deal, just tell the internship student to be more careful next time." Although Beth did not want to get the student into trouble with the agency and did not want to cause a rift with the chair, she knew that there were bigger issues at stake. She decided to notify both the student and the agency about the CD. The agency convened an emergency meeting to deal with the HIPAA (Health Insurance Portability and Accountability Act of 1996) violation and developed a plan to address it.

Have you ever been placed in a situation where you felt the ethics of someone in charge were questionable? Have you ever felt tempted to minimize an ethical issue?

The Fire Dog

The Fire Dog is ready on the spot and jumps to actions without consideration of the long-term ramifications and consequences. The Fire Dog shoots from the hip. His motto is "Any action is better than inaction."

When a state auditor visited his agency and reported irregularities regarding client files, the agency director, David, jumped into action with a new agency policy requiring case notes to be submitted only during regular business hours so they could be reviewed for compliance. Several contract professionals found that they were no longer able to complete case notes if they worked late. Since they were scheduled to work only twice a week, they were forced to come in to complete paper work during times they were not scheduled to work. If they waited until their next scheduled work day, their paperwork would be late, and they would be assessed a fine per another agency policy designed to ensure timeliness with record-keeping. These professionals had a record of exemplary work and felt punished because of others' mistakes. David, in his well-intentioned desire to remedy the ethical irregularities, ended up creating a solution that demoralized some of his best employees.

Have you ever completely overreacted to an ethical issue out of fear, creating a more difficult situation for others?

The Bee

The Bee is just too busy to be bothered with an ethical concern. She has her own agenda that does not take time to reflect on the complexity of an ethical dilemma. The Bee's motto is "Can't you see that I am just too busy to deal with that right now?"

Kara worked as an elementary school counselor serving 2,400 students in five buildings, which meant that she spent one day each week in each one of the five buildings. She had a waiting list of at least 15 students in each one of her buildings and was feeling quite overwhelmed. No matter how hard she worked, there were always unhappy people tracking her down with issues that would take up even more of her time. She even tried to time her escape at the end of each day, sneaking out the back door to her car to avoid teachers. What Kara failed to see was that by ignoring these ethical concerns, she was not being a responsible practitioner and she was not acting in ways that promoted confidence in the school counseling profession. Had she done a fitness evaluation, she might have realized how the stress was impacting her ability to recognize and address ethical dilemmas.

Have you ever felt so busy and overwhelmed that you couldn't stop to address an ethical issue in a timely manner? Have you ever forced yourself to slow down or take time off to recuperate from stress?

The Wolf

The Wolf is sly, deceptive, and uses ethics for self-promotion. His method of operation is to focus attention on the tiniest mistakes of others while committing his own major violations of the ethical code. His motto is: "Ethics are the cornerstone of the profession. Therefore, I will let other people be cornered by them."

Lars appeared to be a very ethical and conscientious professor and psychologist. He was always monitoring fellow professors' and students' ethical behavior, so most were so intimidated by him that they were afraid to point out some serious ethical violations committed by Lars. When one person courageously brought up some of Lars's behavior publicly, Lars immediately filed ethical charges against that person. He was able to convince administration that these accusations against him were merely a reaction to his heroic actions to demand accountability and excellence. Lars was never held accountable for his ethical violations.

Do you hold yourself to the same expectations you have for others? Have you had experiences with other practitioners whose behaviors are suspect but never seem to be held accountable because they are always accusing others of ethical violations?

APPLYING THE POSTURES TO AN ETHICAL DILEMMA

Consider which of these character postures is most similar to how you deal with stress. Think about what stances best fit your colleagues, supervisees, supervisors, or administrators. Which ones do you find the most difficult to deal with at work? How would a group of mental health professionals handle an ethical dilemma if they each retreated to one of these character postures? Imagine how each one of the characters might react to the following ethical scenario:

You have been counseling an 8-year-old boy, Steven, for about three months. He was brought to counseling by his parents, who were concerned about his reaction to their impending divorce. He seemed somewhat depressed and withdrawn, and his parents were worried about his inability to express his emotions. They felt that counseling would help him. They signed an informed consent document that included a disclaimer that you are not trained to do custody evaluation. Both parents have been equally involved in his treatment. Steven has made progress by opening up in counseling and expressing himself. He trusts you implicitly. Although the parental styles vary widely, with Dad being more structured but less available and Mom being more available and less structured, each parent brings an important dimension to child rearing. After your Saturday appointment with Steven, Dad voices concerns that Steven has been traumatized by an event that occurred at Mom's house a few nights ago. Two of Mom's boyfriends got into an argument at Mom's house, and the police had to be called, as well as child protective services. Steven was home when this happened but was not physically injured in any way. Dad wants you to call his lawyer and reveal what happened in the counseling session and wants you to testify in court on his behalf in order to gain custody of his son. Steven did play out a scene in the dollhouse about the incident, but you believe that he does feel safe now and has not suffered a major trauma. He clearly demonstrated in his play that he loves and needs both of his parents.

How do you answer Dad's request? What might the Turtle do? Can you feel the Hen's anxiety? Do you see the Puppy leaping into the fray in his efforts to help a child and accidentally violating scope-of-practice boundaries? Would the Fire Dog develop yet another policy to cope with this situation? Does the Bee take the time to fully discuss the situation with Dad, or does she buzz off into session with Steven to avoid the matter? Can you imagine what the Wolf might find wrong with your approach to the case so far, even though you've taken all reasonable precautions?

To help us navigate ethical issues, it is time for our final character to make his appearance. The Wise Owl comes to the rescue and inquires, "Why not use an ethical decision-making model?" For purposes of this case, the Welfel Model for Ethical Decision Making (2002) will be used to address the dilemma step by step.

- *Develop ethical sensitivity.* This is done through the examples given in the ethical fitness and readiness statements, such as reading relevant professional codes, regulations, and legal requirements. Before being able to adequately address an ethical dilemma, a person needs to have a basic understanding of the ethics of the profession.
- *Define the dilemma and options.* The dilemma appears to be making a decision regarding whether to testify on behalf of the father in a custody battle. Two options might include agreeing to testify in court against the mother using the child's drawing of the event that happened, or refusing to testify, thereby protecting the child's confidentiality.
- *Refer to the professional standards.* What do the standards say regarding confidentiality? How do the standards address confidentiality with children and parents? How do you resolve differences of ethical standards between professions?
- *Examine the laws and regulations.* Laws clearly state that providing a custody opinion would be outside the therapist's scope of practice. She is not a trained custody evaluator and was merely doing a play therapy session with the child. The incident had already been reported to the police and child protective services and is currently under investigation.
- *Search out ethics scholarship.* What has been written in the field regarding similar ethical dilemmas? Have you searched the latest professional journals, your professional association's Web site, and so on?
- *Apply ethical principles to the situation.*
  - **Respect for Autonomy:** What would the child want independent of parental wishes?
  - **Maleficence:** How would the child be harmed by agreeing to testify or not testify? The child is not asking you to change his custody. The child also believes you are there to do play therapy with him, not use the contents of his confidential session in court. He may have chosen not to share anything at all with you if he thought it would become public information. He would be put into the position of his words being used to take him away from his own mother, whom he dearly loves, and she could treat him differently or refuse to bring him back for therapy again. His father could refuse to bring him back for therapy as well if the therapist agrees not to testify.
  - **Beneficence:** Would it do more good for the child for the therapist to testify or not testify? It might help the mother to know that her behaviors were not acceptable parenting, and it could serve as an impetus for her to look at protecting her child from such scenes. It could help the child by not testifying, as he would not have to endure the ordeal of a custody battle, and he would continue to be coparented by two parents who love him. He was not

injured physically by the event and appears to be dealing appropriately with his upset feelings about what happened.

- **Fidelity:** The parents signed an informed consent document that specified that the therapist would provide play therapy and that she was not trained to do custody evaluation. By refusing to testify, the therapist would remain faithful to her word. Does becoming embroiled in a custody battle and taking sides despite what the signed consent form says cast doubt on the therapist's fidelity?

- **Justice:** How fair would it be to take sides in this custody dispute? Is it fair to the mother, with whom you have had a good relationship, to take sides against her without even talking with her about the event? Is it fair to the father not to help him get custody of his child when he has to deal with the mother's inappropriate behavior? How fair is it to become involved with one side over the other side without the child's permission?

- **Veracity:** How will the child feel after being told that what he shared in a private session is now going to be shared with others, including his mother? Will the child view the counselor as dishonest because of this?

After reviewing these ethical principles, Wise Owl continues with the ethical model:

- *Consult with supervisor and respected colleagues.* Find another mental health professional who has dealt with similar issues to gain his/her insight on the dilemma.
- *Deliberate and decide.* Consider the ethical principles weighing the benefits or consequences of each option, the ethical standards, laws and regulations related to the issues, and the advice of supervisors and colleagues; then make a decision.
- *Inform supervisor, implement and document actions.* Inform your supervisor of your decision, and out of courtesy let your colleague whom you consulted with know what your course of action was. Make sure that you document the ethical decision-making process.
- *Reflect on the experience.* Once you have implemented your decision, reflect on the experience. Did you fully consider all of the options? Did you follow advice or follow a different course? Did the benefits or consequences materialize in the way that you thought they would? How did your client handle the decision? How would you do it differently if the same dilemma happened again? What did you learn from the process?

The process of ethical decision making can become second nature with practice. Gaining an understanding of how mental health care professionals typically respond to ethical issues under stress can provide valuable assistance as we strive to grow into becoming more ethical, competent, and virtuous play therapists doing our best to provide excellent care for both children and their families.

REFERENCES

Corey, G., Corey, M., & Callanan, P. (2007). *Issues and ethics in the helping professions* (7th ed.) Pacific Grove, CA: Brooks/Cole.

Cottone, R. R. (2001). A social constructivist model of ethical decision making in counseling. *Journal of Counseling and Development, 79*(1), 39–45.

Cottone, R. R., & Claus, R. E. (2000). Ethical decision making models: A review of the literature. *Journey of Counseling and Development, 78,* 275–283.

Cottone, R. R., & Tarvydas, V. M. (2007). Counseling ethical decision making (3rd ed.). Upper Saddle River, NJ: Pearson.

Fischer, L., & Sorenson, G. P. (1996). *School law for counselors, psychologists, and social workers* (3rd ed.). White Plains, NY: Longman.

Gottleib, M. C. (2006). A template for peer ethics consultation. *Ethics and Behavior, 16*(2), 151–162.

Herlihy, B., & Corey, G. (1996). *ACA ethical standards casebook* (5th ed.). Alexandria, VA: American Counseling Association.

Hill, M., Glaser, K., & Harden, J. (1995). A feminist model for ethical decision making. *Women and Therapy, 21*(3), 101–121.

Kitchener, K. S. (1984). Intuition, critical evaluation, and ethical principles: The foundation for ethical decision making in counseling psychology. *Counseling Psychologist, 12,* 43–55.

Levy, C. S. (1972). The context of social work ethics. *Social Work, 17,* 95–101.

Mappes, D. C., Robb, G. P., & Engels, D. W. (1985). Conflicts between ethics and the law in counseling and psychotherapy. *Journal of Counseling & Development, 64,* 246–252.

Pope, K. S., & Vasquez, M. J. (1998). *Ethics in therapy and counseling* (2nd ed.). San Francisco, CA: Jossey Bass.

Remley, T. P., & Herlihy, B. (2007). *Ethical, legal, and professional issues in counseling* (2nd ed.). Upper Saddle River, NJ: Pearson.

Sue, D. W., Arrendondo, P., & McDavis, R. J. (1992). Multicultural competencies and standards: A call to the professional. *Journal of Counseling and Development, 70,* 477–486.

VanHoose, W. H., & Kottler, J. (1985). *Ethics in counseling and psychotherapy: Perspectives in issues and decision-making.* Cranston, RI: Carroll.

Welfel, E. R. (2002). *Ethics in counseling and psychotherapy: Standards, research, and practice* (2nd ed.). Pacific Grove, CA: Brooks/Cole.

PART II

MAJOR THEORETICAL APPROACHES

PSYCHODYNAMIC MODELS

Chapter 4

PSYCHOANALYTIC APPROACHES TO PLAY THERAPY

Alan J. Levy

HISTORICAL BACKGROUND

The first examples of play therapy of children were published by psychoanalysts nearly 100 years ago. The first account was published by Hug-Hellmuth (1921). Freud (1908) himself encouraged early analysts to treat children in order to explore and validate psychoanalytic theory. He stated that "every child at play behaves like a creative writer, in that he creates a world of his own, or, rather, re-arranges the things of his world in a new way which pleases him" (pp. 141–154). Marans, Mayes, and Colonna (1993) assert that Freud recognized that play involves a suspension rather than a denial of reality. Freud noted that play also entails a "revolt against passivity and a preference for the active role" (Freud, 1931, p. 264). These are critical attributes because play then sets the stage for action (Marans et al., 1993). Solnit (1993) amplifies this notion and states that, simply, "action can be a trial of thought, especially when, as in play and playfulness, the action is based on the suspension of reality—that is, the use and practice of pretending or of making believe and of trying on." In an important sense, play can be the dramatic expression of what later becomes metaphor in language (p. 39). Metaphors are higher forms of cognition and play an important role in affect regulation and development of self-complexity (Fonagy, Gergely, Jurist, & Target, 2004).

Early child analysts viewed play as a route into the unconscious minds of children, much the way dreams are used therapeutically for adults. In addition to a vehicle for exploration of the unconscious, play was also recognized as a useful medium to treat children who presented with a range of difficulties that were generally characterized as neurotic. Children were unable to make use of the traditional frame of therapy for adults, namely, lying on the couch and engaging in free association. This prompted the analysts of the time to look for avenue(s) that provided the following conditions:

1. A setting that allowed children to relax and loosen the ego's control over the entry of psychically dangerous, conflictual material into consciousness.
2. As in dreams, a medium where this material would be admitted to consciousness in a symbolic, disguised form (in order to minimize the anxiety that would accompany it if its actual meaning were recognized).

3. A setting that was congruent with children's developmental level, in which their wishes, fears, and needs would be expressed naturally.

4. A setting that would permit the analyst to observe, interpret, and engage children therapeutically.

Play filled these conditions and became the primary route for child analysis.

Indeed, Waelder (1932), a member of Freud's inner circle, stated that play

1. Serves to develop a sense of mastery
2. Allows for wish fulfillment
3. Permits the assimilation of overpowering experiences
4. Transforms experience of the individual from passivity to activity
5. Is a vehicle for temporarily moving away from demands of reality and the superego
6. Is a route for fantasizing about real objects (i.e., internalized representation of important people)

The 1930s and 1940s witnessed a growth in the application of psychoanalytic methods to the treatment of children. Given the necessity of adhering to psychoanalytic orthodoxy that predominated in the early periods of psychoanalysis, the goal of psychoanalytic play therapy was to adhere to the frame of adult psychoanalysis as closely as possible. This was seen as ideal. It should be remembered that, during this period, psychoanalysis was a new and exciting method of psychotherapy. The insights and findings of psychoanalysis were startling at the time.

The model of the mind developed by the early analysts was that unconscious conflicts were pressing for expression, but ego controls ensured that whatever was expressed was apparent only after careful and laborious effort on the part of the analyst. One metaphor for psychoanalysis in general was that of archaeology, which also captured the imagination of scientists and the lay public alike at the time. Artifacts of earlier and more "primitive" cultures were unearthed only after painstaking efforts at locating where valuable remains might lie buried. Great care and skill was needed by archaeologists to retrieve and piece together the fragments once they were found. Just as in archaeology, the deeper one dug, the artifacts that were recovered were more ancient and "basic." This became a major tenet of psychoanalysis as well, and its early development could be characterized as "archaeology of the mind." The analyst learned to be adept at unearthing and interpreting fragments of childhood conflicts that lay hidden beneath the surface of consciousness. As in archaeology, the older the fragment, the more basic and fundamental was this material to the development of the patient's psyche, and thus would shed light on the nature of the roots of the patient's conflicts. By bringing these conflicts into the light of day, and by emotionally coming to terms with them, it was posited that patients would be "cured" of their neuroses.

Through play, early analysts recognized that its form and content held great symbolic meaning for children and that the play situation permitted the symbolic expression of early and current conflicts. These child analysts held that the tenets of psychoanalysis with adults were applicable to children, albeit with some modifications.

Early Psychoanalytic Approaches to Child Therapy

Melanie Klein was one of the best-known early analysts who treated children through play. Perhaps more than any other theorist, Klein (1932) viewed interpretation as the sine qua non of analytic treatment of children. Klein asserted that, like adults, children form transference neuroses with their analysts, and, through analysis of their play, the roots of their conflicts are readily discernable. Because of this, Klein (1955) viewed play as the equivalent of free association in analysis with adults. She asserted that play, along with other elements of children's behavior, are means of expressing what adults express through words. Child analysis, therefore, required the interpretation of "phantasies, feelings, anxieties, and expressions by play" (Klein, 1955, p. 124). Interpretation was therefore seen as crucial for the establishment of an analytic frame and was the primary means for helping children to understand the purpose of psychoanalysis and for freeing children's imaginations (Klein, 1932). For Klein, interpretation facilitates contact with the unconscious of child analysands and advances analysis by removing repression of intrapsychic material. Moreover, Klein (1955) asserted that children are able to understand and make use of the analyst's interpretations if they are succinct, clear, and employ children's words. Interpretation of play permitted the analysis of transference and the tracing of conflicts to their origins in the histories of children (1932).

In Klein's approach, if interpretations were accurate, children would experience the interpretation as "proof of confidence and love and help to alleviate (a patient's) sense of guilt" (Klein, 1932, p. 69). Klein believed that interpretation was necessary because of children's weak egos and the resultant massive repression of content and their obsessive preoccupation with reality. Therefore, for Klein, the content of play is a vehicle for interpretation of what she considered deeply unconscious phantasies. While she made pioneering contributions to child analysis, Klein viewed the primary value of play as providing unconscious material for interpretation. Klein did not tend, therefore, to utilize play itself as a therapeutic vehicle (Winnicott, 1971b).

In contrast to Klein's approach, Anna Freud asserted that the meaning of play is more uncertain than that of language and, as such, cannot function as the equivalent of free association in adult analysis. Like Klein, she viewed child analysis as having the same aims as other forms of psychoanalysis, which she defined as increasing ego control by expanding consciousness. However, Anna Freud (1946) believed that children were incapable of forming the transference neuroses that were central to the analysis of adults for two main reasons. Because children's relationships with their original objects (i.e., parents) are contemporaneous with treatment, they precluded children from transposing their neurotic conflicts onto the child analyst. Second, she believed that child analysts cannot be neutral to child analysands (A. Freud, 1965). As such, they cannot function as blank screens upon which children project their internal dynamics. In addition, Anna Freud noted that the analyst's dependence on and close work with parents of child patients and others in the child's environment made the analyst a real object to the child, and this precluded the development of a transference neurosis as well. She also diverged from Klein insofar as she did not consider play as equivalent to free association. She cited the facts that children do not corroborate interpretations as do adults, that play does not occur in the context of a full transference neurosis, and that children's play is not dominated by the same purposive attitudes as in adult free association (A. Freud, 1926, 1945).

Anna Freud asserted that while children do form transferences with analysts, analysts are also new objects to children, not just current manifestations of old ones. This creates a double relationship (A. Freud, 1965). She asserts that the duality of the analytic relationship, the proclivity of children to externalize conflicts, and children's dependence on their environment require analysts to balance between external and internal factors and to recognize when their patients are using them in one or the other manner.

Although she advocated a variety of treatment techniques beyond interpretation, Anna Freud still viewed interpretation as central to child analysis. The focus of initial phases of treatment sought to "induce an ego state conducive to perceiving inner conflicts" via the interpretation of defenses (A. Freud, 1965, pp. 225–226). The role of interpretation was seen as a means to help children become aware of the defenses they employed because they were more rigid than those of adults. Once a child was sufficiently prepared, the analyst may then interpret transference and resistance, thereby widening consciousness and increasing ego dominance. She suggested that the analyst use interpretation judiciously and balance between internal and external elements of the case. In addition to interpretation, Anna Freud employed interventions that included verbalization and clarification of preconscious material, suggestion, and reassurance. In this model, children select from among all of these elements and also utilize the analyst as an object of identification (A. Freud, 1965).

All analytic therapists have recognized that their relationships with their child patients were essential components of therapy. Within the traditional psychoanalytic model, the child analyst's role primarily was still seen as that of bringing unconscious conflicts into conscious awareness, thus strengthening ego control over the child's life. This often was accomplished through the development and subsequent interpretation of transferential elements in the child's relationship with her or his therapist. In order to avoid corrupting the essence of transference material that emerged through children's play, analysts strove to adhere to the principle of analytic abstinence, namely, that the analyst should reflect back to the child only what the child her- or himself has produced. Early child analysts therefore tried to minimize the impact of their own participation in the play setting in order to avoid contaminating the material with their own presence. This view of play therapy became a point of departure for contemporary psychoanalytic child therapists, as they began to redefine the therapeutic nature of their participation in play.

CONTEMPORARY PSYCHOANALYTIC APPROACHES

While more traditional psychoanalytic approaches treated play mainly as a vehicle for the expression and interpretation of preconscious and unconscious material, contemporary psychoanalytic play therapists have recognized that, while maintaining the therapeutic importance of interpretation and other forms of elucidating the inherent meanings in children's play, the engagement of the therapist with the child directly through play itself is therapeutic (Levy, 2008). Perhaps the most prominent analyst who advanced analytic play therapy was D. W. Winnicott (1971a). Winnicott viewed play as a form of "transitional phenomena," where the child's inner and outer realities intermingled. Therefore, for Winnicott, play is never fully intrapsychic, nor is it completely focused on external reality. He viewed play as an essential ability of adults as well as children. Play is, fundamentally, a creative activity where the internal and external realities of child and therapist join one another, where the past, present, and future intermingle. Winnicott's wife, Clare (1945, 1963), herself a noted social worker and child therapist, stated that

> through play, the child is experiencing on two levels. There are his inner personal experiences which satisfy his inner needs, and there is the experience of play itself in relation to the environment. If inner experiences do not get used and related to the environment in this way [*author's comment:* i.e., through play] then the child is in a dangerous position. Either he will concentrate on them and cut himself off from vital effective contact with life around him, or he will concentrate on external activities and become cut off from his own inner life. (p. 114)

Winnicott (1971a) stated that the "area of playing is not inner psychic reality. It is outside the individual, but it is not the external world" (p. 51). Marans et al. (1993) state that, for Winnicott, "play is a reflection of the child's capacity to occupy a space between psychic and external reality in which the child uses elements from both domains" (p. 15). This is especially important since transitional phenomena allow children to internalize their relationships with their caretakers and, with the therapist, cocreate representations of new and more successful ways of experiencing self and others, and of relating.

Winnicott (1958) used interpretation judiciously. The main purpose of interpretation was to shift unconscious transference impediments to therapy and thereby allow play to continue. Winnicott (1971a, 1971b) was careful to present interpretations in a nondogmatic manner, so that children were free to accept or reject them. Although he viewed interpretation as an essential component to treatment, he noted that a key source of therapeutic change from psychoanalytic treatment depended on the analyst's surviving the manifestations of the patient's aggression attacks because it established the analyst as independent of the client's needs and because it facilitated object usage (Winnicott, 1971a). For Winnicott (1971a), play was inherently therapeutic because it opens potential space in the therapeutic relationship. Within this metaphorical space, a child can symbolically destroy, differentiate from, and use the analyst.

Notably, Winnicott (1971a) asserted that it is possible to do deep psychother-apy through play without interpretive work. This is because the pleasurable experi-ence of play is derived from the blending of intrapsychic reality with the control of actual objects, such as the therapist. By participating in the play with this in mind, interpretation outside of the frame of play wasn't necessary. Winnicott's work is significant in many ways for psychoanalysis. For play therapy, Winnicott laid the foundation for expansion of analytic treatment to embrace use of play itself, the therapist/child relationship, and the essentially creative and playful nature of treatment.

Current thinking about psychoanalytic play therapy considers successful devel-opment as a dynamic balance and congruence between the internal representation of self and other with the concomitant recognition of each as independent centers of subjectivity (Benjamin, 1995). Despite various differences among modern psycho-analytic developmental theorists, they tend to emphasize the importance of how people develop representations of the world (Beebe & Lachmann, 1988; Tronick, 2007; Tyson, 2002). These authors posit that a subjective sense of self and other is constructed from the relational experiences that are derived from a complex matrix of factors. It is within this matrix that children's innate endowments encounter the qualities and aptitudes of caregivers as well as others in the environment (Beebe, Knoblach, Rustin, & Sorter, 2005; Beebe and Lachmann, 1988; Spiegle, 1989; Tronick, 2007).

CONTEMPORARY PSYCHOANALYTIC CONCEPTIONS OF PLAY

Contemporary analytic theorists and clinicians have extended these views to the relational and neurobiological spheres (Altman, Briggs, Frankel, Gensler, & Pantone, 2002; Barish, 2004a, 2004b; Bonovitz, 2004; Frankel, 1998; Levy, 2008, 2009, 2011, in press; Spiegel, 1989). In this context, Benjamin (1988) acknowl-edges the importance of symbolic play in expressing the tension that exists in the acceptance of conflicting feelings between self and others. She asserts that play constitutes an essential element in the developmental process of promoting mutual understanding. In this way, play facilitates the development of the capacity to relate to the other as both object and subject. She also notes that play creates the first dia-logic forms of mutual recognition.

Play, as a form of transitional phenomenon, opens "potential space" within the analytic relationship (Winnicott, 1971a). That is, therapeutic relationships become contexts wherein new possibilities may emerge. Through play, anything is possible because the play partners are free to enact any scenario, wish, fear, or self-state. By playing, children are allowed to destroy symbolically, differentiate from, and use the therapist to advance their development. The play partners are able to do this because, within the frame of play, there are no consequences to one's actions since play isn't strictly real. Rather, it is marked as a form of subjunctive communi-cation, that is, possible, but not actually true (Pizer, 1998). Because and in spite of the fact that while play material is not strictly true, in psychoanalytic psychotherapy, play is linked very powerfully to a child's subjective experiences (Levenson, 1985).

Slade (1994) noted that by placing their experiences within play rather than merely in words, children create new psychological structures. The structures derived through play form the basis for children's self-understanding and their view of the relational world. Play develops children's identities and their ability to negotiate their environment. It follows that therapists must strive to help child patients to explore their experiences and integrate them within structures that permit more adaptive functioning (Bonovitz, 2004).

A central tenet in contemporary child therapy is that children need others to form meaning and to respond in ways that recognize their experiences as meaningful (Benjamin 1988, 1995; Fonagy, Gergely, Jurist, & Target, 2004; Frankel, 1998). Slade (1994) notes that "when we play with a child, we let the child know that we are there to be told.... Children learn to represent internal experiences because these experiences are first made real by another's recognition of them" (p. 95). Recognition is a complex process that encompasses both verbal and nonverbal constituents. Slade states that

> the process of naming feelings is a first step in differentiating affect states: distinguishing one affect from another, distinguishing speaking about emotion from acting on it, and distinguishing one character from those of another. It typically accompanies the emergence of narrative. (p. 94)

Therefore, through the medium of play, children's experiences may become "realized, integrated, and accepted into the patient's experience of himself" (Frankel, 1998, p. 154). Therefore, in psychoanalytic play therapy, children are helped to form and re-form their experiences through play and to derive meaning from them in order to develop their self-integrity and coherence. It aims to enhance children's ability to relate to others in deeper, more satisfying ways. Therefore, while play in child therapy long has been seen as a useful medium, psychoanalytic authors have differed regarding the role of play itself as therapeutic and the role of interpretation in child treatment.

Play and Language

Psychoanalytic play therapy significantly involves actions that more or less are tied to spoken language. This fact creates problems as well as opportunities for child therapists. One of the main difficulties in working clinically through play is that the meaning of spoken language is more precise than are other forms of communication. Spoken language is not necessarily so very accurate, but its meaning often is far more apparent than are the meanings of play. Child therapists therefore are much less certain about the meanings of their clients' actions (Sutton-Smith, 1997). Since therapists' constructed meanings of clients' behaviors form the basis for therapeutic decision making and action on the part of clinicians, child therapists are usually less certain about how best to respond to their clients. In contrast to others, child therapists therefore must develop comfort with ambiguity in their work with their clients. They also need to cultivate a facility for understanding the semiotics (i.e., the signs and symbols) of human communication.

Bateson (1972) noted the parallel between therapy and play. He pointed out that both play and therapy occur within a delimited psychological frame and possess temporal and spatial bounding of messages. Bateson asserted that, in both therapy and play, the messages have a particular relationship to a more concrete and basic reality. For Bateson, therapy and play are effective precisely because the interactions and communications are not considered to be "real" within their respective frames and because the material strongly relates to important elements of a person's life outside of these frames (Levenson, 1985). Levenson notes the parallels between speech and action when he states that they are "transforms of each other; that is, they will be, in musical terms, harmonic variations of the same theme" (p. 81).

Play in therapy is immediate (Gaines, 2003). Rather than a child discussing difficulties with his therapist that are seen as occurring outside the therapy space, play treatment often results in enactments of these problems in vivo, through the medium of play itself. Like their colleagues who treat adults, some child therapists believe that it is more efficacious if their clients discuss and focus on past relationships. Indeed, they consider the material from the more remote past as more basic and significant than recent memories. However, as Levenson (1985) asserts, "the patient's past, the patient's present, and his interaction with the therapist (also) become transforms of each other, immensely useful as different parameters of the same experience" (p. 52). Therefore, for modern psychoanalytic child therapists, the use of the present play experience is as essential to therapy as is focusing on past histories of the children they treat.

Although both play and verbal language are forms of communication, they essentially are not equivalent. While play lacks the precision of language (Sutton-Smith, 1997), it affords the clinician certain advantages over other means of communication. In addition to play being children's natural forms of expression, play provides both clients and therapists "plausible deniability" concerning troubling material; that is, it permits the parties to suspend and, if necessary, to disavow its reality. After all, it's "only" a game. Play therefore frees the participants to express and explore these issues in ways that would be far more difficult should one pursue a more exclusively verbal means of communication.

There is literature that asserts that nonverbal processing of experience independently contributes to the ways that people function (Levy, 2009; Lyons-Ruth, 1999). Lyons-Ruth et al. (1998) note that "implicit knowings governing interactions are not language-based and are not routinely translated into semantic form" (p. 285). Since children's play includes more nonverbal elements than do therapies that focus on verbal communication, analytic play therapy provides greater access to implicit relational knowledge and gives therapists a means to develop and expand it with their clients by developing new models for being with others (Levy, 2007).

Because of its immediate and active nature, play demands the participation of therapists in ways that are unimaginable in more verbally oriented therapies. The roles of child therapists therefore necessarily are more active, and they find themselves in situations that allow little time to reflect upon the meaning of what transpires in treatment prior to their actions (Gaines, 2003). While an adult therapist might labor under the illusion that one mainly needs to understand and empathize with one's clients and offer interpretations, such a mind-set would handicap a child therapist. In a way, contemporary psychoanalytic theory now fits better with the action-oriented nature of play therapy, as theorists realize the inherent limitations of a primarily verbal approach to treatment (Barish, 2004b; Frankel, 1998). Modern relational psychoanalytic theorists have emphasized that clients must be encountered—that is, that therapists must do more than listen and interpret (Aron, 1996; Bromberg, 1998, 2006; Levenson, 1985; Mitchell, 1988, 1997; Pizer, 1998; Slochower, 1996).

Mitchell (1988) asserted that analytic therapists must not merely understand their clients but that they must also find a voice to communicate that understanding in order to find a way out of the client's usual patterns of hearing and experiencing others. Indeed, Mitchell (1997) stated further that

> a therapist discovers himself as a co-actor in a passionate drama involving love and hate, sexuality and murder, intrusion and abandonment, victims and executioners. Whichever path he chooses, he falls into one of the patient's pre-determined categories and is experienced by the patient that way. The struggle is toward a new way of experiencing both himself and the patient, a different way of being with the analysand, in which one is neither fused nor detached, seductive nor rejecting, victim nor executioner. The struggle is to find an authentic voice in which to speak to the analysand, a voice more fully one's own, less shaped by the configurations and limited options of the analysand's relational matrix, and, in so doing, offering the analysand a chance to broaden and expand that matrix. (p. 295)

In treating children, psychoanalytic child therapists struggle to engage, to become unhinged, to find one's footing, and to communicate one's understanding of the child's experience. This is all the more essential given the complications engendered by treating children and the essential ambiguity and immediacy engendered by play in psychoanalytic child therapy.

Play thus permits psychologically dangerous thoughts and feelings to be acted upon and then be plausibly denied by the child (Levy, 2008). Play encompasses a paradox: It is both true and untrue at the same time. The duality of actual experience occurring in the subjunctive frame of play permits deeply held feelings and thoughts to emerge and to be engaged therapeutically within the frame of play. Further, play derives its therapeutic value because it fosters integration of diverse modes of processing experience. In order to play, children must engage and coordinate a variety of sensory, perceptual, cognitive, affective, and behavioral processes. Since it encompasses action as well as thought and feeling, play engenders experience of emotionally vivid self-states within the relatively secure relationship with the therapist (see Levy, 2009, for a more extensive discussion).

To maximize the therapeutic value of play, therapists must genuinely have an extraordinary interest in their child patients, in part because it can engender new relational experiences. Such experiences may serve as a template for the construction of new models of self and others or alter existing ones to foster a sense of self-integrity, cohesion, and interpersonal security.

Play therapists must also accept a measure of uncertainty due to the relative ambiguity of the meaning of play (Levy, 2008; Sutton-Smith, 1997). Child therapists must learn to cultivate patience and let the therapeutic relationship emerge and evolve. In modern psychoanalytic play therapy, therapists must be prepared to tolerate uncomfortable states that may be painful, hard to imagine, or even repulsive. These feeling states are seen as a form of implicit communication of the child's experiences and constitute key constituents of the therapist's formulation of the child's experiences (Boston Change Process Study Group, 2002, 2008). In this way, much information regarding children's organization of experiences is embodied in the play relationship. It is important to engage children in creating and recreating their own stories and become a coinvestigator of their experience.

Play treatment, because of its cross-modal nature, may function to help children better integrate their experience (Levy, 2007, 2008). Once a therapeutic relationship is negotiated adequately, challenge and disruption of the relationship almost always occurs as old relational models are enacted within the current therapeutic relationship. Rather than a threat to the therapy per se, psychoanalytic play therapists see these situations as opportunities to engage their child patients and to help them re-regulate their patients' emotional states in new ways. In this way, the patient can symbolically destroy the therapist through play and then rediscover and re-create him or her. In so doing, the patient re-creates him- or herself as well. It is through this process that the therapist becomes a usable object for the child (Winnicott, 1971a). This is a recursive process in which new self/other configurations emerge.

THE THERAPEUTIC RELATIONSHIP IN CONTEMPORARY PSYCHOANALYTIC PLAY THERAPY

By tailoring the therapeutic relationships to maximize the inherent capacities of their patients, psychoanalytic therapists attempt to engage the forward edge of their patients' zones of proximal development, that is, ". . . the distance between the actual developmental level as determined by independent problem solving and the level of potential development as determined through problem solving under adult guidance or in collaboration with peers" (Vygotsky, 1978, p. 86). Through their relationships with children with Asperger syndrome, development can be fostered by the minor impingements engendered by the play relationship and by marking the emotional reactions of the child (Fonagy et al., 2004). The role of interactive repair thus is an essential component in fostering development (Beebe et al., 2005; Tronick, 2007) and in modern psychoanalytic treatment. This entails struggle on the part of the therapist to find a way of authentically communicating his or her subjectivity (Mitchell, 1997) while processing, integrating, and reconstructing the child's experience and then responding in a manner that maximizes the potential that the child also can recognize his or her own experience in the interaction with the therapist (Lichtenberg, Lachmann, & Fosshage, 2002). Through the interactive, dynamic interchange of play, where interactive impingement and repair abounds, children may develop a greater capacity for awareness of self and other, for better affect regulation, and for participating in social relationships in more satisfying ways.

Contemporary psychoanalytic play therapy embodies a sense of emotional resonance (Levy, 2008), that is, "an individual's signal to another that 'I am present
with you, regardless of our differences.'" (Coburn, 2001, p. 309). Coburn sees emotional resonance as a

> prereflective, procedural process that determines the course not just of present and
> future relational patterns within the dyad, but also the lived, affective experiences of
> two or more people that center on the continual checking, probing, questioning, nego-
> tiating, affirming, disconfirming, of experiences of relative certainty about something,
> conviction about something, or both. (p. 312)

The concept of the therapeutic alliance in psychoanalytic play therapy therefore
has evolved with new developments in child development, neurobiology, family
dynamics, and in psychoanalysis itself. It should be clear that the therapeutic alliance generally has moved to a more collaborative approach within the therapeutic
dyad (Aron, 1996; Levy, 2008). Because play allows children's experiences to be
embodied and enacted in a less-than-real play context, child patients express and
explore facets of themselves within the context of a facilitating, generative relationship. Construction of a therapeutic, psychoanalytic relationship permits a sense of
security to develop. This relationship allows unacceptable, psychically dangerous
feelings to emerge and to be addressed in more productive ways (Levy, in press;
Pizer, 1998; Winnicott, 1971a).

Play itself is seen as providing a crucial vehicle for children to develop this
capacity. Increased affect regulation, self-awareness, and self complexity is developed by the process of containing, regulating, and repairing the treatment relationship, the engendering of experimentation, and promoting the experience of new
self-states through play. There is a reciprocal relationship between experiencing
new or dissociated self-states in the therapeutic play relationship and the promotion
of greater complexity in the child's self-organization (Saari, 1993) as unformulated
and dissociated self-states become more elaborated, more flexibly experienced, and
better integrated within the child's personality.

The therapeutic alliance especially is complicated in psychoanalytic child treatment since the therapist must maintain working alliances with the child's caretakers, teachers, school-based mental health professionals, and others. Child therapists
therefore must respond to the multiple demands that emanate from sources beyond
the child her- or himself. One needs to embrace this state of affairs and balance
one's approach based on these multiple inputs. Indeed, child therapists must develop
working alliances with other adults while also keeping the needs and subjectivity of
their child patients central and alive.

CASE EXAMPLE

Connor, a boy of 9, came to the therapist with a diagnosis of an atypical developmental disorder and oppositional behavior. Neuropsychological evaluations
indicated that, although Connor was intellectually gifted, there were indications

of severe deficits in understanding the reactions of others and evidence of cognitive rigidity, especially in ambiguous situations. Connor also manifested deficits in executive functions. According to reports, Connor enjoyed saying "inappropriate things," especially when he was with his parents, who reacted angrily to his behavior. When Connor would say rude and offensive things to others, he outright resisted his parents' attempts to stop him. He experienced periods of severe emotional dysregulation when he perceived impingements that were especially intrusive.

Over the years, Connor's parents enrolled him in numerous therapies. His parents were unsure that many of these therapies had helped Connor (the therapist's work with Connor's parents is beyond the scope of this chapter). Connor and his parents had participated in cognitive-behavioral therapy since he was age 2 to help him with the dysregulation and specific behavioral symptoms such as tics. That therapy focused on redirecting Connor to more prosocial activities and on helping Connor to employ techniques to prevent dysregulation. Connor's parents were skeptical whether psychoanalytic play therapy would be helpful, but they were willing to pursue it if it might help their son.

Connor approached psychoanalytic therapy with understandable apprehension. When he met the therapist for the first time, Connor appeared to steel himself for an onslaught of yet another helping professional making him do something he didn't want to do or telling him how he should do things. The therapist remarked that Connor didn't seem like he wanted to come to therapy. He said that he didn't, and Connor expressed antipathy toward his parents for what he perceived as their unwarranted control of his life, for their restrictions on his free time, and for their arbitrary curbs on his viewing movies that his peers had already seen. The therapist listened carefully to Connor's complaints. Rather than comment on the wisdom of his parents' decision, he instead inquired about and commented on Connor's feelings about his parents, the various "helpers," and explored with Connor what he wished his life would be. During the session, Connor appeared to notice that the therapist was paying careful attention to his reactions and that the therapist refrained from stopping, redirecting, or fixing him. At the end of the hour, the therapist presented a dilemma to Connor. He said that although he wanted to work with Connor, he knew how much Connor disliked participating in any therapy. The therapist said that he didn't want to force Connor to continue to come to treatment, but he also noted that Connor's parents thought that they might work well together. He said that he wasn't sure what to do but that a solution should come from *both* Connor and him. Connor said that he would be willing to continue to attend sessions if they also would be like the current one. The therapist couldn't promise that because he couldn't predict the future, but he said that he would always try to keep Connor's feelings, desires, and needs in mind and genuinely try to help. He also hoped that if Connor believed that the therapist didn't live up to his word, he would feel comfortable enough to tell the therapist so that they could try to work this out. Connor agreed to return.

Early on, Connor said things that he thought were inappropriate to the therapist. He made racist and anti-Semitic comments and said that he intended to be the supreme ruler of the world for the sole purpose of making others suffer. The therapist said that he could understand why Connor would be so angry and want to control others when he saw others unfairly controlling him. Rather than stop him from speaking, the therapist engaged him by exploring how others reacted when he said these things. They laughed together at how people became upset at these comments, and the therapist acknowledged that it might feel good to upset people who Connor felt upset him.

It isn't clear who initiated it (in good play therapy, such things often are unclear), but they spontaneously began to compose "plays" that included material that became increasingly outrageous. At Connor's request, the therapist dutifully recorded them, and even offered measured suggestions for the plot and for dialogue. Connor was careful to make sure that the therapist hid their "plays" when their sessions were over out of concern that his parents might see them. Connor began to anticipate his sessions eagerly, running down the hall to the therapist's office. Intermixed with this activity, Connor began to mention the ways that his parents angered him and talked about fantasies that he had about punishing them and others whom he felt had wronged him. Concurrent with these events, Connor's behavior became more regulated, and he appeared more relaxed and even happy.

Connor then engaged the therapist in competitive board games. This afforded the therapeutic dyad opportunities to address issues of aggression, dominance, defeat, and self-esteem. Because Connor chose games that required a good deal of strategy, his deficits in executive functions were evident. Connor asserted his desire to obliterate the therapist in the game, and he described his fantasies of omnipotent domination of the therapist and of the entire world. The therapist accepted these feelings and playfully responded with acknowledgments of Connor's intentions.

The therapist modified how he played the games based on how well Connor was playing. Connor would become visibly anxious when he seemed to be losing the game. He would become silly, say that he lost interest in the game, or giddily flick his pieces across the board and knock down as many of the therapist's as he could. The therapist recognized how frustrating the game could be and permitted these otherwise forbidden feelings and behaviors to be expressed through the game. He noted how well Connor could manage his frustration and took it as a current indicator of Connor's emotional status. Over some months, Connor's ability to tolerate periods when it appeared that he would lose the game improved, and he began to laugh with the therapist when he became frustrated by his moves. According to parent and teacher reports, Connor was more regulated at home and at school. His oppositional behavior remained, but it decreased in frequency, intensity, and duration. He began to participate more freely in group activities and even began to develop friendships.

Case Discussion

There were two examples of play in this case. The first was verbal and resulted in the cocreation of plays that expressed Connor's subjective needs and wishes. The second was the use of competitive board games. In both instances, play spontaneously developed as the dyad developed ways of working together. While their relationship was truly mutual, it was also asymmetrical in that the therapist was participating in ways to help Connor formulate his experience, especially when it seemed most difficult for him. It was implicitly communicated that, so long as they were expressed through play (i.e., the subjunctive), Connor was free to bring self-states that were otherwise banned, dissociated, or negatively sanctioned into their sessions. Another paradox of psychoanalytic play therapy is that, for therapy to proceed, there must be enough comfort and trust in the dyad to take risks and allow painful material to be enacted in the therapeutic relationship.

Connor's behavior outside of therapy improved as he began to feel deeply understood, and the meanings of his reactions were mutually formulated. Because Connor expressed his anger through play and was accepted by his therapist, both because and in spite of it, Connor had the direct experience of participating in other modes of engaging with others. Also, as the therapist had a deeper understanding of Connor, he was in a better position to help others in Connor's life to be more responsive. Rather than automatically reacting with oppositional or otherwise disruptive behavior, more adaptive options for expressing himself and in engaging others expanded for Connor. Greater adaptability resulted in, and resulted from, greater self-complexity and in multifaceted ways of engaging others.

CONCLUSION

In nearly 100 years of using play therapeutically, psychoanalytic approaches to play therapy have evolved substantially. Psychoanalysis has remained in dialogue with such diverse fields as neurobiology, history, philosophy, and gender studies, as well as the visual, literary, and performing arts. It has used these contacts to refine and enrich its approaches to therapy. Although most students are taught outmoded psychoanalytic theory, mainly as a point of criticism, psychoanalysis actively continues to address a wide range of current issues, such as changing social structures, individual alienation, identity and diversity, political violence, marginalization and exclusion, and emerging cultural realities. In addition, there has been a long tradition of reciprocal influence between psychoanalysis and psychological research, especially in the areas of human development, cognitive science, and social psychology.

Modern psychoanalytic therapy, and therapy with children in particular, emphasizes the collaborative and individualized cocreation of meaning through a creative engagement between patient and therapist. It recognizes that there is no one "correct" interpretation of play or of any other behavior. Rather, it stresses co-construction of meaning within the therapeutic dyad. Psychoanalytic treatment pays close attention to the moment-by-moment interactions within an intimate therapeutic relationship and uses them as cues to develop a deeper, richer understanding of the child's internal and relational world. In this way, new opportunities for experiencing self and others and for new ways of acting are opened for the child, and the child's innate capacities for growth are freed.

REFERENCES

Altman, N., Briggs, R., Frankel, J., Gensler, D., & Pantone, P. (2002). *Relational child psychotherapy.* New York, NY: Other Press.

Aron, L. (1996). *A meeting of minds: Mutuality in psychoanalysis.* Hillsdale, NJ: Analytic Press.

Barish, K. (2004a). The child therapist's generative use of self. *Journal of Infant, Child, and Adolescent Psychotherapy, 3,* 270–284.

Barish, K. (2004b). What is therapeutic in child therapy? *Psychoanalytic Psychology, 21,* 385–401.

Bateson, G. (1972). *Steps towards an ecology of mind.* New York, NY: Ballantine Books.

Beebe, B., & Lachmann, F. (1988). The contribution of mother–infant mutual influence to the origins of self- and object representations. *Psychoanalytic Psychology, 5,* 305–337.

Beebe, B., Knoblach, S., Rustin, J., & Sorter, D. (2005). *Forms of intersubjectivity in infant and adult treatment.* New York, NY: Other Press.

Benjamin, J. (1988). *The bonds of love: Psychoanalysis, feminism, and the problem of domination.* New York, NY: Pantheon.

Benjamin, J. (1995*). Like subjects, love objects.* New Haven, CT: Yale University Press.

Bonovitz, C. (2004). The cocreation of fantasy and the transformation of psychic structure. *Psychoanalytic Dialogues, 14,* 553–558.

Boston Change Process Study Group (BCPSG). (2002). Non-interpretative mechanisms in psychoanalytic therapy—the "something more" than interpretation. *International Gestalt Journal, 25,* 37–71.

Boston Change Process Study Group (BCPSG). (2008). Forms of relational meaning: Issues in the relations between the implicit and reflective-verbal domains. *Psychoanalytic Dialogues, 18,* 125–148.

Bromberg, P. M. (1998). *Standing in the spaces: Essays on clinical process, trauma, and dissociation.* Hillsdale, NJ: Analytic Press.

Bromberg, P. M. (2006). *Awakening the dreamer: Clinical journeys.* Hillsdale, NJ: Analytic Press.

Coburn, W. J. (2001). Subjectivity, emotional resonance, and the sense of the real. *Psychoanalytic Psychology, 18,* 303–319.

Fonagy, P., Gergely, G., Jurist, E., & Target, M. (2004). *Affect regulation, mentalization, and the development of the self.* New York: Other Press.

Frankel, J. (1998). The play's the thing: How the essential processes of therapy are seen more clearly in child therapy. *Psychoanalytic Dialogues, 8,* 149–182.

Freud, A. (1926). The role of transference in the analysis of children. In A. Freud (Ed.), *The psychoanalytical treatment of children* (pp. 28–37). New York, NY: International Universities Press.

Freud, A. (1945). Indications for child analysis. In A. Freud (Ed.), *The psycho-analytical treatment of children* (pp. 67–93). New York, NY: International Universities Press.

Freud, A. (1946). *The psycho-analytical treatment of children.* New York, NY: International Universities Press.

Freud, A. (1965). *Normality and pathology of childhood.* New York, NY: International Universities Press.

Freud, S. (1908). Creative writers and day-dreaming. *Standard Edition, 9,* 141–155.

Freud, S. (1931). Female sexuality. *Collected Papers, 5,* 252–272.

Gaines, R. (2003). Therapist self-disclosure with children, adolescents, and their parents. *Journal of Clinical Psychology, 59*(5): 569–580.

Hug-Hellmuth, H. (1921). On the technique of child analysis. *International Journal of Psychoanalysis, 2,* 287–305.

Klein, M. (1932). *The psychoanalysis of children.* New York, NY: Delacorte Press.

Klein, M. (1955). The psychoanalytic play technique: Its history and significance. In M. Klein (Ed.), *Envy and gratitude* (pp. 122–140). New York, NY: Free Press.

Levenson, E. (1985). *The ambiguity of change: An inquiry into the nature of psychoanalytic reality.* Northvale, NJ: Aronson.

Levy, A. J. (2007, March). *A re-consideration of the therapeutic action of play in the psychodynamic treatment of children.* Paper presented at the biannual meeting of the American Association for Psychoanalysis in Clinical Social Work, Chicago, IL.

Levy, A. J. (2008). The therapeutic action of play in the psychodynamic treatment of children: A critical analysis. *Clinical Social Work Journal, 36,* 281–291.

Levy, A. J. (2009). Neurobiology and the therapeutic action of psychoanalytic play therapy with children. *Clinical Social Work Journal.* Published online at Springer First, August 10, 2009. doi: 10.1007/s10615-009-0229x

Levy, A. J. (in press). Psychoanalytic psychotherapy for children with Asperger's syndrome: Therapeutic engagement through play. *Psychoanalytic Perspectives.*

Levy, A. J., & Frank, M. J. (2011). Clinical practice with children. In J. Brandell (Ed.), *Theory and practice of clinical social work* (pp. 101–122). Woodland Hills, CA: Sage.

Lichtenberg, J. D., Lachmann, F. M., & Fosshage, J. L. (2002). *A spirit of inquiry: Communication in psychoanalysis.* Hillsdale, NJ: Analytic Press.

Lyons-Ruth, K. (1999). The two-person unconscious: Intersubjective dialogue, enactive representation, and the emergence of new forms of relational organization. *Psychoanalytic Inquiry, 19,* 576–617.

Lyons-Ruth, K., Bruschweiler-Stern, N., Harrison, A. M., Morgan, A. C., Nahum, J. P., Sander, L., . . . Tronick, E. Z. (1998). Implicit relational knowing: Its role in development and psychoanalytic treatment. *Infant Mental Health Journal, 19,* 282–289.

Marans, S., Mayes, L. C., & Colonna, A. B. (1993). Psychoanalytic views of children's play. In A. J. Solnit, D. J. Cohen, & P. B. Neubauer (Eds.), *The many meanings of play* (pp. 9–28). New Haven, CT: Yale University Press.

Mitchell, S. (1988). *Relational concepts in psychoanalysis: Integration.* Cambridge, MA: Harvard University Press.

Mitchell, S. (1997). *Influence and autonomy in psychoanalysis.* Hillsdale, NJ: Analytic Press.

Pizer, S. A. (1998). *Building bridges: The negotiation of paradox in psychoanalysis.* Hillsdale, NJ: Analytic Press.

Saari, C. (1993). Identity complexity as an indicator of health. *Clinical Social Work Journal, 21,* 11–24.

Slade, A. (1994). Making meaning and making believe: Their role in the clinical process. In A. Slade & D. Palmer Wolf (Eds.), *Children at play: Clinical and developmental approaches to meaning and representation* (pp. 81–107). New York, NY: Oxford University Press.

Slochower, J. A. (1996). *Holding and psychoanalysis: A relational perspective.* Hillsdale, NJ: Analytic Press.

Solnit, A. J. (1993). From play to playfulness in children and adults. In A. J. Solnit, D. J. Cohen, & P. B. Neubauer (Eds.), *The many meanings of play* (pp. 29–43). New Haven, CT: Yale University Press.

Spiegel, S. (1989). *An interpersonal approach to child therapy.* New York, NY: Columbia University Press.

Sutton-Smith, B. (1997). *The ambiguity of play.* Cambridge, MA: Harvard University Press.

Tronick, E. (2007). *The neurobehavioral and social–emotional development of infants and children.* New York, NY: Norton.

Tyson, P. (2002). The challenges of psychoanalytic developmental theory. *Journal of the American Psychoanalytic Association, 50,* 19–52.

Vygotsky, L. S. (1978). *Mind in society: The development of higher psychological processes.* Cambridge, MA: Harvard University Press.

Waelder, R. (1932). The psychoanalytic theory of play. In S. A. Guttman (Ed.), *Psychoanalysis: Observation, theory, application* (1976 collected works; pp. 84–100). New York, NY: International Universities Press.

Winnicott, C. (1945). Children who cannot play. In J. Kanter (Ed.), *Face to face with children: The life and work of Clare Winnicott* (revised 2004; pp. 112–121). London, UK: Karnac Books.

Winnicott, C. (1963). Face to face with children. In J. Kanter (Ed.), *Face to face with children: The life and work of Clare Winnicott* (revised 2004; pp. 166–183). London, UK: Karnac Books.

Winnicott, D. W. (1958). *Through pediatrics to psycho-analysis.* New York, NY: Basic Books.

Winnicott, D. W. (1971a). *Playing and reality.* New York, NY: Routledge.

Winnicott, D. W. (1971b). *Therapeutic consultations in child psychiatry.* New York, NY: Basic Books.

Chapter 5

JUNGIAN ANALYTICAL PLAY THERAPY
Eric J. Green

> *Childhood is the time when, terrifying or encouraging, those farseeing dreams appear before the soul of the child, shaping his whole destiny.*
>
> *(Jung, 1951)*

Swiss psychologist Carl G. Jung's (1875–1961) analytical theory has not traditionally been viewed in terms of its application to children but seen primarily as an erudite psychology of the adult. Specifically, Jung's theory is known for its focus on the second half of adult life, where he hypothesized *individuation* (or becoming a "psychological individual") occurs. According to Main (2008), however, Jung was indeed concerned with the child as a metaphorical image or archetype and focused on the psychology of "the child" or the symbol/myth inherent within the universal image of childhood. The archetype or image of "the child" is seen throughout Jung's early writings, especially in the *Theory of Psychoanalysis* (Jung, 1913) and *Psychic Conflicts in a Child* (Jung, 1910). In these writings, Jung reveals his views of childhood as being a dependent on caretakers. Through association tests, he demonstrated the far-reaching effects of identification between caretakers and children, with a child's life almost completely shaped by the unconscious or inner world of his parents.

Most of Jung's (2008) writings on children stemmed from his analysis of adult patients remembering their dreams from childhood, including the epic *somnia a deo missa* (dreams sent by God). He determined that much of the underlying psychological content in these dreams from childhood was related to parents' psychopathology. It was not until much later in his studies that he began the process of applying his notion of archetypes to childhood. Eventually, his theory became vulnerable to derision. Specifically, critics were discontent with the soundness of Jung's esoteric theory unless archetypes could be observed in childhood and throughout the life span, and not exclusively in the latter part of adulthood.

For Jung, "the child" does not refer to the human child but essentially refers to the universal symbol or archetype of the child, found in myths, fairy tales, dreams, and fantasies (Fordham, 1994; Jung, 1951; Main, 2008). Jung was not interested in the child's development necessarily but more in the myth-making function of the psyche during childhood. Jung found that the archetype of the child appears in various child motifs, as an archetype by its definition cannot be directly described, such as "the eternal child," "the divine child," and "the child of chaos." Two commonalities in Jung's symbolic view of childhood across all motifs involve autonomy and spontaneity.

Wanting to explore the analytical process with children, Jung encouraged Dora Kalff (1980) to study under Margaret Lowenfield and develop a method for symbolic play in child therapy, which she later termed *sandplay*. Starting in the 1930s, Melanie Klein (1955), a child psychoanalyst, influenced by Jung's work, developed a revolutionary approach to working with children, including the use of play techniques. Inspired by Klein, Michael Fordham (1944) wrote *The Life of Childhood*, where it was argued, for the first time with evidence from actual child analysis and not simply from analyses of adults like Jung had previously undertaken, that archetypes were observable in children and were a significant component in the therapeutic process. Archetypes refer to the predisposition to create images, to organize experience, and to determine an individual's relationship between the inner and outer worlds. Fordham goes on to say that the archetypal content in children is related to drives, instincts, and bodily experiences in relation to the child's mental world. Development and psychological maturation lead the child toward the spiritual end of the archetype, where he can cultivate individuality and engage in collective thinking.

Later, Sidoli and Davies (1988) compiled a book titled *Jungian Child Psychotherapy* that encapsulated Fordham's Jungian views on child analysis, as well as the other significant contributions to the topic. John Allan went on to refine Jungian child psychotherapy further by the specificity of incorporating play therapy techniques in child analysis with various applications through his seminal book, *Inscapes of the Child's World* (1988). More recently, J. P. Lilly (2009), and Eric Green (2007, 2008, 2009) write, provide trainings at professional conferences, and advocate for the inherent focus on depth and meaning as espoused through Jungian play therapy into the 21st century.

BASIC CONCEPTS, GOALS, AND TECHNIQUES

The conceptual basis of Jungian analytical play therapy (JAPT) is that during children's development, either by introjection (internalizing beliefs of others) or identification (strongly relating to the values and feelings of others), feelings, thoughts, and traits of primary caretakers are acquired (or internalized) as well as any associated dysfunction or trauma(s) related to those significant primary relationships. Therefore, the practice and scope of JAPT is to afford children sufficient space in an emotionally protected environment or *vas* (container) so that personal development (individuation) materializes. Individuation characterizes a progress from psychic fragmentation toward wholeness: the acknowledgment and reconciliation of opposites within an individual (Jung, 1951). Jung believed children's psyches contain a transcendent function, or self-healing archetype (Allan, 1988; Fordham, 1994), that surfaces through symbol production.

Archetypes form the basis of typical activities and behaviors associated with the human existence, which are evolutionary and upon which individual development proceeds. Jung emphasized the feeling-tone nature of archetypes and believed they formed the link between psychic events and the meaning of life. These archetypal themes organize children's behaviors, and their understanding is of paramount importance when engaging in the analytic attitude required to effectively facilitate JAPT.

Therapists enable children's healing through the safety inherent within a nonjudgmental, therapeutic relationship and witness the emergence of the self-healing archetype released from children's psyches throughout therapy. A *self-healing archetype* is an innate symbol that promotes healing by achieving a well-adjusted intrapsychic connection between the *ego* and the *self*. The *ego* is the seat or faculty of reasoning (the "I" as we know it), and the *self* is the central organizing archetype that represents the ego linked with the personality (or perhaps the "soul") (Green, 2009; Peery, 2003). By unifying oppositions that surface within, children achieve equilibrium between the burdens of the ego and external world (e.g., home, school, peers) and the needs of the personal unconscious (inner world of feelings).

The relationship to the symbolic life or how children relate to their inner symbols is the crux of Jung's theory of psychological growth (Jung, 1964). Jung believed that inner development occurs when an individual acknowledges and creates symbols from dreams and fantasies and follows these symbols wherever they lead through the process of *active imagination*. Jung's psychology centers around the contrast of the dissent of the ego going down to the underworld and its natural assent up to the external world.

Jungian play therapists focus on the psyche's role in child personality development. *Psyche* is defined as the child's center of thought that regulates conscious experiences, such as behaviors and feelings. Jung (2009) explained that the evolving nature of the child's psyche is affected by the collective unconscious as the images within the collective influence the process of individuation. Jung's concept of the collective unconscious was less person specific than Freud's term *unconscious*. Jung (1964) replaced Freud's theory of a personal unconscious—a reservoir of individual unconscious memories and repressed emotions—with a *collective unconscious* containing shared images that surpass an individual's personal (or conscious) experience. The collective unconscious consists of primordial images and mythological motifs often manifested in fairy tales, Greek myths, and ancient legends. Fordham (1994) took this a step further and stated that childhood, not just the latter part of adult life as Jung initially argued, is a time of individuation when children tap into the archetypes within the collective unconscious to grow and assimilate to their culture. In children, the growth process revolves around the ego separating from the self; and in late adulthood, growth occurs from the reintegration and alignment of the self with the ego. Individuation in childhood is simply maturing, or moving away from the *primary identity* (Astor, 1988). Primary identity is when children behave toward objects as if their fantasies about them were reality, and they do not have the consciousness to perceive the "as if" quality.

Jung believed there was no ego consciousness at birth, with ego being the center of the conscious mind. Jung stated that the ego is embedded in the self. Fordham (1994) stated that at birth, ego deintegrates (dissolves), exemplified by eye moving, the calming of a distressed infant, sucking, being comforted, and crying, all of which form ego. Deintegration of the ego is followed by reintegration if the infant is comforted by a caretaker. When the child is adequately cared for (i.e., fed when hungry, held when scared, diaper changed regularly), positive parental *introjects* (internalized images) emerge, creating a sense of secure attachment. With secure attachment, children are positioned to develop healthy coping skills and ego strength to resolve typical adverse events in the external world. In some instances, the infant's primal needs are not mediated by a caretaker, and the infant introjects (internalizes) negative images of the mother and father imagoes. These negative images are internalized as *not good enough parents*, which creates rigid ego defenses (Allan, 1997). Ego defenses become inflexible because they must guard the child's delicate ego from extermination due to the myriad feelings of desertion, denial, and wretchedness (Alan, 1988; Green, 2009).

Jungian therapists stay *at the feeling level* of the child (Allan, 1997). Ego therapists want to rush in, but Jungian analysts are patient observers. Jungians recognize that children must be treated in their own right as individuals and not viewed merely as a symptom within a dysfunctional family system. Before moving into the working phase in clinical work, a therapist must build trust with the child and accept the child's personality. Once trust is formed, the child's unconscious is free to enter into the symbol, and the symbol deintegrates or is reduced to a conscious feeling or recognizable image. For example, if an introverted child presents with anxiety or attention deficit/hyperactivity disorder (ADHD), the analyst will witness what image surfaces with the child's neurosis by assisting the child in switching off the ego's energies and painting the image of anxiety. Jungians believe that by entering the feeling, the child changes the affect. The Jungian approach to play psychotherapy depends on children trusting and allowing the symbols to lead them into healing by containing images. Moreover, the successful nature of Jungian play psychotherapy depends on the cultivation of the *transference*, or as Jungians describe it, *working in the transference*. Psychotherapy is only as good as both the analyst and child are changed within the transferential projections, out of which healing and growth occur.

Model of Psychopathology

An infant's ego defenses rely on nascent defensive structures that create breaks in the hypothetical ego–self axis when an infant's physiological and emotional needs are inadequately supported. The *ego–self axis* is a Jungian term for the negotiation between the child's inner and outer worlds (Alan, 1997). With the introjection of the *bad parent image*, the child may recognize the world as dangerous and unbalanced. With this insecure attachment come feelings of degradation and being *not good enough* (Winnicott, 1971). Because of the nascent functioning of the ego in early childhood, rigid ego defenses develop to protect the insubstantial ego, which creates a psychopathology of defensive splitting of the self from the ego for preservation (Green, 2009).

A child's autonomous personality may encounter extinction when faced with an imminent, sustained level of hyperarousal or extreme traumatic anxiety (Jung, 1964). To avoid this eradication, Kalsched (1996) speculated that an *archetypal self-care system* comes to the child's aid—an archaic mechanism that creates a defensive splitting to encapsulate the child's delicate personal spirit in safety by banishing it to the unconscious. The child's psychic defense against insufferable pain sends an archetypal daimon, or an image from the self-care system, to protect the child's *transitional space*. According to Kalsched, the transitional space is the realm between the inner and outer worlds where the child learns how to play creatively and utilizes symbols. Traumatic anxiety interrupts the transitional space and may temporarily quench the child's capacity to be imaginative through symbolic play.

Children are guided toward healing and fulfillment by the process of connecting the unconscious psyche to the ego, which Jung (1959) stated may be provisionally detached during extreme trauma. Psychopathology in children appears when a tenuous connection between the unconscious and conscious develops. This typically occurs because of the destruction of the *transitional space* between the outer and inner worlds due to the subversion of the *good enough parental introjects* (e.g., images and the feelings associated with those images of the good mother or good father archetypes that offer containment). A *significant* integration must occur in order for the child's ego to resolve the effects of trauma. Significance is defined when children's somatic symptoms are provided with mental illustration by transitional archetypal figures so that they eventually attain symbolic expression (Kalsched, 1996). Jungians assist the child in recovering the feeble transitional space so that his or her creative dimensions are reinstated. This involves the enrichment of the linkage between the unconscious and conscious through interpretation, which fosters psychological growth and psychic healing (Allan, 1997; Jung, 1951).

Goals

The predominant goal of Jungian play therapy is activating the individuation process through an analytic attitude where images can be produced freely. Once images and elements within the unconscious are made conscious, analysts believe children can better regulate their impulses by maintaining equilibrium of energy between their inner and outer worlds. Individuation is the lifelong development of personality from the inception of life (Stein, 2006). The goal of Jungian play therapy with children, individuation, is operationalized through the transformation of symbol—the process of the child's inner symbols being generated throughout therapy. Jungian play therapists observe symbol production and transformation in children throughout the clinical process predominantly through artwork, sandplay, and dreams. Children speak through actions and metaphor in symbols, so Jungians pay close attention to the things not talked about or enacted during a session, as part of reaching goal attainment.

JAPT's goals differ from those of other treatment approaches. First, therapists maintain an analytical attitude. Fordham (1994) describes the analytical attitude as a technique that provides conditions for children to freely express themselves while the therapist emphasizes interpretative rather than directive methods. The essential feature of the analytical attitude is that it is impartial and seeks to illuminate the child's conflicts from the framework of resolving the conflicts in the present moment. Moreover, the therapist resolves complex feelings into their simplest components by taking into account the transference and countertransference. The analytical attitude of the therapist permits the child to move from impulse or action to the symbolic life, where emotions and images are contained. By conceptualizing and containing rage, therapists facilitate children's transformative process, sublimating aggression into assertiveness, which brings forth containment. Through the safety of the therapeutic dyad, aggression moves into assertiveness to help children articulate "I do not like or I am mad" instead of violently attacking toys or others.

Another goal of JAPT that may differ from that of other paradigms is to *ground* (stabilize or reorient) the child back to the external reality at the end of each session through artwork. The transition of art at the end of a play session helps the child move from impulse and action to metaphor and symbol. The Jungian play therapist dialogues with the child on a symbolic stage, as too much external reality may inhibit the child's ego. Therapists should block self-destructive processes, but aggression must come out both symbolically and behaviorally. Effective therapists *carry* the child's aggression. Another goal of therapy is for children to carry images of the good mother and father so they can nurture themselves. Through self-nurturance, an internalization of a positive self-image may emerge.

Jungian play therapists assist children in reconciling the meaning of their symbols by (a) asking what the symbol means to the child and by (b) asking the child to externalize the accompanying inner dialogue associated with the symbol. This typically works well with children over the age of 8 due to developmental and cognitive implications. If a child is under age 8, perhaps the reconciliation of the meaning of the symbol may be inferred through artwork analysis and viewing the gestalt of the child's psychology. For example, if a 6-year-old draws variations of an eagle, which may represent wisdom or perceived authority, the therapist may ask questions related to the eagle. Second, the therapist may attempt to amplify (explore) the symbol by asking the child questions or comments such as, "Let's talk about the eagle and what its purpose is in this drawing. Does the eagle live alone or with others?" "Is the eagle ever afraid or brave or both? When?" With the therapist actively dialoguing with the symbols within the artwork of children, their ego is provided a voice to inner longings, desires, and hidden or unknown qualities perhaps necessary to fully relate and ultimately acclimate to the constraints of the external social world.

Techniques

Though not an exhaustive list, the sections that follow are examples of Jungian play techniques practitioners may use with children. Most of these techniques are projective in nature to cultivate a child's interior life, where a sense of depth and meaning are honored.

Jungian Sandplay

Sandplay typically involves the child's playing in a sand tray and choosing sand miniatures to create a world, with no direction or guidance and with little or no *processing* (resolving) afterward. Therapists permit children to draw, depict, or create whatever world they choose. The therapist may say, "Create a sand world.

There's no right or wrong way to do this. It's completely up to you. After you finish, we may talk a little about your sand world. I'll be quiet while you play." After children finish creating their sand worlds, therapists might inquire about the sand world's name or title. Second, therapists may ask, "If you were in this world, what would you feel like?" Third, therapists may probe children further by asking how they felt while forming the world. Sample questions for processing sandplay worlds could include (a) What were you feeling when you placed that castle there? and (b) If this symbol (or object or person) were talking, what would they be saying and to whom? A therapist may utilize Jungian sandplay techniques to facilitate containment of the child's affect in the sand tray. Additionally, some children will ask the therapist to devise a new game or activity for sandplay, which should signify to the therapist a specific need for emotional containment.

Create Your Mandala

This is a semidirective technique used to facilitate sandplay therapy with children (Green, 2009). In *Create Your Mandala*, the Jungian play therapist first asks the child to spend a couple of minutes relaxing. With eyes closed in a comfortable seated position, the child is led through a guided imagery technique, with the therapist assisting the child to release through deep breathing any frustrations or anxieties accumulated throughout the school day. Also, therapists may ask the child to manipulate Play-Doh® or clay as an anxiety-releasing technique while deeply breathing. After a couple of minutes, the therapist asks the child to draw a large circle in the sand. The child is then instructed to depict, draw, or create a world within the circle in the sand tray. Once the child finishes, the therapist and the child contemplate the images in silence.

Jung (2008) believed the *mandala*, or an object (perhaps a circle) with an image contained within, represents unity or wholeness. From a Jungian perspective, unity or wholeness is commensurate with psychological healthiness, because Jung believed a reconciliation of opposites has occurred in the individual (*individuation*). In individuation, the child functions outside of the constraints of the ego, operating from the true center of being—the autonomous self. Jungians believe that a mandala in sand depiction is representative of the child's rich interior life (Kalff, 1980).

After the therapist facilitates the child's concretization of the unconscious, the child then progresses toward wholeness through *ego-based reliability* (depending on the ego to differentiate emotional polarities uncovered from within). The healthy change a child experiences through sandplay occurs within the warm, therapeutic relationship and the experiencing of the sandplay scene, not necessarily through specific sand techniques or interpretations. Therefore, Jungians honor the process of sandplay by attending to the individuality of the child with complete acceptance, and do not focus on providing clever interpretations to the child. As Kalff (1980) and De Domenico (1994) confirmed, the healing is in the doing.

Fairy Tales in the Sand (FTS)

A second Jungian sandplay technique is *Fairy Tales in the Sand* (Green, 2009; Green & Gibbs, 2010). FTS recognizes archetypical displays in the child through fantasy imagery and fairy tale depictions. The FTS process begins with the therapist reading a fairy tale to the child. The therapist may bring 8 to 10 prese-lected fairy tales with a variety of themes commensurate with the child's current psychosocial struggles. Jungians believe the self leads the child in the right direction for healing. After the child selects a fairy tale, the therapist reads the fairy tale and asks the child to identify a particularly important component of the fairy tale—an image, a theme, a plot, or a character. After the child has identified a portion of the fairy tale, the child depicts the image or feeling associated with that symbol in the sand. The therapist silently observes while the child creates a world in the sand.

After the child finishes the fairy tale sand creation, the therapist *processes* the creation with the child by asking questions similar to those listed previously in this chapter. FTS allows the child—through *active imagination*—to identify with myths and inherent archetypal realities that may provide *numinous* (spiritual) change. Specifically, children consciously connect to meaningful myths and mythical fig-ures in fairy tales that carefully capture their personal struggles or origin of their emotional predicament. As with *Draw Your Mandala*, FTS enables healing through a trusting, caring relationship with a therapist, where the children identify, express, and connect to the myth out of which they live. Once children become aware of the myth and symbols that they are living out, they are able to more accurately form effective coping mechanisms to understand and transform pain and suffering.

Serial Drawings

Serial drawing is an art therapy technique infused with Jungian impressions that involves a child producing images through various art media over a period of time, therefore providing an assessment of the child's interior life to the therapist (Allan, 1988; Green & Hebert, 2006). After a therapeutic relationship and/or trust are formed between the therapist and child, problems are expressed symbolically (or sometimes concretely) in the artwork, and healing and resolution of inner (and outer) conflicts occur (Furth, 1988). The serial drawing technique involves a therapist meet-ing with a child regularly and asking him to "draw a picture while we talk." Jung (1964) believed that in times of significant crisis, children could turn inward toward the unconscious for dreams and images that carried within them the potential for healing. Jung himself turned toward playing with stones by a lake for self-healing after his period of disorientation following the ideological break from Freud.

In serial drawings, the Jungian play therapist does the following:

- Encourages the child to make the images independently by providing little or no instruction
- Permits the child to observe the image fully so that the self can lead the child wherever he may need to go toward self-healing
- Links the meaning of the symbols with the child's outer world at the point the child's ego can accept and integrate the bridge between "transitional spaces"

The serial drawing technique in and of itself does not heal (for further expla-nation, please refer to the case illustration later in this chapter), but rather the self-healing archetype in children is galvanized through a restorative coalition with a nonjudgmental therapist. The serial drawing provides for a safe expression and exploration of feelings associated with the child's psychological experience.

While individual children move at their own pace in self-healing according to their developmental stage and also the nature of their psychopathology, typical designs in manufacturing images through the serial drawing technique have been observed by Allan (1988) and Green (2008) and are listed in Table 5.1.

In addition to open-mindedness for vagueness, therapists should offer an atmosphere that contains unconditional positive regard, trust, authenticity, warmth, and understanding, which may assist children to draw freely and produce unconscious symbol imagery through various media. To process (resolve) the serial drawing and amplify its symbols, Allan (1988) suggested that the therapist ask the child one or more of the following questions:

- Does this picture tell a story?
- I'm wondering if you can tell me what is happening in this scene?
- If you could give this picture a title, what would it be?
- If you were inside this picture, what would it feel like?
- What went on in the story before this scene occurred? What happens next?
- Could you tell me what you were thinking or feeling as you drew this?
- What does (identify certain object or symbol in the picture) mean to you?

Table 5.1   Stages in Serial Drawings

Initial Stage (1st–4th Sessions)	Middle Stage (5th–8th Sessions)	Final Stage (9th–12th Sessions)
Drawings (a) provide a glimpse of the child's interior illustrated by symbols that reflect the source of trauma, (b) reflect loss of internal or external control with feelings of despair, and (c) establish initial rapport between the therapist and child.	Drawings reflect (a) a pure expression of intense emotion, (b) struggles between conflicting internal polarities (loss of control vs. mastery), and (c) the deepening of the therapeutic relationship between the child and therapist, which is exemplified by the child's talking directly about a traumatic issue or disclosing private and painful memories of the crisis to the therapist.	Drawings reflect (a) images that reflect a sense of mastery, self-control, and valuation; (b) scenes with positive imagery; (c) a depiction of the self (intact self-portraits or mandalas [circular shapes connoting wholeness/integration]); (d) scenes that are humorous with no macabre references; and (e) artwork representing autonomy from the therapeutic relationship.

During the processing of artwork, it is important for the therapist to remember that verbal and nonverbal communications to the child should reflect support, as the child will come to realize that both good and horrible feelings are acceptable to convey in the therapeutic relationship.

THERAPEUTIC POWERS OF PLAY UNDERLYING THE MODEL

Therapeutic change in the analytic process relies not only on the analyst's interpretation and understanding, but also on his or her feelings and personality. From a Jungian perspective, the power of the archetypal imagery in the child's personal and collective unconscious will invariably affect the therapist. Therefore, the therapist needs to receive (or have received) personal analysis and clinical supervision.

The central component to the play therapy relationship in uniquely Jungian terms is based on the dialectical interpersonal (observable behaviors and associated feelings) and intrapersonal (unconscious or inner drives) communication between analyst and child. Within the therapeutic exchanges, the analyst is just as much affected as the child. According to Samuels (2006), therapists must be flawed, recognize those flaws, and constructively work on those limitations in relation to the child. The therapist must accept that some of the child's interpretations are not merely transference projections but may be accurate assessments of the flaws within the therapist that need fixing. Jungian play therapists realize that the child needs opportunities to help or heal the therapist as well in this dynamic therapeutic relationship so that the child's full developmental potential to heal others and oneself may be realized.

Through a symbolic creation of their world or how their unconscious projects that world through the metaphor of play, children access available ego energies and rely on their imagination and creativity to bring forth unconscious conflicts. When intraphysic conflicts are made conscious, the ego constellates (activates) the difficult feelings and behaviors, and the child is able to resolve them within the "sheltered space" (Kalff, 1980) of the playroom and therapeutic relationship. This process of symbolically connecting the ego to the self through play engenders growth and reparation in children who are grieving or suffering, as they are able to integrate the shadowy aspects of their personality through the acceptance of the projections.

In addition to a variety of multicultural, interreligious, and archetypal sand tray miniatures (see Figure 5.1), the Jungian playroom contains a puppet or playhouse, where the child may hide (see Figure 5.2). This is essential to the playroom so that children may perceive a sense of emotional safety by banishing their ego to a concealed place that is impermeable should they meet difficult raw material while playing out themes in the playroom. Another reason to maintain a hiding place in a clinical playroom is if a child wants to relax and ease the psyche from the frenzied pace of the external world. The "hidden place" permits the child's ego to escape from the external environment temporarily and regenerate itself in its solitude. The playhouse puppets are multicultural and contain representations from various

Figure 5.1   Examples of Jungian Sandplay Miniatures

Figure 5.2   Hiding Place for Child's Ego in a Jungian Playroom

professions. Moreover, the play therapist ensures that sexist stereotypes are not reinforced in the playroom, and male and female puppets represent different professions, including doctors, firefighters, police, and so on.

Play Therapy Process

The Jungian play therapy process resembles the metaphorical process undertaken by the ancient alchemists, in which the interpersonal and intrapersonal aspects of therapy are honored (Samuels, 2006). Alchemists (1400–1700) projected their internal processes into the melding of items of little value into something precious, such as iron into gold ("the philosopher's stone"). Also, alchemists believed that by converting base elements into spirit, the soul would be freed from its bodily prison. The alchemists always worked in relation to someone else to complete their mineral and spiritual transformations, referring to this "other" as the *soror mystica* (mystical sister). This is akin to there being no play therapy without an analyst and a child. The stages of the alchemical process inform the therapeutic aspects throughout the course in play therapy:

- *Fermentatio* is when something is brewing up as the chemical reactions of the therapy process get under way. This involves changes in both the analyst and child and is often seen at the onset of the psychotherapy.
- *Nigredo* is a blackening due to the realization of imminent dangers ahead. We sometimes see this in children when they begin to display highly reactive behaviors during therapy before they begin to stabilize.
- *Mortificato* is something that must be extinguished and die. A change or shift in both the client and therapist must occur before healing and containment begin.

JAPT's treatment plan involves three steps: (1) counseling a child 50 minutes per week in an emotionally and physically safe environment, (2) conducting one family play therapy session with caretakers every two weeks or so, and (3) consulting with a multidisciplinary team of school and community-based professionals to provide holistic care.

ROLE OF THE THERAPIST

The play therapist's role is that of observer-participant, utilizing an integrative approach comprising a baseline of nondirective philosophy intertwined with the ability to incorporate techniques that harness the child's creativity in spontaneous drawings, dream interpretation, coloring mandalas, or sandplay. The therapist may use directive techniques to determine the archetypal (or universal) *complex* the child's psyche is captivated in, which often encompasses polarities (Alan, 1997; Green, 2009). Complexes are generalized, internal relationship patterns that imply a reactive state between one's ego and another individual (Kast, 2006).

It is part of the therapist's role to facilitate children's unearthing and incorporation of their *shadow* side in order to maintain psychic evenness and encourage spiritual well-being. Jung's *shadow* term refers to any aspect of the psyche that has been excluded from conscious awareness. For example, a 4-year-old girl, Danica, was maltreated by her primary caretakers as an infant. Danica exhibited a variety of symptoms, cognitions, and feelings in the playroom, including irrational fears of abandonment; attention-seeking, maladaptive behaviors; clinginess; and insecurity of the world around her. She was functioning out of a broken attachment complex, which could be treated by the therapist's providing her psyche the freedom to enact these dysfunctional behaviors without judgment. Therefore, the psychotherapy process serves as containment and a nurturing environment where the maternal or mother archetype is activated through the transference unto the therapist. After the child's psyche has an opportunity to display its broken and abandoned nature within an accepting and permissive atmosphere, the therapist introduces activities, offers interpretations, and expresses genuine feelings of security, safety, and contentment. These interpretations provide a curative function so that the child's psyche may begin to fully realize and ultimately internalize the healing potential within itself.

The role of the Jungian play therapist includes the following:

- Making sense of symbols through an extensive process of personal analysis with a Jungian analyst
- Conceptualizing rage ego-syntonically (i.e., a broken attachment turns into rage and if not remedied, depression and ultimately withdrawal) and helping children symbolize it
- Maintaining an analytical attitude that is both involved and detached
- Possessing the ability to direct children's raw material by carrying some of their psychological poison
- Using sandplay, artwork, and dream analysis to amplify symbols and follow the child's self wherever it leads (Green, 2009, p. 91).

ROLE OF THE PARENT

Parents or caretakers play a crucial role in the psychotherapy process with children. The play therapist needs to know what sort of transference is present and what is likely to develop in parents (Fordham, 1988). Therapists need the coparticipation of parents throughout the counseling process. Depending on the parents' psychopathology, a therapist may recommend that the mother and/or father receive individual counseling from another therapist. Parents are needed to manage any transitory regressions that may appear in the child during therapy, and their ego strength must be bolstered to cope with this task. Therefore, many therapists incorporate parents into the play therapy process through either family therapy or family play therapy. Typically, parent consultations and/or family play therapy are interwoven throughout the clinical process, perhaps every two to three weeks (but only after an initial period when the analyst and child meet individually in the playroom to develop therapeutic rapport). It is not uncommon for the presenting problems initially observed in a child not to be entirely remediated unless systemic attention is given to the relationship between the parents and the child and the family system as a monolithic functioning unit.

CLINICAL APPLICATIONS

Table 5.2 contains some of the most current information found in the literature related to diverse applications of Jungian play therapy. The list of citations contained within the table is predominantly from a select group of recent book chapters

Table 5.2   Jungian Play Therapy Clinical Applications

	Elementary School–aged Children	**Adolescents**	**Adults/Family**
Jungian Applications		**Citations**	
Bereavement	Bertoia (1993); Green and Connolly (2009)		
Disruptive Behavioral Problems	Fordham (1988); Green and Gibbs (2010)	Green (2010)	
Disaster Mental Health Counseling	Green (2007)		
Group Play Therapy	Bertoia (1999); Kestley (2001)		
Psychosis	Allan (1988); Feldman (1988); Gabreillini and Nissim (1988)		
Sandplay	Allan and Berry (2003); Carey (1999); De Domenico (1994); Kalff (1980); McNulty (2007)	Boik and Goodwin (2000); Kalff (1980); Pearson and Wilson (2001)	Botkin (2000); Carey (1994, 1999, 2006); Kalff (1980); Mitchell and Friedman (2003)
Suicide or Death	Bertoia (1993); Walsh and Allan (1994)	Allan (1988); Allan and Bertoia (1992)	Green (2008)
Treating Sexual Trauma	Allan (1988); Allan and Bertoia (1992)		

and books specific to the field of play therapy from a Jungian perspective and is by no means comprehensive to all work involving Jungian perspectives in the more general field of child analysis.

EMPIRICAL SUPPORT

Both Allan (1988) and Green (2007) identified JAPT as a beneficial treatment modality when counseling elementary school aged children. Additionally, several qualitative investigations and anecdotal data obtained through case study analyses have demonstrated JAPT as a beneficial therapeutic modality with young children struggling with difficult feelings and behaviors (Allan; Allan & Bertoia, 1992; Green, 2008, 2009).

In the current child psychotherapy literature, a significant emphasis is placed on behavioral, evidence-based treatment approaches, which many clinicians decry as cold, standardized cures. Evidence-based and evidence-informed treatment approaches often are validated by rigorous control studies and utilize a manualized approach to treat individuals with specific symptoms at specific intervals. Most notably, cognitive behavioral therapy (CBT) has received substantial attention in the mental health field over the past several years as being the "gold standard" in psychotherapy for multiple childhood disorders and issues. In his recent meta-analysis in the *American Psychologist*, Jonathan Shedler (2010) stated that psychodynamic therapies, those approaches that include not only symptom remission (which is the primary aim of many evidence-based behavioral approaches) but also the distinguishing feature of fostering positive psychological capacities (i.e., creating meaningful relationships, relating to symbols in one's fantasies and dreams, healing complex emotional scars from childhood to promote resilience and positive self-worth, etc.) demonstrate high effect sizes in the treatment of mental health disorders compared with CBT. Shedler identified multiple factors specific to the psychodynamic (or modalities that use principles and are derived from the psychodynamic school such as "depth" or "analytical" psychology) approaches that may be anomalous to new, scientific, and primarily behavioral evidence-based treatment approaches: (a) focus on affect and expression of emotion, (b) identification of themes and recurring patterns, (c) focus on the therapy relationship, and (d) exploration of fantasy life. There are numerous recent studies that demonstrate support of psychodynamic and analytical approaches to mental health care that provide scientific validation (Shedler, 2010). However, the author is unaware of any specific experimental designs for the use of Jungian play therapy with children. Before an experimental design can be devised, a Jungian play therapy treatment handbook would need to be created. The author of this chapter is currently creating a handbook for Jungian play therapy. With a manualized approach, replication of experimental studies can be completed, and researchers can report the findings and treatment effect size (ES) of a theory. One of the most notable limitations in designing an experimental design with a control group for Jungian play therapy is that it relies heavily on projective techniques and qualitative, theoretical information to inform its scope that may be difficult to quantify.

CASE ILLUSTRATION[1]

An 18-year-old male relative (uncle) sexually assaulted "Jana," an 8-year-old girl living in a subsidized housing section of an urban city in the southern portion of the United States. Jana was a trauma survivor of child sexual abuse (CSA). She was molested on weekends over six months while her mother was away from the home and at work. The perpetrator assaulted Jana repeatedly and asked her to keep it a secret. He manipulated Jana through fear by stating that the police would be called to remove her from her mother's home if anyone found out about the sexual assaults. This paralyzed Jana with fear, as she and her mother lived alone, and their extended family was located in another part of the country. Jana was dependent on her mother for all of her financial, emotional, and practical needs. Jana's father died when she was 3 years old from a gunshot wound related to gang activity, and her mother worked two part-time jobs to maintain their household.

During and after the abuse, Jana's grades declined, and her behavior at home and with male peers became *disordered*. She displayed avoidance of trauma-related stimuli by becoming hyperaroused around adult males. Specifically, she became defiant when attending science class taught by Mr. Smith, the only male teacher at Jana's elementary school. Eventually, Jana disclosed the sexual abuse to a female teacher, and a child protective agency was notified. After the forensic interview, child protective services referred Jana to a play therapist. Upon intake, her presenting problems were (a) numbing of her general responsiveness at school and at home and (b) defiant behaviors in Mr. Smith's class.

Jana's Jungian play therapist utilized spontaneous drawings from the initial counseling session to develop the therapeutic relationship and begin the *extended developmental assessment* (EDA), which lasted approximately five sessions. The EDA (Gil, 2006) is a comprehensive and sensitive assessment that involves (a) a caretaker intake with a complete cognitive-behavioral assessment of the child; (b) obtaining historical, medical, and behavioral traits of the child post- and preabuse; and (c) conducting several individual *play* sessions, utilizing both directive and nondirective assessments and play-based methods to inform and initiate treatment planning.

Throughout the EDA, the therapist observed Jana's artistic abilities. Jana symbolically depicted many of the issues related to CSA that she had difficulty expressing verbally. For example, Jana drew images of a white fantastical castle surrounded by a moat that was excavated for additional fortification. Her drawings typically contained a bright yellow sun and sometimes smiling, beautiful fairy princesses appeared in the castle's windows. Staying with the metaphor, the therapist asked Jana what the fairy princesses were viewing outside their window. Jana replied, "They are waiting for a handsome prince to come and marry them. He will be nice to them, and they will be rich and happy."

---

[1] The case illustration is adapted from the following journal article with the express permission of the Association for Play Therapy: Green, E. J. (2008). Re-envisioning Jungian analytical play therapy with child sexual assault survivors. *International Journal of Play Therapy 17*(2), 102–121.

The therapist observed that Jana's drawings and verbalizations of the meanings of the drawings conveyed wish fulfillment, which possibly depicted her need to feel love in a safe, nonsexualized way. Jana inserted a dark unicorn-like figure looming behind one or more trees in many of her drawings. Moreover, Jana reported that the dark figure was "an evil unicorn trying to hurt people with his horn because he was hungry and wanted food." The therapist further amplified the symbol of the dark unicorn by asking Jana to draw a new picture with the same castle but with a unicorn that had enough food and did not need to puncture anyone with his horn. She drew a unicorn that found berries and nuts on the ground, and his color changed from dark and ominous to a lighter, more whimsical brown. She then appeared less intense, as her affect changed from serious and concerned to relieved. She began to regain mastery and control over her feelings. Without a probe from the therapist, Jana replied, "My uncle was bad and used to hurt me, and I used to be scared. I always thought it was my fault because he told me it was. But now he's hurting 'cause he's in trouble for what he did to me, and it was bad. But I'm not bad." After talking about the pictures and exploring her individual perspective, the therapist conceptualized Jana's drawings as internalizing positive effects of hope and stability in a fantastic, mythical world that she created. Jana also began to articulate her trauma narrative.

This example demonstrated the notion of *intrinsic processing* of the traumatic event (Briere & Scott, 2006). Specifically, Jana's mind repeatedly relived disturbing features or memories of the trauma symbolically through her artwork, which may have represented an evolutionarily derived attempt to promote cognitive and affective accommodation to the reality of the trauma. By systematically desensitizing or extinguishing emotions and cognitions from the event through mastery of the feelings and thoughts associated with the event, Jana was able to change her conditioned responses to the traumatic event. This clinical judgment follows the trauma theory promulgated by Briere and Scott (2006) that stipulates that emotional processing of traumatic events occurs when "erroneous perceptions, beliefs, and expectations ("pathological fear structures") associated with trauma-related fears are activated and habituated in the context of new, more accurate information" (p. 121). In other words, because Jana processed evocatively or resolved painful emotional material in the presence of a nonjudgmental therapist and was able to pair positive emotions and cognitions with painful, previous trauma-relevant stimuli, she experienced a reduction in the cascade of trauma-focused symptoms.

Treatment Plan: Goals and Procedures

One of the primary goals when using Jungian play therapy with maltreated children is to restore a child to preabuse functioning. The spontaneous drawing technique was a significant component of Jana's EDA because it informed the treatment planning as Jana began the process of restoring hope to her insecure outlook on life through individual creative expression in the presence of a caring counselor. Jana conveyed her unconscious or tacit psychic longings to be loved in a safe way through spontaneous drawings. In several of her drawings, she illustrated and seemed connected to one or more of the fairy princesses, and her self-healing arche-type emerged.

After *sitting with,* or contemplating, the images and providing the therapist with her own interpretation of the images in the drawings, Jana began to internal-ize feelings of security and contentment. These feelings were compromised previ-ously by the sexual assault. Once Jana internalized positive cognitive attributions of her world as stable, meaningful, and ordered and connected those internalizations to her outer world, Jana's reactive symptoms began to dissipate. Combined with several cognitive behavioral strategies such as cognitive restructuring and disput-ing irrational beliefs about Jana's complicity in the abuse, Jana and her therapist made slow progress in reducing Jana's emotional numbing and cognitive distor-tions. Because of the bad dreams Jana regularly reported to her therapist, he regu-larly conducted the Jungian technique "Draw Your Dream On" (see the worksheet at the end of this chapter). Jana found this technique helpful as she reported feel-ing empowered by taking control or mastery of difficult images that haunted her unconscious.

Jana's mother and teacher, through Filial Therapy and consultation, respectively, began praising Jana for her prosocial behaviors and offered suggestions for cop-ing mechanisms when she became distraught. The teacher expressed concern to the therapist that because the school did not perform any type of psychoeducation to the children regarding fending off sexual predators or normalizing the disclosure process, this may have contributed to Jana's abuse continuing for several months. The teacher, collaborating with the therapist, petitioned a new psychoeducational program on CSA to the school's principal and county, and it was approved for execu-tion. Also, Jana's teacher and school counselor conveyed their skills were augmented after their consultations with the therapist. They brokered peer relationships by con-ducting more group work in class and placing Jana with young girls who were psy-chologically adjusted and socially appropriate. Jana developed the capacity to reach out to her same-sex peers and re-form friendships, and she began evidencing an ele-vation in prosocial behaviors and an increased level of positive peer interaction.

A second goal of JAPT with children affected by sexual trauma is to facilitate resiliency through the recognition and utilization of effective coping mechanisms. The traditional paradigm of counseling children that utilizes talking methods, often associated with adult psychotherapy, is often insufficient to guide abused children through self-healing (Landreth, Baggerly, & Tyndall-Lind, 1999). Spontaneous drawings are a nonverbal technique utilized in Jungian play because drawings assist children in artistically externalizing emotions stemming from sexual assault. Drawings and interpretations of drawings may enable the child's psyche to con-sciously identify the self-healing potential that talking alone cannot accomplish. Spontaneous drawings are one way to encourage a child affected by CSA to pen-etrate deep psychic substrates, where hidden fears and ambivalent feelings are made conscious, thereby generating psychic healing.

Through spontaneous drawings and the contemplation of symbols, Jana identi-fied with the beautiful and happy fairy princesses who were safe in the castle and protected behind a moat. These princesses and prince may have represented Jana reconciling the anima and animus archetypes (female traits within a male and male traits within a female, respectively) that had been activated by the premature sexual encounter. Her identification of the self-healing archetype encouraged her inner relatability to coping mechanisms, such as her ability to be lighthearted with a sense of humor to handle pain, something that had lain dormant since the assault occurred.

The third central goal of JAPT with this population is to incorporate nonoffending caretakers in filial and/or family play therapy and to coordinate services with other significant adults in the child's home, school, and community through consultation and collaboration. Jana's therapist evaluated her environmental support structures, and a multidisciplinary team was formed to assist Jana and her family following the crisis of the CSA disclosure. The therapist met with (a) Jana's academic teachers, including Mr. Smith; (b) ancillary support staff, including her resource specialist; (c) medical and mental health personnel (e.g., school nurse, social worker); and (d) the administrative staff (e.g., assistant principal) to answer the questions they posed on the potential behavioral effects of CSA. The school team also cooperated on formulating practical solutions to complex issues, such as allowing Jana to switch science classes until she felt comfortable returning to a classroom with a male teacher, which she eventually did. Also, Jana's mother attended Filial Therapy sessions with the play therapist every two weeks. During these filial sessions, the play therapist listened to the mother's concerns, validated her feelings, and provided practical strategies to increase her patience with and understanding of the healing process.

Case Analysis and Conclusion

Throughout the clinical process of bridging the unconscious to the conscious, and by connecting her inner world to her outer world, Jana's self-healing archetype became activated by the therapeutic relationship and subsequent interpretations. Jana's self-healing archetype emerged when she shared her individual creative art expressions in the presence of an accepting, permissive therapist. After six months of weekly individual psychotherapy sessions, Jana's therapist, teachers, and family noticed a decrease in her emotional pain and a reduction in her morbid self-alienation stemming from the shame she felt regarding the sexual assault.

The potential for dissociation in extreme cases of child trauma, predominantly due to unbearable psychic pain sometimes associated with CSA, can result in a defensive splitting (Kalsched, 1996). In Jana's case, part of the defensive splitting was her idealization of fantasy, depicted in the drawings of the castle with the beautiful princesses high atop in secure windows and green trees while she was feeling *ugly on the inside.* She included, frequently, a dark, ominous figure representing danger, or possibly her *shadow*, that lurked outside the moat of the castle. After the archetypal self-care system took over, Jana's idealizations faded, and the harsh reality of coping with her psychogenic pain began. This would be an example of the *nigredo* (or "darkening") stage of play therapy mentioned earlier. From a Jungian perspective, Jana's personal spirit was defended, for her ego–self-reliability was strengthened due to the recognition of her inner resiliency.

At the beginning of treatment, Jana began to self-heal her emotional wounds while smoothing out the roughness of her exterior—evidenced by her improvement in grades and increased social connections. Part of this process was evidenced by Jana's ability to reconcile her emotionally numbed outer world with her turbulent inner world. This occurred partially because the play therapist articulated to Jana that the abuse was just one small part of who she was and did not define who she was. Jana eventually internalized this accurate appraisal. Jana created several picture journals of all of the pieces that made her who she was, not just the assault, and this began to change positively her self-concept. After the defensive splitting lost its negative valence in Jana's psyche, the negative effects associated with the trauma appeared, and she began to resolve the internalized guilt. The guilt, stemming from her cognitive misattributions of culpability in the sexual assault, manifested externally as emotional numbing and defiance in a male teacher's classroom setting.

Once the recognition of opposites occurred within the protection of the therapeutic relationship, Jana felt empowered and engaged in positive self-talk: "This (therapy) wasn't so bad after all, and I feel better now and know that what he did to me was not my fault." Furthermore, the therapeutic relationship facilitated Jana's inner healing because of the frequency of the play therapist's affirmations— consistent verbal acknowledgements of Jana's heroic struggle with overcoming self-condemnation. The play therapist's affirmations were praises of Jana's efforts: "Jana, you are placing so much effort and energy into this exercise. I just wanted to acknowledge that I appreciate your commitment to this process, even though I know it may be scary at times. I can't say for sure I know how things will work out, and I don't know if everything will be OK. But I do know that I will be here with you." This is an example of the transference providing a holding environment or nurturing containment.

While Jana was sometimes disquieted by nightmares after treatment ended, she became aware of the slow, *numinous* transformation going on within. From a Jungian point of view, Jana had relied upon the transcendent power of the self to countercondition pain and desolation invoked by the sexual assault and to formulate accurate cognitive appraisals and symbolic interpretations of the event. The new feelings and healthy images associated with the event allowed Jana to generate a new perspective. In an archetypal underworld, Jana felt free to integrate conflicting symbols and images associated with the assault to produce a more accurate, meaningful trauma narrative.

CHALLENGES IN IMPLEMENTING THE MODEL

The most significant challenge to implementing this model is the lack of a manualized treatment approach or succinct handbook that offers specificity for addressing dependent variables within clinical populations. Once a manualized approach is created, then practitioners may face fewer challenges when facilitating this paradigm. Many practitioners find Jung's theory and concepts to be dizzying and often intellectually ambivalent, especially in this modern age with a behavioral emphasis of effective and practical solutions to problems. A third central challenge is implementing the model in elementary schools. Currently, there is a nationwide push for school counselors to utilize behavioral and evidence-based treatment (EBT) to remediate children's psychological issues (New Freedom Commission on Mental Health, 2003). Jungian play therapy has not yet been a part of a randomized, experimental design to test its effectiveness. Therefore, some practitioners, insurance companies, clients, parents, and administrators may be averse to its implementation in educational systems due to the recent trends in EBT.

CONCLUSION

The central aim of Jungian analytical play therapy is for children to individuate, which is to say they must become more and more of who they really are, distinct from others (e.g., parents), yet learn about themselves in relation to others. This process is facilitated by a series of dialogues within the safety of a nonjudgmental therapeutic dyad in which children uncover who they are in relation to the rest of the world through symbolic play. Once the unconscious is brought up to the conscious level, mainly through play and amplifying symbols, children are less controlled by irrational forces and begin to mediate more rational behaviors aligned with the needs of a healthy ego. Through the transformation of affect (emotion) to image, the natural healing function of the child's psyche emerges. As Chodorow (2006) states, a child's imagination, constellated (activated) through spontaneous and symbolic play, replaces raw affect with images and stories that express the mood and emotion of the child that is more comprehensible. The understanding of inner images and the associated feeling tones guides the process of psychological development. Finally, in his posthumously published *The Red Book*, Jung (2009) states the importance and healing nature of identifying the child archetype within himself during conflict toward the end of his life: "The spirit of the depths taught me that my life is encompassed by the divine child" (p. 234). Jung recognized the importance of the child archetype as compensating the one-sidedness of consciousness in adulthood and therefore facilitating psychological wholeness through a joining of opposites.

REFERENCES

Allan, J. (1988). *Inscapes of the child's world*. Dallas, TX: Spring Publications.

Allan, J. (1997). Jungian play psychotherapy. In K. J. O'Connor & L. M. Braverman (Eds.), *Play therapy: A comparative presentation* (pp. 100–130). New York, NY: Wiley.

Allan, J., & Berry, P. (2003). Sandplay. In C. Schaefer & D. Cangelosi (Eds.), *Play therapy techniques* (2nd ed., pp. 161–168). Northvale, NJ: Aronson.

Allan, J., & Bertoia, J. (1992). *Written paths to healing: Education and Jungian child counseling*. Dallas, TX: Spring Publications.

Astor, J. (1988). Child analysis and individuation. In M. Sidoli & M. Davies (Eds.), *Jungian child psychotherapy: Individuation in childhood*. London, UK: Karnac Books.

Bertoia, J. (1993). *Drawings from a dying child: Insights into death from a Jungian perspective*. London, UK: Routledge.

Bertoia, J. (1999). The invisible village: Jungian group play therapy. In D. Sweeney & L. Homeyer (Eds.), *Group play therapy* (pp. 86–104). San Francisco, CA: Jossey-Bass.

Boik, B. L., & Goodwin, E. A. (2000). *Sandplay therapy*. New York, NY: Norton.

Botkin, D. (2000). Family play therapy: A creative approach to including young children in family therapy. *Journal of Systemic Therapies, 19*(3), 31–42.

Briere, J., & Scott, C. (2006). *Principles of trauma therapy: A guide to symptoms, evaluations, and treatment*. Thousand Oaks, CA: Sage.

Carey, L. (1994). Family sandplay therapy. In C. E. Schaefer & L. J. Carey (Eds.), *Family play therapy* (pp. 205–219). Northvale, NJ: Aronson.

Carey, L. (1999). *Sandplay therapy with children and families*. Northvale, NJ: Aronson.

Carey, L. (2006). Short-term family sandplay therapy. In H. Kaduson & C. E. Schaefer (Eds.), *Short-term play therapy for children* (pp. 202–215). New York, NY: Guilford Press.

Chodorow, J. (2006). Active imagination. In R. Papadopoulos (Ed.), *The handbook of Jungian psychology* (pp. 215–243). London, UK: Routledge.

De Domenico, G. (1994). Jungian play therapy techniques. In K. J. O'Connor & C. E. Schaefer (Eds.), *Handbook of play therapy: Advances and innovations* (2nd ed., pp. 253–282). New York, NY: Wiley.

Feldman, B. (1988). Analytical psychotherapy of a psychotic child. In M. Sidoli & M. Davies (Eds.), *Jungian child psychotherapy: Individuation in childhood* (pp. 207–220). London, UK: Karnac Books.

Fordham, M. (1944). *The life of childhood*. London, UK: Routledge.

Fordham, M. (1988). Emergence of child analysis. In M. Sidoli & M. Davies (Eds.), *Jungian child psychotherapy: Individuation in childhood* (pp. 19–29). London, UK: Karnac Books.

Fordham, M. (1994). *Children as individuals*. London, UK: Free Association Books.

Furth, G. M. (1988). *The secret world of drawings: Healing through art*. Boston, MA: SIGO Press.

Gabriellini, G., & Nissim, S. (1988). Sand play with a psychotic child. In M. Sidoli & M. Davies (Eds.), *Jungian child psychotherapy: Individuation in childhood* (pp. 221–232). London, UK: Karnac Books.

Gil, E. (2006). *Helping abused and traumatized children: Integrating directive and nondirective approaches*. New York, NY: Guilford Press.

Green, E. (2007). The crisis of family separation following traumatic mass destruction: Jungian analytical play therapy in the aftermath of hurricane Katrina. In N. B. Webb (Ed.), *Play therapy with children in crisis: Individual, group, and family treatment* (3rd ed., pp. 368–388). New York, NY: Guilford Press.

Green, E., & Hebert, B. (2006). Serial drawings: A Jungian play therapy technique for caregivers to utilize with children between counseling sessions. *Play Therapy, 1*(4), 20–24.

Green, E. J. (2008). Re-envisioning Jungian analytical play therapy with child sexual assault survivors. *International Journal of Play Therapy, 17*(2), 102–121.

Green, E. J. (2009). Jungian analytical play therapy. In K. J. O'Connor & L. D. Braverman (Eds.), *Play therapy theory and practice: Comparing theories and techniques* (2nd ed., pp. 83–122). Hoboken, NJ: Wiley.

Green, E. J. (2010). Jungian play therapy with adolescents. *Play Therapy*, *5*(2), 20–23.

Green, E. J., & Connolly, M. (2009). Jungian family sandplay with bereaved children: Implications for play therapists. *International Journal of Play Therapy*, *18*(2), 84–98.

Green, E. J., & Gibbs, K. (2010). Jungian sandplay for preschool children with disruptive behavioral problems. In C. Schaefer (Ed.), *Play therapy for preschool children* (pp. 223–244). Washington DC: American Psychological Association.

Jung, C. G. (1910). Psychic conflicts in the child. In H. Read, M. Fordham, & G. Adler (Eds.), *The collected works of C. G. Jung* (Vol. 17). Princeton, NJ: Princeton University Press.

Jung, C. G. (1913). The theory of psychoanalysis. In H. Read, M. Fordham, & G. Adler (Eds.), *The collected works of C. G. Jung* (Vol. 4). Princeton, NJ: Princeton University Press.

Jung, C. G. (1951). The psychology of the child archetype. In H. Read, M. Fordham, & G. Adler (Eds.), *The collected works of C. G. Jung* (Vol. 9). Princeton, NJ: Princeton University Press.

Jung, C. G. (1959). *Collected works 9: The archetypes and the collective unconscious*. New York, NY: Pantheon.

Jung, C. G. (1964). *Man and his symbols*. Garden City, NY: Doubleday.

Jung, C. G. (2008). *Children's dreams: Notes from the seminar given in 1936–1940*. Princeton, NJ: Princeton University Press.

Jung, C. G. (2009). *The red book*. New York, NY: Norton.

Kalff, D. (1980). *Sandplay: A psychotherapeutic approach to the psyche*. Boston, MA: Sigo Press.

Kalsched, D. (1996). *The inner world of trauma: Archetypal defenses of the personal spirit*. New York, NY: Routledge.

Kast, V. (2006). Anima/animus. In R. Papadopoulos (Ed.), *The handbook of Jungian psychology* (pp. 113–129). London, UK: Routledge.

Kestley, T. (2001). Group sandplay in elementary schools. In A. Drewes, L. Carey, & C. Schaefer (Eds.), *School-based play therapy* (pp. 329–349). Hoboken, NJ: Wiley.

Klein, M. (Ed.). (1955). *New directions in psycho-analysis*. New York, NY: Basic Books.

Landreth, G. L., Baggerly, J., & Tyndall-Lind, A. (1999). Beyond adapting adult counseling skills for use with children: The paradigm shift to child-centered play therapy. *Journal of Individual Psychology*, *55*(3), 272–288.

Lilly, J. P. (2009). *Jungian analytical play therapy: Theory and practice*. Proposal presented at the Annual Association for Play Therapy International Conference, Atlanta, GA.

Main, S. (2008). *Childhood re-imagined*. New York, NY: Routledge.

McNulty, W. (2007). Superheroes and sandplay: Using the archetype through the healing journey. In L. C. Rubin (Ed.), *Using superheroes in counseling and play therapy* (pp. 69–89). New York, NY: Springer.

Mitchell R. R., & Friedman, H. S. (2003). Using sandplay in therapy with adults. In C. Schaefer (Ed.), *Play therapy with adults* (pp. 195–232). Hoboken, NJ: Wiley.

New Freedom Commission on Mental Health. (2003). *Achieving the promise: Transforming mental health care in America*. Final Report (DHHS Publication No. SMA-03-3832). Rockville, MD: Department of Health and Human Services.

Pearson, M., & Wilson, H. (2001). *Sandplay and symbol work: Emotional healing and personal development with children, adolescents, and adults.* Melbourne, Victoria: Australian Council for Educational Research.

Peery, J. C. (2003). Jungian analytical play therapy. In C. E. Schaefer (Ed.), *Foundations of play therapy* (pp. 14–54). Hoboken, NJ: Wiley.

Samuels, A. (2006). Transference/countertransference. In R. Papadopoulos (Ed.), *The handbook of Jungian psychology* (pp. 177–195). London, UK: Routledge.

Shedler, J. (2010, February/March). The efficacy of psychodynamic psychotherapy. *The American Psychologist, 65*(2), 98–109.

Sidoli, M., & Davies, M. (Eds.). (1988). *Jungian child psychotherapy: Individuation in childhood.* London, UK: Karnac Books.

Stein, M. (2006). Individuation. In R. Papadopoulos (Ed.), *The handbook of Jungian psychology* (pp. 196–214). London, UK: Routledge.

Walsh, D., & Allan, J. (1994). Jungian art counseling with the suicidal child. *Guidance & Counseling, 10*(1), 3–10.

Winnicott, D. (1971). *Playing and reality.* New York, NY: Basic Books.

Draw Your Dream On

Population

This Jungian art therapy technique can be used with most children but is especially beneficial for elementary school-aged children coping with anxiety or trauma.

Rationale

The process of transferring a "picture" from a child's imagination or unconscious onto a blank slate (i.e., plain white paper) permits the child the opportunity to master difficult feelings or thoughts associated with a nightmare. Specifically, the process of bringing unconscious material forward and drawing the dream allows the child to bridge the material to his or her consciousness awareness, where psychical healing occurs. The process of actualizing the unconscious through artistic recreations typically leads to *externalization*—the transformation of the internal to the external. This technique assists in relieving distressing symptoms and empowers a child to take ownership of disturbing thoughts and change them. Depending on the child's age and level of cognitive development, the therapist decides on appropriate action or coaches the child accordingly. It is important for the therapist to convey a nonjudgmental, nonevaluative, warm demeanor and hopeful attitude and to convey genuinely that this technique benefits children with nightmares.

Materials

Plain white paper, colored pencils, thin markers or crayons

Procedure

- **Engagement:** Greet the child and clarify your role as someone who helps children with worries. Explain that many children and even adults struggle with nightmares when sleeping. Normalize bad dreams by telling the child that you work with many children who also have bad dreams at night and that you know strategies to help get rid of them. Gauge the child's reaction as he or she will often want to ask questions. Typically, traumatized children's dream content may be unrecognizable, so helping the child to articulate the feelings associated with the images is of paramount importance.

- **Draw the Dream:** Give the child markers, crayons, and paper and ask him or her to draw the scariest part of the dream. During the drawing process, it is important for the therapist to remain quiet and silently respect the child as the unconscious is produced on paper.

- **Dream the Dream On:** Ask the child to identify what the image is and what feelings occurred as he or she was drawing it. Then, direct the child to "Dream the Dream On" by giving out another sheet of paper and asking the child to draw the dream again except with the ending he or she would like. If a scary image is in the initial drawing, ask the child to redraw the dream the way he or she would like to dream it.

- **Resolution:** After the action is completed say, "This activity helps lots of children, and sometimes bad dreams go away. Now that you have imagined the dream the way you want it to be, you will hopefully have a good night's rest. You're courageous to want to overcome your nighttime worries, and I know you will do it!"

Chapter 6 ─────────────────────────────────

ADLERIAN PLAY THERAPY
Terry Kottman

Adlerian play therapy is an active and rather directive approach to working therapeutically with children using play (toys, stories, art, drama, puppets, and role-playing) as the vehicle for communication. Adlerian play therapy combines the theoretical constructs and some of the therapeutic intervention strategies of Alfred Adler's Individual Psychology with the basic premises of play therapy (Kottman, 1993, 2003, 2005, 2009, 2010, 2011). In Adlerian play therapy, the therapist does the following:

1. Establishes an egalitarian relationship with the child, parents, teachers, and other important people in the child's life
2. Explores the child's thoughts, feelings, behaviors, relationships, and attitudes
3. Explores the child's perceptions of self, others, and the world
4. Explores the thoughts, feelings, behaviors, relationships, and attitudes of parents and other influential people in the child's life
5. Develops a conceptualization about the intrapersonal and interpersonal dynamics of the child and his or her parents, other family members, and/or teachers
6. Generates a treatment plan for the child (and for parents and teachers if necessary)
7. Works toward helping the child gain insight into his or her intrapersonal and interpersonal dynamics and make new decisions about self, the world, and others
8. Helps the child learn and practice new interpersonal skills
9. Provides consultation for parents and teachers aimed at helping them cultivate positive perspectives on the child and practice more constructive ways of relating to the child

BASIC CONSTRUCTS, GOALS, AND TECHNIQUES

The important theoretical constructs of Adlerian play therapy are based on Adler's assertion that people are socially embedded, goal-directed, subjective, and creative beings (Adler, 1927/1954, 1931/1958, 1956; Carlson, Watts, & Maniacci, 2006; Mosak & Maniacci, 2010). These four principles are the foundation of the theory and practice of Individual Psychology.

Basic Constructs

People Are Socially Embedded

Adlerians believe that people are socially embedded, which means that they have a need to belong (Adler, 1956; Carlson, Watts, & Maniacci, 2006; Eckstein & Kern, 2009; Mosak & Maniacci, 2010). By observing the reaction of others to their behavior, children decide how to gain significance for themselves and fit into different groups. Adlerian play therapists spend time observing children in the context of their families and gathering information about family dynamics because the family is the first group to which children belong. If children do not experience success in their attempts to find a place in their families or in other groups of people in prosocial, constructive ways, they begin striving to belong in negative, self-destructive ways. In Adlerian play therapy, therapists continually assess how children make connections and gain a sense of significance in their families, schools, and communities in order to be able to design intervention programs to help them improve their ability to positively connect with others (Kottman, 2003).

Adlerian play therapists explore how the child has learned to belong by considering the family constellation and family atmosphere (Kottman, 2003). Family constellation is based on the concept of birth order and the child's perception of how his or her birth order influences behavior, attitudes, and so forth (Eckstein & Kern, 2009). Adlerian play therapists use the concept of family constellation to explore the assets and liabilities of the child client in the context of the typical assets and liabilities of a child in a similar birth order position. Family atmosphere is based on the family mood, the structural hierarchical relationships within the family, and the patterns of interaction within the family (Eckstein & Kern, 2009). The Adlerian play therapist considers the family atmosphere in which the child is living because the atmosphere of the family influences how the child views self, others, and the world and how the child gains a sense of belonging and significance.

By the time children are 7 or 8 years old, they have developed ideas about who they are, how others will treat them, how the world works, and how they can belong and find significance. They weave these ideas into a picture of themselves, others, and the world, basing their behaviors on the premise that these perceptions are true. In Adlerian terms, these perceptions and the behaviors based on them create the child's lifestyle, which is defined as "the characteristic way that we act, think, and perceive and the way we live" (Carlson, Watts, & Maniacci, 2006, p. 12). Although individuals always have choices about the way they live their lives, this lifestyle remains relatively stable throughout the life span unless the individual has some kind of psychological intervention or experiences a life-changing crisis of some kind. The lifestyle

> organizes and simplifies coping with the world by assigning rules and values; it selects, predicts, anticipates; its perceptions are guided by its own "private logic"; it selects what information it allows to enter, what it will attend to, what affects will be aroused and what its response will be. (Watts, 1999, p. 3)

Most of the time, individuals are not consciously aware of the elements of their lifestyles. Lifestyles are like maps for navigating through life's experiences that usually remain out of awareness. In Adlerian play therapy, the therapist observes clients' interactions and behaviors with the mission of understanding the lifestyles of the child clients and their parents so that the therapist can help clients become more aware of their patterns of thinking, feeling, and behaving and change them if they so desire.

One tool Adlerian play therapists use to organize their ideas about the lifestyles of children and parents and guide their therapeutic interactions is personality priorities (comfort, pleasing, control, and superiority) (Kefir, 1981; Kottman, 2003). Personality priorities can be defined as the most important aspect in a person's efforts to belong. Adlerian play therapists use personality priorities as a vehicle for understanding child clients, parents, and teachers. In determining a person's personality priority, a therapist examines (a) his or her personal reaction to the client, (b) the client's behaviors, (c) the client's presenting problem and/or complaints about life, (d) the client's goals in interacting with others, (e) the client's assets, and (f) the aspects of life the client tries to avoid. Play therapists can use their understanding of personality priorities as a way to guide their interactions with clients and help them develop treatment plans—both for child clients and the adults involved in their lives. While personality priorities seldom change significantly once a child is older than 8 or 10, the therapist can help the client move from destructive manifestations of his or her priorities to more constructive manifestations.

Adlerians label the sense of being connected to others as social interest (Adler, 1931/1958, 1956; Carlson, Watts, & Maniacci, 2006). Adler suggested that every individual is born with an innate capacity and a longing to connect with others but must be taught how to build relationships and gain significance positively. Many of the children who come to play therapy have not developed a strong sense of social interest and tend to lack the social skills necessary to establish a constructive connection with others. The Adlerian play therapist works with children in ways designed to increase their ability to positively connect with others. Initially, the play therapist models connecting in the play therapy relationship, talks about the value of positive interactions with others, and works with parents and teachers to foster the social interest of child clients. As the therapy progresses, the play therapist teaches prosocial skills to the child and makes suggestions about ways to apply those skills in relationships outside the play room. At times, it is even helpful to bring parents, siblings, or a friend into the playroom so that the child can practice appropriately interacting with others in a safe environment with the play therapist able to observe and make suggestions about how to refine the application of social skills.

People Are Goal Directed

Another key construct in Adlerian play therapy is that all human behavior is purposive and directed toward goals (Carlson, Watts, & Maniacci, 2006; Kottman, 2003; Thompson & Henderson, 2006). In contrast to other psychological theories based on the premise that people are motivated by instincts or that people are formed solely by experience, heredity, or environment, Adler believed that people are motivated by their desire to move toward a variety of life goals and choose their behaviors as a means to forward their movement toward these goals (Mosak & Maniacci, 2010; Sweeney, 2009). The Adlerian therapist examines clients' behavior to discover the underlying goals of the behavior. As the therapist helps clients explore the purposes of their behavior, clients have the opportunity to consciously decide whether to continue striving toward those purposes. Dreikurs and Soltz (1964) developed a way of classifying the goals of discouraged children's misbehavior into four distinct categories: attention, power, revenge, and proving inadequacy. To determine the goal of the child's misbehavior, the therapist considers (a) the child's behaviors, (b) the child's feelings and beliefs, (c) other people's reactions to the child's behaviors, and (d) the child's reaction when corrected or punished (Dreikurs & Soltz, 1964; Kottman, 2003).

Attention-seeking children believe that they do not belong unless they are the center of attention. Examples of typical behaviors of children whose goal is attention include whining, bothering others, showing off, being the class clown, repeatedly asking for approval, being overly solicitous or helpful, seeking constant reassurance, striving for perfection, being shy or highly anxious, and being excessively messy, lazy, or clingy. Adults feel mildly irritated or annoyed by many of the behaviors of the attention-seeking child but do not usually move toward anger or extreme frustration because, when corrected, these children temporarily cease their misbehavior.

Power-seeking children believe that their significance and belonging depend on dominating others and making sure that others cannot control them. The active form of power-oriented behavior includes behaviors such as arguing, contradicting others, having tantrums, being dishonest, being defiant, engaging in an inordinate number of power struggles, and being disrespectful. A more passive form of power-seeking behavior includes being lazy, stubborn, or disobedient; forgetting even routine responsibilities; doing little or no work at home or school; or acting in a passive-aggressive manner. When adults encounter children whose goal is power, they get angry, and they often feel challenged, threatened, or provoked by the behavior of these children. If corrected or punished, power-oriented children usually escalate behavior designed to assert their control over themselves and others. Kottman (2003) makes a distinction among three separate types of power-seeking behavior, based on the atmosphere and discipline methods in children's families (children with too much power, children with too little power, and children from chaotic families in which no one has appropriate power).

Children whose goal is revenge believe that others will hurt them and that no one will like or love them. They try to push others away with their hurtful behavior. With some of these children, their behavior is a self-defeating attempt to protect themselves from being vulnerable to hurt from others. Some revenge-seeking children seem to believe that hurting others is a normal way to connect and gain significance. The behaviors of children whose goal is revenge are designed to hurt other people. These children are often malicious, violent, and cruel. They frequently lie and steal. In a more passive mode, these children are moody and withdrawn. They may bully or threaten others for real or imagined transgressions. Adults who interact with revenge-seeking children feel hurt by their behavior and usually either want to get even or withdraw from the relationship with these children. When corrected, children whose goal is revenge work harder to hurt those who they believe inflicted hurt on them.

Children whose goal is proving inadequacy believe that they are failures. They give up easily. They do not take risks, avoiding any behavior where they are not guaranteed success. Adults who interact with these children feel hopeless and powerless. Although they seldom exhibit inappropriate behavior, if corrected, these children become even more discouraged.

Adlerian play therapists can use Dreikurs and Soltz's (1964) goals as a way of guiding how they are going to respond to the child in the playroom. For example, in the playroom, children who are striving toward power may argue with the therapist, refuse to abide by limits, and/or try to control every aspect of the play. When the Adlerian play therapist realizes that the child's goal is power, he or she works harder to make sure that power is shared in the play room, emphasizing taking turns, treating others with respect, and so forth. The Adlerian play therapist also uses these goals of misbehavior as a way to help parents learn to interact differently with the child. For example, with a child who gives up easily and is striving to reprove to himself that he is worthless and inadequate, the therapist would help parents look for very small accomplishments and encourage the child for effort and progress, not for perfection.

Another strategy used by Adlerian play therapists is encouraging children to substitute positive, constructive goals in the place of negative, destructive goals (Dinkmeyer & McKay, 2007; Lew & Bettner, 1996, 2000). Lew and Bettner (1996, 2000) suggested four goals (the Crucial Cs) that lend themselves to promoting positive behavior: (a) connecting with others (the positive goal of cooperation), (b) being capable (the positive goal of self-reliance), (c) believing that they count and are inherently valuable (the positive goal of contribution), and (d) being courageous (the positive goal of resiliency). The Adlerian play therapist helps children move toward learning to connect with others, believing that they are capable, believing that they count and gaining their significance in appropriate ways, and having courage to take risks and try new things. The Adlerian play therapist strives to move children toward positive goals of behavior by fostering the Crucial Cs in play therapy sessions and consulting with parents and teachers to help them establish family and classroom atmospheres that foster the Crucial Cs.

People View Reality Subjectively

Adlerians believe in a phenomenological view of the world, where people have unique interpretations about specific situations and interactions (Carlson, Watts, & Maniacci, 2006; Eckstein & Kern, 2009). This means that every person involved in an experience has his or her own way of interpreting the circumstances and relationship. Parents, children, and teachers each have different views of relationships and situations. The Adlerian play therapist must always be aware of all of these subjective interpretations. As the play therapist sifts through the various perspectives, it is essential to remember that there is no one correct interpretation of reality. The child is the primary client, and the play therapist should give extra weight to the child's perspective in an effort to understand how he or she is interpreting the events and interactions in his or her life.

Because people tend to see what they expect to see, their interpretation of reality reinforces their beliefs, whether those beliefs are accurate or not, and they "act as if" their perception is the "truth." The Adlerian play therapist looks for ways that children, parents, and teachers are setting up situations in which they reprove to themselves negative things (mistaken beliefs) they already believe about themselves (Kottman, 2003). People often behave as if their own subjective negative picture of themselves is true, evoking a negative reaction from others, which confirms their mistaken beliefs. It is the job of the Adlerian play therapist to "spit in the client's soup" by pointing out these self-defeating patterns in beliefs and behaviors and to help clients find new ways of thinking about themselves and learn more appropriate behaviors.

People Are Creative Beings

Another key concept in Individual Psychology is the belief that each person is unique, constantly expressing a creative ability by making choices (Carlson, Watts, & Maniacci, 2006; Mosak & Maniacci, 2010; Sweeney, 2009). Adlerians stress self-determination in the therapeutic process, recognizing that each individual has the ability to make choices about his or her own unique interpretation of situations and relationships and to act as if those interpretations are true. H. Ansbacher and Ansbacher (1956) summarized this tenet of Adler by saying, "the important thing is not what one is born with, but what use one makes of that equipment" (pp. 86–87). Both children and adults are always free to make new and different decisions and interpretations, exercising their creativity and uniqueness.

Adlerian play therapists' faith in clients' ability to make creative decisions is the basis for working with children, parents, and teachers in changing their lifestyle patterns, increasing social interest, making shifts toward more positive goals of behavior, capitalizing on their assets, and learning new behavior and relationship patterns (Kottman, 2003, 2010). Adlerian play therapists explore the ways that children express their unique and special selves. Part of the process of Adlerian play therapy and consultation with parents and teachers is helping children learn to appreciate their own uniqueness and helping parents and teachers learn to celebrate their own strengths and the strengths of the children.

Goals and Techniques of Adlerian Play Therapy

The goals and techniques of Adlerian play therapy can best be understood in the context of each of the four stages of the therapeutic process. In each of the phases, the general goals of therapy are usually the same across clients. However, the play therapist works with parents and teachers (and sometimes child clients) on specific goals appropriate for that particular child and his or her family. Based on the goals of therapy and the needs of the individual child, the play therapist specifically tailors the play therapy process, resulting in a unique and individual interaction with the child in the playroom. Adlerians are technically eclectic, custom-designing treatment goals and interventions to the particular needs and circumstances of the client and the client's family (Carlson, Watts, & Maniacci, 2006). Because of this, the process of Adlerian play therapy is actually quite similar to the process advocated by prescriptive play therapists (Gil & Shaw, 2009; Schaefer, 2003), except that Adlerians consistently conceptualize the child and his or her issues using Adlerian methods for understanding clients (e.g., Crucial Cs, goals of misbehavior, personality priorities, etc.).

First Phase: Building an Egalitarian Relationship

The primary goal of the first stage of Adlerian play therapy is building an egalitarian relationship with the child (Kottman, 2003, in press). Adlerians believe that the relationship is a foundation that is essential for successful therapy to take place. In this phase, the play therapist uses tracking, restatement of content, reflection of feelings, returning responsibility to the child, encouragement, limiting, and cleaning the room together to establish a collaborative relationship with the child.

Tracking (telling the child what the child is doing), restating content (paraphrasing and summarizing), reflecting feelings, and returning responsibility to the child are techniques employed by most play therapists, regardless of their theoretical orientation (Kottman, in press). Encouragement is a particularly Adlerian therapeutic strategy. Encouragement is an essential technique in all four phases of Adlerian play therapy. Encouragement involves the following elements:

1. Conveying unconditional acceptance by communicating that the child is valuable just as he or she is
2. Showing faith in the child's abilities by recognizing current achievement and giving the child credit for making progress
3. Giving the child recognition for his or her efforts, without using evaluative words
4. Focusing on the child's strengths and assets
5. Giving the child credit for the positive part of what was done and ignoring the parts that do not come up to standards
6. Demonstrating a sense of caring about the child's interests
7. Letting the child know that it is perfectly acceptable to make mistakes by modeling the courage to be imperfect
8. Helping the child realize he or she can learn from mistakes and that mistakes do not have to be negative or devastating

In Adlerian play therapy, there is a specific method for limiting that is unique to this approach to play therapy (Kottman, 2003). The therapist uses a four-step process to provide limits. In the first step, the play therapist states the limit in a clear, nonjudgmental way. The formula for setting the limit is to say, "It is against the play room rules to ____" (whatever the therapist wants to limit). Next, the therapist reflects the child's feelings and/or makes a guess about the underlying message in or purpose of the limit-testing behavior. For example, the therapist might say, "I can tell you want to show me that you are really mad at me right now" or "You want to show me that I can't tell you what to do." During the third step, the therapist invites the child to help generate acceptable alternatives. This involves a decision-making process in which the therapist and the child collaboratively determine what is and is not acceptable in the playroom. The therapist starts this process by saying, "I bet we can figure out something you can do that isn't against the playroom rules." Usually, this is as far as the limit-setting process proceeds because when a child is actively engaged in redirecting his or her own behavior, power struggles or limit testing seldom persists. However, some children may continue to break the limit. When this happens, the therapist must proceed to the fourth step in limit setting and engage the child in setting up appropriate logical consequences. In the generation of logical consequences, the therapist continues to build an egalitarian relationship in which the child has input into the rules and the process of the playroom.

Adlerian play therapists believe that cleaning the room together can also build the relationship with the child. By establishing a collaborative partnership with the child in taking responsibility for the toys and materials in the playroom, the play therapist can further strengthen the positive connection with the child. To start the cleanup process, the therapist stands up and says, "It is time for us to clean up the room together. What do you want to pick up, and what do you want me to pick up?" Some children, especially younger children, may need a little more structuring than this, so the play therapist may ask, "Do you want to pick up the blocks or the dinosaurs? Whichever ones you don't want to pick up, I will pick up."

Second Phase: Exploring the Child's Lifestyle

During the second stage, the goal of the play therapy process is to explore the child's lifestyle so that the play therapist can gain a clear understanding of the child's interpersonal and intrapersonal dynamics (Kottman, 2003, 2010). To do this, the play therapist uses art techniques, questioning strategies, observation of play patterns, and solicitation of early recollections to investigate goals of behavior, Crucial Cs, family constellation, and family atmosphere and gather information about the child's attitudes, perceptions, beliefs, feelings, and behaviors.

Drawing techniques such as the Kinetic Family Drawing and the Kinetic School Drawing (Burns & Kaufman, 1970; Knoff, 1985), the Family-Centered Circle Drawing (Burns, 1990), the Rosebush drawing (Oaklander, 1992), and other art techniques (Kottman, 2003, Malchiodi, 2003) can reveal patterns in family interactions; images of self, others, and the world; mistaken beliefs; and ways of gaining belonging and significance. With children who do not like to draw, the therapist can exercise flexibility and ask the child to use some other medium to explore these factors. It is essential to match the inclinations of the child with the mode of expression—clay, painting, puppet shows, and pipe cleaner sculptures are just a few ways of inviting the child to use sensory means to communicate about his or her situation and relationships (Kottman, 2003).

Other important techniques in the process of investigating the child's lifestyle are asking questions and observing the play. Sometimes, the therapist chooses to ask questions about drawings or other forms of expressive arts. Other times, the therapist asks the child direct questions about his or her life. More often, the therapist asks questions about the child's life through a metaphor in the play of a story the child is telling (Kottman, 2003). Observation of play patterns is an important strategy for gathering information. All children will express what is happening in their lives through their play. The play therapist must simply observe patterns and themes in the child's narratives to gain insight into what is happening with the child.

A uniquely Adlerian technique for learning about a child's world is the solicitation of early recollections (Eckstein & Kern, 2009; Kottman, 2003). Early recollections are memories of moments—usually from the first 4 to 6 years—a person chooses to remember from all the possible life experiences. It is important to gather enough early recollections (usually six to eight) so that a pattern emerges. Interpretation of early recollections helps the counselor understand clients' lifestyles. Many Adlerian play therapists ask children to tell, draw, or paint their early recollections as a means to help them understand children's lifestyles, mistaken beliefs, social interactions, Crucial Cs, personality priorities, and goals of behavior (Kottman, 2003).

Gathering this information during the second phase prepares the play therapist for developing a conceptualization of the child that will guide the rest of the play therapy process (Kottman, 2003, 2010). The play therapist integrates the information into an organized picture of the child and his or her relationships, a summary of the child's lifestyle, which includes (a) strengths and assets; (b) functioning at home and school; (c) play themes; (d) perceptions of the child's birth order position and the ways in which those perceptions affect his or her attitudes and functioning; (e) perceptions of the family atmosphere and the ways those perceptions affect his or her attitudes and functioning; (f) themes in the child's early recollections that give a picture of views about self, others, and the world; (g) goals of misbehavior; (h) Crucial Cs; (i) personality priorities; and (j) mistaken beliefs. Based on this conceptualization, the play therapist develops a treatment plan for working with the child and his or her parents (and possibly teachers as well, depending on the presenting problem). The treatment plan includes goals and play therapy strategies for helping the child in acknowledging and capitalizing on assets; improving functioning at home and school; making shifts in negative, self-defeating beliefs about self, others, and the world; moving from negative goals of behavior to positive goals of behavior; capitalizing on all of the Crucial Cs; and maximizing on the assets of his or her personality priority (Kottman, 2003).

Third Phase: Helping the Child Gain Insight into Lifestyle

The goal of the third phase of the Adlerian play therapy process is helping the child gain insight into his or her lifestyle through an enhanced understanding of interpersonal and intrapersonal dynamics (Kottman, 2003, 2010). Techniques used in this phase include metacommunicating, delivering metaphors, "spitting in the soup," and drawing techniques to convey essential information about lifestyles, mistaken beliefs, goals of misbehavior, Crucial Cs, and assets to the child. As the child gains insight into his or her dynamics, the therapist helps the child decide which attitudes, beliefs, and behaviors to continue and which to replace with more constructive attitudes, beliefs, and behaviors.

In metacommunication, the therapist steps outside the interaction between himself or herself and the child to communicate about the communication.

Metacommunicating involves the play therapist making interpretations about (a) patterns in the interactional patterns between the therapist and the child, (b) nonverbal communication on the part of the child, (c) the child's reactions to the counselor's statements and questions, and (d) the underlying meaning in the child's play and verbalizations. Children are often not aware of their communication patterns nor can they articulate their thoughts and feelings about their patterns of interacting with others. Adlerian play therapists can use metacommunication about these patterns to help children become more aware of communication patterns to give them the opportunity to make shifts in how they interact with others.

In the "spitting in the soup" technique, the therapist points out situations in which the child is acting as if self-defeating beliefs about self, others, and the world are true even when they are not. Often, the best way to spit in a child's soup in play therapy is to use gentle humor or teasing to let the child know that his or her perceptions and behavior may not be helpful.

The therapist capitalizes on children's natural communication by using metaphoric techniques to help children gain insight into their lifestyles (Kottman, 2003; Kottman & Ashby, 2002). When a child is using metaphors or stories to relate information about experiences, the play therapist enters the story the child is telling in order to ask questions, metacommunicate about lifestyle themes, and make suggestions for different ways of handling situations. Adlerian play therapists often design new therapeutic metaphors for specific children to help them gain a new perspective on themselves and their lives. In the Adlerian version of mutual storytelling, play therapists will listen for lifestyle themes and patterns, Crucial Cs, personality priorities, and problem-solving strategies in children's telling of the story and use the retelling to emphasize assets, teach problem solving, suggest more prosocial goals of behavior, and foster the Crucial Cs. Two other ways to use storytelling to help children gain insight are superhero stories (Rubin, 2007) and bibliotherapy—the use of children's books as an indirect vehicle for encouraging children to reexamine their attitudes and behaviors (Kottman, in press; Malchiodi & Ginns-Gruenberg, 2008).

Fourth Phase: Reorientation/Reeducation

The reorientation/reeducation phase is designed to help the child learn and practice more positive attitudes, perceptions, beliefs, feelings, and behaviors (Kottman, 2003, 2010). The therapist uses a variety of teaching strategies (such as modeling, brainstorming, role-playing, therapeutic metaphors) to help the child grow in positive directions. This phase includes many directive techniques designed to help the child learn problem-solving skills, social skills, negotiation skills, and any other skills that are lacking in his or her behavioral repertoire.

THERAPEUTIC POWERS OF PLAY

Schaefer (1993) and Schaefer and Drewes (2009) generated lists of therapeutic powers of play, suggesting that each of these factors has specific beneficial outcomes for clients. Some of these therapeutic factors are self-expression, access to the unconscious, direct and indirect teaching, abreaction, stress inoculation, mastering of fears and counterconditioning of negative affect, catharsis, positive emotion, competence and self-control, sublimation, attachment formation, rapport building, relationship enhancement, moral judgment, behavioral rehearsal, empathy, power/control, sense of self, creative problem solving, reality testing, and fantasy compensation. Adlerian play therapy makes use of all of these therapeutic elements, with a special emphasis on direct and indirect teaching, competence and self-control, rapport building and relationship enhancement, behavioral rehearsal, power/control, and creative problem solving.

ROLE OF THE THERAPIST

Through the process of Adlerian play therapy, the role of the therapist is that of partner, encourager, and teacher with children, parents, teachers, and siblings. However, manifestation of that role changes depending on the phase of the therapeutic process (Kottman, 2003, 2010). During the first phase of therapy, the primary task of the therapist is building the relationship with the child and with any important individuals in the child's life, such as parents and teachers. The therapist is usually nondirective with the child during this phase, following the lead of the child. In the spirit of establishing an egalitarian partnership, the therapist encourages the child to make many of the decisions in the playroom, working to create an atmosphere of teamwork and cooperation. In working with the adults in the child's life, the therapist concentrates on building a caring relationship, listening to their concerns, and looking for ways to provide encouragement and guidance.

In the second phase of Adlerian play therapy, the therapist is much more active and directive in the process of exploration of the child's lifestyle, asking questions, observing, making guesses, and requesting that the child tell stories, draw, do puppet shows, and recount early recollections (Kottman, 2003). The therapist solicits information from parents and teachers about their perceptions of the child's lifestyle, information about their own lifestyles, and impressions about the interactions between the child's lifestyle and the lifestyles of other important people in the child's life. The therapist gathers information about perceptions, attitudes, cognitive patterns, emotions, relationships, self-concept, and other factors that could affect how the child sees himself or herself, others, and the world. The therapist uses the information and impressions gathered in this phase to develop a lifestyle conceptualization and treatment plan that informs the rest of the therapeutic process.

During the third phase of Adlerian play therapy, the therapist continues to be active in the playroom, using interpretation, tentative hypotheses, storytelling, and art to help the child gain insight into mistaken beliefs, goals of misbehavior, and other factors that might be causing distress or leading to misbehavior (Kottman, 2003). The therapist is often directive and confrontive, challenging self-defeating patterns and beliefs and making guesses about discrepancies between clients' words and behaviors, between verbal and nonverbal communication.

The main role of the therapist in the fourth phase of Adlerian play therapy is to work in active and directive ways to help reorient and reeducate clients by teaching them new skills and encouraging them for effort and progress (Kottman, 2003, 2010). By using art, storytelling, role-playing, problem-solving strategies, and encouragement support for development of new skills in areas such as assertiveness, negotiation, social interactions, parenting, and classroom management, the therapist can help children acquire new strategies for interacting with others and coping with life.

ROLE OF THE PARENT

Because of the Adlerian emphasis on the importance of family in the formation of the personality, including parents as part of the therapeutic process is a critical component of Adlerian play therapy (Kottman, 2003). Whenever possible, in each phase, the play therapist engages the parents in a process that parallels the therapeutic interaction with the child. During the first phase, the play therapist works to create an egalitarian relationship with parents, striving to build a collaborative partnership designed to provide support for any changes the child decides to make and support for the parents' growth toward positive parenting. In the second phase, the therapist has two different tasks—investigating the parents' perception of the child's lifestyle and the parents' lifestyles, striving for an understanding of both the child and the parents and how they interact with one another. At the end of the second phase, the therapist makes a treatment plan for parents if such a plan would be helpful for the therapy process. The third phase entails the therapist's helping the parents gain insight into their child and into themselves. The therapist helps parents learn more positive ways of thinking about and interacting with the child while they explore how their own issues might be getting in the way of their effectively providing the nurturing and structuring that is necessary for children to grow up mentally healthy and strong. The focus of the intervention with parents during the fourth phase is teaching them parenting skills, teaching them new ways to conceptualize their children, and helping them work on personal issues that might be interfering with their ability to be the best parents they can be.

CLINICAL APPLICATIONS

Because Adlerian play therapy is tailored to the specific client and his or her presenting problem, family circumstances, and ongoing life experiences, it can be used with children who are experiencing a variety of difficulties. Based on anecdotal reports (Ashby, Kottman, & Martin, 2004; Kottman, 1993, 1997, 2003, 2009; Kottman, Bryant, Alexander, & Kroger, 2008; Kottman & Stiles, 1990; Morrison, 2009; Snow, Buckley, & Williams, 1999), empirical research (Meany-Whalen, 2010), and the author's clinical experience, Adlerian play therapy seems to be particularly effective with children who exhibit behavior problems, acting out behavior, and difficulty with peer relationships; children who have difficult life situations (e.g., divorce of parents, death in the family, etc.); children with issues related to power and control; children who are struggling in school; children with low self-esteem; children who are depressed, perfectionistic, or anxious; and children who have experienced some kind of trauma.

EMPIRICAL SUPPORT

According to a survey conducted by Lambert and colleagues (2007), Adlerian theory is the third most widely used theoretical orientation applied to play therapy. However, there is little empirical support for Adlerian play therapy. This has been, at least in part, due to the difficulty in defining exactly how a clinician would go about doing Adlerian play therapy because treatment is custom designed for the child and his or her situation. However, this problem has recently been resolved by the development of a treatment manual developed for the express purpose of facilitating the pursuit of empirical research into the efficacy of Adlerian play therapy. This treatment manual (Kottman, 2010) was used to conduct the first randomizing control group pretest/posttest design study in Adlerian play therapy (Meany-Whalen, 2010). In this study, Meany-Whalen compared the effectiveness of Adlerian play therapy with an active control group (reading mentoring). Participants were 67 children in kindergarten through third grade who had been identified by teachers as exhibiting disruptive behaviors in the classroom. These children were randomly assigned to the experimental (Adlerian play therapy) or the active control (reading mentoring) groups. Teachers did not know in which group children were placed in order to avoid halo effects. Adlerian play therapists followed the Adlerian play therapy treatment protocol outlined in the treatment manual, working with the children for sixteen 30-minute sessions that were conducted twice weekly. Before and after the treatment, the Caregiver–Teacher Report Form (C-TRF) and the Direct Observation Form (DOF) were used to measure children's externalizing behavior problems, and the Index of Teacher Stress (ITS) was used to measure teachers' stress related to the teacher–student relationship. The C-TRF and the ITS were completed by teachers and the observations for the DOF were completed by objective observers who were blinded to the study. The results from a two (group) by two (measures) split plot analysis of variance (ANOVA) indicated that the children who participated in Adlerian play therapy (compared with the children who participated in the reading mentoring program) had statistically significant decreases in disruptive behavior and total behavior problems. They also demonstrated improvement on in-class on-task behavior, and their teachers reported a reduction in teacher–student stress. The Adlerian play therapy group demonstrated a moderate treatment effect on the teacher-reported measures (CTRF and ITS) and a large treatment effect for instruments completed by independent observers blinded to the study. Approximately 70% of the children in the Adlerian play therapy treatment group had reduced the level of concern about their disruptive and off-task behaviors from the borderline or clinical ranges to less severe levels of concern following the treatment.

Several other researchers have examined the use of Adlerian interventions with children, but not with a specific focus on Adlerian play therapy. In an empirical study, Statton (1990) explored the use of early recollections in working with children and suggested that this practice can be helpful. Rotter, Horak, and Heidt (1999) explored the use of children's drawings in gathering early recollections and found that it is often easier to gather early recollections from children if they are asked to draw a picture along with telling the story of the early recollection. However, these were the only studies found related to using Adlerian interventions with children.

Now that there is a method for manualized treatment in Adlerian play therapy (Kottman, 2010), hopefully more research will be conducted as a means for establishing Adlerian play therapy as an evidence-based treatment (EBT). If a treatment modality is to be considered evidence based, it has to have a foundation in scientific evaluation through rigorous research and not rely on anecdotal evidence, belief in the specific procedure, or tradition (U.S. Department of Health and Human Services, Substance Abuse and Mental Health Services Administration, 2009). By following the path pioneered by Meany-Whalen (2010) and the research strategy outlined by the Association for Play Therapy (2009) that calls for researchers to conduct "well-designed, experimental outcome studies that examine benefits from a manualized play therapy treatment as compared to either a comparison treatment and/or a control group on targeted population or symptoms" (p. 1), researchers in the future could establish Adlerian play therapy as an evidence-based treatment.

CASE ILLUSTRATION

"You hate me! I am never coming here again, for the rest of my life!" This was the way Liam ended his first session with Andrea, his Adlerian play therapist. She decided that the first phase of the play therapy process might take a while. Liam was a boy who had never received much consistent nurturing. His father had left his mother, Caitlin, before he was born. Caitlin struggled with drug abuse and abusive relationships until Liam was 5, when she left him with her mother and entered drug rehabilitation. When Caitlin got out of rehab, she was determined to "do right by my boy," but 6-year-old Liam was a handful. He talked back, he tested limits, he called his mother names, he threatened to run away from home, and he repeatedly informed his mother that she "just did not love him enough." At school and in aftercare, he formed strong attachments with teachers but was very emotional, crying with little provocation and regularly having hour-long tantrums.

In the first several sessions, Liam spent much of each session burying soldiers and small animals in the sandbox and stacking and unstacking a pile of cardboard bricks. He did little with any of the other toys, though he occasionally made towers of Legos and drew pictures and painted. Andrea concentrated on building the relationship with Liam, using tracking, restating content, reflecting feelings, encouraging, setting limits, and cleaning the room. She used humor to show him that he did not always have to take everything so seriously. She also provided practice in learning to share power with others by taking turns with Liam deciding on what they were going to do in the session. Liam tested the limits often in the playroom, and Andrea worked to be consistent, friendly, but firm with him, setting logical consequences when he chose to ignore or violate the rules of the playroom. She noticed that he had difficulty acknowledging his assets and used encouragement to help him feel more comfortable about his strengths. Andrea had parent consultation sessions with Caitlin every time she saw Liam. During these sessions, she worked to establish a collaborative and supportive relationship with Caitlin.

During the third session, Andrea began to investigate Liam's lifestyle by asking him to draw a picture of everyone in his family doing something (the directions for the Kinetic Family Drawing). Liam drew a picture of his mother, his absent father, and his grandmother. He did not include himself in the picture. When Andrea asked him where he was, he acted surprised and told her that he was "outside waiting for someone to come and play with me," and then he drew himself on the back of the piece of paper. He drew a similar picture during the next session when Andrea asked him to draw a picture of himself, a teacher, and a classmate or two at school. He drew his entire class, but he reported that he had run out of room and had to put himself and one other child on the back of the paper. When Andrea asked him about this, he said, "Probably no one will notice I am gone since I am not yelling or pitching a fit."

After the sessions in which he drew the kinetic drawings, Liam seemed more open to allowing Andrea to know more about his life and his relationships because he started playing with the small animal families and the puppets and telling stories about their adventures. He would never answer direct questions about the characters in his stories, so Andrea observed the play themes in the stories and asked questions through the metaphor. Through Liam's continuing story about a bird that always got left behind by the other members of his family, Andrea came to the conclusion that Liam felt no one loved him enough to stay with him. He was really struggling with the Crucial Cs of connect and count. Through his pattern of always wanting his way manifested in their sessions and reported by Caitlin and Liam's teacher, Andrea recognized that his personality priority was control. Liam had many assets—he was intelligent, creative, and cared about other people—he just wasn't confident that others cared about him.

Caitlin reported that she was an only child whose father had died of liver problems caused by acute alcoholism. Her mother had worked several jobs to keep the family afloat, and Caitlin was often left to care for herself. She married at 16, was pregnant with Liam at 18 and deserted by her husband, and developed an addiction to cocaine at 20, when Liam was 2 years old. She had tried to be a consistent parent for Liam, but her addiction interfered with her ability to parent. She seemed to be determined to stay clean and sober and wanted very much to learn to be a good parent. Caitlin confessed that she did "not really understand" Liam. She was frustrated by the power struggles that they so often had and wasn't sure how to cope with them.

By the seventh session, Andrea was confident that she had a clear conceptualization of Liam and his issues, and she began the process of helping him and his mother gain insight. Her priorities in working with Liam were to help him develop a sense that he could connect with others and that he was significant, important, and lovable. She believed that the goal of his misbehavior was usually control and that this goal was related to his sense that his life had (up until this point) been out of control. She also attributed his tendency to engage in power struggles and tantrums to his control personality priority. Andrea believed that Liam had many strengths, and she wanted to help him recognize how capable and courageous he was.

During the third phase, Andrea used spitting in the soup and metacommunicating extensively to point out times when Liam was engaging in self-defeating attitudes and behaviors. She metacommunicated whenever he began to act as if he did not know how to connect with others or that he was insignificant and unlovable. She used encouragement to stress Liam's assets. Andrea developed several different therapeutic stories for Liam, using the mutual storytelling approach and featuring the bird that got left behind. In her retellings, the bird did not always get left behind, and he learned to ask for what he needed more clearly. The bird also learned to express his feelings without resorting to tantrums or power struggles. Liam and Andrea played games in which they took turns talking about feelings and ways to connect with others.

Andrea consulted with Caitlin, helping her gain insight into the destructive patterns in which she and Liam had been engaged. Andrea taught Caitlin about how her own personality priority of pleasing and comfort might be sabotaging her ability to set consistent limits and boundaries for Liam. Caitlin explored her own Crucial Cs and came to understand that her own struggles with the Crucial Cs of connect and count were contributing to the problems she and Liam were experiencing. She was very receptive to having some of Liam's behaviors reframed and seemed to want to learn how to encourage him for his assets.

In the fourth phase of the play therapy process, Andrea invited Caitlin to join her and Liam in the playroom. They worked on setting limits, expressing feelings, generating problem-solving strategies, negotiating for compromise, and making positive connections. In several individual sessions with Liam, Andrea helped him polish his social skills in preparation for participating in a friendship group with the school counselor. By the 20th session, Liam had made enough progress that Caitlin, Andrea, and he decided that they were ready to terminate the play therapy. Although things were not always perfect, Liam and Andrea lived mostly happily forever after.

CONCLUSION

Adlerian play therapy is an active process in which the therapist uses toys, art materials, stories, puppets, and role-playing to build an egalitarian relationship with the child, explore the child's lifestyle, help the child gain insight into his or her lifestyle, teach the child new skills and attitudes, and provide a forum for the child to practice these skills and attitudes in the safe space of the playroom. Simultaneously, the play therapist consults with parents, helping them gain insight into themselves and their children and learn constructive parenting strategies, and (when appropriate) teachers, helping them learn more effective ways of interacting with children who are struggling in school.

REFERENCES

Adler, A. (1954). *Understanding human nature* (W. B. Wolf, Trans.). New York, NY: Fawcett Premier. (Original work published 1927)

Adler, A. (1956). *The Individual Psychology of Alfred Adler* (H. Ansbacher & R. Ansbacher, Eds.). New York, NY: Basic Books.

Adler, A. (1958). *What life should mean to you*. New York, NY: Putnam. (Original work published 1931)

Ansbacher, H., & Ansbacher, R. (Eds.). (1956). *The Individual Psychology of Alfred Adler: A systematic presentation in selections from his writings*. San Francisco, CA: Harper & Row.

Ashby, J., Kottman, T., & Martin, J. (2004). Play therapy with young perfectionists. *International Journal of Play Therapy, 13*(1), 35–55.

Association for Play Therapy. (2009). *Research strategy*. Retrieved from www.a4pt.org/download.cfm?ID=28318

Burns, R. (1990). *A guide to family-centered circle drawings*. New York, NY: Brunner/Mazel.

Burns, R., & Kaufman, S. (1970). *Kinetic family drawings: An introduction to understanding children through kinetic drawings*. New York, NY: Brunner/Mazel.

Carlson, J., Watts, R., & Maniacci, M. (2006). *Adlerian therapy: Theory and practice*. Washington, DC: American Psychological Association.

Dinkmeyer, D., & McKay, G. (2007). *The parent's handbook: Systematic training for effective parenting (STEP)*. Atascadero, CA: Impact.

Dreikurs, R., & Soltz, V. (1964). *Children: The challenge*. New York, NY: Hawthorn/Dutton.

Eckstein, D., & Kern, R. (2009). *Psychological fingerprints* (6th ed.). Dubuque, IA: Kendall/Hunt.

Gil, E., & Shaw, J. (2009). Prescriptive play therapy. In K. O'Connor & L. M. Braverman (Eds.), *Play therapy theory and practice: Comparing theories and techniques* (2nd ed., pp. 451–488). New York, NY: Wiley.

Kefir, N. (1981). Impasse/priority therapy. In R. Corsini (Ed.), *Handbook of innovative psychotherapies* (pp. 400–415). New York, NY: Wiley.

Knoff, H. (1985). *Kinetic drawing system for family and school: Scoring booklet*. Los Angeles, CA: Western Psychological Services.

Kottman, T. (1993). The king of rock and roll. In T. Kottman & C. Schaefer (Eds.), *Play therapy in action: A casebook for practitioners* (pp. 133–167). Northvale, NJ: Aronson.

Kottman, T. (1997). Building a family: Play therapy with adopted children and their parents. In H. Kaduson, D. Cangelosi, & C. Schaefer (Eds.), *The playing cure: Individual play therapy for specific childhood problems* (pp. 337–370). Northvale, NJ: Aronson.

Kottman, T. (2003). *Partners in play: An Adlerian approach to play therapy* (2nd ed.). Alexandria, VA: American Counseling Association.

Kottman, T. (2005). Adlerian case consultation with a teacher. In A. M. Dougherty (Ed.), *Psychological consultation and collaboration in school and community settings: A casebook* (4th ed., pp. 53–68). Belmont, CA: Thomson.

Kottman, T. (2009). Adlerian play therapy. In K. O'Connor & L. M. Braverman (Eds.), *Play therapy theory and practice: Comparing theories and practices* (2nd ed., pp. 237–282). New York, NY: Wiley.

Kottman, T. (2010). *Adlerian play therapy treatment manual*. Unpublished manuscript.

Kottman, T. (2011, in press). *Play therapy: Basics and beyond* (2nd ed.). Alexandria, VA: American Counseling Association.

Kottman, T., & Ashby, J. (2002). Metaphoric stories. In C. Schaefer & D. Cangelosi (Eds.), *Play therapy techniques* (2nd ed., pp. 132–142). Northvale, NJ: Aronson.

Kottman, T., Bryant, J., Alexander, J., & Kroger, S. (2008). Partners in the schools: Adlerian school counseling. In A. Vernon & T. Kottman (Eds.), *Counseling theories: Practical applications with children and adolescents in school* (pp. 47–84). Denver, CO: Love.

Kottman, T., & Stiles, K. (1990). The mutual storytelling technique: An Adlerian application in child therapy. *Journal of Individual Psychology, 46,* 148–156.

Lambert, S., LeBlanc, M., Mullen, J., Ray, D., Baggerly, J., White, J., & Kaplan, D. (2007). Learning more about those who play in session: The National Play Therapy in Counseling Practices Project (phase 1). *Journal of Counseling and Development, 85,* 42–46.

Lew, A., & Bettner, B. L. (1996). *Responsibility in the classroom.* Newton Center, MA: Connexions Press.

Lew, A., & Bettner, B. L. (2000). *A parent's guide to motivating children.* Newton Center, MA: Connexions Press.

Malchiodi, C. (2003). *Handbook of art therapy.* New York, NY: Guilford Press.

Malchiodi, C., & Ginns-Gruenberg, D. (2008). Trauma, loss, and bibliotherapy. In C. Malchiodi (Ed.), *Creative interventions with traumatized children* (pp. 167–185). New York, NY: Guilford Press.

Meany-Whalen, K. (2010). *Adlerian play therapy: Effectiveness on disruptive behaviors of early elementary-aged children.* Unpublished dissertation, University of North Texas, Denton, TX.

Morrison, M. (2009). Adlerian play therapy with a traumatized boy. *Journal of Individual Psychology, 65*(1), 57–68.

Mosak, H., & Maniacci, M. (2010). Adlerian psychotherapy. In R. Corsini & D. Wedding (Eds.), *Current psychotherapies* (9th ed., pp. 67–112). Belmont, CA: Brooks/Cole.

Oaklander, V. (1992). *Windows to our children: A Gestalt approach to children and adolescents.* New York, NY: Gestalt Journal Press.

Rotter, J. C., Horak, R. A., & Heidt, H. M. (1999). Incorporating children's drawings as early recollections in Adlerian psychotherapy. *Journal of Individual Psychology, 55,* 316–327.

Rubin, L. (Ed.). (2007). *Using superheroes in counseling and play therapy.* New York, NY: Springer.

Schaefer, C. (Ed.). (1993). *The therapeutic powers of play.* Northvale, NJ: Aronson.

Schaefer, C. (2003). Prescriptive play therapy. In C. Schaefer (Ed.), *Foundations of play therapy* (pp. 306–320). New York, NY: Wiley.

Schaefer, C., & Drewes, A. (2009). The therapeutic powers of play and play therapy. In A. Drewes (Ed.), *Blending play therapy with cognitive behavioral therapy: Evidence-based and other effective treatment and techniques* (pp. 3–15). Hoboken, NJ: Wiley.

Snow, M. S., Buckley, M. R., & Williams, S. C. (1999). Case study using Adlerian play therapy. *Journal of Individual Psychology, 55,* 328–341.

Statton, J. (1990). Adlerian counseling and the early recollections of children. *Dissertation Abstracts International, 851*(05).

Sweeney, T. (2009). *Adlerian counseling and psychotherapy: A practitioner's approach* (5th ed.). New York, NY: Routledge.

Thompson, C., & Henderson, D. (2006). *Counseling children: A developmental approach* (7th ed.). Belmont, CA: Brooks/Cole.

U.S. Department of Health and Human Services, Substance Abuse and Mental Health Services Administration. (2009). *National registry of evidenced-based programs and practices.* Washington, DC: U.S. Department of Health and Human Services.

Watts, R. (1999). The vision of Alfred Adler: An introduction. In R. Watts & J. Carlson (Eds.), *Interventions and strategies in counseling and psychotherapy* (pp. 1–13). Philadelphia, PA: Accelerated Development.

Chapter 7

RELEASE PLAY THERAPY

Heidi Gerard Kaduson

INTRODUCTION

Release Play Therapy (RPT) is an extension of the work of David M. Levy known as release therapy. Release therapy contrasted with what was called "pure" psychotherapy because it was used in the treatment of specific problems, and it focused on that problem alone. Levy proposed and implemented this type of therapy for treating children's problems by capitalizing on children's own methods of healing themselves. He also maintained that there were different types of release:

1. Simple release consisted of allowing the child to release feelings of aggression (throwing, pounding, screaming) or infantile pleasures (sucking water from a bottle, spilling water on the floor, sitting in the water or splashing the water by jumping in it, etc.)
2. Release of feelings in standard situations, which would include, among other things, general issues of family interaction, social interactions (sibling rivalry, parents alone together, etc.)
3. Release of feelings in a specific situation by having the therapist create or facilitate the creation of situations by the use of play methods in which anxieties of the child are given expression (set up to resemble a definite experience)

Release therapy used children's play as the medium for healing or change, but the therapist did not focus on interpretation as was usually done in psychoanalytical treatment at that time. Each of the different types of release therapy would utilize children's play in somewhat different ways but would always follow the children's lead.

Simple release allowed children the freedom to release any and all destructive behaviors, including just plain "naughtiness" (Levy, 1939). The *situational release* (as in sibling rivalry) was more structured in that Levy might set up the play by selecting the characters and then give it over to the child to take the play forward. In this case, Levy facilitated the play and increased the child's insight in his own way. The *specific release* utilized various forms of restoration of the situation out of which the anxiety and its accompanying symptoms arose (Levy, 1939).

RPT is very similar to release therapy, although it incorporates more of the therapist's involvement to have techniques ready for use by children when they are incapable of playing by themselves. Some of these children are within the preoperational stage of development (Piaget, 1951), when pretend or imaginative play is at its peak. However, other children might be either in latency age or older, and the play therapy techniques used in RPT allow children to release their aggression, anxiety, or sadness through playing and having fun. The choice of techniques or therapeutic modes of RPT (specific or situational) are at the discretion of the play therapist based on the individual child, situation, and goals.

Children often handle their emotional difficulties by using pretend or imaginative play. This is an important method of eliminating tensions. Children's daily lives are filled with situations over which they have no control, and while there are children who let their feelings be heard (screaming, crying, speaking), many other children hold them inside, unable to release the feelings for many reasons. Under certain circumstances that are anxiety provoking, children can show the fear or shut down and look "brave." If children's affect had been appropriate during an event that caused the anxiety, no tensional residues would have remained (Levy, 1939). When a young boy named Joey had to go to the emergency room for stitches, instead of screaming or crying, he became totally compliant while the doctor gave him a needle right in the top of his lip. Joey saw the needle coming, and he seemed to "be fine" (as reported by parents). After that, however, the family had difficulties getting Joey to the dentist or doctor. It was impossible for them to get him in the car. This resistance grew and generalized to other events, and then the parents brought him to treatment. It was through playing out the event that had happened, and having the affect he would have had during the procedure, that Joey returned to a more compliant child. This is just one example of how the tensions or anxieties remain with children if they can't release them at the time of the event.

There are numerous other reasons why children may not be able to "play it out" without the assistance of a therapist. Certainly, any or all of the following characteristics would make it difficult, if not impossible, for a child to naturally abreact through play:

1. If the strength of the stimulus is too strong, children might be unable to cope with it.
2. Children may have fears influenced by varying intensity and duration. Greater intensity and/or longer durations might interfere with children's abilities to being able to face the situation again by themselves.
3. The summation of past events can be too close together or very similar, all of which would be too frightening for children to revisit.
4. Children's unique sensitivities to a specific stimulus might make the stimulus much more powerful than expected.
5. Children's sensitization to a stimulus through a specific past experience might make it too strong to handle alone.

When any of these factors are connected with an event, and the child is reported to have been "brave" (which usually involves the shutting down of affect) by the caretakers, there is a possibility of developing posttraumatic stress disorder (PTSD).

Piaget's (1954) theory on cognitive development of children indicates the stages of play that begin in infancy. The preoperational stage of development (approximately ages 2 through 7) is the stage when children begin pretend play. They typically use pretend play to work through emotional or other difficulties that they have encountered. In many cases, the pretend play facilitates the healing of children without intervention by a psychotherapist. However, when children encounter a traumatic experience in which the conditions are intense or extreme, children may shut down emotional responses, thereby leading to aftereffects such as PTSD or oppositional defiant disorder.

RPT involves play activities and techniques, as well as pretend play, to help children to express whatever they are feeling through the play. The play activities give children the ability to release aggression, fear, and other difficulties that they have not been able to resolve on their own either through talking about it or using imaginative play.

This chapter illustrates how the use of RPT can help children to overcome psychological difficulties through various methods and techniques. RPT allows children to have the necessary components to release difficult feelings or play through traumatic responses that have impaired the child's psychological development.

BASIC CONCEPTS, GOALS, AND TECHNIQUES

RPT has had a significant impact on helping children heal. Certain criteria must be met before this treatment can be used with children, however. RPT must offer children a sense of safety and support so that they feel their feelings. With the ego strength of the therapist involved in the play, the child can revisit a traumatic event and simply play it out without closing down the feelings that needed to be expressed in the actual past experience. Certain types of RPT can be done so that children have fun while releasing feelings of anxiety, anger, or other negative reactions, thereby allowing for the psychological healing to begin. While allowing children the freedom to play it out, the therapist must also play an important role in the facilitation of the play in order for children to assimilate the traumatic event slowly and evenly. If children jump into the play too fast, they can be retraumatized by the play or become too anxious to go forward. Children in the preoperational stage of development are at risk of being retraumatized by their play. When the children are older, the pretend play is not their first choice of play. At these stages, children might prefer games with rules or more activities to choose from. In either case, the play therapy environment, along with the therapeutic relationship, allows reenactment or release of emotions to happen easily so that children can let go of the psychological difficulties that could impact their healthy development and move on. The success of RPT has been consistently shown through clinical work, and while it is not totally "nondirective" (Axline, 1947), it still follows the lead of the child with all the characteristics of child-centered play therapy's relationship guidelines (VanFleet, Sywulak, & Sniscak, 2010).

Criteria for Using RPT

The criteria for using RPT with children depend on what is needed for a specific child in a particular situation. When children are referred for behavioral issues, the type of treatment is decided after following the lead of that child (are they pre-schoolers, are they able to do pretend play, are they withdrawn or highly anxious, do they appear comfortable in the playroom, etc). It must be decided at first whether the RPT will be used for general release or specific release. General Release Play Therapy (GRPT) is used when children are in latency age or older and their symptoms are behavioral in nature (whether the behavior is seen as externalizing (symptomatic of attention deficit/hyperactivity disorder, oppositional defiant disorder, conduct disorder, etc.) or internalizing (depression, generalized anxiety disorder, obsessive-compulsive disorder, etc.). Specific Release Play Therapy (SRPT) uses abreactive play and creates or facilitates the creation of specific situations that children had experienced. Through SRPT, the children can replay the event in the safety of the play therapy room with a trained play therapist and allow the expression of anxieties and/or anger that were thwarted when the original trauma occurred.

The criteria for the two different types of release differ in very important ways. When using GRPT, there is very little restriction on what is used and how it is done. GRPT relies on techniques that provide children with fun, thereby allowing the expression of feelings in a safe and protected environment. While most children may be treated by GRPT at first, only some will then switch to SRPT treatment. When SRPT is needed, it is of utmost importance that the following criteria be considered so that children do not get retraumatized by their play (Terr, 1990):

1. The presenting problem should be a definite symptom picture precipitated by a specific event, in the form of a frightening experience, such as divorce of parents, hospital visits, natural disaster, and so on.
2. The problem should not be of too long a duration.
3. Most importantly, the event or problem that happened must be in the past.

Children who are referred for treatment and are still within the experience (i.e., maternal neglect, alcoholic parents, continued hospitalizations, etc.) would not benefit from SRPT but would still benefit from the GRPT approach.

Goals for the Child

The goals for children in treatment with any form of RPT are to (a) develop understanding of their own feelings; (b) be able to express feelings in order to meet their own needs better; (c) increase mastery of past events or traumatic situations; (d) work through and overcome their problems; (e) release hostility toward parents, siblings, or others in the child's life; (f) alleviate guilt feelings that might be attached to thoughts they may have had or have at the present time; (g) have the opportunity to express freely all fantasies; and (h) most importantly, desensitize children to past events by means of repetition. The therapeutic aspects of RPT include the ability of children to air their own thought processes and to overtly express the hostilities or fears they have harbored within and also to incorporate therapeutic suggestions.

The methods that are used in RPT actually use the "acting-out principle in play to the highest degree" (Levy, 1939). Children are often seen playing out events in their lives whether they are traumatic or not. Because of its intrinsic motivational properties, play is done for the sake of play alone. Adults do not have to motivate children to play because the play itself seems to satisfy an inner desire of the child (Schaefer, 1997). Play offers children an experience of power and control rarely afforded them in other situations (VanFleet, et al., 2010), and through playing and having fun, children are able to overcome many psychological difficulties.

Piaget (1951) wrote of the stages of play that a child goes through developmentally. Practice or sensory motor play in infancy begins as early as 2 months. This type of play starts with infants playing with their own bodies until approximately 5 or 6 months, and then they can change their actions of play to reproduce interesting consequences, such as kicking one's feet to move a mobile suspended over the crib. The next stage is construction play (ages 18 months to 3 years) which allows children to put things together to create a third object or situation. Symbolic or pretend play is the next level that a child goes through. This is a very important form of play and certainly the place where children spend a great deal of their time from ages 2 to around 7. Using fantasy play, children change themselves into people, objects, or situations other than themselves. Piaget believed that this form of play was assimilative, rather than accommodative, in that children adapt reality to fit their own needs. Children copy what they see or things that they have no control over, and then they can play it out being the person who has authority (mother, father, sister, etc.) and feel empowered by that experience. Children learn how to live through pretend play. Therefore, when children have gone through something that they don't even understand, whether traumatic or not, the reenactment they do in the play therapy room must be followed and facilitated to allow for the processing of the emotions through their play.

For RPT to be effective, the sessions are devoted entirely to the release of anger, fear, or other negative emotions that manifest themselves through oppositional behavior either at home or in the school. Many parents who bring their children for treatment do so because of the misbehaviors at home or in school. These parents often have no idea what might have triggered the behavior because, in some cases, it develops slowly over time. But once RPT treatment begins, often parents report that the children's misbehaviors slowly begin to disappear, and many children's behaviors revert back to relative compliance. There have been many cases in which this behavior actually dissipates over time, yet there are also numerous cases in which SRPT was used with a child, and in two sessions, the issues were gone. The mastery that a child feels over the traumatic event by playing it out influences whether the child's behaviors are difficult or positive. The goal is to allow the release of emotions that were thwarted during an event that a child experienced, even if the parents did not perceive the event as particularly stressful. In fact, many times children who are referred because of an acute onset of behavioral problems are described as having been "very brave" during some event they had experienced because they didn't cry or carry on. That might be a red flag for the play therapist because children are supposed to be crying and complaining when in an extremely frightening situation.

Social Support

Children's posttrauma difficulties sometimes arise when they don't receive the social support needed while experiencing the trauma. Parental distress or inability to parent during or after the trauma can also increase the risk of PTSD, as well as the degree to which the child perceives significant others to be in physical danger. Children need to be in the presence of adults who handle the trauma with authority in order for children to let go and feel. If the support system of children breaks down, they cannot lean on the adults to help them get through the trauma or event.

A striking example is Gary, a 5-year-old boy who was brought to treatment due to oppositional behavior. Six months prior to the intake, Gary was in a traumatic car collision with his mom driving. He was in the back in his car seat when another car swerved into their lane and hit their car head-on. Immediately after the accident, Mom held herself together and projected strength for Gary. She kept him calm by saying they were okay and safe, and the police would be there soon. She did this even though the steering wheel was crushing her chest. For 5 to 10 minutes she was his support system, and he expressed his fear by crying and letting out his emotions. Then Gary said to his mom that he had to go to the bathroom. This was the trigger for Mom because she could not help her son, and she began to scream and cry for help. His trauma started at that point and not before. During RPT, he initially would not do any pretend play about the accident, and therefore, GRPT was begun. He was able to release his anger through a game using dart guns with a target. Gary had to shoot at the target and say something he hated. After a couple of sessions, he was able to play out the car accident. The abreactive play or SRPT could not be done until Gary was ready to do that, and first he had to get his anger expressed through the dart-shooting technique. Once he played that game, he began to play out his trauma of the rescue rather than the entire car accident. It became clear that Gary had shut down his emotions when Mom began to scream and cry. Over time, he played out the entire accident and rescue, and his behavior at home and at school improved significantly.

There are several factors that have been found to increase the risk of children developing PTSD. As indicated by Gary's case, lack of social support when experiencing the trauma created Gary's PTSD. He seemed to manage the event until his mother could no longer support his emotional release. Some other factors are as follows (Schaefer, 1994):

1. Traumas that are man-made versus natural disaster. Children can play out the hurricane or thunderstorm as long as their social support is strong.
2. Traumas involving human aggression (domestic violence or physical abuse).
3. Traumas that are life threatening or involve great destruction of property.

4. Parental distress or inability to parent after the trauma. In Gary's case, his mother's initial reaction to the car accident allowed him to maintain his barrier against the psychic trauma.
5. The degree to which the child perceived significant others to be in physical danger. Gary did not know his mother was in any danger until she started to scream and cry.
6. Lack of parent–child communication about the trauma.

Another example of how the criteria affect the outcome is with relation to the summation of events and/or the child's sensitivity to the stimulus. Maggie was referred for oppositional defiant behavior. Family history was unremarkable, and it seemed that she was "all of a sudden" behaving badly. Maggie was one of four young girls. She was 5 years old and the third born. All of her sisters had blonde hair, and she had red. In the intake, I was told that she just started being very defiant, but there appeared to be no significant antecedent. When I asked about gross motor and fine motor abilities, the parents reported that she was very independent, and she even started riding a bike by herself. At 5 she was able to get herself dressed, and she could button, zip, and snap on her clothes. They did say that her younger sister, Haley, had a small accident when Maggie was 3. Haley was on the back of Daddy's bike in the child seat when she was about 13 months old. They were all riding their bikes together, and Daddy hit something slippery, and the bike slipped out from under him. Haley flew out of the baby seat and was screaming on the road. Mom was there and crying, but Maggie was brave and helped Mommy with the baby. Everyone healed, and this story was set aside. When asked if anything else happened, Mom said that was the only scary thing that Maggie had experienced. With further discussion, Mom also said that Maggie had to have the regular vaccinations, but she had swollen up like a balloon with some rare allergic reaction. But she was fine after being given the correct antibiotic. Mom said that Maggie didn't even remember it. But it was at the age of 5 that she started being so defiant.

The intake for Maggie was on the next day. She came right into the playroom without any difficulty, and she immediately went to the play hospital situated on the floor. She asked for a bike for this little boy, and she began to have him ride the bike back and forth in front of the hospital. Maggie told me he had his helmet on because it was safe to do that. Then she said, "Watch out," and she had the little boy fall off the bike onto the street. She then said to me, "Quick, get the ambulance. We have to go to the hospital." I grabbed an ambulance and made the siren. When it got to the boy, she said, "Put him in there, his knee is growing bigger and bigger." We put him in and rushed to the hospital, where Mommy and Daddy appeared. They took the boy to the emergency room, and a doctor came and said, "What do we have here?" Then the doctor took a very, very long needle (Maggie illustrated with her hands that it was about 2 feet long and wide), and he put it into the little boy's knee. I could see that this had to be a very scary event, so I put the emotions to the play and started crying and yelling. Maggie laughed the entire time, but then the doctor said, "OK, that wasn't so bad was it?" Then the parents took the boy home.

When the intake was over, I called the parents and asked if there was any way something like this could have been in Maggie's life, or could she have seen something like this? They said that did happen when she was 4, but she was fine and never cried. She was very brave. At that moment, I told them that the series of stressful events in the past, i.e., the vaccinations creating a frightening experience that Maggie could see on her parents' faces, the bike accident when Maggie was 3, and now this bike accident at the age of 4 could all have come together and produced a traumatic experience for her. The only way that Maggie could deal with it was to try to take control in inappropriate ways so that she could control what happens. As soon as this session was completed, Maggie was beginning to appear happier at home, and she became more compliant.

For some children, however, the release must happen through a more directive approach. Some children cannot easily play, and they might just stand in the center of the playroom indicating that there is nothing fun to do or even rejecting the play materials. This is commonly seen with the latency age group (8 to 10 years). In these cases, GRPT techniques are used to get them more relaxed and comfortable. Any event that might have occurred when they were younger might have to be resolved through the pretend play, but first they have to feel more comfortable in the playroom and have fun.

There are several different levels of release used in GRPT, some of which are just to enhance the expression of feelings (Level 1), and others are to feel the release of feelings (Level 3). The first level of release is done with dart guns with suction cups, which are used to shoot at a whiteboard that has a target on it. The target has rings, each of which has a score increasing from the outside ring (10 points) to the center ring (100 points). This is usually used first in treatment, except in schools or other locations where the use of toy guns is prohibited. The client is given a dart gun, and the therapist explains, "We will take turns shooting at the dart board to get a high score. This is a bit different than other dart games because we will be saying what we hate as we shoot at the board." These feelings are most often called their "mads." The therapist illustrates this by shooting first and saying something generic that she hates. A common example would be "I hate homework." The therapist needs to illustrate that the louder the client says it, the more fun it will be. After a few tries, the client typically ends up throwing it with all of his or her strength, and the release is felt immediately. Children and/or adults will express this feeling by saying such things as "wow" or "that felt good" or "can I do that again?" This becomes "so much fun" school, and then the therapist follows the lead of the child as to topic or severity. This opens up the topic and lets the child release the anger within a fun and nonthreatening environment. Dart guns are helpful in releasing the anger statements, and generally the children enjoy the game, while it enhances their ability to express themselves.

An equivalent level of release can be done with straws and spitballs. These objects can be used in lieu of the dart guns, and children and adults enjoy this type of release. In order for this GRPT treatment to be successful, the therapist should not discuss anything that the client expresses, unless initiated by the client. Level 2 release is when the clients throw something onto the whiteboard but it cannot break at all. The most effective toys to use are called Sports Wall Rollers (sold by Rhode Island Novelty Corp.). The difference between the guns (Level 1) and Wall Rollers (Level 2) is that the children use all of their body to throw the Wall Roller at the whiteboard. Wall Rollers cannot break, so the impact is what entices the children to throw again and again. Children are still required to say what they hate when they throw the Wall Roller. Just throwing is not necessarily therapeutic, but with the verbalization of feelings, the play therapy begins.

The highest level of release (Level 3) is with splat balls (sold by Oriental Trading Company) (Kaduson & Schaefer, 2001). Splat balls resemble chicken eggs that are made of translucent rubber skin on the outside, with water and a yellow ball (similar to a yolk) on the inside. This technique has been used not only with latency-aged children but also teenagers and young adults. The client is given a splat ball (also called "egg splats"), and the therapist explains that these are used to get out feelings that are bothering us. Again it is explained that these feelings are most often called "mads." The therapist illustrates this technique by taking the egg splat ball and throwing it at a whiteboard while saying what she hates. Since they have shot and thrown at the dartboard before, most children are easily engaged. The therapist needs to illustrate that the harder they throw and the louder they scream, the more fun it will be. After a few tries, the clients typically end up throwing it with all their strength, and the release is felt immediately. The most fun is when the egg splat ball breaks. That causes the water in the egg to go anywhere in the room, and the children are thrilled at their own physical strength. (Some children have said, "I am so strong," "I must really hate that," "I want to do that again.") Children and/ or adults will express this feeling after throwing the egg splat ball by saying such things as "wow" or "that felt good" or "can I do that again?" This becomes so much fun that children readily and easily tell all the items they hate. The therapist has a turn after each of the child's turns, and that is when the prompting might occur by the therapist saying that she "hates when school is too long." This line will prompt issues that the child has at school, and then the therapist follows the lead of the child as to topic or severity. This opens up the topic and lets the child release the anger in a fun and nonthreatening environment. Once it is out in the open, even a child who is older will have an easier time of playing it out with the miniatures, if need be. A key to having this release be effective is that the therapist never discusses what the child has said but might agree with it so that the child can feel safe and validated. Just allowing the simple release begins the process that the child needs. Whether it is situational or specific release that follows does not matter. The goal is to release the anger, fear, or other feeling; enhance the verbalization of the same; and then abreact through play as long as the child needs to. When the child is done, the play discontinues, and in most cases, parents report better behavior at home and/or in school.

THERAPEUTIC POWERS OF PLAY

As is clearly stated in Schaefer's book titled *The Therapeutic Powers of Play*, play all by itself can help children communicate since play is the language of the child

(Schaefer, 1993). Even when children have experienced something that has frightened them, they play because it is the play itself that is rewarding and intrinsically motivating (Kaduson, 1997). When it is in relation to RPT, there are several therapeutic factors at work.

Overcoming Resistance

When children walk into a playroom, they are walking into their own world. Play allows them to dive into their own issues without questions being asked. Children who come to treatment are wary of talking to a strange adult, but through play they can express themselves without being questioned. Play is the best way to create an alliance with a child who needs treatment.

Communication

Children use play as their language. They do not use words to convey feelings easily until at least the formal operations stage of development around the age of 11 or 12 (Piaget, 1951). They easily can play or express difficult feelings as long as the environment feels emotionally safe or if it is "only a game." Play is a special form of communication because it is primarily nonverbal and constitutes a language quite different from verbal language. According to Piaget (1954), pretend play "provides the child with the live, dynamic, individual language indispensable for the expression of his subjective feelings for which collective language alone is inadequate" (p. 166). It is also important to understand that the communication through play is done on two levels: one is the conscious level, when a child plays out events, thoughts, and/or feelings that he or she is aware of but cannot express in words perhaps due to a limited vocabulary. This is often seen in children who have been sexually abused, and they cannot necessarily say what happened to them, but they can play what happened to them. On the other level, children use play to express their unconscious conflicts. They may not be aware at all verbally, but they express their emotions through play—emotions that they can be totally unaware of.

While many children seem to use language well to communicate, this is not the case with emotions. But if a child plays it out, one can see what he or she is or was feeling underneath his or her verbal ability. This generation has many verbal children who seem to express themselves very well, but cognitive ability and social and/or emotional growth are not the same. Using language and being highly verbal does not mean that a child understands the emotional expression at all.

What is very interesting is the process in which communication develops through play. On the conscious level, play allows children to express things that they cannot express in words or that they do not have the words to even describe. On the unconscious level, play allows children to express their own wishes and conflicts without even being aware of doing so. Therefore, play is a very powerful tool for children in treatment.

Mastery

Because play is self-motivated, it satisfies children's innate need to explore and master their environment (Berlyn, 1960). Children rarely have the experience of control in their lives except when they are playing. In play, children are in control of the events, and by playing out similar situations that they had experienced in real life, they can achieve mastery over them. In play, this feeling of mastery or efficacy enhances children's self-esteem, allows for events to be less threatening, and helps children feel that they are the masters of their own fate. Because play is intrinsically motivating, it allows children to steadily play with something until it is mastered, leaving them with a great sense of competence.

Abreaction

Certainly, the most important power of play with respect to RPT is the ability to do *abreactive* play. Abreaction is the reliving of a past experience with the safety of play and therefore allows children to express emotions that were thwarted at the time of the original situation. When children have anxiety about some past stressful event, they will play it out slowly and assimilate pieces of the event at a pace that they can control. When this is done, children are able to gain a sense of mastery over an event that previously might have traumatized them. In pretend play, it is "as if" it were real, but children can project feelings onto the dolls, cars, or whatever they are playing with, and they are in control of the outcome.

Catharsis

Catharsis is defined as the arousal and discharge of strong emotions (positive and negative) for therapeutic relief (Schaefer, 1994). Just releasing affect is therapeutic for most children. It provides children with comfort through the release of tension and affect on inanimate objects (punching bags, balloons, bobo dolls). Children can release tension, anger, grief, or any other negative feeling in the playroom without concern for retaliation. Catharsis is a core therapeutic factor shared by many schools of psychotherapy (Greencavage & Norcross, 1990). The release gives children a feeling of relief. Since anxiety is usually associated with past experiences or current experiences that create discomfort for children, the release of that anxiety can be done through the fun and laughter associated with the play. Many children find that this alone relieves their tension, and it provides almost immediate enhancement of the therapeutic relationship because the therapist is joining in the event.

Desensitization

Play by itself can reduce anxiety by the process of systematic desensitization. Through the repetition of the play in RPT, children feel relaxed and safe, and that counteracts and neutralizes the fearfulness so that children perform the desired behavior of being able to play about the traumatic event (Schaefer, 1994). While many children do this on their own, in SRPT, the therapist must be able to facilitate the play so that children can feel the ego strength of the therapist and play out the experience that had caused them so much distress. Play allows the child to assimilate as little of the past experience as he or she wants, and by doing so over and over again, the child is able to resolve the psychological difficulties associated with the trauma or event.

ROLE OF THE THERAPIST

The play therapist has to be well versed in child development, as well as the therapeutic powers of play, in order to help children heal through any type of play therapy. Specifically, in RPT the therapist must be able to shift his or her role to that which is needed at the moment during the treatment. The most important task, of course, is to have rapport with children in treatment. In fact, RPT must not be done until rapport is established. Without a therapeutic relationship, there is no therapy. If a child is referred for anger issues, anxiety, or the like, the therapist might need to be more directive in the play at first in order to introduce techniques after rapport is established. This could begin the process that the child needs to reduce his or her behavior that is emotionally charged. Once the child is familiar with this release, it can be done every week (which is usually the case with preteens and teenagers). The therapist introduces this technique, but then follows the lead of the child. Many times in treatment, a child will choose this technique because it feels good and it is fun. Those two qualities allow the child to go deeper into any psychological disturbance he or she may have and get to the point where he can let go of the negative thinking and/or behavior that is shown outside of the playroom.

The other role of the play therapist is similar to that in child-centered play therapy. The therapist follows the lead of the child to help resolve psychological difficulties. Through both types of play therapy, it is the ego strength of the therapist that helps children to explore deeper into a past experience. In RPT, the therapist sets up the play prior to the child coming into the playroom and provides the child with miniature toys that can replicate as much as is known from the perspective of the adults in that child's life. By providing a miniature of a hospital along with doctors, nurses, and so on, as well as having knowledge of the procedures that were done, the therapist can help a child play out a previous trauma slowly. However, many children who have PTSD or even just a behavioral change do not have the ability to express the feelings that the dolls are having during the event. The therapist's role is to enhance that experience by being the "child" in the play, and when something looks scary, the therapist might say or show how scared that child would have been, including the expression of words and affect. Children find it very funny when a therapist does pretend "screams" or "crying," and it allows the child to continue the play without the anxiety that might be associated with the stronger emotions that the child had experienced in the past but never expressed.

Carl, a 5-year-old boy with Asperger's syndrome, was required to have a battery of tests in a hospital. Although his mother was by his side in the room, when many of the tests were done, Carl was alone. The experience of being in the hospital was so frightening for Carl that he shut down all his feelings whenever he was removed from his mother for testing. As Carl began to play out the experience in the hospital, he was identifying with the doctors in order to play out his experience. The therapist then joined the play and took the role of Carl, expressing all the emotions—anger as well as fear—by screaming and complaining while the doctors took him to different parts of the hospital. In particular, Carl had to have a procedure where he was given a shot of dye so that the doctors could see the contrast when viewing his magnetic resonance imaging (MRI). As Carl rolled the hospital bed into the procedure room, the therapist began screaming and crying very loudly. Carl began to laugh when the therapist was crying, and he took the bed out of the procedure room and then quickly reentered into the MRI so that the therapist would do it again. This part was repeated several times, and Carl was able to enhance the play even more, processing bits of additional information as it occurred in his play. By the time the RPT was completed, Carl was able to tell the story of what happened and play any portion of it as the child and/or doctors.

The therapist must also be able to facilitate the play when children pull back but be very aware of the child's psyche so that the child does not go too fast into his play. Children may start out totally engaged in the play, having fun showing what might have happened to them. However, children can sometimes jump into the play too quickly, and they will "pull back" from the play. This is seen when children seem to completely change the direction of the play or begin to play with other things that don't reflect the play that they were just fully engaged in. This pulling back can be for several reasons. Children may become uncomfortable and seem to pull out of the play that they started when they become anxious. If the play creates more anxiety, children cannot tolerate it, so they may start talking about something else or shift position to another location in order to manage the increase of the feeling. It is the therapist's job to follow the child's lead and connect with whatever is now being focused on. The therapist must respect this retreat from the play but needs to have the child reenter the therapeutic play at a slower pace. This is done within the play. The therapist comes out of role when the child pulls back, and perhaps discusses whatever the child brought up, but then goes back into role and tries to reengage the child in the original play. Most of the time, the child easily returns, but if the anxiety is too strong, the play might be discontinued at that time. It is only with the help of the therapist that children can do what is necessary to play out many stressful problems or traumas that have occurred.

The other very important role the therapist would play is to stop play when it retraumatizes a child. There is much literature on what is called "retraumatizing" play (Terr, 1991). It is not the same as regular play, and it actually is harmful for a child. This type of play is robotic, and there is no expression of any sort from the child, but he or she keeps repeating the exact same play over and over again. Many children might show this play right after a traumatic event, and if so, they are compelled to do it, but they are scaring themselves during this process. When RPT is used, the therapist must be well educated in this type of play in order to know when to completely drop the play and redirect the child to something else. The therapist must make sure that safety is followed at all times in the playroom, and retraumatizing play is not a safe place for a child to be.

ROLE OF THE PARENT

Parents' involvement in RPT has to do mainly with being supportive, open-minded, and understanding of the difficulty a child has had. Parents are very proud of their children who act "brave" during some event, but acting "brave" doesn't help the child cope. Parents who take charge during an event that is frightening for a child typically can provide a safe environment psychologically for the child, and, therefore, the child is able to show and/or say whatever feelings that child has at the time of the event. When a child experiences the opposite due to either parents being unavailable or the child being alone at the time of the event, then it is more likely that PTSD will appear.

Parents are sometimes the most important piece of treatment. If they are able to provide the support the child needs, then they can help facilitate the child's therapeutic experience by following some of the guidelines set out by the RPT play therapist.

While a child is in RPT, the parents are asked to be effusive in attending to the positive behaviors of the child in order to balance out the child's emotions while working through an event. The parents are given instructions to keep a "good behavior book" for the child. The instructions are to list the expected behaviors that a child does, as well as the other good behaviors noticed. In many cases when a child needs RPT, that child's behavior might be difficult at best when at home. Therefore, the shift of the parenting to a more positive approach is necessary.

The parents are given a stenographer's pad to keep the record of behaviors, and a sample of how to record the behaviors is presented to the parents alone. They are to say aloud to the child and write the behavior at the same time. This reinforces the positive behaviors as being heard and seen. They are to start with "got up" (out of bed) on the first line, and then end on the last line of that page with "went to bed," and in between are the behaviors that the parents report and record. The parents are told to write only two to four words because children do not attend to more than that at a time. Then they are to share the recorded behaviors with a significant other (mom, dad, grandmother, etc.) of the child. When this is being done, the child needs only to be in the home but not right next to the parent who is sharing. If done by phone, then the person who the parent called to share will ask to speak to the child just to reinforce that it was heard. The last reading of the good behavior book to the child is done before bed during the normal bedtime routine. All of this is in addition to what the parents normally do, but does not replace it. Overdoing the positive allows the child to feel more secure as he or she does his or her RPT work in the playroom.

Difficulties that the parents might encounter are reviewed after the first week, and many seem to have the same comments. When parents say that their children do not like hearing the same stuff every day, the therapist reassures them that the behaviors that they are listing are "really good" behaviors, but no one had paid attention to them before. These might also be known as expected behaviors. If the parents continue past the child's resistance, the positive attention will be appreciated. Unfortunately, it is difficult for many parents to switch the way they are parenting, so if children complain, it gives the parents the easy way out. Children will want status quo, even if it is negative attention. The therapist has to be a model of attending to these expected behaviors with the excitement needed to heighten children's acceptance of what is truly their good behavior.

CLINICAL APPLICATIONS

Since RPT can be used for many different types of disturbances, a brief summary follows of how each aspect of RPT can be beneficial for several different presenting problems.

Anxiety is underlying many of children's psychological difficulties. While most people experience some anxiety, it can become debilitating when it overwhelms children and behaviors begin to change. It is not as simple as just saying "you'll be fine" because most children who are referred for treatment do not believe that line. They don't feel fine. Therefore, the cathartic release, as with the egg splat balls, provides a welcome relief to children who tend to hold everything in or are not encouraged to let out their anxiety in any manner. Many parents do not want their children to be afraid of them, but in past generations it was a "normal" way of parenting. Although many times irrational, under this form of parenting, children did what they were told without question. This generation's children are very verbal. Parents did not want their children to be afraid of them, and so they encouraged their children to express their feelings. The problem with that change was that there was no innate way to handle this. Parents really only know the parenting they were given, and when they are trying to parent a verbal child, they do not necessarily handle the situation successfully.

Most parents don't want their children to feel anxious or act angrily toward others. However, there are parents who show their own anger and anxiety so much that the child feels compelled to hold it all in. When a child begins to have behaviors that disturb others, most parents will take their child for treatment. The freedom of saying what you "hate," without discussion afterward, allows children to process the information and externalize it, instead of holding it all in and thinking about it sometimes constantly. It is very important that the therapist allows children to say anything, without discussion. The verbal discussion about different items may once again shut children down. When this technique is used, children decide if they want to do it alone or have the therapist take turns. Either way is effective. Following children's lead is of utmost importance so that they feel safe and can release their feelings at their own rate.

Anger management is a common phrase for treatment of children who exhibit behaviors associated with what adults might refer to as "destructive," "disruptive" behaviors or lack of self-control. There are many books about anger management; however, they are instructional in nature, and most children know what to do when they are angry, but they don't do it. In the treatment of children, one can ask a child what to do if something happens that would result in an explosive response, and most children know exactly what to do. They just don't do it. RPT allows them to get the anger out and be validated. It is difficult for parents to do this when the child has done something extremely aversive to someone in school, at home, or in public. Many times during those situations, parents show their own anger and frustration when the child begins to show his or her own feelings of the same. Parents want their children to manage their own feelings, but the use of words does not help children if the thoughts are still running in their head. Allowing a child to say anything in the playroom gives a venue in which that child can let it out and get rid of the negative thinking that produces the anger, whether it is from something irrational, divorce of parents, school failure, learning disabilities, or anything else that the child brings to the session.

PTSD is not always seen at first with a referral from a parent or teacher. But it is the play that allows it to be seen when the child feels safe enough to play it out. RPT provides this so naturally to a child. A child can enter a therapeutic playroom and be drawn immediately to toys that are necessary for his or her own psychic healing. The therapist follows the child's "hints" through the play to determine what the child needs. Interestingly, it can also be used with young adults if the traumatic experience was when they were children and could not play it out at that time. RPT facilitates the psychological work needed to resolve issues such as these. Pretend play has the power of making the situation appear "as if" it were real. This aspect of play can give a child the psychic distance from the event that he or she needs to play it out. It also allows adults to "see" what the child went through in his or her past.

EMPIRICAL SUPPORT

Release therapy has been used since the 1930s. David Levy described a series of three experiments with children in standardized situations for the study of sibling rivalry. "There is abundance of evidence that the behavior of children in play therapy . . . affects the relationship with the real mother and child" (Levy, 1939). He also described much of his work with night terrors of children. Levy's papers also emphasize that in all cases, there is no pat formula, and the methods "are modified primarily by the therapists' immediate understanding of the child's own response" (Levy, 1976, p. 182). There are numerous articles now published about how play therapy can help children with psychological difficulties. Much of the current research illustrates the efficacy of play therapy (Ray, Bratton, Rhine, & Jones, 2001).

CASE ILLUSTRATION

Mr. and Mrs. L. brought their son, Joey, to treatment when he was 5 years old. Joey's parents were amicably divorced about a year prior to the beginning of treatment, and they attributed Joey's oppositional and challenging behavior to that fact. They were referred to treatment by their pediatrician, who felt that Joey could express his anger through play therapy and his parents could learn better parenting skills. During the intake, Mr. and Mrs. L. were very open about how their relationship might have affected Joey, and they were equally concerned with this oppositional behavior, as they were both having difficulty parenting him. All developmental milestones were in the normal range, although Joey did walk and talk early. Joey seemed to be a very easy child until about a year ago, when his parents divorced. There was no fighting that Joey experienced, and since he spent half his time with each parent, they were convinced that it must have been the divorce that Joey was acting out against. Joey was in preschool and academically ahead of his peers. Both parents said that many people thought Joey was older because of his height and his verbal ability, so expectations were sometimes too high. They seemed to be very cognizant of developmental issues, but they were unclear on how to help Joey. The intake with Mr. and Mrs. L. was done without Joey, and all information was given regarding his first 4 years of life.

In the following session, Joey was to come into the playroom by himself, and an initial intake play session was conducted. Joey easily separated from his mother and father and came into the playroom without any difficulty. He was told that he could play with whatever he wanted to play with, and the only rule was that he couldn't clean up. He seemed to take that in stride, and he went right to the cars and trucks. He took them out and started to line them up so that the racing cars were first, then the family cars, followed by the tractor-trailers. Since Mr. and Mrs. L. had told me of his fascination with these types of toys, there was nothing that seemed to stand out in his play. He did want to play with me, and he told me to line up the cars to get ready for the race. He then used the pull-back cars, and he began the race. Each time he let go of two cars at the same time, I was instructed to clap when they got over the finish line. This repeated numerous times, and Joey was certainly in charge of the playroom. Joey directed me on what to put in what order, and when the race began, he told me to use the gun to shoot up in the air so that they would know when to go. He obviously had a strong knowledge of car racing, and it became evident that this was a love shared by his dad and mom. The play continued without interruption, and then I gave the 3-minute warning that the time was almost over. It was clear that Joey understood, as he began to bring the cars back to the "lot" where they would be parked for another racing day to come.

Joey had no difficulty transitioning out of the playroom back to his parents. On the way, he said to me, "Wow, that was really fun. Maybe next time we can play about how I swallowed the quarter." This was not mentioned in the intake, but when I called each of his parents on the phone later that day, they both agreed that he had indeed swallowed a quarter when he was at his grandmother's house, but it was all taken care of and he never even cried about it. They both admittedly said that he was amazingly brave for a 4-year-old (at about the same time as the divorce was finalized). They said that he was taken to the hospital, of course, and the quarter was removed, but grandmother could not go because she was confined to a wheelchair, and while each finally did get there (phone service was not working properly), he had indeed gone to the hospital in the ambulance alone. They met him at the hospital, and then they were with him throughout the rest of the event. I asked each of them to give me as much detail as they could remember so that I could set up the play before Joey entered the playroom. I wanted to be able to produce as much of a realistic look in miniatures so that Joey could play out what happened. Both parents said that he never played anything about it at the time of the event, so they thought nothing bothered him. I told them that perhaps they were right, but since he requested it, I wanted to allow him to play it out.

In the next session, Joey came into the playroom with me and was all smiles when he saw the entire hospital, house, ambulance, and other vehicles that he "needed" to play out what happened. In order to facilitate the play, I took the lead, picking out a 4-year-old little boy from the Playmobil™ characters, and said, "This little boy had something bad happen at his grandmother's house—something to do with a quarter." Joey joined right in and said, "I know what happened. I will show him." I asked what the little boy's name was, and I immediately suggested "little boy." This was to keep the play at enough of a distance so that Joey could play out slowly what happened without it being "Joey" as the main focus. He liked the name "little boy," and he said, "Quick we have to get the ambulance ready to get him. The little boy swallowed a quarter and broke his leg." I then followed his lead and brought an ambulance to him. Joey wanted it to be as real as he remembered, so he said, "We need the *ambulancers* to get him from his grandmother's house and get to the hospital." The *ambulancers* were the EMTs who came to her house when she called 911. Grandmother was not capable of coming in the ambulance with Joey because she was disabled and in a wheelchair. This clearly was not the best of circumstances, but it seemed fine until there was a real emergency. I had to get two Playmobil™ people who looked like the EMT people, and I handed them to Joey, who took them and put the little boy on the gurney. He strapped the boy in, but he had trouble getting the Playmobil™ figures' hands around the gurney to carry it. He asked for help, and I did as instructed.

Then he said, "Quick, get him in the ambulance. We have to get the quarter out." I entered into the play what I supposed was a major piece that had been missing, and I said, "Is his mommy or daddy there?" He acted very surprised and said, "Mom, Dad, yeah, yeah, they're here." At this time, Joey began to make the sound of an ambulance siren even though it was only the rescue people carrying him into the ambulance. He then asked me, "Do you know what they call these people (pointing to the *ambulancers*)?" I said I did not, and he continued and said, "They call them hospitals!" I agreed with whatever information he gave me. I did find out that while he was in the ambulance, alone, he heard the two EMTs talking back and forth about which hospital to take him to. I knew that this was an event that would have been difficult to take even if his parents were around, but both had been called, and neither got the call in time.

As soon as Joey got the little boy into the ambulance, he then made the siren sound again, and this time the ambulance traveled to the hospital. As soon as he said we were there, he told me to get the nurse to take the little boy in. Again I asked, "Is Mommy or Daddy going with him?" He responded with surprise again,

"Mommy, Daddy, where? Oh yeah, they are." I then picked out what might have been a nurse, but he meant the two EMT people who drove him to the hospital. They then took the boy into the hospital, and they put him in a wheelchair. He had another nurse take him in the wheelchair to check his "heartbeat." As the nurse was pushing the little boy, Joey made the siren sound again. It was clear that this was part of the trauma, if not the entire trauma, but I facilitated the play to allow him to play out what he had to show and process. After hearing the heartbeat (from an electrocardiographic machine that was part of the hospital toy pieces, and not really something he went through), he said, "Get him into the bed now."

I then rushed the play too much with "Doctor, are you going to take the quarter out?" He said, "Yeah, yeah." But then he pulled out of the play a bit and said, "The hospital had a playroom, and they had some toys." I went with him and reflected, "They had toys at the hospital." He asked, "What is this?" He was holding a hospital bed, but it had a broken wheel, and then he quickly picked up another item and asked, "Hey, what is this?" He did not need to know what they were, but it was clear that he needed some distance from the play at that moment. I joined him in this piece of play, so that he could feel secure and know he could continue doing whatever he wanted.

Within another few minutes, he hesitated, and I said, "Doctor, will you be taking the quarter out?" He then moved back into the play and said with confidence, "Yeah, yeah—do you know how to do this?" I began to answer, and he just continued, "I know, I know. I heard it before. It gets dark out and then we take the quarter." I could see that his reentry into the play was strong, and he actually did quite a bit of prepping for the operation. He told me that the boy could stay in his bed, and he had to open his mouth and say "Ahhhhh." I did that portion, and he pulled the quarter out and said, "Okay, we got it. He is good now."

I waited to see what his next move would be, and he spoke for the doctor and said, "Now, this boy will have to stay here in the hospital for 10 more days with his mom and dad staying the whole time, too." Joey laughed at his own idea and said to me, "That's how it happens." I laughed and said that I see that. He then said, "That was really fun. Can we do it again?" I told him he could do whatever he wanted, and he played out the first few scenes two more times. These were when he was put in the ambulance alone and when he was taken out of the ambulance and went into the hospital alone. Each time he played it, a little more of the real trauma came out, which was the ambulance ride without either parent. He ended his play with his parents being required to be with him together for the 10 days, and he found this to be the best ending and laughed about it.

Following the session, Joey went back home with Mom, and both parents reported that he seemed so much happier after that. He was no longer fighting every command they were giving, and each reported that in each of their homes, Joey was more compliant and happier. He had to do what he did in play to get rid of the traumatic experience, and then he was done and back to the way he was before this event happened. Although both parents were sure that he started being oppositional as soon as the divorce was final, it just seemed to coincide with the traumatic event of going in the ambulance alone knowing that he swallowed a quarter.

CHALLENGES IN IMPLEMENTING THE MODEL

RPT is a very powerful therapy, and it must be done with a trained play therapist specifically trained in RPT to guide and facilitate the play. There are many traumas that are not as clear as Joey's experience was, and as was done in the example, a therapist can go too fast into the play. I was aware of this and therefore could stabilize Joey to see if he could continue with the play. The most important part of this work is to be well versed in retraumatizing play. Retraumatizing play is actually harmful to a child. It is important to know that this type of play involves the repetitive and compulsive reenactment in play of episodes of the trauma or the repetition in play of traumatic themes. This type of play stirs up feelings of helplessness and terror, and if not stopped, the driven quality of this play may continue for years (Terr, 1981). Therefore, the cycle must be broken by active intervention.

There is a driven quality to retraumatizing play. The child is not in control of the play but seems driven by a compulsion to play in a way that produces the same terrifying outcome. This play is very literal, devoid of enjoyment or variety, and lacks freedom of expression. This type of play reflects a compulsion for traumatized children to repeat the repressed experience. It is this repetitive and compulsive reenactment in the play that fails to provide resolution for children, and the therapist needs to discontinue it right away. The cycle must be broken by active intervention from the play therapist, who would direct the trauma play so as to create a sense of mastery. To achieve this, the following has to be accomplished: Children have to feel in control of the outcome of the play, children need to play out a satisfactory ending to the play, children need to feel free to express and release negative affect, and children have to exhibit a cognitive reappraisal of the event (Schaefer, 1994).

In general, this play would not be seen in treatment except in crisis intervention where there has been no distancing from the trauma. But when it comes to how to do RPT, there isn't an actual guideline to say when a therapist should move toward more realistic play or stay just in pace with the child. In RPT, the therapist is the ego strength of the child, and with the combined egos of both client and therapist, children are empowered to play out what they need to do. Therefore, the play therapist must be aware of the possibilities that could happen during the play and know intuitively when to move the play along.

Another challenge for any play therapist implementing this model is the child who cannot play. With regard to this possibility, the play therapist must become attuned to the client to know how to open the child up to work through the past experiences. Bringing the egg splat balls into the beginning of a session or having silly balloons or any other means of opening the child up to laughter would be the beginning of treatment. Sometimes a child can take weeks before actually going to the miniatures to play out what happened, but will use the egg splat balls every session to say things that he or she hates or that scare him, or any other feeling, before he or she can feel safe enough psychologically to begin the pretend play and abreact with the help and guidance of the therapist. During this time, it is difficult for a therapist to know when to open the child up to play, but once again the intuition of the play therapist who is trained in RPT is what guides the treatment. One must follow the lead of the child when the pretend play begins.

It is also challenging to know when to push the play in RPT, but with children who have had traumatic experiences, they are more likely to jump into the play too fast, rather than the therapist pushing them into it. Children do not allow us to do the wrong thing or say the wrong thing. Whenever a play therapist makes a suggestion or even interprets, if the therapist is wrong, the child will usually tell him or her so. Therefore, it is part of the treatment to encourage the play to the extent that the child can do it. The relationship between the child and therapist is the most important part of the treatment, and it is through that trust that the rest can be done.

CONCLUSION

David Levy introduced release therapy in the 1930s, and at that time there was quite a bit of research and clinical work along the same lines as his treatment. It did not receive the same attention as child-centered play therapy, which was popularized initially by Virginia Axline (1947). The premise is the same in that all who use any type of play therapy need to be "child-centered" and accompany children through their discoveries or process to regain their mental health. RPT is the treatment of choice for PTSD for children, and it helps the child do what he or she would have done if the child could have done it alone. With RPT, more and more children return to their prior state of comfort after working through the therapeutic process through play in a short-term format. Play is their language, play is their way, and so play is what we use to help them heal.

REFERENCES

Axline, V. (1947). *Play therapy.* New York, NY: Houghton Mifflin.

Berlyn, D. E. (1960). *Conflict, arousal and curiosity.* New York, NY: McGraw-Hill.

Greencavage, L. M., and Norcross, J. C. (1990). Where are the commonalities among the therapeutic common factors? *Professional Psychology, 21,* 372–378.

Kaduson, H. G. (1997). Play therapy for children with attention-deficit hyperactivity disorder. In H. G. Kaduson, D. Cangelosi, & C. E. Schaefer (Eds.), *The playing cure* (pp. 197–227). Northvale, NJ: Aronson.

Kaduson, H. G., & Schaefer, C. E. (2001). *101 favorite play therapy techniques.* Northvale, NJ: Aronson.

Levy, D. M. (1939). Release therapy. *American Journal of Orthopsychiatry, 9,* 713–736.

Levy, D. M. (1976). Release therapy. In C. E. Schaefer (Ed.), *The therapeutic use of child's play* (pp. 173–186).

Piaget, J. (1951). *Play, dreams and imitation in childhood.* London, UK: Routledge & Kegan Paul.

Piaget, J. (1954). *The construction of reality in the child.* New York, NY: Basic Books.

Ray, D., Bratton, S., Rhine, T., & Jones, L. (2001). The effectiveness of play therapy: Responding to the critics. *International Journal of Play Therapy, 10,* 85–108.

Schaefer, C. E. (1993). *The therapeutic powers of play.* Northvale, NJ: Aronson.

Schaefer, C. E. (1994). Play therapy for psychic trauma in children. In K. O'Connor & C. E. Schaefer (Eds.), *Handbook of play therapy* (Vol. 2, pp. 297–318). New York, NY: Wiley.

Terr, L. (1981). Psychic trauma in children: Observations following the Chowchilla school-bus kidnapping. *American Journal of Psychiatry, 140,* 1543–1550.

Terr, L. (1991). Childhood traumas: An outline and overview. *American Journal of Psychiatry, 148,* 10–20.

VanFleet, R., Sywulak, A. E., & Sniscak, C. C. (2010). *Child-centered play therapy.* New York, NY: Guilford Press.

HUMANISTIC MODELS

Chapter 8

CHILD-CENTERED PLAY THERAPY

Daniel S. Sweeney and Garry L. Landreth

Although child-centered play therapy receives its title because of its foundation in person-centered theory, the appellation fundamentally points to the simple reality that child-centered play therapy *centers* around *children*. While the majority of adults in the lives of hurting children focus on behavioral and emotional symptoms, or perhaps its causation, the child-centered play therapist refuses to lose sight of the child who has reluctantly come in for treatment. The focus on the person of the child is the foundation and goal of this approach. The play therapist is not a diagnostician and therapeutic director but rather a facilitator and fellow explorer on a journey with a child on a mission of self-discovery. Thus, unlike many other approaches, the child-centered play therapist does not focus on diagnosis, symptoms, or prescriptive treatment techniques. Sweeney and Landreth (2009) summarize:

> Child-centered play therapy is not a cloak the play therapist puts on when entering the playroom and takes off when leaving; rather it is a philosophy resulting in attitudes and behaviors for living one's life in relationships with children. It is both a basic philosophy of the innate human capacity of the child to strive toward growth and maturity and an attitude of deep and abiding belief in the child's ability to be constructively self-directing. Child-centered play therapy is a complete therapeutic system, not just the application of a few rapport-building techniques. (p. 123)

The therapy model was originally developed by Carl Rogers (1951) and adapted by Virginia Axline (1947), a student and colleague of Rogers, as a child-centered model of play therapy. The child-centered approach to play therapy, like client-centered therapy, is based on a process of being with children as opposed to a procedure of application. It is not so much a process of reparation as it is a process of becoming (Landreth & Sweeney, 1999; Sweeney & Landreth, 2009).

BASIC CONSTRUCTS, GOALS, AND TECHNIQUES

Child-Centered Theory

The theoretical constructs of child-centered play therapy are not related to the child's age, physical and psychological development, or presenting problem. Rather, they are related to the inner dynamics of the child's process of relating to and discovering the self that the child is capable of becoming (Sweeney & Landreth,

2009). Development is viewed in the child-centered approach as a flow—a sinuous, dynamic journey and maturing process of *becoming*.

The child-centered approach embraces a belief that children can grow and heal when a growth-producing climate is provided for them, free from agenda and constriction. It is recognized in client-centered work that all persons have a formative tendency, meaning that the appropriate environment leads to development of personal and relational capacity. To begin a look at the foundation of child-centered work, it is important to look at the fundamental constructs of personality as described by Rogers (1951): (1) the person, (2) the phenomenal field, and (3) the self.

The *person* (or organism) is all that a child is, consisting of self-perceptions including thoughts, feelings, and behaviors, as well as the physiology. The developmental process in children is emphasized, as every child "exists in a continually changing world of experience of which he is the center" (Rogers, 1951, p. 483). Children interact with and respond to this personal and continually changing world of experience.

As a result, a continuous dynamic intrapersonal interaction occurs in which every child (person), as a total system, is striving toward actualizing the self. Sweeney and Landreth (2009) suggest that this dynamic and animated process is an internally directed movement toward becoming a more positively functioning person; toward positive growth; toward improvement, independence, maturity, and enhancement of self as a person. Thus, the child's behavior in this process is goal directed in an effort to satisfy personal needs as experienced in the unique phenomenal field that for that child constitutes reality (Landreth, 2002).

The *phenomenal field* consists of everything that is experienced by the child. These experiences include everything happening within a person or organism at a given time—whether or not at a conscious level, internal as well as external—including perceptions, thoughts, feelings, and behaviors. Essentially, the phenomenal field is "the internal reference that is the basis for viewing life; that is, whatever the child perceives to be occurring is reality for the child" (Landreth & Sweeney, 1999, p. 41). This points to a basic tenet in child-centered play therapy, which is that the child's perception of reality is what needs to be understood if the child and the behaviors of the child are to be understood.

Whatever the child perceives in the phenomenal field, therefore, assumes primary importance as opposed to the actual reality of events. Since reality is essentially determined individually and subjectively, the therapist therefore intentionally avoids judging or evaluating even the simplest of the child's behaviors (i.e., a picture, stacked blocks, a scene in the sand) and works hard to try to understand the internal frame of reference of each child in the group (Sweeney & Landreth, 2009). If the therapist is to connect with the person of the child, the child's phenomenal world must be contacted and understood. Children are not expected to meet predetermined criteria or fit a set of preconceived categories (Landreth, 2002).

The *self* is the third central construct of the child-centered theory of personality structure. Self is that differentiated aspect of the phenomenal field that develops from the child's interactions with others. The consequence of how others perceive a child's emotional and behavioral activity and accordingly react involves the formation of the concept of "me." This is a natural and continuous process in which children positively value those experiences that are perceived as self-enhancing and place a negative value on those that threaten or do not maintain or enhance the self.

This process of evaluation—by parents, others, and self—points to one of the key benefits in child-centered play therapy. As children develop, they experience reaction and evaluation of parents and others and symbolize themselves as good or bad dependent on these evaluations. In order to preserve a positive self-concept, the child may distort such experiences and block from awareness the satisfaction of the experience (Rogers, 1951). The child-centered play therapy experience provides the opportunity for children to be viewed by the therapist as a positive and growing self within an atmosphere of permissiveness and acceptance. Rogers hypothesized that the self grows and changes as a result of continuing interaction with the phenomenal field. The play therapy experience becomes a phenomenal field through which children can discover self. Not only is a child's behavior consistent with the concept of self, but the play therapy experience facilitates positive change in self-concept.

Rogers (1951, pp. 483–524) proposed concepts of personality and behavior that reflect the philosophical core of person-centered therapy. Sweeney and Landreth (2009) summarized these concepts in the description of child-centered play therapy and a child-centered view of children:

> Every child exists in a continually changing world of experience, of which he or she is the center. The child reacts as an organized whole to this field as it is experienced and perceived, which for the child is reality. As the child develops and interacts with the environment, a portion of the child's total private world (perceptual field) gradually becomes recognized as "me" (differentiated as the self), and concepts are formed about himself or herself, about the environment, and about himself or herself in relation to the environment. The child has a basic tendency to strive to actualize, maintain, and enhance the experiencing self. The resulting behavior is basically the goal-directed, emotionally influenced attempt of the child to satisfy his or her needs as experienced, in the field as perceived. Therefore, the best vantage point for understanding the child's behavior is from the internal frame of reference of the child.

> Most of a child's behavior is consistent with the child's concept of self, and behaviors inconsistent with the self-concept are not owned. Psychological freedom or adjustment exists when the self-concept is congruent with all the child's experiences. When this is not the case, tension or maladjustment is experienced by the child. Experiences that are inconsistent with the self-concept may be perceived as a threat resulting in the child's becoming behaviorally rigid in an effort to defend the existing self-concept. When there is a complete absence of any threat to the perception of self, the child is free to revise his or her self-concept to assimilate and include experiences previously inconsistent with the self-concept. The resulting well-integrated or positive self-concept enables the child to be more understanding of others and thus to have better interpersonal relationships. (pp. 126–127)

Child-Centered Play Therapy

Based on these premises, child-centered play therapy involves a journey with the child to engage in self-discovery and self-exploration. A definition of play therapy is provided by Landreth (2002):

> Play therapy is defined as a dynamic interpersonal relationship between a child (or person of any age) and a therapist trained in play therapy procedures who provides selected play materials and facilitates the development of a safe relationship for the child (or person of any age) to fully express and explore self (feelings, thoughts, experiences, and behaviors) through play, the child's natural medium of communication, for optimal growth and development. (p. 16)

Consistent with person-centered theory and therapy, the foundational element in this definition is the focus on *relationship*. The success or failure of therapy in fact rests on the development and maintenance of the therapeutic relationship. Moustakas (1959) believed that "through the process of self-expression and exploration within a significant relationship, through realization of the value within, the child comes to be a positive, self-determining, and self-actualizing individual" (p. 5).

In the child-centered approach to play therapy, the child is focused upon rather than the presenting problem. Therapists who concentrate on diagnosis and evaluation have a greater likelihood of losing sight of the child. Symptoms are important, but the focus must remain on the child. Although interpretation of play behaviors is interesting, it generally serves the need of the therapist and not the child (Homeyer & Sweeney, 2010; Sweeney, 1997). This therapeutic relationship, therefore, should be focused on a present, living experience (Landreth, 2002):

person of the child	rather than	problem
present	rather than	past
feelings	rather than	thoughts or acts
understanding	rather than	explaining
accepting	rather than	correcting
child's direction	rather than	therapist's instruction
child's wisdom	rather than	therapist's knowledge (p. 86)

Goals of Child-Centered Play Therapy

It should initially be established that the term *goal* is somewhat inconsistent with child-centered philosophy. The reason is that goals are evaluative and also imply specific achievements required of the client that have been externally established. Children should be related to as persons to be understood as opposed to goals to be checked off or persons to be fixed. Since a central hypothesis of child-centered philosophy is that the therapist has an unwavering belief in the child's capacity for growth and self-direction, the establishment of treatment goals is somewhat contradictory.

There are, however, broad therapeutic objectives that are consistent with the child-centered theory and approach. Landreth (2002) suggests the following:

The general objectives of child-centered play therapy are consistent with the child's inner self-directed striving toward self-actualization. An overriding premise is to provide the child with a positive growth experience in the presence of an understanding, supportive adult so the child will be able to discover internal strengths. Since child-centered play therapy focuses on the person of the child rather than the child's problem, the emphasis is on facilitating the child's efforts to become more adequate, as a person, in coping with current and future problems that may impact the child's life. To that end, the objectives of child-centered play therapy are to help the child

1. Develop a more positive self-concept
2. Assume greater self-responsibility
3. Become more self-directing
4. Become more self-accepting
5. Become more self-reliant
6. Engage in self-determined decision making
7. Experience a feeling of control
8. Become sensitive to the process of coping
9. Develop an internal source of evaluation
10. Become more trusting of himself (pp. 87–88)

Movement toward these objectives occurs as the therapeutic relationship unfolds. This type of relationship emerges as the therapist communicates acceptance and understanding. Children begin to recognize their inner value when the play therapist responds sensitively to the inner emotional part of their person by accepting and reflecting feelings, whether verbally or nonverbally expressed. As part of this process, the child-centered play therapist generally avoids asking questions. Questions tend to move children (or clients of any age) from the world of emotion into the world of cognition, which essentially defeats the developmental rationale for using play therapy. Questions also structure the relationship according to the therapist's agenda, thus placing the focus on the therapist rather than the child.

Evaluation of any kind is avoided in child-centered play therapy. Children are encouraged, not praised, because praise establishes an evaluative pattern. Evaluative statements deprive the child of inner motivation, since the lead would at that point belong to the adult. Accordingly, the therapist allows the child to lead and diligently avoids interfering with the child's play. This should never eliminate participation in the child's play, but this participation should be done at the direction of the child. Participation involves the child's being the director and choreographer of the play experience, with the therapist taking cues from *only* the child. Interference in the child's play may involve asking questions, offering solutions or suggestions, or allowing the child to manipulate the therapist into becoming a teacher or doing things for the child. Children do not learn self-direction, self-evaluation, and responsibility when the therapist evaluates or provides solutions. Landreth (2002) provides an important reminder:

> In this view, no attempt is made to control a child, to have the child be a certain way, or to reach a conclusion the therapist has decided is important. The therapist is not the authority who decides what is best for the child, what the child should think, or how the child should feel. If this were to be the case, the child would be deprived of the opportunity to discover his/her own strengths. (p. 89)

Child-Centered View of Maladjustment

While the child-centered philosophy is essentially incongruent with conceptualizations of maladjustment and a focus on problems, it is helpful to take a brief look at this topic. This is done with the recognition and reminder that the child-centered philosophical position is that there is an inherent tendency within children to move in subtle directedness toward adjustment, mental health, developmental growth, independence, autonomy of personhood, and what can be generally described as self-actualization (Landreth & Sweeney, 1999).

According to Rogers (1951), maladjustment exists when the person denies significant experiences to awareness, which therefore do not get symbolized and organized into the structure of self. The existence of "psychological tension" then becomes a potential. Raskin and Rogers (2005) summarize:

> [Rogers] assumes that very young infants are involved in "direct organismic valuing," with very little or no uncertainty. They have experiences such as "I am cold, and I don't like it," or "I like being cuddled," which may occur even though they lack the descriptive words or symbols for these examples. The principle in this natural process is that the infant positively values those experiences that are perceived as self-enhancing and places a negative value on those that threaten or do not maintain or enhance the self ... The situation changes once children begin to be evaluated by others (Holdstock & Rogers, 1983). The love they are given and the symbolization of themselves as lovable children become dependent on behavior. To hit or to hate a baby sibling may result in the child's being told that he or she is bad and unlovable. The child, to preserve a positive self-concept, may distort experience ... expression of anger comes to be experience as bad, even though the more accurate symbolization would be that the expression of anger is often experienced as satisfying or enhancing ... This type of interaction may sow the seeds of confusion about self, self-doubt, and disapproval of self, and reliance upon the evaluation of others. Rogers indicated that these consequences may be avoided if the parent can accept the child's negative feelings and the child as a whole while refusing to permit certain behaviors, like hitting the baby. (p. 142)

The child's inner drive toward affirmation of self-worth and self-realization are basic needs, and each child is striving continually to satisfy these needs. Axline (1947) argues:

An adjusted person seems to be an individual who does not encounter too many obstacles in his path—and who has been given the opportunity to become free and independent in his own right. The maladjusted person seems to be the one who, by some means or other, is denied the right to achieve this without a struggle. (p. 21)

All maladjustments are viewed as resulting from an incongruence between what the child actually experienced and the child's concept of self. If a child's perception of an experience is distorted or denied, a state of incongruence between the self-concept and experience exists, resulting in psychological maladjustment. Incongruence between the child's self-concept and experience fundamentally results in incongruence in behavior (Sweeney & Landreth, 2009). This is where the referral for play therapy comes from and where child-centered play therapy provides a climate for change.

Therapeutic Limit Setting

Any discussion of child-centered play therapy must include an exploration of therapeutic limit setting. Limit setting is facilitative, as children do not feel safe or accepted in a completely permissive environment. Moustakas (1959) summarized the importance of limits as a vital and necessary part of relationships:

Limits exist in every relationship. The human organism is free to grow and develop within the limits of its own potentialities, talents, and structure. In psychotherapy, there must be an integration of freedom and order if the individuals involved are to actualize their potentialities. The limit is one aspect of an alive experience, the aspect which identifies, characterizes, and distinguishes the dimensions of a therapeutic relationship. The limit is the form or structure of an immediate relationship. It refers not only to a unique form but also to the possibility for life, growth and direction rather than merely to a limitation . . . In a therapeutic relationship, limits provide the boundary or structure in which growth can occur. (pp. 8–9)

The purpose for limits in the play therapy process emphasizes the child-centered play therapist's focus on the process rather than specific behaviors. The basic rationales for setting limits in the playroom include the following:

1. Limits define the boundaries of the therapeutic relationship.
2. Limits provide security and safety for the child, both physically and emotionally.
3. Limits demonstrate the therapist's intent to provide safety for the child.
4. Limits anchor the session to reality.
5. Limits allow the therapist to maintain a positive and accepting attitude toward the child.
6. Limits allow the child to express negative feelings without causing harm and the subsequent fear of retaliation.
7. Limits offer stability and consistency.

8. Limits promote and enhance the child's sense of self-responsibility and self-control.
9. Limits promote catharsis through symbolic channels.
10. Limits protect the play therapy room and materials.
11. Limits provide for the maintenance of legal, ethical, and professional standards (Ginott, 1961; Landreth, 2002; Sweeney, 1997; Sweeney & Landreth, 2009).

Landreth (2002) provides a pragmatic and therapeutic limit-setting model, based on the acronym ACT. This in itself is therapeutic, as it is appropriate to *act* rather than *react* in response to behaviors requiring a limit. The model involves:

1. **A**cknowledge the child's feelings, wishes, and wants. This recognizes that it remains crucial to respond to children with reflection and acceptance. Limits are responded to more readily when the child's emotion and intent are recognized.
2. **C**ommunicate the limit—in a nonpunitive and nonauthoritative manner.
3. **T**arget acceptable alternatives. This recognizes that children still have the need to express self and should be able to do so within acceptable boundaries.

The play therapy relationship is not a completely permissive relationship. The child is not allowed to do just anything he or she may want to do. Limits do need to be set on (a) harmful or dangerous behavior to the child and therapist, (b) behavior that disrupts the therapeutic routine or process (continually leaving playroom, wanting to play after time is up), (c) destruction of room or materials, (d) taking toys from playroom, (e) socially unacceptable behavior, and (f) inappropriate displays of affection (Sweeney & Landreth, 2009).

It is important to note that limits should not be set until they are needed. Providing a list of prohibited activities at the beginning of the play therapy process would clearly not encourage or facilitate exploration and expression by the children. When limits are needed, the therapist should take a matter-of-fact and firm approach. This is necessary so that children do not feel chastised, as the therapist should not be parental and authoritative but rather facilitative yet structured. Limits should also be specific, rather than general (generality makes for unclear boundaries); limits should be total, rather than conditional (conditional limits are confusing and can lead to power struggles); and limits must be enforceable.

TOYS AND MATERIALS

Because toys are considered to be children's words and play is their language, there should be careful and deliberate selection of toys and materials that facilitate the child-centered play therapy relationship and process. Materials should promote children's self-directed activity and facilitate a wide range of feelings and play activity. Not all toys and materials encourage children's expression or exploration of their feelings, needs, and experiences. Using a deck of cards or a board game, for example, does not guarantee a growth-promoting play therapy experience for the child. In fact, it can be argued that games are more likely to promote competition, which contradicts the development of relationship. Play materials that are mechanical, complex, highly structured, or require the play therapist's assistance to manipulate typically do not facilitate the expression of children's feelings or experiences. They can be frustrating to children, and may foster dependence in children who already feel helpless or inadequate.

The materials recommended by Landreth (2002) for a "tote bag playroom" constitute the core of play materials in the playroom: crayons, newsprint, blunt scissors, clay or Play-Doh®, popsicle sticks, transparent tape, nursing bottle, doll, plastic dishes and cups, bendable Gumby® (nondescript figure), doll family figures, dollhouse furniture, dollhouse (open-top type on floor), Lone Ranger®–type mask, rubber knife, dart gun, handcuffs, toy soldiers, car, airplane, hand puppets, telephones (two), cotton rope, and costume jewelry. It is obviously important for play therapists to be sensitive to issues of culture and diversity in the toy selection process.

ROLE OF THE THERAPIST

The role of the child-centered play therapist is simple yet powerful. He or she is a facilitator, encourager, and fellow explorer for the child in the playroom. While it is important to discuss what the therapist's role is, it is equally important to identify what it should not be. The child-centered play therapist is *not* a director, teacher, preacher, peer, parental figure, police officer, babysitter, investigator, or playmate. The child-centered play therapist is *not* a problem solver, rescuer, interpreter, inquisitor, or explainer. To take on these roles would be to deprive the child the occasion for self-exploration, self-creativity, self-evaluation, and self-discovery.

The child-centered play therapist is mindful that process comes before procedure and that presence comes before prescription. The therapist's role can be summarized in Axline's (1947) eight basic principles, which are revised and extended by Landreth (2002):

1. The therapist is genuinely interested in the child and develops a warm, caring relationship.
2. The therapist experiences unqualified acceptance of the child and does not wish the child was different in some way.
3. The therapist creates a feeling of safety and permissiveness in the relationship, so the child feels free to explore and express him- or herself completely.
4. The therapist is always sensitive to the child's feelings and gently reflects those feelings in such a manner that the child develops self-understanding.
5. The therapist believes deeply in the child's capacity to act responsibly, unwaveringly respects the child's ability to solve personal problems, and allows the child to do.

6. The therapist trusts the child's inner direction, allows the child to lead in all areas of the relationship, and resists any urge to direct the child's play or conversation.
7. The therapist appreciates the gradual nature of the therapeutic process and does not attempt to hurry the process.
8. The therapist establishes only those therapeutic limits necessary to anchor the session to reality and which help the child accept personal and appropriate relationship responsibility. (pp. 84–85)

While this is an attempt to define the therapeutic role, it is important to remember that being a play therapist is not really a role at all—it is a way of being with children. The child-centered play therapist's objective is "to relate to the child in ways that will release the child's inner directional, constructive, forward-moving, creative, self-healing power. When this philosophical belief is lived out with children in the playroom, they are empowered and their developmental capabilities are released for self-exploration, and self-discovery, resulting in constructive change" (Sweeney & Landreth, 2009, p. 123).

ROLE OF PARENTS

The legal guardians and primary caretakers of most children are their parents. Too many play therapists focus exclusively on children, to the exclusion of involving their parents in a meaningful way. This involvement is imperative because "any effort by the therapist to be helpful to children must begin with consideration for the parameters of the relationship to be established with the parent" (Landreth, 2002, p. 151). *Whether* the parents should be involved in the therapeutic process is never the issue but rather *how* the parents should be involved.

When parents bring their children to therapy, they are usually feeling overwhelmed and out of control. Having already made attempts to resolve the presenting issue, parents have this overwhelmed feeling compounded by the decision to bring their children in for therapy, which adds to feelings of loss of control. It is crucial that therapists remain aware of this dynamic and that they employ the very empathic skills needed in the playroom with the parents. This not only helps the parents on an emotional level but also models therapeutic responses in which they eventually should be trained to employ with their children.

Parents need to be interviewed prior to the therapy process. It can be argued that an informed therapist is a more empathic therapist, but it should also be cautioned that it is easy for a therapist to become biased against or toward aspects of a child's presentation. This bias would be at odds with child-centered philosophy because information given to the therapist before or during the therapy process should not call for any change in therapeutic approach. A possible resolution to this potential dilemma would be for another therapist to interview the parents, which would avoid bias on the part of the child's play therapist. Crane (2001) suggests that the goals of the initial interview should be "to (a) establish rapport, (b) obtain background information, (c) assess the situation, (d) discuss expectations for therapy, (e) set goals, and (f) explain the play therapy process" (p. 86).

There is another reason why parents should be involved—for legal and ethical considerations. Sweeney (2001) notes: "When working with children, it is imperative to remember that while the child may be the focus of treatment, the legal guardian is essentially the client from a legal and ethical perspective" (p. 65). Parents must be made aware of the purpose and process of the play therapy, and appropriate informed consent secured.

The degree of direct therapeutic involvement of the parents is a clinical decision made by the play therapist. When children are seen individually, parents should be involved on a peripheral basis continually. They should be kept informed of the therapeutic process and routinely interviewed along the way regarding developmental progress and emotional/behavioral change. Change is never the goal of the child-centered play therapist because this goal would change the therapist's manner in the playroom. The fact that change is the goal of the parents, however, cannot be forgotten.

Parents may need a referral for individual, conjoint, or family therapy. It is not uncommon for children to be engaging in internalizing or externalizing behaviors in response to marital conflict, for example. It may be a more expedient use of time and money for a parent or both parents to engage in an "adult" therapeutic experience as opposed to individual child play therapy.

Frequently, another child-centered play therapy intervention with the parents is needed: Filial Therapy. Chapter 9 describes the rationale and process. Because the majority of child referrals are for issues of noncompliance, a parent training intervention such as Filial Therapy makes considerable sense. Filial Therapy is a parent training intervention designed to build and enhance the parent–child relationship through teaching child-centered play therapy skills so that the parents become the agents of therapeutic change. A 10-session model of Filial Therapy has demonstrated significant positive results in multiple research projects (Landreth, 2002; Landreth & Bratton, 2006). These are briefly discussed in a later section of this chapter.

CASE ILLUSTRATION

The following transcript of interactions in a play therapy session provides specific examples typical of the child-centered approach to play therapy. The objective of the therapist is to understand, accept, allow the child to lead, facilitate development of the child's creative coping abilities, and help the child to assume responsibility for self.

> **Kevin**: I'm gonna make you something, okay? What do you want me to make?
>
> **Therapist**: In here, that's something you can decide. (Therapist returns responsibility to Kevin and allows Kevin to lead in the relationship.)
>
> **Kevin**: OK, OK. I'll make a heart. No, I don't want this.

Therapist: You don't like that one. (Therapist conveys understanding of Kevin's feeling.)

Kevin: I hate brown. (He gets another color and finishes painting.) Would you take this sheet off here? (Points to clip holding paper.)

Therapist: That's something you can do if you want it off.

(Children should be allowed to struggle and in so doing discover their strengths.)

Kevin: OK.

Therapist: You got that side off. You did it.

Kevin: (as the newsprint falls down) Oh, shoot! Hold this. (He gives the therapist his picture and replaces paper on easel.)

Therapist: You didn't like the way that came down.

Kevin: I hate it. (He takes his picture over to the counter.) Can I stick this in the trash can?

Therapist: The trash can is right there. (Points to it.)

Kevin: No, thanks. (He leaves the picture on the counter and comes back and starts another picture.) I hate orange. I'll try it.

Therapist: There are some colors you really don't like.

Kevin: I hate colors I hate!

Therapist: The ones you hate, you really hate!

Kevin: Yeah. I'll try black. Now, black is a little bit good, but brown—I'll try brown. Red looks like the one I like! (He gets a paper towel and wipes off the brown paint.) I'll need 10,000 of these. I'm gonna wipe it. Okay, here's my picture. This is mine. (He picks up a toy gun and pretends to shoot the therapist.)

Therapist: You were pretending to shoot me.

(Pretend behaviors are accepted in the playroom. A dart gun with a dart in the barrel of the gun would not be pretend and would necessitate the setting of a limit.)

Kevin: I never wanted to shoot you.

Therapist: You were just shooting.

Kevin: I'll just practice my target shooting. (He goes over to the shelf and picks up the dart gun.) I'll use this for target practice, also. (He walks over to the two-way mirror and starts to shoot at the mirror.)

Therapist: Kevin, I know you want to shoot that, but the mirror's not for shooting; you can shoot at all these other places over here (pointing).

(The ACT model of limit setting discussed previously is implemented here. Identifying and pointing toward acceptable alternatives facilitates Kevin's being able to achieve satisfaction by expressing himself in an acceptable manner.)

Kevin: OK. You mean like . . . (He gets up and shoots at the blackboard.)

Therapist: Like right there.

Kevin: Anywhere I want, but not the mirror.

Therapist: Umm . . . so you know which things you can shoot at. (Gives Kevin credit for knowing what is appropriate. Responses that build self-esteem are a part of the child-centered approach.)

Kevin: (Picks up gun, looks angry, and pretends to shoot therapist.)

Therapist: You're mad at me. (Therapist reflects child's feelings and shows understanding.)

Kevin: I'm not mad at you.

(Kevin may feel that anger is not acceptable and so corrects the therapist.)

Therapist: Oh, you're not mad at me.

Kevin: But I am really sick of it.

Therapist: So, you're not mad at me, you're just sick of it.

Kevin: (Puts gun down and gets plastic knife.)

Therapist: You just don't like it at all.

Kevin: (Takes knife and starts cutting therapist's arm.)

Therapist: Now you're pretending to cut my arm with that.

(Tracking of play behaviors needs to continue throughout the session to show interest and involvement.)

Therapist: (He pushes knife hard against therapist's arm.) I know you want to do that, but I'm not for hurting.

Kevin: Well, see, I got to do this.

Therapist: Hmmmmmm.

Kevin: (Starts cutting hard.)

Therapist: Kevin, I'm not for hurting. You can pretend one of those dolls is me and cut with that.

Kevin: (Walks over and cuts doll.)

(Kevin accepts responsibility for bringing himself under control and plays out his anger in an acceptable manner.)

Therapist: So, you decided you're going to pretend that's me and you're cutting with that really hard.

Kevin: Yeah. (Picks up two small child dolls and moves them toward door of building labeled Schoolhouse.)

Therapist: (as doll figures go through the door) They're going inside there.

(Therapist avoids labeling. It's not a schoolhouse until the child labels it a schoolhouse.)

Kevin: Yeah. They're going to see their friend in the hospital.

Therapist: So they're going to visit their friend in the hospital.

Kevin: Yeah. He's got cancer. (Picks up boy doll with no hair.) All his hair came out when they gave him medicine.

Therapist: So he looks kinda like that doll.

Kevin: Before, he had lots of long hair.

Therapist: He looks different now.

Kevin: His mom said it would grow back, but he can't ride bikes with us for a long time (sounds sad and grimaces).

Therapist: Some day he will have hair again, but you feel sad, and you miss him.

(Therapist's empathic responses show understanding and identify Kevin's feelings.)

Kevin: (picks up doctor kit) I'll try to, um, do something here on your wrist. (He goes over to therapist and puts the blood pressure toy on therapist's wrist.) Check you.

Therapist: You want to see how I am. (Acknowledges Kevin's intent and shows understanding.)

Kevin: Here. Wait. (He works the blood pressure toy.) Pretty low.

Therapist: So I'm pretty low.

Kevin: (He puts the blood pressure toy back in the kit.) Just because I'm playing doctor doesn't mean that it's real.

Therapist: Oh, even though it seems like it's low, it doesn't mean I'm really sick.

(Therapist senses that Kevin's response is directed toward the therapist in a personal way and, therefore, personalizes the acknowledgment of understanding.)

Kevin: That's right, because I'm just playing doctor. (He gets the stethoscope out of the kit and listens to therapist's heart.) Looks like doctors use this thing. Nothin' to it!

Therapist: Nothing to it. You know just how to use it.

(The continued giving of credit to Kevin communicates acceptance and affirms his ability and capability. A child who receives such affirmation builds problem-solving and coping skills through the play therapy relationship.)

Kevin: Yeah . . . kind of. (He gets out the syringe from the kit.) Here's that thing. A shot! (He goes over and gives the therapist a shot.) Right here. (He shows her the syringe.) Look at all this. (He gives therapist another injection.)

Therapist: You just gave me a shot right there.

Kevin: OK, let's put this on and let's just see here. Hold your hand out straight. (Puts Band-Aid on therapist's hand.)

Therapist: Got that finished.

(Therapeutic responses in the playroom should be short, succinct, and interactive with the child's feelings and actions.)

> **Kevin:** (uses stethoscope) OK, deep breath, another one, another one, another one—deep breath, another one, another one. OK!
> **Therapist:** Sounds like you're pleased with that.

(Therapist responds to nonverbal cue and reflects Kevin's feeling. The child's feelings and reactions are considered more important than the details of the child's play.)

> **Kevin:** Yep, I am. (Uses syringe to draw blood from therapist's arm.) OK, got to put it in a bottle for tests.
> **Therapist:** Ummmm, you're doing a lot of blood tests.
> **Kevin:** OK, you're fine. The blood test results said you're doing great, and you don't need any more checkups until Monday.
> **Therapist:** You made me better.

(Such responses empower a child.)

> **Kevin:** (picks up can of Play-Doh) What do you do with this?
> **Therapist:** In here you can decide.

(Therapist returns responsibility to Kevin, allows him to make a decision and use his own creativity.)

> **Kevin:** Hey, it's a bomb! (He drops the can of Play-Doh on top of a small car in the sandbox.) Blam! Did you see that car!
> **Therapist:** Just blew that car up!
> **Kevin:** (grabs sand scoop, quickly digs hole, and buries car) Blew such a big hole it covered the car up.
> **Therapist:** Yep, that was a big hole. The car can't be seen anymore.
> **Kevin:** The people aren't hurt. They're hiding in the car, and the guy who dropped the bomb doesn't know.

(Therapist's reflective responses show understanding and acceptance and continue to allow the child to lead and for his story to unfold.)

> **Therapist:** They're safe, and the guy doesn't know.
> **Kevin:** If he knew they were hiding in the car, he would drop another bomb, but the father digs out of the car (Kevin picks up father doll from dollhouse) and shoots the guy.
> **Therapist:** They're safe now.
> **Kevin:** They decided to drive the car home. (Kevin picks up the handcuffs.) Now put these handcuffs on. Here, stick your hands back here.
> **Therapist:** You want my hands behind my back, but my hands are for keeping in front.

(The therapist acknowledges what Kevin wants and sets a limit on behaviors that make the therapist feel uncomfortable. This declaration of self is essential in the child-centered approach.)

> **Kevin:** OK.
> **Therapist:** You're putting them on me right there.
> **Kevin:** (writes on board) How do you spell math?
> **Therapist:** In here, you can spell things any way you want to.

(A major objective of the child-centered approach is to empower the child. This response returns responsibility to Kevin and grants permission to be creative.)

> **Kevin:** (writes Mh) No, that's not it, wrong—h is wrong—m.
> **Therapist:** Doesn't look like it's right to you. You want it to be a certain way.
> **Kevin:** Yeah. Who owns this school?
> **Therapist:** You would like to know what this place is all about.

(Responding to the underlying meaning avoids answering a question that hasn't really been asked, communicates understanding, and frees the child's expression to go on beyond the initial question.)

> **Kevin:** I think this place is just about playing.
> **Therapist:** Mmm. So, you're not really sure if it's a school or just a place to play.
> **Kevin:** I think it is a school.
> **Therapist:** Mmm.
> **Kevin:** If I want it to be a school, I can let it be a school.

(Kevin recognizes the uniqueness of the play therapy relationship and feels empowered.)

> **Therapist:** So you can just decide what you want it to be.
> **Kevin:** Yep.
> **Therapist:** Kevin, we have 5 minutes in the playroom and then it will be time to go to the waiting room where your mom is.

(A 5-minute warning allows Kevin to complete play sequences that are important to him and to get ready to leave the playroom.)

> **Kevin:** Oh, nuts!
> **Therapist:** Mmm. Sounds like you don't want to leave.
> **Kevin:** I hate it.
> **Therapist:** You really don't like it. (pause) You're really trying hard to get that on there. If they don't go in one place, you'll just find another place for them.

Kevin: I'm locking 'em up (in the trunk). I have troubles at school. (Identifies the difficulty he is having at school.)

Therapist: Mmm. So you have troubles at school sometimes.

Kevin: Is there a key to this (the trunk)?

Therapist: You would like to have a key, but there isn't one.

Kevin: (throws dolls in trunk) Get in here! Everybody! In here!

Therapist: You're angry and you're telling them where to go.

Kevin: Gotta get out here with your stinky . . . old heads. You have to take a bath. Just get in there! (in the trunk)

Therapist: You think they're pretty smelly . . . need to have a bath.

Kevin: That's why I'm locking 'em in here. They're trying to get out. They'll never get out (looking at the trunk). Are y'all ready to get out? (mumbles)

Therapist: Mmm.

Kevin: Did you wash up? Okay, you smell pretty good.

Therapist: You want to make sure they're clean. But you decided they must be. Seems like you like the way they smell now.

Kevin: Now, get to work, y'all, or I'm not gonna ever let you out.

Therapist: Hmm. You're warning them that they better do what they're supposed to do or you're just not gonna let them out.

Kevin: Uh huh. That's what I want . . .

Therapist: Sounds like you like to be in charge.

Kevin: I wanta be the king.

Therapist: Mmm.

Kevin: But I can't be.

Therapist: You wanta be . . .

Kevin: God likes me.

Therapist: Mmm. So God likes you. Kevin, our time is up for tonight.

Kevin: Now?

Therapist: Mmm. Sounds like you're not ready for it to be up, but our time is up.

Kevin: Can I have this big thing?

Therapist: You would like to take that with you, but the toys are for staying in the playroom so they will be here when you come next time.

(Therapist reflects Kevin's feeling; sets a limit by generalizing to all the toys, thus avoiding having to verbalize the same limit in reference to every item in the playroom; and shows great respect for Kevin by communicating that the toys will be there when he comes next time.)

Kevin: Does all of this stay in the room?

Therapist: Sounds like you'd like to take some of it, but it all stays here. (Reflects the feeling beneath the question.)

Kevin: I don't want . . . to go yet.

Therapist: You're just not ready to go, even though it's time to go.

(The therapist demonstrates great patience. The objective is that Kevin will assume responsibility and talk himself out of the playroom.)

Kevin: It's time to go, but . . . (looking on the shelf).
Therapist: Kevin, I know you want to look at those things, but our time is up for tonight . . . you just don't want to go.
Kevin: My socks . . . and my shoes. (Picks them up.)
Therapist: Mmm. Just picked those up to take with you. (They walk out together.)

CLINICAL APPLICATIONS

Child-centered play therapy is not limited in its clinical application to children. Because the child-centered play therapy model does not focus on diagnosis or maladjustment, its applicability is considered widespread. There is a philosophical belief that children have an inherent tendency to move in either subtle or obvious paths toward adjustment, emotional health, developmental growth, independence, autonomy, and personhood. The focus of the child-centered play therapist is not only on the person of the child but also on what the child is capable of becoming. The etiology of the problem, the problem itself, or the evidential symptoms are not limitations and are not in fact pertinent to the development of a therapeutic relationship with the child.

Sweeney and Landreth (2009) noted that the child-centered approach has broad clinical applications in terms of child background:

> The child-centered approach is uniquely suited for working with children from different socioeconomic strata and ethnic backgrounds, because these facts do not change the therapist's beliefs, philosophy, theory, or approach to the child. Empathy, acceptance, understanding, and genuineness on the part of the therapist are provided to children equally, irrespective of their color, condition, circumstance, concern, or complaint. The child is free to communicate through play in a manner that is comfortable and typical for the child, including cultural adaptations of play and expression. (p. 135)

The clinical applications of child-centered play therapy are evident in the play therapy literature. The following discussion attests to the extensive applicability of the child-centered approach.

EMPIRICAL SUPPORT

Contrary to the myth that child-centered play therapy is a long and meandering process, the research literature supports its efficacy in short-term usage. Raskin and Rogers (2005) reported that with person-centered therapy, significant changes in self-acceptance and the individual's ability to move toward internal self-evaluation have been demonstrated in single sessions and in short-term therapy. In a recently published text on child-centered play therapy research (Baggerly, Ray, & Bratton, 2010), the authors note a significant fact:

> You will notice that all the research studies described are based on the child-centered play therapy (CCPT) theoretical orientation and filial therapy approach. This focus is because virtually all play therapy research studies that were published in a professional journal since the year 2000 were CCPT or filial therapy. (pp. xiii–xiv)

Axline (1948) reported significant progress using CCPT with a selective mute child. This progress was reported by the child's mother by the fifth play therapy session. Bills (1950) studied the effects of CCPT on children with reading difficulties, noting a significant improvement in reading skills as compared with the control group.

Oualline (1975) demonstrated the effectiveness of CCPT with hearing-impaired children, reporting significant reductions in behavioral problems in comparison with the control group. Barlow, Strother, and Landreth (1985) reported significant progress with a child with trichotillomania, noting significant hair growth by the seventh session. Working with elementary school children, Crow (1989) reported significant improvement in self-concept and internal locus of control as compared with the control group following a CCPT intervention. In a study of 60 elementary school–age children diagnosed with attention deficit/hyperactivity disorder (ADHD), the CCPT intervention demonstrated significant improvement on ADHD and anxiety symptoms, as well as reductions in teacher stress (Ray, Schottelkorb, & Tsai, 2007).

Using CCPT with a grieving child, LeVieux (1994) reported positive changes by the seventh session, including improved behavior and ability to more easily discuss the loss. Johnson, McLeod, and Fall (1997) examined the effects of six CCPT sessions on children with emotional or physical challenges affecting school performance. Improvement was noted by the researchers, teachers, and parents. Webb (2001) reported the efficacy of one to three sessions with children affected by the Oklahoma City bombing. Danger and Landreth (2005) demonstrated positive results employing child-centered group play therapy with children with speech difficulties.

Kot, Landreth, and Giordano (1998) investigated use of an intensive model of short-term CCPT with child witnesses of domestic violence. Children in the experimental group demonstrated a significant decrease in behavior problems and a significant increase in self-concept. Tyndall-Lind, Landreth, and Giordano (2001) researched the same population using intensive short-term child-centered sibling group play therapy and found the same significant positive results. Jones and Landreth (2002) investigated the efficacy of intensive play therapy for chronically ill children, demonstrating positive results. An exploratory study of the use of CCPT with aggressive children also demonstrated significant efficacy (Ray, Blanco, Sullivan, & Holliman, 2009).

Consistent significantly positive results also have been found in research with Landreth's (2002; Landreth & Bratton, 2006) 10-session Filial Therapy model. As previously noted, Filial Therapy is a parent training intervention that involves training parents to use child-centered play therapy skills in addressing challenging child and family issues. This model has been demonstrated to improve children's self-concepts, reduce children's behavioral problems, improve children's emotional adjustment, and increase children's desirable play behavior. Additionally, the 10-session model has been demonstrated to significantly decrease parental stress, increase parental empathy and acceptance, and improve the family environment.

Using a pre- and posttest control group design, the Landreth Filial Therapy model has been studied and demonstrated to be effective with a wide variety of child and parent populations. These include single parents (Bratton & Landreth, 1995), incarcerated mothers (Harris & Landreth, 1997) and fathers (Landreth & Lobaugh, 1998), nonoffending parents of sexually abused children (Costas & Landreth, 1999), learning-disabled children (Kale & Landreth, 1999), chronically ill children (Tew, Landreth, Joiner, & Solt, 2002), and child witnesses of domestic violence (Smith, 2000). Several studies have also been done with nonparent paraprofessionals with significant results, including teachers of deaf and hard-of-hearing students (Smith & Landreth, 2004), teachers and teacher aides (Helker & Ray, 2009), undergraduate student trainees (Brown, 2000), high school students conducting play sessions with at-risk preschool and kindergarten students (Jones, Rhine, & Bratton, 2002), and training fifth graders to work with kindergarteners (Robinson, Landreth, & Packman, 2007).

Cross-Cultural Research

Child-centered play therapy has been demonstrated to have broad cross-cultural applications. Numerous research projects have shown child-centered play therapy to be effective across diverse cultures: school-based CCPT with Hispanic children (Garza & Bratton, 2005), short-term CCPT training with Israeli school counselors and teachers (Kagan & Landreth, 2009), group play therapy with Chinese earthquake victims (Shen, 2002), CCPT with Japanese children in the United States (Ogawa, 2006), brief CCPT training for professionals working with vulnerable children in Kenya (Hunt, 2006), and nondirective play therapy with Iranian children with internalized problems (Bayat, 2008).

Multiple studies have also demonstrated the benefits of Filial Therapy with diverse parent populations: Chinese parents (Chau & Landreth, 1997; Yuen, Landreth, & Baggerly, 2002), Korean parents (Jang, 2000; Lee & Landreth, 2003), Israeli parents (Kidron & Landreth, 2010), Native American parents (Glover & Landreth, 2000), African-American parents (Sheely, 2009), and Hispanic parents (Ceballos, 2009).

CONCLUSION

Child-centered play therapy is a dynamic process of relating to children on their own terms in developmentally appropriate ways, consistent with their natural medium of communication. Just as trees change color in the autumn—which involves an internal process of resources already existent, responding to a climatic change—children have internal resources that blossom in the environmental change of a self-led play experience in the presence of a therapist communicating child-centered responses. This is a process of continual discovery as the play therapist consistently portrays understanding and acceptance, which creates a relationship of safety and is internalized by the child in ways that free the child to express and explore dimensions of self that have typically not been shared with other adults. The child-centered play therapist has the opportunity to be perhaps the only adult who is focused fully upon the child as opposed to his or her "problem."

The content and direction of the child's play are determined by the child. The child-centered approach is not a prescriptive approach dependent on the identified problem of the child. A central issue is that the key to behavior is how a child feels about himself or herself. Behavioral interventions, while certainly having value, do not change self-perception. Therefore, the play therapist works hard to understand the child's perceptual view. The child's behavior must always be understood by looking through the child's eyes. Child-centered play therapy is one of the most thoroughly researched theoretical models, and the results are unequivocal in demonstrating the effectiveness of this approach with a wide variety of children's problems and in time-limited settings involving intensive and short-term play therapy. Child-centered play therapy has and will continue to focus on the process of being and becoming.

REFERENCES

Axline, V. (1947). *Play therapy: The inner dynamics of childhood.* Boston, MA: Houghton Mifflin.

Axline, V. (1948). Some observations on play therapy. *Journal of Consulting Psychology, 11*, 61–69.

Baggerly, J., Ray, D., & Bratton, S. (Eds.). (2010). *Child-centered play therapy research: The evidence base for effective practice.* Hoboken, NJ: Wiley.

Barlow, K., Strother, J., & Landreth, G. (1985). Child-centered play therapy: Nancy from baldness to curls. *School Counselor, 32*(5), 347–356.

Bayat, M. (2008). Nondirective play-therapy for children with internalized problems. *Journal of Iranian Psychologists, 4*(15), 267–276.

Bills, R. (1950). Nondirective play therapy with retarded readers. *Journal of Consulting Psychology, 14*, 140–149.

Bratton, S., & Landreth, G. (1995). Filial Therapy with single parents: Effects on parental acceptance, empathy, and stress. *International Journal of Play Therapy, 4*(1), 61–80.

Brown, C. (2000). Filial Therapy with undergraduate teacher trainees; child–teacher relationship training. *Dissertation Abstracts International, 63*(09A), 3112.

Ceballos, P. (2009). School-based child parent relationship therapy (CPRT) with low income first generation immigrant Hispanic parents: Effects on child behavior and parent–child relationship stress. *Dissertation Abstracts International, 69*(8-A), 3042.

Chau, I., & Landreth, G. (1997). Filial Therapy with Chinese parents: Effects on parental empathic interactions, parental acceptance of child and parental stress. *International Journal of Play Therapy, 6*(2), 75–92.

Costas, M., & Landreth, G. (1999). Filial Therapy with nonoffending parents of children who have been sexually abused. *International Journal of Play Therapy, 8*(1), 43–66.

Crane, J. (2001). The parents' part in the play therapy process. In G. Landreth (Ed.), *Innovations in play therapy: Issues, process, and special populations* (pp. 83–98). Philadelphia, PA: Brunner-Routledge.

Crow, J. (1989). Play therapy with low achievers in reading. *Dissertation Abstracts International, 50*(9A), 2789.

Danger, S., & Landreth, G. (2005). Child-centered group play therapy with children with speech difficulties. *International Journal of Play Therapy, 14*(1), 81–102.

Garza, Y., & Bratton, S. (2005). School-based child-centered play therapy with Hispanic children: Outcomes and cultural considerations. *International Journal of Play Therapy, 14*(1), 51–79.

Ginott, H. (1961). *Group psychotherapy with children: The theory and practice of play therapy*. New York, NY: McGraw-Hill.

Glover, G., & Landreth, G. (2000). Filial Therapy with Native Americans on the Flathead Reservation. *International Journal of Play Therapy, 9*(2), 57–80.

Harris, Z., & Landreth, G. (1997). Filial Therapy with incarcerated mothers: A five week model. *International Journal of Play Therapy, 6*(2), 53–73.

Helker, W., & Ray, D. (2009). Impact of child teacher relationship training on teachers' and aides' use of relationship-building skills and the effects on student classroom behavior. *International Journal of Play Therapy, 18*(2), 70–83.

Homeyer, L., & Sweeney, D. (2010). *Sandtray therapy: A practical manual* (2nd ed.). New York, NY: Routledge.

Hunt, K. (2006). Can professionals offering support to vulnerable children in Kenya benefit from brief play therapy training? *Journal of Psychology in Africa, 16*(2), 215–221.

Jang, M. (2000). Effectiveness of Filial Therapy for Korean parents. *International Journal of Play Therapy, 9*(2), 39–56.

Johnson, L., McLeod, E., & Fall, M. (1997). Play therapy with labeled children in the schools. *Professional School Counseling, 1*(1), 31–34.

Jones, E., & Landreth, G. (2002). The efficacy of intensive individual play therapy for chronically ill children. *International Journal of Play Therapy, 11*(1), 117–140.

Jones, L., Rhine, T., & Bratton, S. (2002). High school students as therapeutic agents with young children experiencing school adjustment difficulties: The effectiveness of a filial therapy training model. *International Journal of Play Therapy, 11*(2), 43–62.

Kagan, S., & Landreth, G. (2009). Short-term child-centered play therapy training with Israeli school counselors and teachers. *International Journal of Play Therapy, 18*(4), 207–216.

Kale, A., & Landreth, G. (1999). Filial therapy with parents of children experiencing learning difficulties. *International Journal of Play Therapy, 8*(2), 35–56.

Kidron, M., & Landreth, G. (2010, April). Intensive child parent relationship therapy with Israeli parents in Israel. *International Journal of Play Therapy, 19*(2), 64–78.

Kot, S., Landreth, G., & Giordano, M. (1998). Intensive child-centered play therapy with child witness of domestic violence. *International Journal of Play Therapy, 7*(2), 17–36.

Landreth, G. (2002). *Play therapy: The art of the relationship* (2nd ed.). Philadelphia, PA: Brunner-Routledge.

Landreth, G., & Bratton, S. (2006). *Child parent relationship therapy (CPRT): A 10-session Filial Therapy model.* New York, NY: Routledge.

Landreth, G., & Lobaugh, A. (1998). Filial Therapy with incarcerated fathers: Effects on parental acceptance of child, parental stress, and child adjustment. *Journal of Counseling & Development, 76*(2), 157–165.

Landreth, G., & Sweeney, D. (1999). The freedom to be: Child-centered group play therapy. In D. Sweeney & L. Homeyer (Eds.), *Handbook of group play therapy.* San Francisco, CA: Jossey-Bass.

Lee, M-K., & Landreth, G. (2003). Filial Therapy with immigrant Korean parents in the United States. *International Journal of Play Therapy, 12*(2), 67–85.

LeVieux, J. (1994). Terminal illness and death of father: Case of Celeste, age 5½. In N. B. Webb (Ed.), *Helping bereaved children: A handbook for practitioners* (pp. 81–95). New York, NY: Guilford Press.

Ogawa, Y. (2006). Effectiveness of child-centered play therapy with Japanese children in the United States. *Dissertation Abstracts International, 68*(02B), 0158.

Oualline, V. (1975). Behavioral outcomes of short-term nondirective play therapy with preschool deaf children. *Dissertation Abstracts International, 36*(12A), 7870.

Moustakas, C. (1959). *Psychotherapy with children: The living relationship.* New York, NY: Harper & Row.

Raskin, N., & Rogers, C. (2005). Person-centered therapy. In R. Corsini & D. Wedding (Eds.), *Current psychotherapies* (7th ed., pp. 130–165). Belmont, CA: Brooks/Cole.

Ray, D., Blanco, P., Sullivan, J., & Holliman, R. (2009). An exploratory study of child-centered play therapy with aggressive children. *International Journal of Play Therapy, 18*(3), 162–175.

Ray, D., Schottelkorb, A., & Tsai, M-H. (2007). Play therapy with children exhibiting symptoms of attention deficit hyperactivity disorder. *International Journal of Play Therapy, 16*(2), 95–111.

Robinson, J., Landreth, G., & Packman, J. (2007). Fifth-grade students as emotional helpers with kindergartners: Using play therapy procedures and skills. *International Journal of Play Therapy, 16*(1), 20–35.

Rogers, C. (1951). *Client-centered therapy.* Boston, MA: Houghton-Mifflin.

Sheely, A. (2009). School-based child-parent relationship therapy (CPRT) with low income Black American parents: Effects on children's behaviors and parent–child relationship stress. A pilot study. *Dissertation Abstracts International, 69*(8–A), 3045.

Shen, Y-J. (2002). Short-term group play therapy with Chinese earthquake victims: Effects on anxiety, depression and adjustment. *International Journal of Play Therapy, 11*(1), 43–63.

Smith, D. M., & Landreth, G. (2004). Filial Therapy with teachers of deaf and hard of hearing preschool children. *International Journal of Play Therapy, 13*(1), 13–33.

Smith, N. (2000). A comparative analysis of intensive Filial Therapy with intensive individual play therapy and intensive sibling group play therapy with child witnesses of domestic violence. *Dissertation Abstracts International, 62*(7-A), 2353.

Sweeney, D. (1997). *Counseling children through the world of play.* Eugene, OR: Wipf & Stock.

Sweeney, D. (2001). Legal and ethical issues in play therapy. In G. Landreth (Ed.), *Innovations in play therapy: Issues, process, and special populations* (pp. 65–81). Philadelphia, PA: Brunner-Routledge.

Sweeney, D., & Landreth, G. (2009). Child-centered play therapy. In K. O'Connor & L. Braverman (Eds.), *Play therapy theory and practice: Comparing theories and techniques* (2nd ed., pp. 123–162). Hoboken, NJ: Wiley.

Tew, K., Landreth, G., Joiner, K., & Solt, M. (2002). Filial Therapy with chronically ill children. *International Journal of Play Therapy, 11*(1), 79–100.

Tyndall-Lind, A., Landreth, G., & Giordano, M. (2001). Intensive group play therapy with child witness of domestic violence. *International Journal of Play Therapy, 10*(1), 53–83.

Webb, P. (2001). Play therapy with traumatized children. In G. Landreth (Ed.), *Innovations in play therapy: Issues, process, and special populations* (pp. 289–302). Philadelphia, PA: Brunner-Routledge.

Yeun, T., Landreth, G., & Baggerly, J. (2002). Filial Therapy with immigrant Chinese parents. *International Journal of Play Therapy, 11*(2), 63–90.

Chapter 9

FILIAL THERAPY
Strengthening Family Relationships With the Power of Play
Risë VanFleet

INTRODUCTION

Children with a wide range of difficulties often respond well to play therapy. While most play therapists wisely involve parents in the process through behavioral consultation and regular meetings, they sometimes are frustrated that parents do not make the changes necessary to maintain the progress achieved in play therapy. Filial Therapy (FT) offers a solution that involves parents more fully in the process, helps them make lasting changes, and better ensures that child progress continues. FT is first and foremost a form of family therapy, but it relies heavily on the power of play to strengthen parent–child relationships, resolve problems, and encourage healthy psychosocial development into the future.

The term *filial* derives from Latin meaning "son" or "daughter," loosely translated as "parent–child." Filial Therapy was the creation of Drs. Bernard and Louise Guerney in the late 1950s and early 1960s and developed and researched by them throughout their careers (Guerney, 1964; Guerney, 1983; VanFleet, 2005, 2006b, 2008a; VanFleet & Guerney, 2003). Although initial reception of this novel approach by the professional community was not enthusiastic, its refinement over time and increasing empirical support have made it one of the most sought-after forms of play therapy by therapists and families today. Its respectful empowerment approach and adaptability have increased its use in multicultural environments and throughout the world.

In FT, the therapist involves parents as the primary change agents for their own families. This is accomplished by training and supervising parents as they conduct special nondirective play sessions with each of their children. As parents become competent and confident in conducting the special play times, they move them to the home environment while the therapist continues to monitor progress. Prior to discharge, the therapist helps parents generalize the skills employed during the play sessions to daily life. Some families continue to hold the special play sessions long after therapy ends, simply because they enjoy them and they help strengthen their relationships and prevent future problems from developing.

FT often is a relatively short-term intervention, requiring between 10 and 20 sessions for many families. It can be used as a primary prevention for strengthening family ties, as a means to offset potential problems in at-risk families, and as a full form of therapy for families experiencing mild to severe problems. VanFleet (2005, 2006b, 2008a) has described the use of FT with individual families in detail. The Guerney group FT model remains a viable intervention today (Guerney & Ryan, in preparation; VanFleet & Sniscak, in press), and other short-term formats have arisen, including the empirically supported parent education adaptation known as Child–Parent Relationship Therapy (CPRT) (Landreth & Bratton, 2006), the 12-week program developed for Head Start families (Wright & Walker, 2003), and the 12-week group FT program developed for Philadelphia's Children's Crisis Treatment Center and more recently used with families devastated by Hurricane Katrina (Caplin & Pernet, in press; VanFleet & McCann, 2007). VanFleet and Sniscak have adapted the Guerney group model for use with highly traumatized and attachment-disrupted children in foster care and adoptive families, a program that runs for 18 weeks to accommodate the multiple needs and deeper levels of distress often found in this population of children and families.

BASIC CONCEPTS, GOALS, AND TECHNIQUES

FT is a theoretically integrative approach, drawing from the contributions or precursors of humanistic, psychodynamic, behavioral, interpersonal, cognitive, family systems, developmental/attachment theory, and community psychology orientations. The specific ways in which these theories are represented within FT are described in detail elsewhere (Cavedo & Guerney, 1999; Ginsberg, 2003, 2004; Guerney, 1997, 2003; VanFleet, 2009a, 2009b) and are discussed further in the Therapeutic Powers of Play section of this chapter.

Conceptually, FT was developed far ahead of its time. It fits much better in today's climate of family and community interventions, expressive therapies, and play therapy. Play therapists were among the first to embrace it fully, but broader professional interest by family therapists, psychologists, psychiatrists, social workers, counselors, and educators is growing rapidly.

Concepts

At its core, FT is a *psychoeducational intervention*. Psychoeducational approaches are predicated on the idea that problems arise when people lack knowledge or skills needed to cope with situations they face. The implications of this approach contrast with the prevailing medical or expert models, in which problems are diagnosed, often seen as a dysfunction of the individual or family, with treatment driven by the relevant professional. While one can use psychoeducational approaches within a medical model, the assumptions and methods are quite different. In a psychoeducational model, the therapist thinks more as an educator. Intervention consists of determining knowledge and skills that would be potentially helpful to the client, teaching that knowledge and those skills, and helping the person or family adapt and use them in their own lives. Psychological, emotional, behavioral, social, and developmental problems are addressed in this manner. A clinical background is valuable to this process, helping the practitioner determine the knowledge and skills most helpful to the family's difficulties.

FT is a *process-oriented approach*. This means that therapists trust that if they create an empathic, accepting, and client-focused environment, clients will often resolve many of their own problems. Although FT is designed to meet various child, parent, and family goals, this is done by strengthening the family relationships. It is through this process that the goals are accomplished, so therapists focus on relationship building through the use of play rather than on specific goals. If the process is well designed, as it is in FT, and if it is well executed by a properly trained therapist, then the specific goals will be met. It is the therapist's job to maintain the integrity of the process so it can do its magic.

Related to this, FT *empowers children, parents, and families*. Therapists focus on the process, allowing children and their parents to resolve many of their own problems. Children are given considerable freedom in the play sessions in which they can freely express their feelings and desires, communicate their wishes, solve problems, and master their fears or traumas. Parents are provided with the tools they need to realize their full potential as parents, but specific parenting decisions are left to them. Better equipped with the skills developed during the FT process, parents are more likely to make decisions and behave in ways that ensure the healthy psychosocial development of their children. Therapists must create a safe and accepting environment for the parents, just as they teach parents to create a safe and accepting environment for their children. It is in this climate of empathy, respect, skills training, and support that parents gain confidence and balance in their approach (as in Baumrind's [1971] recommended authoritative parenting style), and children reap the benefits.

Therapists using FT *engage parents are true partners* in the process. Therapists learn to value the information and insights that parents bring to the process. Parents truly are the world's best experts on their own children. Perhaps they have not treated their children well. Perhaps they have conflictual and damaged relationships. Perhaps they have very poor parenting skills. Even so, they know their children and what to expect of them far better than any therapist will ever know. Parents know their children's habits, tendencies, preferences, and reactions by virtue of living with them. Their relationships are intimate, even if less than ideal. In essence, parents have an understanding of the *context* in which they and their children live, and this is vital information for therapy. In FT, the therapist treats parents with the respect, sensitivity, and empathy they deserve, and this helps form a truly collaborative therapeutic relationship. The therapist brings his or her specialized training in child development, family therapy, and play therapy to the equation, while parents supply the on-the-scene "intelligence." Such partnerships can sometimes be difficult to forge, especially with parents who are court-ordered to attend or who are suspicious of therapy, but efforts to engage and support parents throughout the FT process are rewarded with true parent involvement and change that ensures better outcomes for their children as well.

Clinicians who use FT also *appreciate the value and use the power of play* for building healthy attachment, strengthening relationships, and resolving individual and family problems. Play is the primary way that children learn about the world, express themselves, and develop their physical, social, cognitive, and emotional skills (Brown & Vaughan, 2009; Elkind, 2007; Ginsburg, 2007; Sutton-Smith, 2008; VanFleet, 2000). VanFleet (2008b) has defined play therapy as "a broad field that uses children's natural inclination to play as a means of creating an emotionally safe therapeutic environment that encourages communication, relationship-building, expression, and problem resolution for the child" (p. 15). Play therapy is considered by many to be the developmentally sensitive treatment of choice for most child problems.

Goals of Filial Therapy

Although FT is a process-oriented therapy, it is designed to accomplish a number of goals. In general, the goal of FT is to help families become stronger, achieving more satisfying relationships built on love, understanding, trust, security, loyalty, belonging, compassion, companionship, and enjoyment (Cavedo & Guerney, 1999). Problems tend to disappear when such needs of family members are satisfied. Furthermore, the goals of FT are consistent with studies of the most effective parenting styles (i.e., Baumrinds [1971] authoritative parenting approach). Guerney (1997) has suggested that FT shows parents how to develop the same attitudes and behaviors that are associated with parents of socially competent children. Her research also suggests that when parents provide empathy during free play, children tend to be more behaviorally compliant with their parents' wishes (Guerney, 1997). The opposite was also found to be true: Children were the least compliant when their parents exerted a great deal of control or were intrusive during free-play periods.

More specifically, the goals of FT can be divided into three areas. First, FT is designed to help *children* (a) recognize and express their feelings in a constructive and accurate manner, (b) increase their self-esteem and confidence, (c) eliminate their maladaptive behaviors, (d) develop problem-solving skills, (e) achieve mastery over their fears and other feelings, (f) increase self-regulation, (g) develop prosocial behaviors, and (h) strengthen their trust in their parents.

Second, FT aims to help *parents* (a) establish more realistic expectations of their children; (b) improve their knowledge of child development; (c) improve their ability to understand their children's feelings, thoughts, perceptions, and behaviors; (d) value their children's play as part of their healthy development; (e) increase their confidence as parents; (f) develop closer, more attuned, more secure, and mutually satisfying relationships with their children; (g) strengthen their trust in their children; (h) improve their coparenting; (i) improve their capacities to show empathy and acceptance of their children; (j) improve their abilities to establish structure and set and enforce limits when needed; (k) communicate better within the family; and (l) play more frequently with their children and enjoy them more.

Third, FT aims to help the *entire family* (a) find more enjoyment with each other; (b) resolve the presenting problems at the most fundamental level; (c) improve communication and interpersonal problem solving; (d) enhance their interactions with each other; and (e) be empowered to function more independently, cohesively, and with greater satisfaction with family life. In essence, FT focuses on strengthening the parent–child relationships within the family, but the process simultaneously improves marital cooperation and whole-family psychosocial functioning.

Treatment plans with behavioral objectives are valuable, not only because some organizations, insurance companies, and government agencies require them but because they represent a dialogue between therapist and parent resulting in specified objectives against which progress can be measured. Because FT as described here is family therapy, it is possible to open files and create treatment plans for the child, for one of the parents, or both. This author often discusses with parents where it makes the most sense to place the diagnosis. Often, because the child's problem reflects broader family dynamics, the case may be opened under one of the parent's names. At other times, it makes sense to open a file for the child, documenting those sessions when the child participates, and another for the parent, documenting those sessions during the training phase and later during the home session phase when only the parents meet with the therapist. Regardless of these practicalities, FT practitioners check regularly with parents to determine progress or setbacks in the child's presenting problems and behavior in the "real world." This is considered one of the most important measures of FT's impact.

Techniques

In FT, the therapist uses a variety of methods to accomplish the ambitious goals outlined previously. The therapist teaches parents how to conduct special child-centered play sessions with their own children. The therapist also supports parents as they develop a fuller understanding of their children's communications and needs as expressed in their play and helps parents work through some of their own reactions and feelings as they participate in this new way of interacting with their children.

Because FT is based on a theoretically integrative model, it combines methods drawn from the various theories represented within it. Therapists develop their empathic attitudes and skills so they can convey understanding and acceptance to parents as they work together to resolve the family difficulties. They use behavioral and learning principles to empower parents to master the play session skills. They help parents gain an understanding of the symbolic meaning of their children's play themes and then support parents with empathy and cognitive restructuring when they must face the (sometimes) difficult messages their children share.

On a practical level, FT therapists must first develop competence in child-centered play therapy (CCPT) before embarking on a path using FT (see, e.g., Cochran, Nordling, & Cochran, 2010; Landreth, 2002; VanFleet, 2006a; VanFleet, Sywulak, & Sniscak, 2010; Wilson & Ryan, 2005). Therapists must also have highly developed empathy skills, with the ability to show understanding of children's and parents' deepest feelings in a sensitive and safe manner. They must also have strong knowledge of family systems work so that they can effectively engage all family members in the process and work on difficult family dynamics. Group leadership skills are also important if one wishes to conduct FT or one of its adaptations in a group format, of which there are several (Caplin & Pernet, in press; Guerney & Ryan, in press; Landreth & Bratton, 2006; VanFleet & Sniscak, in press; Wright & Walker, 2003).

After the assessment phase, FT therapists demonstrate a CCPT session with each of the family's children while the parents observe. This is followed by a training phase in which parents learn to conduct the CCPT sessions themselves. Next, as parents begin to conduct the play sessions one-on-one with their own children, the therapist observes and later gives the parents feedback, focusing on the things that they did well and offering one or two suggestions for improvement until parents become competent in conducting the special play sessions. It is also during this time that therapists help parents learn to recognize and understand the children's play themes. This is done cautiously, considering the child's play themes in a variety of contexts. Therapists also help parents with their own emotional reactions to the play themes, which can reflect some of the core family dynamics. Once parents confidently and competently conduct the play sessions, the process is shifted to the home environment. Parents hold weekly half-hour play sessions with each child and meet with the therapist weekly or biweekly to discuss them. During these meetings, the therapist helps them begin to generalize the skills used in the play sessions to everyday life. Additional problem solving based on parents' newfound understanding of their children's and their own dynamic issues also takes place at this time.

FT therapists teach parents five basic skills, four of which are employed during the nondirective parent–child play sessions and one that focuses on understanding play themes. The four skills that are employed during nondirective parent-child play are as follows:

Structuring. This skill is used to set the tone of the play sessions, one of openness and acceptance. It also establishes the broad boundaries around the play sessions, such as the use of 5-minute and 1-minute warnings before the play session ends.

Empathic listening. This skill is designed to help parents pay close attention to their children's actions and feelings during the play and to convey their understanding and acceptance to the child. The parents use empathic listening skill whenever children are engaged in solitary play. Usually, there are no limits placed on what the child says or on the imaginary play of the child, as those things represent the child's work. All behaviors and feelings are accepted using empathic listening skill unless they are dangerous or destructive in real time.

Child-centered imaginary play. This skill is used when children invite their parents to enter their pretend play. Parents learn to take on roles that are assigned to them, following their children's lead as to how to play those roles. Parents can act in an animated way, using faces or voices to play the characters they are assigned, but they always attempt to determine what the child really wants. Sometimes children correct their parents or give more detailed directions, and parents then adjust their role accordingly. In many ways, use of this skill represents another form of attunement, acceptance, and empathy for the child.

Limit setting. This skill is used sparingly but is important for maintaining the safety and integrity of the play session. Whenever children are playing in a manner that is potentially unsafe to themselves or their parents, or whenever they are destroying expensive or many toys, parents learn to set limits firmly and specifically. A three-step approach is used to ensure that children comply with the limits. If children cannot exert self-control over the forbidden behavior, parents may eventually end the play session to establish safety and their ultimate authority during the sessions. Children are given a great deal of freedom within these boundaries, but parents must be prepared to handle situations in which children challenge the rules. This skill is designed to put parents quickly back into the driver's seat when needed.

The four skills outlined above are described in greater detail elsewhere (VanFleet, 2000, 2005, 2006a, 2006b; VanFleet, Sywulak, & Sniscak, 2010). They are used in accordance with Axline's (1947, 1969) principles of CCPT in which parents must follow the child's lead, providing a safe and accepting environment in which children can express themselves and work through their feelings and dilemmas in their play. Whenever parents are conducting their FT play sessions, they are using one of these four skills.

The fifth skill is used after each play session has ended. At this time, the therapist helps parents determine what *play themes* may have been present and discusses what those themes might mean to the child. This is where parents' knowledge of the context of family life is very useful in honing the therapist–parent hypotheses about the meanings to a more accurate interpretation. This skill involves learning to recognize when play themes are present (e.g., repetitious, very focused, or sequential play) and how to develop at least a basic understanding of them. Therapists encourage parents to share their knowledge of the child and their home or school situations to cast light on possible meanings of the play.

To teach the four play session skills, FT therapists use an effective training model. They explain each of the skills, demonstrate them, and then practice them with parents, providing feedback. Much of the practice takes place during mock play sessions in which the therapist pretends to be a child and plays so that parents can practice the skills. The therapist gives some feedback immediately during the mock play session and then provides a dedicated time at the end to discuss the process in more detail. Parents' impressions of the practice experience are elicited, and therapists provide positive feedback about the things parents did well. Using basic behavioral shaping, the therapist recognizes and encourages little steps in the right direction. Suggestions for improvement are also shared, but only one or two are given at a time in order to avoid overwhelming the parents. This approach gives the therapist considerable control over the learning *process*, and most parents learn quite quickly in this way.

When parents begin the supervised play sessions with their children, the therapist observes without interfering and then meets with the parents alone afterward to go through the feedback process once again. Usually by parents' third or fourth play sessions with their children, they are showing considerable improvement. Typically, parents begin to master the skills after the therapist has observed them five or six times, and plans turn toward the home sessions.

During the debriefing periods that follow the parent–child play sessions, the therapist invites the parents to share their impressions of the play. It is at this point, after the skill feedback has been completed, that they discuss possible meanings of the play and parents' reactions to it. The therapist offers empathic understanding to the parents throughout this process, creating a safe and accepting environment for the parents to think about what they are learning about their children and themselves.

When two parents or caregivers are involved in the FT process, they observe each other's training sessions and parent–child play sessions, including the debriefing periods. They can learn from each other's experiences, and child, parenting, and family issues can be discussed openly with the therapist.

THERAPEUTIC POWERS OF PLAY

Because of its theoretically integrative nature, FT incorporates many of the therapeutic powers of play. Relevant powers are listed here, with brief explanations of how FT involves them.

- *Overcoming resistance.* Children are rarely resistant during FT, both because they enjoy the emotional safety of play and they are eager to have fun with their parents. Parents are less resistant in the atmosphere of empathy and acceptance offered by the FT therapist.

- *Communication.* Children in FT communicate a great deal through the metaphors of their play. They often open up quickly with their parents, perhaps because they already know them and have intimate relationships, even though they may be damaged ones. Parents are given ample opportunity to communicate their newfound understanding to their children, and the therapist offers understanding and acceptance, which encourages their communication about their own thoughts and feelings.

- *Clinical and developmental mastery.* This comes for children through their play. In this climate, they can freely play out their concerns, worries, and traumas, eventually gaining mastery over the frightening or distressing feelings involved. This typically happens quite naturally in the context of their relationship and during the nondirective play sessions. Much of their play reflects developmental themes and mastery as well. Mastery for parents comes in the form of learning the skills, successfully changing their own behaviors, and feelings of satisfaction as their interactions with their children become happier and healthier.

- *Creative thinking.* For children, this happens during the child-directed play sessions. They have the freedom to take the play where they need to, and they do. They find their own, creative solutions to many of their own problems. For parents, the creativity comes as they discover new ways of interacting with their children and solving problems. They can think and plan more freely with the acquisition of new skills and the therapist's continual and non-judgmental support.

Catharsis and abreaction. Children typically play out their strongest feelings and reenact traumatic events because of the safe and accepting environment created by their parents. Play can be very expressive. Parents are able to express their doubts, frustrations, anger, and joys to the therapist with assurance of an empathic response. Sometimes, children's play sequences or themes result in parents' own abreaction about shared traumatic events or their hidden feelings about their children and themselves.

Role-play, fantasy, and metaphor. Children frequently use role-play during FT. They often involve their parents in dramatic imaginary play that also gives parents insight into their children's inner worlds. With the therapist's help, parents often gain new understandings of their family dynamics and the way forward because the children's metaphors and imaginary play can be like a mirror held up to the family. It is often quite empowering for children to play various imaginary roles, and parents feel empowered when they can join in that play with skill and understanding.

Attachment formation and relationship enhancement. Play provides a strong foundation for healthy attachment. In the FT sessions, parents learn to provide a secure base for their children, allowing them to explore first the playroom and later the world, knowing that the children will return to them for support and encouragement. The primary purpose of FT is to create strong attachment bonds and relationships, because little true change is possible without them. Parents' use of the play session skills coupled with the freedom of children's play offer new opportunities to overcome relationship difficulties and create new, caring, reciprocal relationships.

Enjoyment. This is perhaps the most beneficial "side effect" of play sessions. When parents and children can learn to enjoy the play sessions together, they draw closer together. Enjoyment becomes the "glue" in their relationships. Many families continue to hold the play sessions long after formal therapy ends. When asked why, they frequently say, "because they're fun."

ROLE OF THE THERAPIST

Therapists serve as both clinicians and educators. They teach parents how to conduct the CCPT play sessions and encourage and support them throughout the process. They help parents process their own reactions while coaching them in the skills and facilitating their understanding of their children. Therapists also serve as models: They continuously try to demonstrate the genuine attitudes and skills of acceptance and safety that they wish parents to employ with their children.

Therapists who use FT typically gain their greatest satisfaction as they watch the unfolding relationship between parents and their children. While most FT therapists also value direct play therapy with children, seeing the children's responses to their parents in the play sessions is even more rewarding. Watching the moments when parents "get it" is priceless because therapists know they have had an impact that goes far beyond the therapy sessions.

ROLE OF THE PARENT

Parents serve as the primary change agents for their own children. They are welcomed as true partners in the therapeutic process. Parents do not become "therapists," but in their use of the therapeutic CCPT skills, they learn to become better parents. Although they can be skeptical or overwhelmed when FT is first presented to them, parents typically respond quickly and positively to the affirming and friendly relationship that develops with the therapist. The therapist's use of humor and a lighthearted atmosphere during sessions help create collaborative relationships with parents who have sometimes had years of difficulties with other professionals. Perhaps one of the most remarkable features of FT is how quickly parents "rise to the occasion" and eagerly transform themselves. This speaks to the power of self-fulfilling prophecy. FT therapists learn to see and expect the strengths in parents and to use those strengths in very pragmatic ways to overcome child and family difficulties.

CLINICAL APPLICATIONS

FT has been used with a wide range of child and family problems. Because it is a family- and process-oriented approach, it has broad applicability. FT has been used successfully with the following problems: anxiety and fear, conduct disorders, depression, trauma, attachment problems, attention deficit disorders, anger and aggression, oppositional behaviors, obsessive-compulsive and perfectionistic tendencies, grief and loss, chronic medical illness, children on the autism spectrum, and family problems such as domestic violence and substance abuse (VanFleet, 2005; VanFleet & Guerney, 2003). FT has been used to form a bridge between foster care and adoption as well as for family reunification (VanFleet, 2006c; VanFleet & Sniscak, in press). While there are some situations in which FT would not be used, or might be applied later in the treatment process, it has wide applicability. Most parents can learn to conduct the sessions if the FT therapist has been fully trained in the methods to do so. FT can be used for the vast majority of presenting problems.

FT has the flexibility to be used in many settings, too, including private practice, community mental health, in-home or mobile services, child protective settings, residential programs and shelters, educational settings (with parents or teachers conducting play sessions), Head Start and early intervention programs, child/family crisis centers, and hospitals (see VanFleet & Guerney, 2003).

FT also has cultural applicability and adaptability. In North America, FT has been used with many diverse cultural groups, including African American, Latino-American, Native American/First Nations, Asian-American, and other families. It has also generated considerable and growing interest in many different countries, including those in Europe, the Middle East, Africa, the Far East, Australia/New Zealand, and South America. The reason for its transcultural appeal is threefold. First, play is universal in children. Wherever they are living, as long as they are permitted to, children play, and they play within the culture, events, and circumstances of their lives. The nondirective nature of the play sessions permits play that reflects children's cultural background. Second, while family practices and traditions vary from culture to culture, most, if not all, cultures value strong families. Third, because parents are involved as partners, they bring knowledge of the family context with them. They provide information and understanding that might be difficult or impossible for a therapist to attain without their collaboration. Parents often provide important clues that help determine possible meanings of children's play themes in a cultural context. Perhaps one of the most important features of cultural competence in psychotherapy is being able to talk freely about cultural beliefs and practices and for clients to be respected for their own unique experiences. The FT process, with its emphasis on empathy, acceptance, and empowerment, honors and incorporates the uniqueness and individuality of the children and families involved, and cultural considerations play a large part in that uniqueness.

EMPIRICAL SUPPORT

FT is one of the most researched forms of play therapy. Throughout the 50 years of its history, research has been conducted on its effectiveness and process. Research has also been conducted on the parent education group form of FT, known as CPRT (Landreth & Bratton, 2006). A meta-analysis of play therapy and FT clearly showed that parent involvement, especially in the form of FT, dramatically improved the outcomes of play therapy (Bratton, Ray, Rhine, & Jones, 2005). A summary of the FT research shows the robustness of this integration of play therapy and family therapy (VanFleet, Ryan, & Smith, 2005). In general, controlled studies of FT have consistently demonstrated the following: improvements in child behavior and presenting problems, parental acceptance/empathy, parent skill levels and parent stress levels, and increased satisfaction with family life.

CASE ILLUSTRATION

In the case illustration that follows, all identifying information has been changed to protect the privacy of clients. Furthermore, this case represents a composite of three families in similar circumstances. Even so, it offers a realistic picture of the process and impact of FT.

Marli was 4 years old when she was placed in foster care after her alcoholic mother left her alone numerous times with a male friend who beat her repeatedly because she wouldn't stop crying when she was with him. There was a history of neglect, and although Marli was very attached to her maternal grandmother, her grandmother was not deemed a suitable guardian because her own abuse of alcohol led to erratic behaviors as well. Marli liked her foster family, a young husband and wife, but she had trouble controlling her trauma-reactive rages and presented them periodically with serious behavior problems. Marli unexpectedly flew into rages in which she yelled, threatened to injure her foster parents or burn down their house, and punched holes in the walls. She sometimes tried to kick or hit her parents as well. Originally, the couple had expressed interest in adopting Marli should that become possible, but their difficulties in managing her behavior began to give them second thoughts. At a loss for how to handle her, they often threatened to send her to a residential placement if she did not behave.

Marli and her foster parents were referred for play therapy services by the foster care agency. After an intake and full family assessment, the therapist recommended FT as the core of a larger treatment plan including some individual play therapy for trauma work as well as parent consultation to manage the home environment. It was believed that FT would provide the foster parents with the tools they needed to help stabilize the placement, ease the tensions, and create a nurturing yet structured environment for Marli. Marli was likely to benefit from the play sessions as she worked through feelings related to her trauma history and disrupted attachments while forming a healthier relationship with her foster family.

The foster parents, Steve and Lauren, were eager to learn to conduct the play sessions and turn around the negative atmosphere of their home. They expressed a continuing wish to adopt Marli if her extreme behaviors could be controlled and eventually eliminated. They learned the play session skills rapidly in three 1-hour training sessions. The therapist added one additional mock play session in which she helped them learn ways to respond to highly emotional or aggressive material during the play sessions and gave them extra practice in setting limits.

Marli was delighted to have her first session with Lauren. At first, she played cautiously with the plastic food and kitchen dishes, but after a few minutes, she spotted the water. She opened the container and tried to throw the water on Lauren. Lauren stepped aside and set a limit, "Marli, one thing you may not do is throw or pour water on me, but you can do just about anything else." Marli then played with a doll, saying, "This is an evil baby. She can do whatever she wants." She then pretended to have the baby throw the water on Lauren. With just a bit of hesitation, Lauren moved to the second phase of limit-setting, "Marli, remember I told you that you cannot get water on me. If you try that again, we will leave the playroom." Marli retorted, "It wasn't ME! It was the EVIL BABY!" Lauren was silent at this point, but Marli did not try it again. Instead, she played with the baby in the corner with her back turned to Lauren.

During the debriefing session at the end, the therapist discussed the many good points of the play session with Lauren. She praised her use of empathic listening, including her ability to recognize some of Marli's feelings and her firmness with the limit-setting. The therapist then suggested ways to reflect even Marli's angry feelings and a response to use if Marli tried to blame the evil babies or something else for her misbehavior: "Marli, I know you wanted to get me wet, but it doesn't matter if it's you or the evil babies. If I get wet again, we will have to leave the special playroom." Lauren said she was relieved to know how to handle this situation. Marli did not push it further.

Marli's play remained challenging during the next session with Steve, although she chose different behaviors to test the limits, such as throwing things at him and trying to climb up on the table. The therapist discussed with Lauren and Steve how these aggressive play themes were not only testing the limits but perhaps expressing some of Marli's pent-up angry feelings from her difficult past. Both parents were able to see this possibility.

Marli's third play session, which was with Lauren, shifted somewhat. She tried to break just one limit at the start and then played with the baby dolls for the rest of the session. She told Lauren that they had to go buy some babies and that they should pick out the "good ones." Lauren, in the role Marli had assigned to her, went to the imaginary shop and asked the shopkeeper (Marli) if she had any good babies to sell. Marli produced one, and they exchanged some play money for the doll. Marli then told Lauren (both still in role) how she should take good care of her new baby.

In the postsession discussion, Lauren and Steve (who had watched the session from the corner of the room) expressed amazement that Marli would play this type of adoption scenario. They were eager to continue as they began to see the potential of the play sessions to release some of Marli's feelings and experiences.

In her next play session with Steve, Marli announced that the baby she had purchased was very bad. She proceeded to spank the baby very hard for an endless list of wrongdoings. Steve did an excellent job reflecting how angry she felt toward the baby, how the baby just couldn't seem to do anything right, and how frustrating that made her feel. During the later discussion, he said that he had been able see her feelings very clearly and to sense how intense they were.

Because Marli was so difficult to handle, Steve and Lauren asked the therapist to watch several more sessions before they began holding them at home. It was during these sessions that Marli began talking like a baby, sitting on their laps, and asking them to sing her songs and tell her bedtime stories. A nurturance theme had emerged. She also played regularly with a small groom figure dressed in a black suit, calling him the "evil guy." In her play, the evil guy caused great unpleasantness for a variety of characters, but in the end he was sent to jail (a small structure made from blocks). This play seemed reminiscent of her anger toward her mother's male friend who had treated her badly.

With so much relevant information unfolding before them, Lauren and Steve became very invested in holding the play sessions. They had become proficient in conducting them, and the therapist urged them to begin the more independent sessions at home. They each planned to hold one 30-minute special play session with her each week.

During her first home play session with Steve, Marli tested two limits, finally settling down to "feed" the dolls. She then prepared an imaginary meal for Steve to eat, which he did with great gusto. Near the end of the session, she began pretending she was a scary monster who startled and attacked all the innocent people, including Steve. In subsequent sessions, she asked Lauren and Steve to be the monster by putting on masks. She told them to be scary, but not too scary. They tried to play as she wished. Tentative at first, she grew bolder in her efforts to vanquish the monster. She pretended to shoot it and stab it with the rubber knife. Both parents made monster pain noises that pleased her greatly.

After several home play sessions, Steve and Lauren reported that Marli had been behaving much better and seemed more able to be emotionally connected with them. Her play sessions still involved power and control themes, but her attempts to control the household had diminished noticeably. Marli also asked each of her parents, in turn, to put on the monster masks and to "act really scary." It appeared that she was working toward mastering some of her fears.

The therapist continued to supervise Marli's FT sessions at home while helping Lauren and Steve determine new ways of dealing with her challenging behaviors. Both parents agreed that her meltdowns were diminishing. As the parents understood her play better and became more understanding, Marli pretended she was an "older" child who tried to help her parents with new baby dolls that they were to adopt. She told them that if they spanked the babies, they would have to go to "Mommy school" or "Daddy school."

Because of the intensity of her trauma and attachment problems, Marli's FT lasted approximately 35 sessions. At the close of therapy, her behavior at home, school, and in the community had improved dramatically. Lauren and Steve were very pleased, realizing that their understanding of her intense feelings and past traumas helped them make better parenting decisions. The play had brought them all closer together, and once again, the parents were embracing the idea of eventually adopting Marli.

In this case, Marli was able to play out the clinical and developmental aspects of her life in a climate of safety and acceptance created by her parents. Their acceptance helped her begin to accept herself, including the "bad" parts that were related to her maltreatment history. Her behaviors in daily life improved considerably as her relationships with Steve and Lauren flourished. Marli seemed to make a good adjustment at home and school. Steve and Lauren described a more peaceful and less stressful home environment, and they also acknowledged that they were working together as parents much better. The parents had a more realistic view of the possible challenges ahead, but they faced them with greater confidence, knowing that they had mastered tools that would help them deal with them effectively. They felt that their attachment with Marli was enriched by the play sessions, and they were hopeful about their future together.

CHALLENGES IMPLEMENTING THE MODEL

There are several challenges to implementing FT, although they usually can be overcome. In the initial stages, parents often have questions about the value of play therapy and/or why they should be involved. Some parents are so frustrated with the failure of all the things they have tried that they hope that the therapist can take care of the problem without their involvement. Parents might be skeptical about the power of play to resolve behavior problems in particular, and they are not expecting that they themselves would be conducting special play sessions. With excellent empathy skills, FT therapists are accepting of parents' doubts, but therapists typically can overcome these doubts by explaining the rationale for FT and the relevance it has for parents' problems. It is often part of the more intensive or advanced FT training programs to learn how to overcome parent resistance or uncertainty in the early phase of therapy.

FT is not a long-term approach, and often is relatively short term or time limited. The length of therapy is not usually a problem. The logistics are more likely to interfere with use of the model, although once again, they can usually be worked out. One of the biggest difficulties occurs when parents begin their home sessions without the direct supervision of the therapist. By this time, families have usually experienced some improvements and relief from their initial stress, and they sometimes do not follow through well at home. FT therapists monitor this and work closely with parents to keep them involved in the play sessions with their children. Therapists have created an open and honest relationship with parents, and they help parents find ways to incorporate the play sessions into their lives by drawing on the collaborative nature of this therapeutic relationship.

When fully trained in FT, most therapists learn how to overcome the implementation challenges that are common with FT. Although working out the logistics of sessions and the transfer to home play sessions can be challenging, once therapists see the power of the approach, they are motivated to work through these issues. In reality, most parents become excited by the play sessions and the results, and the primary challenge is how to build the play sessions into their daily lives.

CONCLUSION

Filial Therapy is a unique and effective intervention that combines play therapy with family therapy. Many child problems are addressed in the context of the parent–child relationship, which is strengthened in the FT process. In FT, therapists train and supervise parents as they conduct special nondirective play sessions with their own children. As parents develop their competence and confidence in holding the play sessions, they conduct them more independently at home with ongoing therapist monitoring. Some families continue to hold play sessions long after the formal therapy process has ended.

This approach blends two critical features in creating lasting change for children: the emotional safety and acceptance of the play sessions within the context of the most important relationships of their lives—those with their parents. Decades of clinical experience and research have clearly demonstrated the power of FT to effect lasting family change, and worldwide interest in this method is growing rapidly.

While it takes considerable training and supervised experience to master the FT approach, many clinicians have found it well worth the effort as they help parents and children overcome problems and strengthen their relationships.

REFERENCES

Axline, V. M. (1947). *Play therapy.* Cambridge, MA: Houghton Mifflin.

Axline, V. M. (1969). *Play therapy* (Rev. ed.). New York, NY: Ballantine Books.

Baumrind, D. (1971). Current patterns of parental authority. *Developmental Psychology Monograph, 2,* 1–103.

Bratton, S. C., Ray, D., Rhine, T., & Jones, L. (2005). The efficacy of play therapy with children: A meta-analytic review of treatment outcomes. *Professional Psychology: Research and Practice, 36*(4), 376–390.

Brown, S., & Vaughan, C. (2009). *Play: How it shapes the brain, opens the imagination, and invigorates the soul.* New York, NY: Avery.

Caplin, W., & Pernet, K. (in press). *Group Filial Therapy for at-risk families: A leader's manual for an effective short-term model.* Boiling Springs, PA: Play Therapy Press.

Cavedo, C., & Guerney, B. G. (1999). Relationship Enhancement® (RE) enrichment/problem-prevention programs: Therapy-derived, powerful, versatile. In R. Berger & M. T. Hannah (Eds.), *Handbook of preventive approaches in couples therapy* (pp. 73–105). New York, NY: Wiley.

Cochran, N., Nordling, W., & Cochran, J. (2010). *Child centered play therapy: A practical guide to developing therapeutic relationships with children.* Hoboken, NJ: Wiley.

Elkind, D. (2007). *The power of play.* Cambridge, MA: Da Capo Lifelong Books.

Ginsberg, B. G. (2003). An integrated holistic model of child-centered family therapy. In R. VanFleet & L. Guerney (Eds.), *Casebook of Filial Therapy* (pp. 21–48). Boiling Springs, PA: Play Therapy Press.

Ginsberg, B. G. (2004). *Relationship Enhancement family therapy.* Doylestown, PA: Relationship Enhancement Press.

Ginsburg, K. R. (2007). The importance of play in promoting healthy child development and maintaining strong parent-child bonds. *Pediatrics, 119*(1), 182–191.

Guerney, B. G., Jr. (1964). Filial Therapy: Description and rationale. *Journal of Consulting Psychology, 28*(4), 303–310.

Guerney, L. F. (1983). Introduction to Filial Therapy: Training parents as therapists. In P. A. Keller & L. G. Ritt (Eds.), *Innovations in clinical practice: A source book* (Vol. 2, pp. 26–39). Sarasota, FL: Professional Resource Exchange.

Guerney, L. (1997). Filial Therapy. In K.J. O'Connor & L. M. Braverman (Eds.), *Play therapy theory and practice: A comparative presentation* (pp. 131–159). Somerset, NJ: Wiley.

Guerney, L. (2003). The history, principles, and empirical basis of Filial Therapy. In R. VanFleet & L. Guerney (Eds.), *Casebook of Filial Therapy* (pp. 1–20). Boiling Springs, PA: Play Therapy Press.

Guerney, L. F., & Ryan, V. M. (in press). *Manual of Group Filial Therapy.*

Landreth, G. L. (2002). *Play therapy: The art of the relationship* (2nd ed.). Philadelphia, PA: Brunner-Routledge.

Landreth, G. L., & Bratton, S. C. (2006). *Child–parent relationship therapy: A 10-session Filial Therapy model.* New York, NY: Taylor & Francis.

Sutton-Smith, B. (2008, January–February). To play or not to play. *The Pennsylvania Gazette,* 18–19.

VanFleet, R. (2000). *A parent's handbook of filial play therapy*. Boiling Springs, PA: Play Therapy Press.

VanFleet, R. (2005). *Filial Therapy: Strengthening parent–child relationships through play* (2nd ed.). Sarasota, FL: Professional Resource Press.

VanFleet, R. (2006a). *Child-centered play therapy* [DVD]. Boiling Springs, PA: Play Therapy Press.

VanFleet, R. (2006b). *Introduction to Filial Therapy* [DVD]. Boiling Springs, PA: Play Therapy Press.

VanFleet, R. (2006c). Short-term play therapy for adoptive families: Facilitating adjustment and attachment with Filial Therapy. In H. G. Kaduson & C. E. Schaefer (Eds.), *Short-term play therapy interventions with children* (Vol. 2, pp. 145–168). New York, NY: Guilford Press.

VanFleet, R. (2008a). *Filial play therapy* (part of Jon Carlson's DVD series on children and adolescents). Washington, DC: American Psychological Association.

VanFleet, R. (2008b). *Play therapy with kids & canines: Benefits for children's developmental and psychosocial health.* Sarasota, FL: Professional Resource Press.

VanFleet, R. (2009a). Filial Therapy. In K. J. O'Connor & L. D. Braverman (Eds.), *Play therapy theory and practice: Comparing theories and techniques* (2nd ed., pp. 163–201), Hoboken, NJ: Wiley.

VanFleet, R. (2009b). Filial Therapy: Theoretical integration, empirical validation, and practical application. In A. A. Drewes (Ed.), *Blending play therapy with cognitive behavioral therapy* (pp. 257–279). Hoboken, NJ: Wiley.

VanFleet, R., & Guerney, L. (Eds.). (2003). *Casebook of Filial Therapy*. Boiling Springs, PA: Play Therapy Press.

VanFleet, R., & McCann, S. (2007). The road to recovery: Using Filial Therapy to promote healing after traumatic events. *Play Therapy*, *2*(3), 16–19.

VanFleet, R., Ryan, S., & Smith, S. (2005). Filial Therapy: A critical review. In L. Reddy, T. Files-Hall, & C. Schaefer (Eds.), *Empirically based play interventions for children* (pp. 241–264). Washington, DC: American Psychological Association.

VanFleet, R., & Sniscak, C. C. (in press). *Filial Therapy for child trauma and attachment problems: Leader's manual for family groups*. Boiling Springs, PA: Play Therapy Press.

VanFleet, R., Sywulak, A.E., & Sniscak, C.C. (2010) *Child-centered play therapy*. New York, NY: Guilford Press.

Wilson, K., & Ryan, V. (2005). *Play therapy: A nondirective approach for children and adolescents* (2nd ed.). Philadelphia, PA: Elsevier.

Wright, C., & Walker, J. (2003). Using Filial Therapy with Head Start families. In R. VanFleet & L. Guerney (Eds.), *Casebook of Filial Therapy* (pp. 309–330). Boiling Springs, PA: Play Therapy Press.

Chapter 10

GESTALT PLAY THERAPY
Violet Oaklander

Gestalt therapy is a process-oriented mode of therapy that is concerned with the healthy, integrated functioning of the total organism—the senses, body, emotions, and intellect. Gestalt therapy, developed by Frederick (Fritz) and Laura Perls, has at its root principles from psychoanalytic theory, Gestalt psychology, and humanistic theories, as well as aspects of phenomenology, existentialism, and Reichian body therapy. From these sources, a large body of theoretical concepts have evolved underlying the practice of Gestalt therapy (Latner, 1986; Perls, 1969; Perls, Hefferline, & Goodman, 1951).

All the concepts and principles presented in the body of Gestalt therapy literature can be related to healthy child development, as well as child psychopathology.

There are some differences between child and adult clinical work, which will be discussed in a later section.

BASIC CONSTRUCTS, GOALS, AND TECHNIQUES

A therapeutic process has been developed by this therapist that emerged from her clinical work over a span of many years—a process that fits organically with the philosophy, theory, and practice of Gestalt therapy. The process is not linear, though the relationship between the client and therapist is a vital prerequisite.

The I/Thou Relationship

Although given somewhat passing reference in Gestalt therapy literature, the *I/Thou relationship* concept has great implication in work with children. This type of relationship, derived from the writings of Martin Buber (1958), involves the meeting of two people who are equal in entitlement. That is, the therapist, regardless of age and education, is not a better or more important person than his or her client. Therapists bring themselves fully to the sessions, genuinely and congruently. Therapists respect and honor clients as they present the self, without judgment or manipulation. At the same time, therapists must respect their own limits and boundaries and not lose themselves in the face of a client's situation. Therapists may have goals and plans they bring to a session, but there are no expectations. Each session is an existential experience. Therapists never push children beyond their capacity or willingness; therapists create an environment of safety. Though therapists accept children as they present themselves, they are ever cognizant of clients' potential for health and growth.

This relationship, itself, can be therapeutic—it may be the only time that a child has had an experience of this kind. It is not described in words; it is an attitude, a stance; and children, as well as adults, respond viscerally.

When children are unable to form even a thread of a relationship, the focus of the therapy becomes one of finding some way to form one. Therapists must creatively find a way to do this. Without even this thread, further therapeutic intervention is fruitless.

Example: Jenna, age 14, was a court referral as part of a special program to divert children to therapy rather than incarceration. She refused to talk or even look at the therapist but sat silently, head bowed, hands on her lap. This continued for three sessions. The therapist made efforts to engage Jenna to no avail and considered referring her to another therapist. At the next meeting, the therapist went into the waiting room and noticed that Jenna was reading a magazine, something she probably had done at each visit. The therapist sat down next to Jenna and asked her what she was reading. Jenna showed the magazine to the therapist quickly. When the therapist told her she didn't have time to see what it was, Jenna held it up again. This was the first time that Jenna had ever responded to the therapist in any way. The therapist noticed that it was a music magazine and invited Jenna to bring it to the meeting room so that they could look at it together. This was the beginning of what turned out to be a solid relationship.

This is an example of the therapist paying attention to the client (what she was doing), meeting the client where she was (her interest in the magazine), and making contact (looking at the magazine together).

ASSESSMENT AND TREATMENT PLAN

The therapist in this model does not do a formal assessment and treatment plan. However, in work with children, the therapist does need a guideline in order to determine what kinds of interventions are required. It cannot be emphasized enough that the treatment plan is merely a guide to help the therapist provide activities and materials to further the therapy. It is not something the therapist follows religiously and can be discarded at any time. There are no expectations.

The best way to set up a treatment plan is to follow the assessment categories, which are based on the therapeutic process. The therapist then would look at these categories in relation to the individual child: relationship, contact functions, expression, cognitive abilities, sense of self, and so forth. It is essential to be familiar with child development models (ages and stages), Eric Erikson's stages of development, and Piaget's Theory of Intellectual Development. Focusing on issues related to any trauma and other life experiences is important as well. For example, a child who has become desensitized due to physical trauma will need a variety of sensory experiences. A child who evidences a poor sense of self will need many self-enhancing activities.

CONTACT AND RESISTANCE

Contact involves the ability to be fully present in a particular situation with all the aspects of the organism vital and available. Healthy contact involves the use of the senses (looking, listening, touching, tasting, smelling), awareness of and appropriate use of the body, the ability to express emotions, and the use of the intellect in its various forms such as learning new things and expressing ideas, thoughts, curiosities, and wants and needs, as well as dislikes and resentments. When any of these modalities is inhibited, restricted, or blocked, good contact suffers. Fragmentation, rather than integrated functioning, occurs. Children who have troubles—who are grieving, worried, anxious, fearful, or angry—armor and restrict themselves, inhibit themselves, and block healthful expression. They literally cut off parts of the self.

Healthy contact involves a feeling of security with self, a fearlessness of standing alone. When the senses, body, emotional expression, or intellect is restricted in any way, the self becomes weak and undefined. Good contact also involves the ability to withdraw appropriately rather than become rigidified in a supposedly contactful space. When this happens, it is no longer contact but a phony attempt to stay in contact. The child who maintains a fixed contact posture, such as requiring constant attention, never able to play alone, or talking constantly, shows evidence of a fragile sense of self (Oaklander, 1988).

Contact abilities in any particular session are never constant. When a child who has shown the capacity for good contact appears distracted, the therapist can assume that something has happened before this time. Children, too, often break contact; that is, suddenly the child's energy appears to fade, and he or she is no longer involved during a session. This may indicate that the child has reached a point of discomfort and suddenly closes down. This kind of resistance must be respected and honored because it is the only way the child knows to protect the self, and it is an indication that the child does not have enough ego strength or self-support to continue at this time. Behind this kind of resistance is fertile material that will emerge or can be addressed later. When this happens, the therapist can suggest a pleasant activity or game to finish out the session.

Some children have difficulty making any contact at all, and again it is the therapist's responsibility to find means for the child to sustain some contact, which becomes the focus of the therapy. Although evidence of a relationship is felt, a child who, for example, may have autistic tendencies needs assistance to stay in contact. Joining the child in his or her space or providing sensory experiences can be helpful.

Sometimes children appear to be in contact but actually are not. For example, a 15-year-old boy the therapist was seeing as part of a court-ordered mandate appeared very contactful—smiling, answering questions, quite cooperative. But something appeared to be missing, and the therapist felt very uneasy about the interaction. So one day when this boy came in, she told him about her uneasiness. He became quite agitated, saying, "I've done everything you've told me to!" The therapist agreed, responding, "But you're heart's not in it." The boy started to cry and then talked about how frightened he was about what was going to happen to him after the mandated number of therapy sessions. After this, there was a decided shift in his ability to be present in the sessions. Again, we learn how important it is for the therapist to pay attention to his or her own feelings.

Organismic Self-Regulation

Gestalt therapy emphasizes the process of *organismic self-regulation.* Fritz Perls (1973), one of the founders of Gestalt therapy, wrote:

> All life and all behavior are governed by the process which scientists call homeostasis, and which the layman calls adaptation. The homestatic process is the process by which the organism maintains its equilibrium and therefore its health under varying conditions. Homeostasis is thus the process by which the organism satisfies its needs. Since its needs are many, and each need upsets the equilibrium, the homeostatic process goes on all the time. (p. 4)

A variety of what are often called in Gestalt therapy vocabulary *contact-boundary disturbances or resistances* are seen in most of the children who come into therapy. In their quest for survival, children inhibit, block, repress, and restrict various aspects of the organism: the senses, the body, the emotions, and the intellect. These restrictions cause interruptions of the natural, healthy process of organismic self-regulation. In its everlasting quest for health, the organism seeks homeostasis. We are constantly faced with needs, whether physical, emotional, or intellectual, and we experience discomfort until some way to satisfy each need is accomplished. The organism appears to strive for equilibrium by, for example, reminding us when to drink water or eat or sleep.

Children react to traumas, family dysfunction, crises, and loss in common developmental ways. They tend to blame themselves and take responsibility for whatever happens. They fear rejection, abandonment, and having their basic needs met. So, in their everlasting quest for health and thrust for growth and life, they will do anything to get their needs met. Often, due to lack of emotional and intellectual maturity, they develop inappropriate ways of being in the world—ways they assume will serve to make life better and meet their needs. One child may become quiet and withdrawn—behavior that is often positively reinforced. As this child grows, withdrawn and quiet behavior becomes his or her process and way of being in the world, particularly in reaction to stress. Another child may repress much anger, having learned that anger is an unacceptable emotion, but the organism, in its crusade for equilibrium, appears to cause the child to express this anger in a harmful way.

When the child inhibits the organism, adversarial behaviors and symptoms develop. Some children retroflect (i.e., pull in) the energy that should be thrust outward. In essence they do to themselves what they might like to do to others. They have headaches and stomachaches, tear their hair out, or gouge themselves. Other children deflect their feelings, turning away from the true feelings of grief or anger. They have tantrums, punch and hit others or generally engage in acting out behaviors. Some children avoid their painful emotions by spacing out, daydreaming, or fantasizing. Other become hyperactive. The child attempts to adapt by engaging in these inappropriate behaviors—they are attempts to survive and cope.

All these behaviors and symptoms affect the child's healthy contact with the environment, and the sense of self is diminished.

When children restrict and inhibit aspects of the organism, particularly emotions, the sense of self always becomes diminished. The major developmental task of children, from birth to adolescence, is to separate and develop their own boundaries and self-support. However, children have very little self-support, or inner strength. They lack the ability to deal with the environment on their own. It is terrifying for a child to imagine he or she might be disapproved of, be rejected and abandoned, and not get basic needs met. Yet the struggle for separation is essential. When children are thwarted in this endeavor, they attempt to find a semblance of self in any way they can. Sometimes deflection, such as hitting or outbursts of anger, gives them a feeling of energy; however, the feeling quickly dissipates. A child never says, "What I am doing isn't working, isn't meeting my needs. Maybe I can try something better." Instead, the child continues and even accelerates the inappropriate behavior.

Gestalt therapy is considered a process-oriented therapy. Attention is paid to the what and how of behavior rather than the why. Gestalt therapy is not generally a problem-solving therapy, although problems may be used as examples of the child's process. Self-awareness of process can lead to change. When the therapist can help clients become more aware of what they are doing and how they are doing it within the context of dissatisfaction, clients then have the choice to make changes. In work with children, experience becomes the key to awareness. Providing varied experiences for children is an essential component of the therapeutic process. Examples of these experiences are presented in the case studies.

THE USE OF PROJECTION

Projection is a powerful tool in work with children and helps provide many of the experiences children may need. In this context, we think of projection contained in stories, artwork, role-playing, and so forth. Actually, everything we do is a projection—a connection with one's own experience. As you read these words, you combine something of your own experience to understand and make sense of them. When a child tells a story or draws a picture, he brings aspects of himself and his experience to the story or picture. When he can own those aspects, he strengthens the self. Sandtray work, drawings, clay sculptures, storytelling, metaphors, and puppet work are some of the play mediums that provide excellent opportunities for projective work. When the therapist can say, "Does anything in your story remind you of you or your life?" much fertile material is presented.

DIFFERENCES BETWEEN CHILD AND ADULT WORK

Some therapists who work with children see children exclusively. Generally, a Gestalt therapist has a varied practice including individual adults, couples, and families, as well as children of all ages. There are some differences between adult and child work that are helpful to understand.

The work with children is in small segments. It may seem that the bulk of the session is spent in enactment or play or some kind of game. All of this may lead up to the child's making one statement such as "Yes, I get mad like that tiger sometimes" and then closing down and breaking contact. Exploring that anger may need to wait for a subsequent session. Resistance in children must be honored. When children close down, it means they don't have the support they need to go further. Adults can handle much more than children. The therapist might say to an adult, "Stay with that resistance—where do you feel it in your body?" or "What are you afraid of?" These kinds of questions cause children to further lose contact.

Sometimes a child does not understand what the therapist means if he or she says, "Does this fit for you?" The child might appear to break contact and appear resistant. Sometimes the therapist needs to explain, "The tiger in your story is mad. Do you feel that way sometimes?"

Children need prompting when asked to imagine things for a fantasy exercise. It is not enough to say, "Imagine you are a rosebush." The therapist needs to provide some ideas for the rosebush, such as "You can be small or full; notice if you have thorns," and so forth.

Children do not come into sessions saying, "I need to work on my stepfather who abused me" or "I need to work on my anger." Sometimes the therapist must be directive: "Today I want you to make your stepfather out of clay." Therapy with children is like a dance; sometimes the therapist leads and sometimes the child leads.

Asking a child how she or he feels is likely to lead to a vague answer such as "fine" or "I don't know." If the therapist asks, "What are you thinking?" there is often a more congruent response.

Example: An 11-year-old boy was dealing with his grief over the death of his brother. He was severely depressed and unable to verbalize his feelings. The therapist asked him to make his brother out of clay, and he did so, placing him in bed in the hospital. When asked to talk to his brother, the boy began to restrict himself. "I can't," he said. "What are you thinking about now?" asked the therapist. The boy vehemently and loudly shouted, "I hate those doctors! They wouldn't let me come into the hospital." After expressing his anger by smashing a lump of clay representing the doctors with a rubber mallet, the boy was able to talk to the clay brother.

Since children do not have the self-support that most adults have to do emotional work, the therapist must help strengthen the child's sense of self. "Self work" is a vital component of the therapeutic process in working with children.

Adults may respond easily to questions; children often feel put on the spot when asked questions. The therapist must ask any questions casually, quietly. With very young children, the therapist makes a statement: " I bet you were mad when your father didn't show up to pick you up the other day." The child either agrees or disagrees. Generally, the therapist is right in an instance such as this, and the child feels known and heard in listening to his feeling articulated.

If a child cries, especially an older child, it is not productive for the therapist to focus on the tears. Older children hate to cry in front of the therapist and tend to close down if the therapist makes any comment. With an adult, the therapist might say, "Stay with the feeling." With a child, the therapist might say, "That's hard" or nothing at all. The therapist needs to just keep the dialogue going.

Example: A 13-year-old girl bursts into tears when the therapist asks, softly, "Do you ever feel lonely like that snake in your picture?" "All the time," she says through her deep sobs. "Tell me about your loneliness," the therapist says, and though crying hard, the girl talks about the loneliness in her life.

STRENGTHENING THE SELF

Children need support within the self to express blocked emotions. Children who have experienced trauma—whether molestation, abuse, the death of a loved one, or the divorce of their parents—block their emotions relating to the trauma and have little experience in knowing how to express them. Because children are basically ego-centric and take everything personally as part of their normal developmental process, they take responsibility and blame themselves for whatever trauma has occurred. They also take in many negative introjects—faulty beliefs about themselves—because they do not have the cognitive ability to discriminate between what is true and what is not true. These negative messages cause fragmentation, inhibit healthy growth and integration, and are the roots of a self-deprecating attitude and low self-esteem. Helping children strengthen aspects of the self gives them a sense of well-being and a positive feeling of self, as well as the inner strength to express those buried emotions.

The Senses

Giving the child experiences to stimulate and intensify the use of the senses is an important step toward defining the self. Most children who are troubled desensitize themselves as a way of armoring and protecting. Experiences with seeing, hearing, touching, tasting, and smelling—modalities that are actually the functions of contact—focus new awareness on the child's senses. Activities are designed depending on the age of the child.

Brief examples of experiments with the senses for enhanced sensation including the following:

Touching. Finger painting, putting objects in a bag and guessing what they are, describing the feel of various textures, using wet clay, moving hands through sand

Seeing. Looking at various pictures that have much detail, doing simple sketches of flowers and fruit

Listening. Painting while listening to music, matching sounds with percussion instruments, using a toy xylophone and hitting various tones to see which are higher or lower, louder or softer

Tasting. Tasting segments of an orange and comparing that taste with the therapist's segments, talking about favorite and not-so-favorite tastes, tasting something sweet and something sour

Smelling. Providing experiences with smelling flowers, fruit, grass, and so forth; placing distinctive aromas such as perfume, mustard, banana, apple slice, and onion in opaque containers and asking the child to identify the smell (Oaklander, 1988)

The Body

Consistent with Gestalt therapy's attention to all aspects of the child's organism, attention is paid to the child's use of the body. Troubled children restrict and disconnect themselves from their bodies, particularly children who have been molested and abused. The therapist can provide numerous experiences to help children heighten awareness of their bodies. Pantomime games, for example, are useful for this kind of awareness. Children learn to exaggerate the movements of various parts of the body to get the message across. Games that require controlled use of the body, such as Twister, and participation in a therapeutic body movement group are useful. In the safe boundary of the therapy setting, children can experience various self-enhancing activities.

Example: In a group of children, ages 8 and 9, the therapist placed many large, soft pillows in the center of the room. A child fell on the pillows in a particular way of his choosing. The other children then took turns imitating the first's child's fall.

FURTHER EXPERIENCES TO STRENGTHEN THE SELF

Defining the Self

To empower the self, a person must know the self. Many experiences are provided to help children make "self" statements. Children are encouraged to talk about themselves through drawings, collage, clay, puppets, creative dramatics, music metaphors, and dreams—any technique that helps them focus on the self. "This is who I am" and "This is who I am not" is what children are learning and integrating into their awareness. The more children can be assisted in defining themselves, the stronger the self becomes.

Choices

Giving children many opportunities to make choices is another way to provide inner strength. Many children are fearful of making the wrong choice in even the most insignificant situations.

Mastery

Children who live in dysfunctional or alcoholic families or who have been abused, neglected, or molested often grow up too fast and skip over many important mastery experiences vital to healthy development. In some cases, the parents may do too much for their children, thereby thwarting their need to struggle; other parents are so rigid they don't allow their children to explore and experiment. Some parents believe that frustration improves staying power. Children never learn to accomplish tasks through frustration. There is a fine line between struggle and frustration, and it is important to be sensitive to that point. Babies struggle to put the smaller box into the larger one, but when frustration sets in, they cry. Older children lose energy and cut contact. The therapist can provide many mastery experiences for children, such as figuring out a new game together or an interesting puzzle or building something together. It is important that the therapist participate in these activities to help the child sustain interest and energy.

Sometimes a mastery experience presents itself.

Example: An 11-year-old boy is trying to make a bird fly in the sand tray by placing it on top of a stick. He attempts to tie the bird on top of the stick with string. The therapist knows that the string is too flimsy and will not work but says nothing. The boy struggles with this but then begins to lose energy and interest in the task. The therapist says, "I have an idea. Do you want to hear my idea?"

The boy perks up. "Some picture wire here on the shelf might do it. Would you like to try that?" The boy nods and cuts off some wire. He begins to work at tying the bird on the stick with the wire and succeeds! His feeling of achievement is evident in his body posture. (*Note:* The therapist does not remind the boy that it was her idea!)

Owning Projections

Many of the techniques used are projective in nature. When children make sand scenes, draw pictures, or tell stories, they are tapping into their own individuality and experience. Often, these expressions are metaphorical representations of their lives. When they can own aspects of these projections, they are making a statement about themselves and their process in their lives. Their awareness of themselves and their boundaries intensifies.

Interpretation

Although many of the techniques encourage projection, they are not used for the purpose of interpretation. The therapist's interpretation is of little value toward a child's healing process. Although it is difficult for therapists to avoid interpretations, they can present them as tentative translations, guesses, and hunches for the child to verify or disclaim. Through this process, the child can feel listened to and understood and thereby gain strength.

Power and Control

As children begin to feel trusting and safe, they often take over the sessions. Most children in therapy feel very little power in their lives. They often fight for control, engaging in power struggles, but actually these children feel a terrible lack of power. Others just give up trying and become passive and meek. When they begin to take over the sessions, that is, make decisions about what activities they want to engage in and give directions to the therapist, it is one of the most self-affirming actions that takes place in the therapeutic session. The kind of control that happens in these sessions is not the same as fighting for power. It is a contactful interaction, but one in which the child, in the play (and the child always knows that it is play), has the *experience* of control. The therapist is always actually in charge, and appropriate limits are abided by.

EMOTIONAL EXPRESSION AND AGGRESSIVE ENERGY

A core goal of psychotherapy with children is helping them uncover and express blocked emotions. Helping children define the self and feel more self-support assists in this. Another important aid is a form of aggressive energy (not to be confused with aggression). To take action requires a certain amount of aggressive energy. To meet needs, whether eating or expressing an emotion, involves movement. This kind of energy is more than a sense of power within; it involves action along with the feeling of power. Disturbed children are confused by this kind of energy. They either push it down (retroflect) and present themselves as fearful, timid, or withdrawn, or they express the energy beyond their own boundaries (deflect) through hitting, punching, power struggles, and generally acting aggressively. Helping children feel this energy from a solid place within themselves and be comfortable with it is a prerequisite for the expression of suppressed emotions. Experiences with this kind of internal force are encapsulated in a play setting involving contactful interactions with the therapist. Certain conditions must be met to provide these experiences:

1. The experience must be in contact with the therapist.
2. The child must feel that he or she is in a safe container. The therapist has set clear boundaries, and the child knows he or she is well taken care of.
3. The activity is exaggerated. For example, in puppet play, the alligator may fiercely bite the shark.
4. There must be a spirit of fun and playfulness.

Aggressive energy activities can involve smashing clay, pounding drums, throwing dart guns at a target, or playing games such as Splat. The emphasis is on experience rather than content, with approval by the therapist. Children need opportunities to find the power within themselves to be free from the constraints that inhibit their ability to accept and express their varied emotions and to live freely and joyfully.

Helping children unlock buried emotions and learn healthy ways to express their emotions in daily life is not a simple matter. A variety of creative, expressive, projective techniques assist in this work. These techniques involve drawing, collage, clay, fantasy and imagery, creative dramatics, music, movement, storytelling, the sand tray, photography, the use of metaphors, the use of puppets, and a variety of games. Many of these techniques have been used for hundreds of years by people in all cultures to communicate and express themselves. These techniques give back to children modes of expression that are inherently theirs. These modalities lend themselves to powerful projections that can evoke strong feelings.

Some children need to first approach expression cognitively. Talking about various feelings, making lists of feelings, playing games that involve articulating feelings;

experimenting with feelings through music; drawing happy, sad, or angry feelings; and so forth help some children become familiar and comfortable with the idea of feelings. This, together with self-support activities, helps them toward authentic expression.

A Note About Anger

Anger is the most misunderstood of all the human emotions. We tend to think of anger as basically distasteful and abhorrent—something that we would rather not experience. Actually, anger is an expression of the self. It is a protection of one's boundaries. When a young child says, "No!" in a loud voice, mobilizing all of the energy she has to express a dislike for something that offends her in some way, she is not angry as we have come to know anger; she is expressing her very self. She must use a loud voice because she desperately wants to be heard. Her "no" comes from the core of her being. Since the child does not have the cognitive ability, the language, or the diplomacy to express profound, basic feelings in pleasing ways, she is perceived as angry. The child soon learns that this kind of expression is unacceptable—that she may, if she continues to express the self in this vein, be in danger of rejection or even abandonment. Since her survival depends on the adults in her life, she will make determinations about how to be in the world to ensure that her needs are met. The child's self becomes diminished due to lack of expression, and her deep-felt feelings become buried somewhere inside of her (Oaklander, 2006).

Self-Nurturing

Self-nurturing involves helping children learn to accept the parts of themselves that they hate and to work toward feelings of self-worth and integration. Further, it teaches them skills for treating themselves well. This latter concept is revolutionary for most children because they have learned that it is selfish and bad to treat themselves well. They look, then, to others to do this job and feel disappointed when it does not happen. Adolescents, particularly, feel guilty when they do nice things for themselves, which debilitates rather then strengthens. As Oaklander observes,

> Even a young child, particularly the disturbed child, has a very well developed critical self. . . . He develops powerful negative introjects and often does a better job of criticizing himself than his parents do. This judgmental stance, often well hidden from others, is detrimental to healthful growth. The child may say to himself, "I should be a better boy," but the enactment of this is well beyond his power and comprehension. The will to "be better" enhances his despair. Self-acceptance of all of one's parts, even the most hateful, is a vital component of unimpaired, sound development. (1982, p. 74)

The first part of the self-nurturing process involves digging out those hateful parts of the self, which are usually negative introjects, messages about the self absorbed in early years. Children tend to identify themselves totally with those hateful parts, though, in fact, they cause fragmentation. Realizing that this is only one aspect of themselves is usually a new concept. Once a part is identified, the child may be asked to draw it, to make it out of clay, or to find a puppet to represent that part. The part is fully described, even exaggerated. A dialogue ensues between the part and the child, usually evoking critical, angry statements toward the part by the child. In this manner, the child expresses the aggression outwardly, rather than inwardly toward the self. This provides self-support for the next step, which involves finding a nurturing element within the self. Projective techniques may be used, such as a fairy godmother puppet, to accept and nurture the hateful part. Realizing that the hateful part is actually a belief from a much younger age often helps the child to develop a nurturing stance of self-acceptance.

Role of Therapist

The therapist takes an active role in this type of therapy. Interaction with the child is of utmost importance, although if the child was absorbed in a drawing of a sand scene, for example, the therapist would certainly not interfere. The therapist assesses the needs of the child at each session and plans for suitable activities to give the child new experiences to find lost aspects of the self. However, though the therapist may have goals and plans based on assessment of the child's needs, there are no expectations, and whatever happens in the session is accepted wholeheartedly. The therapy sessions are akin to a dance; sometimes the therapist leads and sometimes the child leads.

Role of Parents

When possible, the therapist meets with the parents and the child together monthly. It is important that the parents understand the principles of this kind of work, and a written summary of the philosophy and practice is given to them at the beginning of the therapy. Often, the therapist makes suggestions to the parents as "homework." The therapist must honor the parents as he or she does the child in service of the I/Thou relationship. Criticism and judgment only sabotage the work. When parents feel they are part of the "team," much progress can be made.

CASE EXAMPLES

The following case examples depict each aspect of the therapeutic process.

The Relationship

Jeannie, age 8, was left in a foster home for almost a year after her birth. The birth mother was unsure if she wanted this baby and was plagued by ambivalence about giving the child up. She took her back when the year was up. Then, when Jeannie was almost 2, the mother finally gave her up for adoption. Jeannie's trust level was severely impaired. She was withdrawn and distant even from her adoptive parents, and they brought her into therapy fearing that she had schizoid tendencies.

The therapist focused treatment on the relationship. Honoring Jeannie's mistrustfulness, the therapist was gentle and cautious in her interactions as she offered activities that the child might enjoy, such as coloring together in an attractive coloring book. Within a few weeks, Jeannie appeared to feel safe enough to chat with the therapist and then to tentatively experiment with more expressive activities. Her adoptive parents were guided toward a mild, sensitive, though loving approach toward Jeannie rather than the effusive and overwhelming stance they had previously employed. Gradually, Jeannie became increasingly responsive.

Contact

Jason, age 10, had many good reasons in his life to avoid contact. He presented himself as extremely hyperactive (medication had no effect). In the therapist's office, he ran around and around the room, picking up one object after another and throwing it down. The therapist attempted, in a gentle, accepting way, to engage Jason. She followed after him, commenting about each object he discarded. He seemed not to hear. At each subsequent session, it appeared that Jason stopped a few seconds longer before running on to the next thing. By the fourth session, he actually responded to the therapist's puppet with a puppet of his own. Gradually, Jason was able to sustain contact and interact with the therapist. He was able then to engage in self-enhancing activities as well as express some deep emotions. His hyperactivity diminished not only in the therapy sessions but also in his outside life.

Strengthening the Self

Ten-year-old Julie had suffered years of sexual and physical abuse before disclosure. She walked woodenly, hunched her shoulders, and had little awareness of any body sensation. Although she progressed well in therapy, her body posture remained the same. Some body movement and body awareness activities helped; the most improvement occurred after she was referred to a therapeutic body movement group.

After several weeks in therapy, Julie, who had never had any control over her life, and, in fact, was rendered utterly powerless, began to take control of the sessions. She invented games with a softball; she directed various play activities such as school, doctor, and restaurant, advising the therapist of her role and dialogue in the games. The therapist energetically submitted to Julie's direction, much to Julie's obvious delight. Though this was a play situation, Julie appeared to revel in her power and her control within the limits of her play. This was a new and valuable experience for her.

Aggressive Energy

Julie, heretofore extremely restricted and timid, was encouraged to exhibit aggressive energy in puppet play. Although many children manifest aggression with puppets, it is usually done in a reactive rather than a contactful way. The therapist attacked Julie's alligator puppet with a shark puppet, the shark advising the alligator with great emphasis, "You'd better not bite me with your big mouth that has all those teeth!" Julie tentatively had the alligator bite the therapist's shark puppet, which "died," making loud screeching and moaning sounds. This scenario was replayed many times at Julie's request. "Do that again!" Julie's alligator was now biting the shark with vigor, and she was obviously enjoying his repeated agonizing "death" scene. Further experiences with this kind of energy were employed through smashing clay, foam bat fights with the therapist, and other energetic games. Becoming comfortable with expressing her inner power helped Julie talk about her years of abuse and move toward the expression of her deep feelings of rage and grief.

Eight-year-old Ivan had witnessed violence in his home until his mother fled, taking him with her and leaving behind everything with which he was familiar. In his new environment, Ivan was disruptive in the classroom, bullied other children, and fought both physically and verbally with his mother. At about the midpoint in Ivan's therapy, the therapist introduced various activities involving the use of aggressive energy. Ivan enjoyed playing games of attack with the therapist using monster figures, shooting at a target with a rubber dart gun, and other similar games. Only then was he able to sort out and articulate his feelings about the trauma and his losses. His behavior at school and at home dramatically improved.

Expressing Feelings

A 13-year-old girl named Susan drew a picture of a rabbit that was alone and lost in the forest. She and the therapist developed a story about this rabbit that found ways to survive in spite of its isolated state. The rabbit, though, was very sad to have lost its mother and father and sometimes sat under a tree and cried and cried. When asked by the therapist if she ever felt like that rabbit, Susan began to cry and talk about her own mother, who had abandoned her.

In another case, 10-year-old Jeffrey made a sand scene with pairs of animals fighting each other. He took the part of each animal, expressing much anger. When asked, "Do you ever feel angry like that lion?" Jeffrey began to express his own anger at his father's death by suicide.

Before engaging in these projective techniques, neither Susan nor Jeffrey would talk about their feelings at all. Often, the techniques will assist the child in direct expression of emotion. The therapist asked Julie, the abused and molested child mentioned previously, to make a figure of her molester out of clay. Both the therapist and Julie began to yell loudly at the figure, and Julie subsequently smashed the clay figure with a rubber mallet (after being assured that this was only clay and that her molester would never know). She took great delight in doing this and actually told the clay figure that he "would get more later."

The brother of 11-year-old John had died, and at the therapist's request, John made a clay form of his brother. Tears came down his face as he told his brother how much he missed him, and then, on his own, he said good-bye to his brother as he picked up the clay figure and kissed it.

Not only do these devices provide concrete objects that the child finds easier to address, but also the very act of creating them helps the child open to deeper places within the self. Children can express themselves through creative media in ways that would be difficult for them to merely articulate.

Nine-year-old Gina made a graveyard scene in the sand try and said the divorce of her parents was like a death. Eleven-year-old Michael arranged army men and army vehicles in the sand and said the divorce of his parents was like a war. In both cases, the creations led to expression of deep emotion and, subsequently, to feelings of relief and calm.

Self-Nurturing

Stephen, age 10, was asked by the therapist to draw a part of himself that he didn't like. He drew a figure that he named as the clumsy part of himself. He claimed this part could not do anything right and fell down and bumped into things all the time. When asked to talk to this part, he expressed much disgust and anger. The therapist directed him to choose a fairy godmother puppet from among the many puppets available who would speak to this clumsy part in a fairy godmother way. He did so, and she said, in Stephen's own words, of course, "You fall down because you're not afraid to try things and I like that!" Stephen turned to the therapist with wonderment and shouted, "That's right! I try things!" Integration was achieved at that very moment. The therapist directed Stephen to imagine that the fairy godmother was sitting on his shoulder each time he fell, telling him that she liked him even when he fell and that she was glad he tried. Stephen reported in subsequent sessions that he really was not as clumsy as he originally thought.

Julie admitted that deep down she felt that she was a bad person and deserved her abuse. She made a clay figure of a 4-year-old Julie, the age that she first remembered abuse. It was not difficult for her to see that this concrete little figure could not have deserved such treatment, and Julie was able to talk to her little girl self in a nurturing way. Julie was directed by the therapist to designate one of her stuffed animals at home to be her 4-year-old self and to hug her and tell her she loved her every night. Julie followed these instructions happily and appeared to be strengthened by this exercise.

CONCLUSION

The varied theoretical concepts and principles of Gestalt therapy fit well in working with children. The therapist respects the uniqueness and individual process of each child while at the same time providing activities and experiences to help the child renew and strengthen those aspects of the self that have been suppressed, restricted, and perhaps lost. The therapist never intrudes or pushes but gently creates a safe environment in which the child can engage in a fuller experience of himself or herself.

Many expressive, creative, and projective techniques are used, such as graphic art forms, clay, sandtray scenes, music, storytelling, puppets, fantasy and imagery, sensory experiences, and body movement exercises. These techniques, combined with the Gestalt therapy approach, have been used with great success with various populations, such as adults, senior adults, adolescents, and children of all ages. They have been used in various settings other than individual work in the therapist's office, such as in the classroom, with therapeutic groups of all kinds, and with families. Further, this approach has crossed many cultural boundaries as evidenced by the fact that *Windows to Our Children: A Gestalt Therapy Approach to Children and Adolescents* (Oaklander, 1988) has been translated into 13 languages, including Chinese, Korean, and Spanish. In addition, the English version has been used extensively in South Africa, as well as many other English-speaking countries. Children all over the world are being guided to claim their own rightful, healthy path to growth.

REFERENCES

Buber, M. (1958). *I and thou.* New York, NY: Scribner.

Latner, J. (1986). *The Gestalt therapy book.* New York, NY: Center for Gestalt Development.

Oaklander, V. (1982). The relationship of Gestalt therapy to children. *Gestalt Journal, 5,* 64–74.

Oaklander, V. (1988). *Windows to our children.* New York, NY: Gestalt Journal Press.

Oaklander, V. (2006) *Hidden treasure: A map to the child's inner self.* London, UK: Karnac Books.

Perls, F. S. (1969). *Ego, hunger and aggression.* New York, NY: Scribner.

Perls, F. S. (1973). *The Gestalt approach & eye witness to therapy.* Ben Lomond, CA: Science & Behavior Books.

Perls, F., Hefferline, R., & Goodman, P. (1951). *Gestalt therapy.* New York, NY: Julian Press.

Chapter 11

EXPERIENTIAL PLAY THERAPY

Carol C. Norton and Byron E. Norton

INTRODUCTION

A young child enters the playroom and walks over to the toys. He picks up two swords, gives one to the therapist, and keeps one for himself. They begin a fierce battle. Eventually, the child overcomes the skills of the therapist, and the therapist loses his sword. The child shouts triumphantly, "I am *much* stronger than you. You will *never* hurt me again." This child is a victim of abuse. He is working in Experiential Play Therapy (EPT) to regain the empowerment he lost at the hands of his abuser. Play scenes such as this will be played out numerous times before the child completes his therapeutic journey toward health. EPT allows the child to experience his trauma in a nonthreatening way and enables him to regain his sense of safety in the world. In the process, he creates his world through fantasy and allows the therapist to enter it with him. Throughout the process, he knows he is safe and can rely on the therapist to respect and encourage him toward regaining his sense of well-being. He will reclaim trust in others and will learn that he has the ability to affect the world around him and have others respond positively to him.

BASIC CONCEPTS

Role of the Experiential Play Therapist

Experiential Play Therapy is based on the concept that children encounter their world in an experiential rather than a cognitive manner. They process by getting all their senses involved in encountering their doubts, questions, fears, anger, and other unresolved emotions (Perry, Pollard, Blakely, Baker, & Vigilante, 1995). Activity is necessary for them, since their language and cognitive skills are not yet fully developed and they are unable to reason themselves out of uncomfortable emotions. The activity also enables them to engage in behaviors they were unable to perform during the precipitating event(s). Play is children's natural medium of expression. It is their means of moving through developmental periods and mastering certain skills. However, whenever life becomes difficult and throws hindrances in their path, some critical learning periods may be lost, as they must spend time attempting to resolve their emotions relative to situations over which they have no control. However, play without therapeutic intervention becomes nonproductive, repeating itself with no resolution (American Psychiatric Association [APA], 1994).

With intervention from a responsive therapist, the child can approach his struggles with a partner who allows freedom of expression so the child can slowly approach his fears at his own pacing. As the child conquers the fears on one level with this support, he next can approach them at a deeper level. The therapist accepts the child wherever the child is emotionally and behaviorally and honors the child's expression of his emotions, no matter how intense they may be, as long as the child is not hurtful of himself or the therapist.

Play therapy becomes possible when a child gains the capacity for symbolic play, usually around the age of 2. At that time, the child can engage in fantasy play and re-create her difficulties utilizing symbols and metaphors, thus distancing it enough from reality that she does not become overwhelmed (Norton, 2009). As therapy progresses, play may come closer to the reality of the situation. It is the responsibility of the therapist to recognize and accept the meanings inherent in the child's play and to support the child through her efforts toward resolution. Through resolution, the child is no longer overwhelmed by feelings evoked by reminders of the situation. It is through this relationship of support, acceptance, and understanding that the child progresses toward health. The relationship is the essential dimension of healing.

EPT holds a firm conviction in the capacity of the child to heal and to strive health. The child alone knows better than anyone else about his pain and struggles and how best to approach them. Given the freedom and acceptance to direct his own play, he will create a scenario that accurately communicates to the therapist exactly what it feels like to be him. During the initial stages of play, he will put himself in the power position (the position held by others in his life) and direct the therapist to act and react as he himself does. In this way, the therapist learns about the emotional life of the child. This play may be disguised through the use of metaphors and symbols (Norton, 2009), but, nonetheless, as the therapist participates, he finds himself experiencing the feelings presented by the child in the child's reality. Often, these are feelings of powerlessness, ineffectiveness, apprehension, and insignificance.

There are five stages of the EPT process. They are the exploratory, testing for protection, dependency, therapeutic growth, and termination stages.

The *exploratory stage* encompasses the first few sessions. This time is used for becoming acquainted with the playroom, the therapist, and the general tone of time spent together. In most cases, children first enter the playroom somewhat cautiously, as they are uncertain as to what to anticipate and what expectations are on them. Some of them will sit or stand, waiting to be told what to do. Others will begin to explore the toys, often asking questions about what one is or how it is to be used. When no direction is given to the child, she slowly begins to develop her own uses for certain toys. As she grows more comfortable, she expands her circle of exploration. Very little content is added to the play. This time is used more as an overture of what is to come. For example, a child may pick up the telephone, dial it, then say, "No one is there." In later stages, as the child adds more content to her play, we learn how alone and abandoned she feels in her life. But, during the exploratory stage, the child is merely becoming acquainted with the tools she will have available to her for expression of her innermost struggles. She also must come to know that the therapist will be understanding and accepting of her feelings. The therapist builds trust in the relationship by honoring the messages the child is communicating. At this point, the therapist uses more observational statements than reflecting feelings. In this way, the child does not feel vulnerable and yet realizes that the therapist is giving all her attention to the child and accepting whatever the child says or does short of letting the child hurt herself or the therapist.

Occasionally, a child will enter therapy with such a press that she does not take the time to explore or to establish trust before launching into her content play. In these cases, the therapist should follow the lead of the child, realizing that, at a later time, the child will return to determine the trustworthiness of the relationship.

During the exploratory stage in the playroom, the child's behavior outside the playroom improves dramatically. This improvement, however, is temporary, as it will soon change during the next stage. The shift is an indicator of the child's potential for change.

During the *testing for protection stage*, the child has come to realize that he is allowed liberties in his behavior that he may not be allowed outside the playroom. He also understands that he is given undivided attention by the therapist, who honors his expressions of his struggles. At this point, he realizes he must determine if the therapist will honor his full expressions at the deepest levels. Therefore, he tests the therapist to determine if the therapist will stay with him and protect him while he confronts his overwhelming feelings. He must determine if the therapist will allow his feelings to overwhelm him or if the therapist can shelter him as he allows his overpowering feelings to come into his full awareness. The child presents an opposing situation to experience the therapist's support as the child is expressing needs that are in opposition to what the therapist might expect. The therapist must reflect the need system of the child to the extent that the child knows the therapist will accept and understand whatever personal expressions are conveyed in the context of this relationship. The therapist must validate the child's expressions of feelings. He does this in the play context by showing the emotions one would experience in the same situation. This process cannot be a power struggle. Instead, the therapist must reflect a complete understanding of the child and give meaning to the expressions of the child's opposition. Passing through this process gives the child trust that the therapist respects and recognizes the child's need for security and dignity as he enters the internal pain that motivates his struggle for regulation and survival.

Testing may take many forms. Frequently, children test by saying they want to take a toy from the playroom. Most commonly, they resist leaving when the therapist announces that the play time is over for the day. When confronted with these issues, it is important for the therapist to recognize the reason behind the testing while, at the same time, holding firm to the limitations originally set. As an illustration, when the child wants to take a toy, the therapist might say, "I'm glad you really like this toy. I know it is special to you. I'm going to keep it in a safe place for you here in the playroom, so it will be here waiting for you next time you come. Where would you like to put it so you will know it is safe?"

A therapist must be clear in his own mind as to what he can tolerate and what is outside his limits of comfort so he knows exactly when and how to communicate this to the child. It is important to communicate this in such a way as to comfort the child at the same time a limit is set. In that way, the child understands that the limit is set for safety and not for punishment. For example, if the child wants to engage in potentially dangerous behaviors, the therapist may respond, "I know you want to show me how angry you are. It's OK to be angry, but I'm not going to let you do this because one of us might be hurt and I want to keep us both safe."

Once the child capitulates, the goal of the testing for protection stage is reached. That goal is the establishment of the relationship. At that point, the child is ready to disclose to the therapist, through his play, the turmoil he has been experiencing. It is also at this point that the child's behavior outside the playroom may become more disruptive as he begins to face his unpleasant feelings. It awakens all his uncertainties, even knowing he has the support of the therapist and (hopefully) of his parents. His emotional state will return him to the age he was when the event occurred or the situation worsened (Norton, 2007; Perry, 2001). The caretakers must be informed, at this time that they will likely see some regression on the part of the child. It is important for them to be tolerant when the child engages in regressive behaviors.

The *dependency stage* is the emotionally intense, working stage of the play therapy process. During this time, since the child knows she is safe, she is prepared to face her emotional turmoil. To do so, she will most often enter fantasy play to disguise the content of the play from her own consciousness. However, the play begins to contain the emotional themes that are personally meaningful to her. Because she has established trust with the therapist, she is willing to invite the therapist into her play. The manner of the child's play may be very intense, with the child appearing to be driven to disclose her concerns. In this case, the therapist gains an emotional understanding of the child's perception of her world. At the end of the session, the therapist will feel what it is like to be this child because, in the play, the child has placed the therapist in her (child's) position and acted on the therapist as the world acts on the child.[1]

The child enters fantasy play in a power stance. She may align with the therapist against an aggressor or she may identify with the aggressor. In either case, the child must possess the power to accomplish through play what she was unable to accomplish in reality, that is, to overcome the aggressor. She accomplishes this first by feeling the power of the aggressor. During this time, the therapist allows the child to dominate in the play, so long as no one gets hurt. Initially, the play may be heavily disguised, such as having cars crash into each other. As therapy progresses, the toys used and the style of play become more similar to reality and more capable of personal interactions. During the personal interactions, the therapist will be assigned the role of the child. As such, the therapist must respond as if she is the child, in the earlier developmental stage where the trauma occurred or began. It is necessary for the therapist to respond in the play as the child would have responded at that young age in those circumstances. These memories, which are sometimes implicit memories, can only be expressed as emotionality or experiences, since there may be no verbal avenue

[1] Some children have been so traumatized in their past that they may have become "frozen" (Levine & Kline, 2006) in their self-protective stance. When this is the case, they will be unable to enter fantasy play and will need more time in the testing for protection stage before they can trust in the relationship enough to enter their pain.

to convey these experiences. Implicit memory is experience dependent (Siegel, 1999), and this subjective experience emerges as body sensations, intense emotionality, and erratic behavior expressed to protect the survival of the self (Schore, 2003a, 2003b). The therapist must use sensory expressions, for example, facial expressions, primitive sounds that may have been emitted during the trauma event, and body movements replicating the child's posture during the event, to convey to the child that an understanding of the meaning of this experience is being received. This style of play will continue as the child attempts to discharge the emotionality of her experiences (Levine & Kline, 2006; B. Norton, Ferriegel, and Norton, 2010). During this stage, the therapist receives the child's experience and conveys understanding and acceptance of these emotions through play. In the role of the victim, the therapist is communicating empathy for the pain the child has endured. With this acceptance also comes empowerment of the child to face the most frightening elements of the experience.

Once the child has regained her sense of empowerment, she can then assign the role of the aggressor to the therapist. At this point, the child creates the response that she was incapable of expressing in the original experience. The child will start changing her internal experiences by enacting the empowerment, sense of security, and control that was taken from her during the trauma. The therapist must act in a mildly degrading manner toward the child, who will immediately counter this attitude with a response that shifts the perpetrator role to submission or total silence (metaphorical death). This process occurs repeatedly as the elements of the remembered experiences change. The child will become more intense and metaphorically aggressive as she plays the motoric responses that have been constricted in her body since the violations were initiated. The therapist must remember that the child can play these expressions only because of the relationship and trust with the therapist.

Two important processes are occurring simultaneously in this play. The child is developing an internal sense of empowerment, a sense of control that represents processes that were disrupted such as object constancy or cause and effect (Winnicott, 1999). The child will shame, ridicule, mock, degrade, humiliate, disgrace, discredit, and humble the perpetrator or fear object role in the play. The therapist must act out these dynamics so the child regains her sense of dignity. This process evolves in the latter part of the dependency stage. It ends with the annihilation or death of the aggressor. One may ask, "Why death?" The first statement of the DSM-IV-R (APA, 1994) on posttraumatic stress disorder states, "The person experienced, witnessed, or was confronted with an event or events that involved actual or threatened death or serious injury or a threat to the physical integrity of self or others" (p. 428). Trauma is a fear of death for the child, and the child must conquer that impending death fear in her play (Levine, 1997). When the fear of death is present, even slightly, the level of cortisol in the child increases (Bremner, 2002). If the role is assigned to her position, the therapist must play the horrendous death. When the annihilation occurs, it represents a spiritual victory for the child. It's the metaphorical equivalent of the pain and struggle of the past being lifted off the child. However, play therapy is not yet completed until the self is totally integrated and functional.

Upon entering the *therapeutic growth stage*, the child briefly grieves the lost trauma persona. During this grieving, he will have flattened affect and will move about the room as in the exploratory stage. Here, the therapist resumes a reflective stance as the child's play slowly evolves into making use of the toys for skill mastery rather than recapitulation of his trauma. He moves into reexperiencing his lost developmental stages from a sense of well-being and a newfound empowerment. During this time, he may ask to suck the baby bottle or to be held and rocked by the therapist. He is seeking the nurturing and security he was unable to receive up to this point in his life. The therapist is the person the child trusts to gauge the new aspects of himself in a relationship. The therapist confirms the value of the child and his newfound sense of self. Only with this feeling of empowerment and safety can he move from fear reactions to the ability to assess situations as safe or dangerous (Norton, 2002; Ogden, Minton, & Pain, 2006). Once this occurs, play assumes the characteristics of age-appropriate mastery, silliness, and laughter. The intense emotional projections of previous fantasy play are no longer evident. Play becomes more interactive and cooperative. The child no longer depends on the therapist for his sense of identity.

Once it has been determined that *termination* is appropriate, the child and the therapist still have some work to do. This stage represents the loss of a significant relationship to the child. It takes several sessions for the child to feel complete closure with the experience and the relationship. It is important for the therapist to introduce termination during the first 10 to 15 minutes of the session. In this way, the child has time to react to the idea of the loss. This is also a time for the child to say good-bye to her play. She may return and review some of her earlier play as if to say, "Look how far I have come."

Trust in the relationship once again becomes an issue. By this time, the child is no longer dependent on the therapist, but she begins to question if she has been as important to the therapist as the therapist has been to her. For that reason, this is a time for the therapist to communicate to the child the importance of the relationship to the therapist. However, this should be followed up with encouragement for the child's ability to move forward without the therapist. Termination should be completed in the process without any promises for future contact as the therapist ushers the child from this relationship into social engagement in her environments. The child has now gained the ability to interact appropriately with others and to allow herself to trust in caring relationships.

The role of the EPT therapist has varying aspects, depending on the stage of the play process. The therapist adjusts to the expressions of the child as the child's intrapsychic needs change throughout her development in the healing process. The responsibility is to accommodate the child at every moment in this process.

THE THERAPEUTIC POWERS OF PLAY IN EXPERIENTIAL PLAY THERAPY

Play is the life of the child. If you want to know a child, enter his play and he will respond to your receptiveness by sharing himself in play. Play is the spirit and the essence of the child. One reason a child plays is to attempt to resolve internal pressures (C. Norton & Norton, 2006; Ogden et al., 2006). The more trust he has in the therapist, the deeper his play moves toward core issues and the closer to reality. A child's play is his perspective of the experiences of his world and of his relationships. A child does not play without expressing the needs and motivations that influence his beliefs in himself and the security and sense of self that guide his responses to the world around him (Moustakas, 1992).

In EPT, the child is allowed to enter a trusting relationship that allows him to express his inner sense of being with respect and dignity. When the sense of self has been disrupted or threatened, the child expresses the inner conflict through play. Sometimes, to convey this experience, the child has to function in ways that are not necessarily acceptable in normal social situations. The play in EPT is therapeutic play, and this play is reserved for therapeutic use in a playroom. Within this therapeutic environment, the child can play any way that serves his purpose to express the internal disharmony that has disrupted his self-expressions and significant affiliations in the world. Once this belief is experienced, the child will enter into fantasy as a defense system to disguise the anxiety created by confusion, doubt, and pain. To do this, the child expresses play through metaphorical expressions (Norton, 2009). Play is a metaphorical expression of meaning for the child. The metaphor of "We're in the jungle and bugs are all over me" expresses greater depth of experience than "I'm scared and don't like the way I feel." Or the role of being "an alien who is lost" has greater internal significance than "nobody plays with me" (Norton, 2009). A metaphor may speak thousands of expressions for a child (Norton, 2009). Metaphors express the core of the child's experiences. Through metaphors, the child can express dynamics and meanings that are beyond their capacity to conceptualize and verbalize through language. The metaphor holds the experience for the child (Norton, 2009; Ferriegel, 2007).

Metaphors also stimulate unconscious processes that facilitate therapeutic movement. When the therapist enters the child's play and accepts the child's metaphors, resistance is reduced and expressions are activated that enhance movement in the therapeutic play process (Norton, 2009). The EPT therapist responds to the contextual meaning of the metaphor as opposed to the content expressions of the play. The therapist plays the affect of the experience to which he is assigned rather than reflecting the content process. The therapist may respond to the toy symbolism, the role assignment, the environmental context, and the fear objects such as animals or persons. With these metaphorical directives, the therapist responds with affect that supports the experiential meaning of the play. The child becomes the creator of his experiences, with needs and fears expressed in a form that he can control, conquer, and change. In this fantasy style of disguised reality, the child is never referred to by name but as the role created for expression. The emotional circumstance the therapist experiences is the child's perspective in his life. The therapist is in the child's frame of experience and conveys that back to the child, who hears the reflection through the play experience. Therefore, the play process is the intervention in EPT. Direct reality is usually out of the child's control and power. Through metaphor, a child can retrieve memories with control over the emotional arousal associated with a fearful event or process.

The therapist does not use the child's name during fantasy play. The experience of the character, role, toy, environment, animal, or process is the focus of what is conveyed. A toy is never just a toy. When it is incorporated into a child's therapeutic play, it becomes a symbol of meaning. The following is an example of symbolic meanings of a toy:

Treasure chest. Self, sense of worth, internal value, affirmation, control, security, hidden, search, validation, gift, future value, hope, lost worth, encouragement, dignity, etc. Trauma responses in the dependency stage: lost sense of worth, undiscovered self-acceptance, seeking lost value, emotionally depleted, and wanting personal confirmation. Corrective responses in the growth stage: future hope, encouragement, sense of value/worth, confirmation, and validating self-acceptance (B. Norton & Norton, 2010b).

An example of the symbolic meanings of a role:

Alien. Lost, outsider, different, misfit, foreign, social outcast, need to belong, nonacceptance, stranger, exclusion, intruder, depersonalized, etc. Trauma responses in the dependency stage: flight, depersonalization, invasion, dissociation, lost sense of self, outsider, rejection, and abandonment (B. Norton & Norton, 2010a).

An example of the symbolic meanings of an environment:

Wedding. Celebration, change, desirable, new identity, chosen, commitment, hope, wanted, anticipation, adored, involved, acceptance, belonging, idealized love, etc. Trauma responses in the dependency stage: identity crisis, domination, jealousy, expectations, acceptable, unrealistic, social pressure, and life's solution.

An example of the symbolic meanings of an animal:

Fox. Calculating, cunning, observant, trickery, alert, manipulation, quick, clever, shady, task-oriented, sneaky, intentional, distrustful, etc. Trauma responses in the dependency stage: self-centered, seductive, betrayal, distrustful, persuasive, deceptive, narcissistic, deceiver, stalking, scheming, and underhanded.

When we accept the metaphors presented by the child, it gives the child permission to continue his expression with greater depth and directness. When the therapist responds accurately to the metaphorical expressions of the child, it gives permission to the child to take the metaphorical play to a deeper level. The more a therapist responds to the child's metaphors, the more profound the level of meaning the child will convey in subsequent metaphors.

PARENTAL INVOLVEMENT IN EXPERIENTIAL PLAY THERAPY

Parental or caregiver involvement as an adjunct to the EPT process is extremely critical to the outcome of therapy. EPT views the parent–therapist relationship as a key supportive component of the play therapy process. Parents are immediately oriented to the child's process in the early stages of EPT and the accommodating aspects the parent will need to contribute and provide. In EPT, the three major components are, first, the capacity of the child to naturally use play, symbolism, and metaphorical expressions to convey his or her internal world and emotions. The second major aspect is the therapist's skills in understanding and relaying the expressions of the child back to the child in an exchange that conveys meaning to the child. The third is the parents' responsibility to learn and engage in the process of their own child as explained in the paradigm of the EPT process.

Since this model deals with the regressive aspects of the child, parents will be introduced to supporting the concept of healing pain in the developmental stage in which it occurred. Most children may need to show younger behaviors that are representative of an earlier age (Perry et al., 1995). Parents and caregivers need to be oriented to this concept. Some parents have difficulty with this belief until they witness the regressive behaviors following therapy sessions. Regression indicates the child is developmentally approaching the irreconcilable internal experiences that motivate his inappropriate attitudinal and behavioral disruptions (C. Norton & Norton, 2002; Perry, 2001; Winnicott, 1999). Parents will need to support this regression and offer nurturing when fearful or reluctant expressions are disclosed by the regressed child. Parents are in the primary relationship to provide security and regulation when a child reexperiences the trauma that needs to be dissipated. EPT therapists teach parents or caregivers to nurture the frightened regressed child inside their child. Parents will need compassionate support from the therapist as they nurture this regressive response. Each regressive episode assists the child in experiencing regulation after emotionally reexperiencing aspects of the disturbing trauma activation. When parents can understand the meaning of these responses that have occurred in the past and that have been framed as misbehavior or defiance, they can provide soothing and nurturing that was lacking in previous reactions. This paradigm shift for parents changes their whole perspective of attunement and nurturing for the child as she confronts her issues in play therapy.

Because this mutual relationship with the parents/caregivers is so crucial, the EPT therapist meets with the parents for 10 to 15 minutes following each play session. The purpose is to convey to the parents the theme(s) their child expressed and the emotional and security needs that will come into play during the interim week. At first, many parents are skeptical, but as they see these needs being expressed, they gain perspective and begin responding with more insight and attention to the nurturing needs of the child. This process is critically important to maintaining the child's sense of security during the interim period between sessions. The therapist literally becomes a coach in motivating and encouraging the caregivers to continue to focus on and be consistent with the child's needs. Making the parents more sensitive to the child's process will hopefully be a sustaining skill for the future. Once caregivers gain an understanding of how important their contributions are to the play process, their cooperation usually shifts to compassionate motivation. How parents respond determines the completeness of the total therapeutic process.

The parent–therapist alliance holds one of the keys to the change process. What the parent/caregiver adapts to during the play therapy period is going to become the sustaining skills after the therapy process has ended.

CLINICAL APPLICATIONS IN EXPERIENTIAL PLAY THERAPY

A prerequisite for a child participating in EPT is the capability of symbolic play. This ability is usually evidenced around the age of 20 months. This is necessary in order for children to express their experiences, since they have neither the cognitive nor verbal skills at a young age to articulate their concerns.

Simply stated, EPT is most effective with disorders in which the child is reacting to a situation around him. These may be termed *reactive disorders*. If one is utilizing diagnostic disorders, it is of ultimate importance to determine an accurate history, as reactions to traumatic experiences may often manifest as categories usually considered constitutional in nature. For example, a child may meet the criteria for attention deficit disorder or attention deficit/hyperactivity disorder (ADHD) when, in fact, he is reacting to chronic, sudden physical or sexual abuse by being hypervigilant.

Most children who present for play therapy are there because they have experienced some form of trauma. EPT offers an exceptional opportunity for these children to approach memories of their trauma at a pace that is not overwhelming to them. Since they are the directors of the play, they may dance around their trauma, entering at the point and to the depth that feels safe for them at that moment. They maintain the power, so they can approach it through their own created metaphor in order to maintain their emotional safety. These children will present with symptoms of oppositional defiant disorder, ADHD, separation anxiety disorder, phobic disorders, elimination disorders, attachment disorder, obsessive-compulsive disorder, or dissociative identity disorder (van der Kolk, 2005). If the abuse has been of lengthy duration and high intensity, they may even demonstrate psychotic features at times.

Children with damaged attachment may benefit from EPT. It is also necessary for the parents to be involved during the work. They may be involved either during or outside the therapy hour or both. Since EPT is so strongly relationship based, the child whose attachment is only mildly damaged may work alone with the therapist during the therapy hour. Outside that hour, the parent may work with the child with other forms of relationship building, for example, regressive time with the child, such as rocking and bottle feeding with eye contact. When the attachment is more severely damaged, the parent may be placed in the playroom with the child while wearing a "bug" in the ear. The therapist can be behind a mirror, feeding verbal cues and responses to the parent. In this way, the parent comes to experience what it is like to be this child, and the child gains acceptance and honoring from the parent. The parents, in turn, also have the advantage of receiving understanding, acceptance, and nurturing from the therapist.

EPT is also very helpful for children who are adjusting to changes in their lives such as divorce of their parents, death of a close family member or friend, relocation of the family home, or remarriage of one or both of the parents. Children with these experiences may present with symptoms of depressed mood, disruptive behavior disorders, ADHD, or even learning disorders due to their temporary inability to focus.

Children with congenital developmental delays will still benefit from EPT, not necessarily to improve the delayed skills, but to address the emotional issues surrounding the delays. These children are capable of symbolic play, so they can benefit from the relationship and the support of their emotional concerns.

If children with pervasive developmental disorders such as autism and Asperger's are not capable of organized symbolic play, they will not benefit from EPT. The same is true for childhood-onset schizophrenia. These children may demonstrate symbolic play, but there is no pattern to their play. It is more ritualized; thus, there is availability to emotional content.

EVIDENCE BASIS FOR EXPERIENTIAL PLAY THERAPY

EPT is a relatively new concept in play therapy (C. Norton & Norton, 1997). The stages of EPT were developed by observing children creating their own process of healing. When the stage development of EPT was compared in research (Lamon, 1999) with other stage analyses of play therapy, these stages of progression were identified as the most accurate in tracking the therapeutic process of children. The findings suggested that the issue of trust was not only an aspect of establishing a therapeutic relationship but a constant recurring process throughout the dependency stage of therapy. An additional recommendation was that the dependency stage should be divided into two stages. The author agrees that two distinct processes occur, with the first focusing on the disclosure of experiences by the child, and the second focusing on "leveling" the fear object or perpetrator, which usually persists longer than the disclosure aspect of therapy.

Knowing these stages is extremely advantageous in identifying the progression of the child's generated play process. The EPT therapist who can identify the location of the child in her process can then respond more accurately with appropriate expressions that match the meanings of the child. Because the progression in EPT is a relatively consistent pattern, the therapist has awareness of what to expect from the child at most points in the process. This is a great advantage in providing accuracy of responding to the child in each stage of therapy.

Several studies of experiential intervention models (Ray & Bratton, 2010) indicate that positive outcomes are derived from these relational focused interventions. These interventions use the relationship as the essential component of the intervention. EPT focuses on the relationship with the child (C. Norton & Norton, 2002) but gives more direct expressions to what the child is expressing in her play. During the play therapy, when the child's dignity is made the primary dynamic of the process (Landreth, 2002), the child responds by becoming more present and interactive, which enhances her sense of significance, and she becomes more responsive to the world around her. Being appreciated and respected extrapolates to relationships in the child's environment and to a more positive worldview.

One of the essential elements of EPT is the understanding of meanings within the metaphorical communication expressed by the child during play therapy. One question is the validity or truth of these metaphors. A significant study (Paley &

Alpert, 2003) reviewed records of traumatic events experienced by children (mean age = 2.5). The records of these events by the rescue professionals were attained and reviewed. These children were provided play therapy three years later (mean age = 5.5). The metaphorical expressions of the children in play therapy regarding the trauma event were symbolically consistent with the anecdotal records obtained from the rescue professionals. This would support the assertion that children are consistent and accurate when expressing their circumstances from implicit or early memory experiences in their play. This is also supported by Levine and Kline's (2007) statement, "Trauma is in the nervous system of the child, not in the event" (p. 4). And this trauma activation remains vibrant in the child's nervous system until it is discharged (Norton et al., 2010; Levine & Kline, 2007). Perry (2001) states that the play process must be active and somewhat repetitive. This allows the child to dissipate the trauma effects on the brain and central nervous system regulatory process.

EPT is a brain-active form of play therapy. The activity of EPT simulates several aspects of the brain processes (Schore, 2003a). The EPT therapist is utilizing integrated right–left and top–bottom processes in the brain (Arden & Linford, 2009). EPT incorporates a developmental perspective of the child. Included in this perspective are the developmental processes of the brain. The implicit memories and sensations of the infant or young child are considered along with the explicit or factual memory processes. Memory processes that affect the brain are assimilated into this method so that the child will reveal and convey her conflict experiences to the therapist. When children regress, the EPT therapist must immediately consider the stage of brain develop being conveyed and the neurological dysfunctions that are effecting or motivating the inappropriate behaviors and thoughts. Authorities in early brain development (Perry, 2002, 2006; Schore, 2003b; Siegel, 2007) have emphasized the importance of accessing these memories in providing plasticity for the brain's future development. These dynamics are addressed in more detail by Norton et al. (2010), who give several examples of infants/toddler reactions to trauma and the brain.

CASE EXAMPLE IN EXPERIENTIAL PLAY THERAPY

An infant was born prematurely at 8 months. The birth was extremely critical both for the mother, who was at risk of dying from the delivery process, and her infant, who was critical and also at risk of not surviving. The medical team focused on connecting an IV in the infant. The procedure was exacerbated by no accessible veins, and he was punctured unsuccessfully over 40 times before the connection before it was successful. Meanwhile, the mother was watching while being attended to by another medical team. She saw her newborn son, Seth, restrained for 20 minutes by three staff members without a single sound being expressed by the infant. This traumatic event is known as "mimicking death" in an infant, which is similar to "feigned death" by animals in threat (Porges, 2001). Seth became frozen or traumatically immobilized with no sounds or movements. The mother and child were united for only a short time before being separated.

At age 4, Seth was referred for play therapy because he had difficulty in several areas. He expressed considerable anger toward his mother and would resist letting her soothe or comfort him. Bedtime was always exasperating and exhausted both parents by the time he collapsed into sleep. He had outbursts of anger at preschool and had difficulty relating to other children, especially because he had to dominate all play activities. Also, he could not lie down and remain still for rest times. Seth had an extremely serious case of asthma that relapsed into severe episodes that required medical treatment every six to eight weeks. His mother also described him as very awkward and uncoordinated, with little awareness of his body and usually falling down two or three times during his daily activities (Gaensbauer, 2002, 2004). He had almost no capacity for empathy or compassion for feelings of others.

Seth's mother asked that she be present in the playroom during his play therapy. She was informed that he was the director of the play process and if she were requested to join the play, she would be required to participate, following his directives.

In the testing for protection stage, Seth tested by refusing to leave the playroom at the end of his third session. The therapist reflected the importance of his presence in this experience and how difficult it was to leave this experience and the importance of his play. After several reflections on how important and meaningful his playtime was to him, he reluctantly separated from his play and the playroom. Trust in his therapy process and therapist was established to begin the depth and disclosure of the dependency stage of therapy.

In the initial part of the dependency stage, Seth rolled on the floor like a newborn infant who was struggling to survive in a constricted prenatal position. This is Seth's unconscious expression of the point in his development the play will take place. Seth proceeded to arm himself with knives, guns, and swords. He placed the therapist in the victim role as he had been as an infant who was helpless in the process that was inflicted on him (medical trauma). Seth assumed the perpetrator role of the doctor and nurses who assaulted him with the needles. Seth spent a number of sessions attacking and stabbing with daggers and swords to convey the intrusion his body experienced. This style of play continued with bullets shot into the therapist's entire body. At other times, the intrusion was expressed as snakebites, bee stings, and electrical shocks. This process continued until he was no longer emotionally or physically overwhelmed by his memories and bodily sensations of the trauma event. In trauma literature, Janet (1889) observed this process, known as the disintegration of experience with the failure of the central nervous system to integrate sensory memory into integrated factual memory (Solomon & Siegel, 2003). At that time, Seth also understood that the experience had been conveyed and validated by the therapist, who reenacted the sensations and emotional responses. Seth had a sense of control of his emotions related to his experience and had expressed in his play what he endured during the event. After he knew that his experience was validated in the play, he shifted roles and placed the therapist in the perpetrator role, and he assumed his position in the experience. It should be noted that the parents are doing the regressive nurturing with Seth at home to promote the experience of regulation that was disrupted and had caused his dysregulatory responses. Also, his mother reports that his asthma attacks subsided during this period of his play therapy.

Seth was beginning to play the responses he could not express in the original event. Again, he rolls on the floor to confirm his developmental age. He attacks the perpetrator from the infant position with power responses. The enactment is meta-phorically the same experience that he endured as an infant with the roles reversed. He ties up his perpetrator, which represents the metaphor of the medical personnel holding him down to insert the injections. He fights against the perpetrator with infant sounds and poop (sand) and pee (water from the baby bottle) being sprayed and dumped on the perpetrator. He is discharging the response his body could not exhibit at the time of the trauma. This response continues with shark and piranha attacks to all parts of the body. He plays that a baby piranha is born and attacks the perpetrator, biting his legs, arms, face, and head. The perpetrator plays that his body is being painfully assaulted and devastated. Seth is becoming more powerful in the play, and his awkward coordination has vanished and is age appropriate, now that the trauma constriction has been dissipated in his body. This style of play continues with intermittent occasions of soothing (Norton, 2010) or developmentally appropri-ate play periods. Seth increased the inclusion of his mother in the play, who fought with him at times against the perpetrators. This was his realization that his mother wanted to help but also was incapacitated in the event. Seth's relationship with his mother improved significantly during this phase of play therapy. At the end of the dependency stage, Seth annihilated the perpetrator by shredding his body with the swords and a piranha attack until he was dead. Seth celebrated with a victory party that fed all the animals that had helped him over the course of his therapy. The party was his spiritual victory over his trauma and gaining a sense of well-being.

The focus of therapy changed as he entered the therapeutic growth stage. Seth hid the jewels in the sandbox and found the valuable lost treasure. He validated himself as rich, wealthy, and powerful. Since the role of the therapist has shifted from fantasy trauma play to relational play, the therapist can reflect, "You're worth a lot" or "You're such a valuable person." Once his value was confirmed, Seth shifted to identity integration. He made statements like "I am the boy king who takes care of the world." Later in his sessions, he said, "I'm going to be a zookeeper and take care of the animals." Seth's nurturing and worldview are being confirmed with his positive identity. Seth integrated his new awarenesses by expressing socially engag-ing and relational perceptions of his being. This would represent the claiming of the self that was lost in his early trauma experience.

CHALLENGES IN IMPLEMENTING THE EXPERIENTIAL PLAY THERAPY MODEL

The therapist in EPT must make a paradigm shift in awareness to understand the meanings children are expressing. Children have wisdom of expression that many adults are unaware of when observing children's metaphorical communications. Besides attending to what the child is playing, the EPT therapist must understand the meaning of each expression from the child's perspective. The toy, the play, the symbolism, the metaphor, and the process bring these expressions together to have special significant meaning to the child. Having an adult recognize meaning at this level inspires the child to express more of her experiences to receive validation of her being. Once a therapist learns this process and recognizes that the child responds by intensifying and moving deeper into her emotions, the therapist enters a perspective that brings the child's world alive with expressions of her life experiences. This phenomenon is the paradigm shift that releases the meaning of the phenomenological world of the child. In this model, the therapist gains such a keen awareness of the child's perspective that it is frequently difficult to maintain credibility with other professionals who serve children.

Because of the depth and intensity of this relationship, the risk of countertransference increases and can become a distraction in the therapeutic process. The EPT therapist must remain receptive to self-examination of her processes when entering the child's world of experience. The growth of the EPT therapist is therefore a constant process of self-examination and collaboration with other EPT therapists and supervisors. However, a therapist who is open to the child's experiential world is usually one who is also open to processing her own experiential world.

Another critical dynamic in EPT is the responsibility of the therapist not to interfere with the child's process and to refrain from directing or leading the child. Once the child has been understood in the context of EPT, she becomes very self-directed and motivated to share her experience in her own style and at her own pacing. At times, the therapist may offer redirection to facilitate the process or provide a safer environment to proceed. When the therapist has a continued propensity to direct the play process, the issue of countertransference becomes a consideration.

Being a play therapist is a lonely profession. Few professionals truly understand the intensity and the depth that children express concerning the experiences they have endured. The EPT therapist is no exception. This model requires that the therapist have colleagues she can consult with on the intricacies of this model in order to protect herself from compassion fatigue.

CONCLUSION

The experiential play therapist facilitates the child's establishment of trust in the therapeutic relationship by accepting and honoring the child's expressions of himself and his life experiences. The therapist recognizes that what may appear as aberrant behavior may be a child's only means of expressing the pain he feels. Once trust is established, the child enters fantasy play, where he metaphorically and symbolically demonstrates his internal turmoil. Within fantasy, the child can approach the pain, control it, and conquer it. By entering the fantasy play with the child, the therapist is able to respond to the child, collaborating with the limbic system of the brain in such a way that the automatic fear response eventually changes. As a result, the child can utilize his experience and judgment to determine if there is actually a threat in the current situation. The healing is through the relationship in play. As the child conquers his fear reactions, he regains self-regulation and the ability to trust in relationships once again. As a result, he can move forward into the world, develop a supportive social network, enjoy intimate relationships, and be a productive member of society.

REFERENCES

American Psychiatric Association. (1994). *Diagnostic and statistical manual of mental disorders* (4th ed., revised). Washington, DC: APA.

Arden, J., & Linford, L. (2009). *Brain-based therapy with children and adolescents.* Hoboken, NJ: Wiley.

Bremner, J. (2002). *Does stress damage the brain? Understanding trauma-related disorders from a mind-body perspective.* New York, NY: Norton.

Ferriegel, M. (2007, April). *Healing images of the psyche in experiential play therapy.* Paper presented at the 13th Annual Meeting of Colorado Association for Play Therapy, Denver, Colorado.

Gaensbauer, T. (2002). Representations of trauma in infancy: Clinical and theoretical implications for the understanding of early memory. *Infant Mental Health Journal, 23*(3), 259–277.

Gaensbauer, T. (2004, May). Telling their stories: Representation and reenactment of traumatic experiences occurring in the first year of life. *Zero to Three*, 25–31.

Janet, P. (1889). *L'automatisme psychoique.* Paris, France: Alcan.

Lamon, K. E. (1999). *Assessing Norton and Norton's model of play therapy through a study of a three-year-old's play therapy experience.* Unpublished thesis, University of Wisconsin-Stout, Menomonie, WI.

Landreth, G. (2002). *Play therapy: The art of the relationship* (2nd ed.). New York, NY: Brunner-Routledge.

Levine, P. (1997). *Waking the tiger.* Berkley, CA: North Atlantic Books.

Levine, P., & Kline, M. (2007). *Trauma through a child's eyes.* Berkley, CA: North Atlantic Books.

Moustakas, C. (1992). *Psychotherapy with children: The living relationship.* Greeley, CO: Carron Publishers. (Original work published 1959)

Norton, B., & Norton, C. (2010a). The symbolic meaning of roles expressed in experiential play therapy. *Journal of the International and UK Societies of Play and Creative Arts Therapies*, Winter, 11–16.

Norton, B., & Norton, C. (2010b). The symbolic meaning of toys expressed in experiential play therapy. *Journal of the International and UK Societies of Play and Creative Arts Therapies*, Spring, 11–17.

Norton, B., Ferriegel, M., & Norton, C. (2010). *Somatic expressions of trauma in experiential play therapy.* Manuscript submitted for publication.

Norton, B. E. (2007, April). *Tracking trauma responses in play therapy.* Paper presented at the Colorado Association for Play Therapy Conference. Denver, CO.

Norton, B. E. (2009, April). *Understanding the use of metaphors in Experiential Play Therapy.* Paper presented at the Colorado Association for Play Therapy Conference, Denver, CO.

Norton, C., & Norton, B. (1997). *Reaching children through play therapy: An experiential approach.* Denver, CO: Publishing Cooperative.

Norton, C., & Norton, B. (2002). *Reaching children through play therapy: An experiential approach* (2nd ed.). Denver, CO: White Apple Press.

Norton, C., & Norton, B. (2006). Experiential play therapy. In C. Scheafer & H. Kuidsson (Eds.), *Contemporary play therapy* (pp. 28–54). New York, NY: Guilford Press.

Ogden, P., Minton, K., & Pain, C. (2006). *Trauma and the body: A sensorimotor approach to psychotherapy*. New York, NY: Norton.

Paley, J., & Alpert, J. (2003). Memory of infant trauma. *Psychoanalytic Psychology, 20*(2), 329–347.

Perry, B. (2001). *Maltreated children: Experience, brain development, and the next generation*. New York, NY: Norton.

Perry, B. (2006). *The boy who was raised as a dog*. New York, NY: Basic Books.

Perry, B., Pollard, R., Blakely, T., Baker, W., & Vigilante, D. (1995). Childhood trauma, the neurobiology of adaptation and "use-dependent" development of the brain: How "states" become "traits." *Infant Mental Health Journal, 16*(4), 271–291.

Porges, S. (2001). The polyvagal theory: Phylogenetic substrates of a social nervous system. *International Journal of Psychophysiology, 42*(2), 123–146.

Ray, D., & Bratton, S. (2010). What the research shows about play therapy: Twenty-first century update. In J. Baggerly, D. Ray, & S. Bratton (Eds.), *Child-centered play therapy research*. Hoboken, NJ: Wiley.

Schore, A. (2003a). *Affect dysregulation and disorders of the self*. New York, NY: Norton.

Schore, A. (2003b). *Affect regulation and the repair of the self*. New York, NY: Norton.

Siegel, D. (1999). *The developing mind*. New York, NY: Guilford Press.

Siegel, D. (2007). *The mindful brain*. New York, NY: Norton.

Solomon, M., & Siegel, D. (2003). *Healing trauma: Attachment, mind, body, and brain*. New York, NY: Norton.

van der Kolk, B. (2005, May). Developmental trauma disorder. *Psychiatric Annals, 35*(5), Psychology Module no. 401.

Winnicott, D. (1999). *Play and reality*. London, UK: Travistock. (Original work published 1971.)

SYSTEMIC MODELS

Chapter 12

FAMILY PLAY THERAPY
Igniting Creative Energy, Valuing Metaphors, and Making Changes From the Inside Out
Eliana Gil

BASIC CONCEPTS, GOALS, AND TECHNIQUES

Family play therapy is the convergence of two major psychotherapy theories: play therapy and family systems. Each distinct and robust field of study has flirted with the other for decades because family and play therapists are often working with the same client populations. Family therapists invite the participation of children and other family members when any single family member (parent, spouse, adolescent) requests help. Even if young children are not the focal point of concern, most family therapists will consider the identified problems in the context of the whole family system; thus, an understanding of everyone's role in the family is considered critical. In my experience, family therapists may become very aware of their own hesitancies, questions, or concerns about working with young children in those cases in which the minor children are under the age of 5. Family therapists seem to be more receptive to the older verbal child or teen who can participate in circular questioning, role-plays, family sculpting, or other interesting family therapy interventions. However, when young children remain disengaged, unreceptive to verbal communication, or simply hesitant to participate, family therapists may exclude young children from family sessions. Chasin and White (1989) noted that in actual practice, children are more excluded than included, particularly because some family therapists want to protect children from certain material they believe might be detrimental for children to hear (e.g., sexual issues). However, Estrada and Pinsof (1995) state that no research exists to determine which specific issues warrant the exclusion of children from family therapy, and Sori and Sprenkle (2004) further postulate that family therapists have lacked sufficient training to develop a sense of competence in working with young children.

Play therapists, conversely, usually receive referrals of young children, whom they are trained to see mostly on an individual basis after they have obtained necessary background information from the parents, who seek counseling for their children. Play therapists obtain necessary historical information and then often move to individual work with the child, confident in their preparation to work with young children. One of the foremost authorities in play therapy, Dr. Kevin O'Connor, suggests that play therapy should be thought of as a continuum from child to family therapy and should not be considered mutually exclusive (O'Connor, 1991), and he includes that basic premise in his own theory, ecosystemic play therapy. However, many play therapists feel more comfortable working with children alone, maybe because they also feel better trained and more competent in their child therapy theories and may feel ambivalent, uncertain, or stymied when meeting with parents who seek direct guidance or who pressure play therapists to participate with their children in therapy.

Bernard and Louise Guerney (1964) likely had the greatest crossover impact for play and family therapists with their creation of Filial Therapy, in which parents were instructed to act as play therapists to their children by using the basic principles of nondirective play therapy (Axline, 1947, 1969) and the relationally based child-centered play therapy (Landreth, 2002). In this way, they sought to *enhance* the parent–child relationship, and this model has been widely utilized and researched and found to have positive benefits (Bratton, Ray, & Rhine, 2005). This pioneering work by Bernard and Louise Guerney is the guiding foundation for an updated, shorter, and manualized treatment model called Child–Parent Relationship Therapy (Landreth & Bratton, 2006).

Probably no other two fields of study are as primed and postured for an integrative approach as these two: Systems thinkers are usually interested in interactional sequences and the impact of change in one family member on everyone else. They are a curious lot—adventuresome, in fact—and over the years, they have developed one strategy after another designed to help in the assessment of underlying problems as well as to deepen an understanding of where windows of opportunities might be opened in order for positive changes to occur. Play therapists, likewise, have a great capacity for playful exploration. They are also more likely to exhibit an exploratory nature, embracing ample forms of communication and expression. Play therapists as a whole tend toward flexibility, humor, and willingness to suspend judgment.

And there is a rich documented history of involving children in family therapy and, as mentioned earlier, bringing parents in to work with their young children. But for some unknown reason, in spite of the obvious commonalities and shared goals, clinicians often tend in one direction or the other, with only a small percentage truly committed to full family play therapy sessions. The preparation of family therapists may be a definitive contributor to this hesitancy to include younger children in therapy sessions (Zilback, 1991), and many family therapists acknowledge this fact (Johnson, 1995). Others suggest the type of training that might be minimally appropriate (Sori & Sprenkle, 2004) for family therapy to begin to develop a base for involving children in therapy sessions. Although no known survey is available of play therapists, from years of training in the field of play therapy, my impression is that play therapists also lack the basic exposure to family systems thinking and family therapy theories to increase their sense of competence in working with parents and other adult family members.

It appears that perhaps the most differential focal point between these two theories is the unique and purposeful attention to specific developmental phases: Play therapists attend more to children's developmental stages and capacities while family therapists attend more to family life cycle issues. Miller (1994) states,

> Generally, play therapy works on the premise of understanding where the child is functioning in a wide range of developmental areas, and tailoring treatment accordingly. Indeed, the whole conception of utilizing play in order to interact within the child's worldview is a developmentally-based concept. (p. 7)

Family therapists are more broadly concerned with developmental issues that face each family member at different times in the life cycle (Carter & McGoldrick, 1989; Zilback, 1989).

Over the years of training both play therapists and family therapists, I have witnessed firsthand the trepidations and inhibitions of trained professionals when they approach an area that seems foreign. It is fascinating and somewhat painful to watch the apparent discomfort that people can experience when the expectation is that they relax, enjoy themselves, and have fun! It might surprise the reader to know how many professionals shiver to hear those words ("relax and have fun") and find this invitation almost chilling and certainly unwelcome. Likewise, play therapists, so calm and secure when in the presence of young children, can feel quite challenged by the inevitable possibilities of having adults in the room or reporting back to parents about how their children are doing or having to provide parents with directives about what to do or not do with their children.

These are some of the reasons why play and family therapists do not travel seamlessly from one theoretical framework into the other. However, there are some sublime exceptions to the rule, and some professionals cross over happily, with sheer joy and with great expectations of positive outcomes (Keith & Whitaker, 1981).

Family play therapy is a blending of two quite solid theories (play therapy and family systems) that can serve to both enhance and inform clinical work. Schaefer and Carey (1994) note that "[f]amily play therapy is the generic name for an extensive and heterogeneous group of treatment interventions that continue to expand each year" (p. xiii).

Once practiced and understood, family play therapy can serve as a bridge between adults and young children as well as a bridge between conscious and deliberate therapy work and access and utilization of the unconscious and less deliberate communications and interactions that are usually available when individuals access the right versus left hemispheres of the brain. In fact, in my opinion, great potential is unleashed when the more analytical, insight-oriented left hemisphere of our brain can evaluate and feel enlightened by the more creative, symbolic workings of the right hemisphere of our brain.

Because family play therapy integrates two distinct theories and fields of study, it can best be understood as an assimilated psychodynamic psychotherapy integration (Stricker & Gold, 2002), which Stricker (2010) describes this way: "Assimilative integration retains allegiance to a single theoretical school but then introduces techniques drawn from other schools, integrated in as seamless a way as possible"

(p. 16). Whether one considers the allegiance to play therapy theory or systems theory, the same effect occurs. For purposes of this chapter, I will discuss family therapy as the primary theory and play therapy as the theory and technique that is integrated.

THERAPEUTIC POWERS OF PLAY UNDERLYING THE MODEL

Play is a universal activity that has been observed in its most pure forms and has been examined in the context of parent–child relationships, clinical settings, and post-trauma release. In fact, Schaefer (2003a) notes that generic play has many curative and therapeutic factors in child development and across the life span. Schaefer (1992) describes the following therapeutic (curative) factors when discussing the potential benefits and functions of play: overcoming resistance, communication, mastery, creative thinking, abreaction, role-play, fantasy, metaphoric teaching, attachment formation, relationship enhancement, enjoyment, mastering developmental play, and game play.

The formal definition of play therapy, devised by the Association for Play Therapy, is as follows:

> Play therapy is the systematic use of a theoretical model to establish an interpersonal process wherein trained play therapists use the therapeutic powers of play to help clients prevent or resolve psychosocial difficulties and achieve optimal growth and development.

Although play that occurs naturally in children includes the preceding therapeutic factors, therapeutic play in a clinical setting can provide yet another dimension of gain that appears promising for children with psychosocial difficulties. Bratton, Ray, and Rhine (2005) conducted a meta-analysis of 93 controlled outcome studies utilizing play therapy and noted that "play therapy has a large effect on children's behavior, social adjustment, and personality" (p. 385). They noted that length of treatment and using parents in (family) play therapy produced the largest effects.

In addition, an area of long-term interest to me and others is the spontaneous use of posttraumatic play in young children who experience trauma. Schaefer (1994) wrote a comprehensive treatise regarding psychic trauma in children and was convincing in his conclusion that children can play out difficult emotions in ways that are both useful and life altering. In fact, recent books (Gil, 2006; Gil, 2010) highlight the occurrence of posttrauma play in the clinical setting of play therapists. Although Terr (1990) described skepticism that clinicians would encounter posttrauma play in their offices because of its inherently secretive quality, it may be possible for clinicians to facilitate this play by establishing a safe environment, offering a therapeutic relationship, and providing toys that are literally related to each child's unique trauma and by placing the objects in the forefront so that children might be inclined to pursue this healing play. Professionals trained in the field of child trauma continue to encounter evidence that many children resist putting their trauma into words, struggle with verbal communication, and yet may possess an inner drive to achieve mastery over difficult experiences. In family play therapy sessions, collective posttrauma play is also feasible and occurs when one person's exposure of trauma material affects and then incorporates others' responses. In fact, the emergence of unresolved trauma frequently makes its way into the rooms of family play therapists, albeit in the form of metaphor, stories, and other types of symbolic language and action.

Irwin and Malloy (1975), in describing a family play therapy technique called the family puppet interview, clearly formulated the ways in which play could provide clarification of assessment issues when working with families:

> The family puppet interview provides many opportunities to observe the visible, as well as the covert, ways that family members communicate with each other. The puppet choices, the conflicts expressed in the fantasy, the post-play discussion when members are invited to associate to the story, the inquiry about the relationship of the story to the family's functioning—all give important clues about the family and the available ego strength for confronting problems. (p. 190)

They also describe the common purpose of play and family therapies "namely to stimulate verbal and nonverbal communication, revealing how a family mobilizes itself towards a goal or task" (p. 180). One other pivotal shared link between family and play therapy is the use of metaphorical work (Keith & Whitaker, 1981), which will be highlighted in the case description that follows. And yet another important aspect valued by both theories and approaches is the goal of decreasing resistance and joining with families (Eaker, 1986; Gil, 1994; Orgun, 1973).

ROLE OF THE THERAPIST

A family play therapist is alert and active and role-models and participates when appropriate. The approach I find useful is to tailor interventions to the client's particular problem, communication style, learning style, and strengths. Thus, a prescriptive approach matches technique or approach to individual problems and uses integration of theories, evidence, and specific models of intervention to address the family's concerns (Gil & Shaw, 2009; Kaduson, Cangelosi, & Schaefer, 1997; Schaefer, 2003b). Especially because a family play therapist is working with family members who range in age across the developmental life span, a basic knowledge of both child development and developmental issues throughout the life cycle is a very useful backdrop for exploring the context of the family's current concerns.

A family play therapist, by definition, must be playful and willing to use his or her sense of creativity and humor, knowing when to push a little and when to retreat. At the basis of this therapeutic work is a strong alliance of trust with clients whose willingness to let go and experiment may be directly related to the confidence in the therapist. Thus, a family play therapist cajoles, encourages, teases, and has a good handle on building a relationship that allows for easy entry and exit within the family system. Chasin (1994) states, "The creative therapist who wishes to work simultaneously with children and adults can invent fresh ways of talking and playing that will serve almost any therapeutic purpose guided by almost any general theory" (p. 68). In fact, Dermer, Olund, and Sori (2006) aptly provide guidelines for integrating play therapy with experiential, structural, and narrative family therapies.

The family play therapist is a risk taker who leads the way gently and with confidence. A willingness to become part of the family system in play is relevant to the success of the work. At times, the family play therapist can sit back and observe but often is called upon to participate, challenge, help in a concrete way, and demonstrate how things might be done.

Most importantly, the family play therapist has a good grasp of not only good family therapy theories and applications (and can be led primarily by any of the grounded family therapy theories) but adds to this knowledge base a comfort with nonverbal communication, movement, the healing potential of power and play, metaphor work (and listening skills that identify and value family metaphors), and a willingness to use amplification questions in order to stay with metaphors long enough to understand the underlying meanings that become available to families as an impetus for change.

In fact, the family play therapist is eager to hear, amplify, enter, and cause reflection through family metaphors and recognizes that the purpose they serve is to externalize issues that need to be addressed at a safe enough distance so that clients can process what is needed on a deeper level than sometimes is allowed with cognitive processing alone. In other words, clients have ways of rehearsing their presentation to clinicians and the responses they wish to give. They may be consciously invested in appearing to be calm, reasonable, patient, and so forth. It is literally disarming for someone to be asked to participate in a way that he or she has have not had the chance to buffer against.

Consider the following example of this unique process: I kept asking a 13-year-old client to tell me a little about her mother and her relationship to her mother. She was hesitant to say much, but it was clear that this mother–daughter relationship was conflictual and a source of distress for the teen. Finally, she agreed to look over my miniature collection and find something to symbolize her mother but after 30 minutes or so, she said, "nothing here works." I gave her some clay and invited her to make something that might show her thoughts and feelings about her mother, and she approached the task with great intensity. She held a jack-in-the-box with a bobbing head in her hand (she had taken apart my ballpoint pen to take out the coil for her use). She then stated with glee, "This is my mom. She's wound up tight, and then eventually, she pops out and screams and yells at everyone." Clearly, this metaphor and my amplification questions[1] allowed us the opportunity to move forward in her treatment.

---

[1] Amplification questions are designed to help the person say more, and thus they are open-ended and directed at the metaphor. As an example, I asked this teen, "What is it like to know a jack-in-the-box that is so tightly wound up?" "Can you see the kinds of things that cause the jack-in-the-box to keep winding up instead of winding down?" "When the jack-in-the-box's lid comes up, how do other who are around react to that?" When this child was able to choose a deer for her father and a butterfly for herself, we continued the discussion of what happens when the deer sees the jack-in-the-box flip the lid, what happens when the butterfly listens to the jack-in-the-box scream and yell, and eventually, what kinds of things would the deer and the butterfly like to say to the jack-in-the-box when the windup is occurring, when the lid comes up, and when the screaming begins. Eventually, in a family therapy session, this teen was able to show her mother the jack-in-the-box, and another layer of helpful therapeutic conversation ensued.

ROLE OF THE PARENT

Over the years, I have had remarkable experiences watching families engage in family play therapy. I admit that the parents' initial responses might include quizzical looks, provocative statements, and/or various levels of unwillingness to participate in play sessions. However, when I can cajole parents by telling them to "trust me" and "see if you can be a little curious about how this goes," the results have been remarkable.

And just as remarkable has been the myriad ways in which parents hesitate to participate in activities or conversations that cause them discomfort. So some parents simply refuse, miss appointments, and speak loudly through actions. For example, one parent "fell asleep" while her family (husband and children) built a sand tray together.

CLINICAL APPLICATIONS

Family play therapy lends itself to ample use when working with children of all ages. Sometimes young children aged 4 to 8 may participate more fully and more quickly, but never underestimate the abilities of older children, preteens, and teens to put aside their hesitancies in favor of doing something new and exciting with their parents. With some older children who withdraw from requests for verbal communication, playing in a variety of dynamic, physical, creative, or artistic ways may be a welcome relief. In my experience working with grandparents and other adult family members, there appears to be an initial self-consciousness or performance anxiety, which appears responsive to constant reassurance that the product is less important than enjoying the process of playing.

EMPIRICAL SUPPORT

I am not aware of any empirical support for family play therapy at this time.

CASE ILLUSTRATION

The Global Nuclear Threat

The phone calls from Mrs. Tracy R. had been cordial and brief. She was referred by the school counselor, who believed that 9-year-old Michelle R. had been abused by her 11-year-old sister, Margie. Mrs. R. was quick to point out that her daughters got along like any normal siblings, that they teased each other a lot, that they fought and then made up quickly, and that they were good at provoking each other. There had been no abuse, she stated emphatically, and she surely would recognize abuse if she saw it. She went on to say that the school counselor was truly exaggerating and overreacting. I told her that I was happy to hear that the girls had a normal relationship and that she would be on alert for abuse, and at the same time I asserted that Michelle's broken arm (and the fact that it was a nonaccidental injury) was sufficient to alarm anyone. Mrs. R. insisted that this was an accidental injury and should not have gotten the attention it did, especially since both girls had been in this school since kindergarten, and the teachers knew what kind of mother she was and what kind of home she had. I empathized with Mrs. R. and then made several appointments, which she was not able to keep for one reason or another. Each time she canceled, she was cordial and brief: Something came up, she was ill, she did not have transportation, or one of her children was ill. I thanked her for calling each time and made another appointment. By the fifth cancellation, I decided that I would make a house call and see if I could make personal contact with this mother, who seemed hesitant to come into therapy as requested by her children's school counselor and child protective services (who had closed the case but encouraged the mother to attend therapy).

She appeared a little startled when I rang her doorbell, stating that she thought I would be coming 2 hours later. I heard that as more ambivalence and did not acquiesce to her request that I come back later. Instead, I told her that I had other appointments to keep, and this was the time we had set up by phone. She was reluctant but slowly warmed up.

She was still angry at the school's referral to me but said she realized that this had nothing to do with me and she shouldn't feel resentful toward me (I agreed wholeheartedly). I told her that no one likes to be told what to do or to be misunderstood. She went on to reiterate that the broken arm had been an accident resulting from a fall. Mrs. R. said that the fall had happened when the girls were wrestling at the top of the stairs. She also said that she had punished Margie for pushing Michelle, even in jest, and that Michelle felt very sorry indeed. Neither child was there in the first half hour of our meeting, even though I had requested that all family members attend. I learned that they would arrive in the middle of my conversation with their mother, and I told her I looked forward to meeting them. I proceeded to talk with Mrs. R. about her life in general and quickly learned that she had many areas of sensitivity, including her family history, her first marriage, her employment history, her current marriage, and her children's relationship to her husband. In other words, it seemed that there was no "safe topic," nothing personal that Mrs. R. wished to volunteer, and no apparent willingness to share her innermost thoughts and feelings with this therapist. I quickly got the feeling that Mrs. R. would be elusive with me in her home, on the phone, or in my office. When the children arrived, it was as if the troops closed ranks, and the three of them together seemed to be defensive and in a happy alliance against outsiders. Or they simply were angered at having to talk to someone about the accident that wouldn't go away.

I greeted Michelle and Margie as I would any other young children. They were very reluctant from the outset. I noticed that they scanned their mother's face when they walked in and seemed to understand that I was from the outside, someone not genuinely invited or welcome to be there. I made a few social comments about their shoes and hair barrettes as well as Michelle's cast, now fully covered by tons of graffiti from schoolmates. There was a beautiful graphic of an electric guitar, and when I asked Michelle, she said that Travis had drawn it for her and that he likes guitars. When I asked who Travis was (and noted that I loved that name), Mrs. R. said, "Travis is their stepfather, well, really, more like their dad than their own dad."

The kids eventually sat politely in their chairs and seemed visibly uncomfortable and uptight. I was a little concerned at how polite they were but proceeded to tell them the following: "I know that your mom told you that I would be coming over at some point to talk with your family about the accident that happened and the fact that Michelle ended up with a broken arm." Silence. "You probably know that the school counselor told your mom that she had to participate in counseling with her family in order to make sure that this kind of accident doesn't happen again." Silence. "Sometimes, unless you know why accidents occur, they are hard to prevent from happening again." Margie chimed up, "Does Travis have to be here, too?" I responded affirmatively and told the girls and their mom that having him participate would be ideal. Mrs. R. noted that she didn't see the point in any of this and said that Travis "wasn't even home" when the accident occurred. I responded that even if he wasn't home, he more than likely had a reaction when he heard the news and may have even gone to the hospital with Michelle (she nodded her head in agreement). I told the family that I am a family play therapist and that usually I meet with families and sometimes we talk and sometimes we do some play activities. The girls perked up momentarily until their mother interrupted with abrupt questions about how much this would cost, what day and time the appointments would be, and how far my office was from her house. My office was located nearby, about 15 minutes away, but when I asked Mrs. R. if she would be driving or taking public transportation, she looked uneasy. Then she told me that Travis would likely be driving them to sessions (the obvious implication that she would not attend). Travis was not expected for a while, so I wrote down some possible times and dates, along with directions. I also clarified that the mother's presence was required. Mrs. R. agreed to come with the family but missed yet another appointment, this time saying that Travis had to work late and they therefore couldn't make it. She called about half an hour into the session, leaving a voicemail message that was polite and very brief. This tendency to cancel appointments in such a polite and dismissive way increased my curiosity because it felt to me to be about more than simple noncompliance.

I called Mrs. R. back and made another appointment for the family. At this time, she told me that the girls thought this was "stupid" and did not know why they had to attend. By this time, Michelle had her cast taken off, everything at home was "fine," and they felt that the accident was long behind them and would not happen again. I insisted that accidents are important to understand and learn from and that the school was also insisting on this. In fact, the school was threatening the mother with calling child protective services again if she did not attend family counseling. I reminded her of how seriously the school took this, especially because Michelle had indicated to the school counselor that there were problems between herself and her sister. Finally, I asked the mother if it would be all right with her if I simply came to their house for the family therapy sessions because it seemed truly difficult for them go get to my office. I told her that I offered this option from time to time to other families and that I would be happy to do this for them. Mrs. R. agreed reluctantly, and within five days I arrived with a basket full of colorful and interesting puppets.

In this, our first official family therapy session, I was happy to meet Travis and to have the whole family together. I repeated some of my initial comments for Travis and noted that as a family play therapist, I would bring toys and art supplies from time to time. "Today, I brought a bunch of puppets, as you can see!" The children seemed legitimately interested now, as Mrs. R. and Travis looked at each other and rolled their eyes. "You're going to have to trust me on this. . . . I work with lots of families, and even though parents may initially have the same kind of questions and reactions that you have right now, most of the time, this can be very helpful work. At least I always like to give it a try because I believe it can be helpful!" Mrs. R. asked if she would have to pay her reduced fee for a meeting that included toys. I said, "Yes, this is just another way to do therapy."

As I was talking with the parents, I started putting all the puppets on the coffee table, and the children seemed excited as they looked around for favorites. I then gave the following directive to the family: "What I would like you to do is (as a family) to make up a story that has a beginning, a middle, and an end." I added that there were few rules, simply "acting out rather than narrating the story," and ensuring that the family was making up a story and they were not retelling a popular story like Cinderella or Pinocchio. I told them that I would like them to have some time together to develop the story and I would move to the other room. I asked them to let me know when they were done making up the story, and I would return (as an audience member) to listen to the story they had created together as a family. I walked into the other room, pulled out a chair at their dining room table, and pulled out paperwork so that I could look busy and appear very unobtrusive. There was a brief period of silence followed by muffled laughter and conversation. I had left the videotape machine "on" and they knew that I would be taping and that, in weeks to come, we would watch the videotaped story together. The children did some initial mugging for the camera, and then the family seemed to focus on the task at hand. What I heard from the other room and what I saw when I played back the camera was a family whose resistance had decreased significantly and a family engaged in playful attempts to follow the assignment I had given them. It took them a full 30 minutes of back-and-forth dialogue from all four members (especially the mother) for the story to unfold to its conclusion. Throughout, I felt great optimism that I had found a way to break through the family's initial hesitancy to family play therapy.

They did not signal me at the completion of their story. Instead, it appeared that their hesitancy to engage with me had resurfaced, as they did some "stalling" as the clock counted down. Finally, when the buzz of talking and laughing had died down, I entered the room, asking, "Are you all ready to start telling me your story?" They agreed that they were, and I began to set the stage for listening to their story by having everyone tell me their puppets' names and what role they were playing in the story. This introduction serves two purposes: To understand what puppets are being used by whom and to give everyone a chance to say something about the role of their puppet in the story.[2]

Some things were immediately apparent when the family introduced their puppets: Each of them had two puppets in hand, and each of them (except the mother) had one puppet whose role was authoritative in nature. Specifically, the father picked a raccoon and a judge; Michelle picked a small lion and a lawyer; and Margie picked a spider and a policeman named Pete. Mother picked an innocent bystander and (Elizabeth H.) Goldilocks.

After introductions that briefly revealed some of the family dynamics (mother leading the way, father compliant and cooperative, Margie with a great deal of energy and power, and Michelle rather disempowered and almost invisible and without a voice), I listened with great interest as their story unfolded.

Father speaks first with a raccoon, using a high-pitched, funny little voice: "I'm Rocky Raccoon and I'm one of the peaceful animals in the forest, and I am always looking for food but generally I just mind my own business and try to get along with everyone!" Then he pulled up his right hand to show the judge, and with a very deep, serious voice, he proclaimed, "And I'm the judge, and I'm here in case anybody needs me or needs my advice." The family laughed a little at Travis's role-plays and funny voices.

Mother followed: "And I'm Goldilocks and I like to go out into the forest, and wait, oh, that's right, I'm Elizabeth H. Goldilocks and I like to go out and see the forest." And using her other puppet, she states, "And I'm the innocent bystander." Michelle goes next and introduces a sock lion on her hand, who moves his mouth gingerly and says, "I'm a lion," in a barely audible voice. She then grabs the other puppet and says, "And I'm Frank the lawyer!" At that point, Margie bursts in with a very loud voice and using a large tarantula puppet on her left hand says, "I'm a spider and I love to eat bugs, and I'm really worried because the nuclear power is making all my plants and bugs turn grody." Then she introduces her second puppet and says, "And I'm Policeman Pete, and I'm here to arrest these people who are involved in a peaceful protest."

At this point, I am intrigued. I think to myself that authority and power must be important in this family. I wonder about the presence of a nuclear threat so powerful that it can contaminate everything on this planet and could threaten the life of animals living in the forest. I also wonder what Goldilocks will explore first and how easy or difficult it will be for the policeman to round up all the peaceful protesters. Finally, the identified patient, Michelle, appears to be barely noticeable in the room (the smallest person) and in the story (she never uses her voice). I also notice that the mother's two puppets reveal an incongruence between being active (Goldilocks) and passive (innocent bystander). These and many other questions loom large as the story

---

[2]Asking family members to introduce their puppets and state their role was originally requested by the originators of the family puppet interview (Irwin & Malloy, 1975). I respectfully acknowledge and honor their original technique of family puppet interviews and have modified it to be more therapeutic in nature (Gil, 1994). In particular, the clinical response to the story is much more amplifying and interested in the family's metaphors and less hurried to invite cerebral activity to the story, such as immediately asking for the name of the story, asking family members for similarities to the story, and so on.

is told, as I try to listen to what is being said and not said, and as I watch as family members move around, negotiate, contribute to the story, withdraw and approach, and participate in the task designed for optimal family participation. I certainly don't have answers to any of the questions that surface for me, but I am filled with curiosity to see where this story goes as the family does a dramatic representation of their story.

The story: The actual story is told very quickly—in less than 10 minutes. However, the preparation to tell the story took about 40 minutes, until I interrupted the laughing and talking to ask if they were ready to tell me their story.

Mother starts the story by turning to the raccoon and the judge and asking them to join her on an adventure to go explore the forest and see about the nuclear power plant and what can be done to fix the problem it is creating for everyone. The judge and raccoon acquiesce, and so they move on together (four puppets) to ask the small lion and "Frank the Lawyer" to join them on their quest to close the Livermore lab so that their bug population and grass won't be contaminated and kill all the animals and everything around them. The little lion makes barely a whimper of agreement and follows the lead of the four energetic puppets now leading the brigade. They come upon a spider and encourage him to join their cause and to come along to engage in a peaceful protest of the Lawrence Livermore Lab. The spider agrees, bemoaning that his bug population is being poisoned. But just as soon as all the creatures are joined as one to conduct a peaceful protest, Policeman Pete comes along and threatens to arrest them all. The arguments from the protesters fall on deaf ears, and Policeman Pete quickly gathers them up to take them to see the judge, who will decide their fate. (This brings to mind how Margie's hitting Michelle rounded the family up for therapy.)

The judge sits back and says, "Well, well, well, what do we have here?" He turns to the policeman and asks him, "What is the problem with these people?" Policeman Pete sounds almost apologetic as he tells the judge that he's "sorry to bother" the judge but that these people have been very disruptive and they are disturbing the peace. He asks the judge to make a decision about what should happen to them. The judge asks, "Who is the ringleader here?" and when Elizabeth H. Goldilocks replies that she is, he asks her for an explanation, Goldilocks explains, "Well, your Honor, the problem is the Livermore Lab and their nuclear power and the fact that they are not taking care of their waste, and consequently, everything is being affected and everything is dying out and their lives are endangered and it's time for the judge to take some action!!"

The judge is rendered completely speechless and tries to get his footing, but then he states, "Well, I don't know what to say. Clearly, there are some problems going on here, and I think I better send this matter to the legislature so that they can make a decision." Elizabeth appears deflated that the matter will not be settled and makes another brief appeal, but the judge holds firm with his prior decision, and then the story comes to an abrupt halt. Suddenly, Michelle, who has not been heard from most of this story, pipes up and says, "What about Frank the Lawyer? I didn't use him." Mrs. R. replies, "That's OK, we didn't need him," and Michelle quickly retreats her puppet.

In the original Irwin and Malloy interview technique (1975), they encourage the clinicians to interview the family members *about* their puppets. My expanded technique instructs clinicians to interview the puppets directly, encouraging the family members to stay in role. In this way, the family members stay with the story metaphor a while longer, and they are not encouraged to shift to a more cerebral activity, losing the potential for amplification of the metaphor.[3]

After this story, I admit to being stifled, not only because I had a feeling that this story was full of relevance and meaning but also because we were about to run over our allotted time. In order to allow myself to sit with the story and learn from it, I told them that I would return next week with a videotape that we could watch so that they could give me their thoughts about the story they had authored and acted out. I must have watched the story 10 times prior to our next meeting, again a home visit to avoid mishaps in scheduling.

When I first came in, the children greeted me happily. I returned the warm greeting and then asked them to take a seat (they seemed on pins and needles to watch themselves on tape). I first asked them what they remembered about the story they had told last week and if they had any thoughts or feelings about anything that happened. Travis spoke first, saying that he felt badly that he had delegated the duty of making a decision to a higher power. "She was *not* happy about that," Travis said, pointing to Mrs. R. with his eyes. She nudged him on the arm and said, "Hey, buddy, that's what you always do, and sometimes you need to stand up for yourself." He pretended to be injured by her punch, and everyone laughed. Tilly and Travis's marital dynamics were on display, and the mother was registering a complaint, following that with laughter, which seemed to decrease its impact.

Michelle said in a small voice, sliding backwards into a big couch, "They were mean to me. They told me that Frank was supposed to talk to the judge, and then they didn't let me talk and told me they didn't really want me to be with them." Mrs. R. said, "Oh goodness, Miss Drama Queen, there was just too much going on. You could have talked if you wanted, but then it was too late—the judge had already passed the problem to someone else." I noticed that Michelle just dug more into her seat, and they moved on quickly. Finally, Margie said, "Well, there was sure a lot of stuff going on with everybody being worried about the bugs they ate. It was kind of weird." When I asked if the spider had been worried about what he ate, she said, "No, not me; those other creatures are scared, not me." I realized then that I had not followed up on Michelle's statement, so I asked her quickly if the lion was worried or scared about the bug population or the forest?" She said, shyly, "No, the lion isn't that hungry and doesn't like bugs." Margie then said, "That's right, that lion is retarded!" It seemed that Margie did not miss a chance to be rude to her little sister, and the teasing did not seem mutual at all.

---

[3] Beginning therapists find it very difficult to generate questions or observations designed to help the clients stay in and expand the metaphors they have introduced. In my opinion, this may or may not come naturally but definitely can be refined with practice. If questions do not come easily, clinicians can thank the family, end the session, or move on to something else, telling the family that it will be useful to spend some time reviewing the videotape to be discussed at the next session. Crafting questions takes practice, and clinicians are encouraged to take the time to do so.

I then said that I wanted them to watch the story and that after they watched it, I wanted them to put on the same puppets and I wanted to chat with them a little more. They watched the puppet story, pointing, laughing, teasing, and feeling alternately fascinated and embarrassed. Finally, I turned it off, and they put their puppets on their hands. By then I had generated a lot of questions and comments designed to amplify this story. The following questions seemed to hit a raw nerve and generated interesting commentary and eventual revelations:

> What is it like for the animals in the forest to feel that their forest is being contaminated by nuclear waste?
>
> What kinds of things have the forest animals done in the past to deal with the threat of nuclear waste?

And the question that got the most response from Margie:

> What was it like in the forest before the animals had to deal with the threat of nuclear waste?
>
> Margie said, "Yeah, mom, was there ever a time when that nuclear threat wasn't there in somebody's mind?"

Mrs. R. looked uncomfortable as I said, "There must have been a time when the animals in the forest didn't have to worry." These questions led to a shift (transition) from the story's metaphor to actual family issues. Once the family makes that shift, I follow.

Margie piped up again, "Go ahead, Mom, tell her, tell her that there is always something to be afraid of and that you're always thinking bad things about everything and that you think everyone is going to hurt us."

I turned to Mrs. R. and Travis and asked them to respond to what Margie was saying. Mrs. R. spoke up first and said, "I keep trying to explain to the kids that they can't be too safe and that there are bad things happening everywhere and they don't seem to want to believe me." Margie spoke up again loudly, "Why do you say 'they,' Mom? You know very well that Michelle is getting just as weird as YOU!" I could tell by the profound silence that entered the room that Margie had just exposed something important.

"Hmmmm," I said, "Margie, what do you mean about Michelle 'getting weird or thinking weird things?'" "Tell her, Mom, tell her, because if you don't, I will." Travis stepped up to the plate, and this time he was not perplexed or ambivalent; he knew just what to do. "Okay Margie, that's enough, you need to chill out and quit yelling at your mother right now."

Travis was elegant as he said simply, "Tilly has a problem with anxiety, she worries too much about everything. She hasn't been able to leave the house for a few years now." In retrospect, I wish I had been able to sound less dumbstruck. "What do you mean, she hasn't left the house in years?" "Just what I said, she stays *in* the house all the time." "Oh," I said. "It feels scary out there to you so you've made a safe enough home for yourself inside." Tilly finally spoke directly to me,

"I'm glad this is out because Margie has been bullying me with this for a long time now. The reality is that they need to understand that if I could go out, I would. I just can't do it. My legs feel heavy, I literally can't pick them up, and my heart feels like it's about to jump out of my chest!"

"Wow," I said, "that's quite a description. It sounds like you have a paralyzing fear. . . . It stops you in your tracks." "That's right," Tilly said, and then she began to wipe away some small tears. Margie said, "And now Michelle is weird like my mom, and like her mom, and I am NEVER going to get weird like them, and I think my mom should just stop being weird like this, or else all of us are going to get weird!!" I immediately wanted to know more, but I felt that this moment of disclosure deserved to be recognized since it was likely not a common event. "Sounds like talking about this with an outsider is a new experience. I thank you for letting me in . . . I mean sharing this with me." I then asked Tilly, "How many others know about this Tilly?" "No one, it's not anything that I feel proud of and other people don't ever get it anyway!" I empathized with everyone about how hard it must be to feel that they don't have any options. "I do," Margie said, "I'm gonna ask my dad to take me to live with him." This was obviously another point of contention, as her mother responded, "That's right, he's never been there for you a day of your life and now you think he's going to take you in, right before he's getting remarried again!" Margie yelled back that her mother didn't know her father anymore and that he might agree to let her live with him. I felt that layers of discontent were coming to the surface for all of us to see.

I decided to include Michelle and asked about her sister's comment that Michelle was turning into her mother. Michelle said, "Well, Mom is right. How about that kidnapping last year right nearby, and what about the robberies in the paper, and what about . . . ?" Her mother interrupted her and said, "There are real things to worry about, but for me, you know, it's too much, I have become like granny." They all looked at each other, and Travis once again took command and stated, "Tilly's mother lives in a trailer in the backyard. She doesn't ever leave that trailer. The girls can visit and Tilly and I can visit, but that's about it." I found my eyes darting to the back window to see if there was really a trailer parked back there. "I can show you," said Margie, "you can't see it from there." Sure enough, as I followed Margie to the window, I saw a small trailer in plain sight, and I wondered about all these folks trapped by their internal and external containers.

"I really, really appreciate you all being *so, so* candid with me and letting me know the kinds of problems you are having in your family," I said earnestly. "Somehow, I now understand a little bit more about your story and the fact that everyone was trying to protest the threat of nuclear waste. I had thought to myself, what a terrible way to live . . . being afraid of global contamination and eventual death by grody bugs!" I don't always understand my sense of humor or plan to say something funny ahead of time. However, luckily for me, that statement came across as funny to the family, and they all began to laugh. It reminded me of something I wanted to tell them (after I finished laughing myself).

"I will come back next time with some ideas of how to proceed. I have great confidence in you as a family. You have the problem well in sight, and I think you have gathered up your energies to come together and put on a protest against the dangers that exist in your lives and in your minds. This is a great start. I also want to tell you that you are all really brave people, and I think you, especially Tilly, have figured out the very best ways you know so far to protect yourself and your family against all the dangers that you feel very deeply. Oh, and I also want to say, Tilly, that it sounds like you grew up watching your mom deal with her fears in this way, so chances are we can work on some other ideas." Finally, I turned to Margie and Michelle. "You two have single-handedly brought some help to your mom. "Do you know how you might have done that?" Margie said, "When I got mad at her for being weird like my mom?" "Yes," I said, "when you became worried that your little sister would have to suffer like your mom and grandmother and when both of you, especially you, Michelle, were willing to bring attention to the problem and tell someone so that eventually, I was asked to come along and try to be of help to you." I sat there a moment and said, "Hmmm, I just realized two things. . . . Tilly, is this why you kept canceling your appointments to come to my office?" She nodded yes slowly.

"And one more thing. Travis, how did you and Tilly meet?" I couldn't resist finding out how these two had met given the fact that the mother did not go out. Travis looked at me with a little twinkle in his eye. "Tilly used to call out for pizza maybe three or four times a week. I was the regular driver who delivered the pizza, and we got to know each other real well. Sometimes I just stayed over for dinner and then, you know, we got to like each other a lot!"

"I love this family," I thought to myself, but I also had the realization that I would need to consult, do research, and get some help to deal with the issues that had arisen and had been called to my attention by an accidental physical injury and a puppet story told deep from the family's collective unconscious.

This and many other family play therapy experiences have strengthened my belief that families who play together have the capacity to cocreate metaphors that can be subsequently revealed, brought from abstract to concrete symbols, and thus explored in a more deep and direct manner.

Without the use of this disarming play technique, I don't know how long it would have taken to bring the truth to the surface. I know from talking with the family for years after this that many had tried. Tilly felt so ashamed and had hidden her mother's condition as far back as she could remember. She was expert at keeping her situation secret and eventually told me that she had no idea how I had figured out what was going on so quickly. I remember saying, "I think you were all ready to show it and talk about it." But the truth is that I am not confident that this situation would have come to light without my trusted puppets.

The Story and My Interpretation

This family's story clearly revealed salient underlying issues: There are animals being endangered by the nuclear power plant and nuclear waste in the forest. The protagonist in the story (mother) has both the desire to take action, mobilize, and set out for adventures (Goldilocks) as well as the need to assert a passive stance (innocent bystander). She does get help from others, however, and is able to organize a peaceful protest, but even though it's peaceful, the policeman has rounded them up and is taking them to the judge. So the mother's efforts are thwarted, and she is in despair about what to do. In this story, the judge is given the ultimate power to evaluate the situation and make the ultimate decision about the fate of the protesters (and possibly resolve the dangers of the nuclear threat). However, the judge cannot be of substantive help and defers to an even higher authority.

I was interested that there were so many symbols of authority, and I wondered whether there was a need for limits, external controls, a more powerful control. I also noted that the story was fraught with an overwhelming, global terror that was potentially deadly and that the danger persisted unabated. The family was in distress, no doubt. Finally, I also surmised that the police officer, Pete, who rounded up the family, was a very powerful person in this family, and sure enough, that turned out to be true since it was initially Margie who spilled the beans.

The Curative Properties of Play

A number of curative properties become available to the family: The ability to "pretend," to develop a story that was far enough away from the reality so that it was safe to tell, and the willingness to laugh, play, and work together so that, eventually, energy makes itself available for the family to work together, face their secrecy, and come forward. In addition, other curative properties are inherently engaged—decreased resistance, communication, mastery, creative thinking, abreaction, attachment formation, and relationship enhancement. When people play together, bonds form, happy memories are created, and the fact that a new, more positive interaction occurs begins to provide a foundation for increased motivation to be together.

CHALLENGES IN IMPLEMENTING THE MODEL

There are obvious challenges in implementation among therapists, including, but not limited to, perceived need of additional equipment, hesitancy about appearing unprofessional when playing, discomfort with the concept of play and playfulness itself, lack of preparedness and training about how to implement play activities with families, and a basic distrust that introducing play could possibly contribute to positive change. In the courses I teach on play therapy, asking participants to do experiential work is a key element in ensuring that clinicians can more fully understand the curative factors of play firsthand. I think the greatest deterrent is fear of the unknown and the anxiety that can set in with lack of familiarity with a technique, activity, or procedure. In addition, when attempting new activities, it takes time for clinical trust to develop about the benefits and gains that can be achieved.

CONCLUSION

Family play therapy can be considered an assimilative psychodynamic psychotherapy integration in which "a clear adherence to a single psychotherapeutic orientation is present, but techniques drawn from other orientations are integrated in as seamless a fashion as possible (Stricker, 2010, p. 66). In the case of family play therapy, clinicians with a primary affiliation to systems theory or play therapy can anchor themselves in one theory and borrow theory or technique from the other. For purposes of this chapter, I began with the foundation of family systems (the desire to work with the family unit versus specific individuals) and then applied play therapy theories and techniques.

Play therapy augments family theory by providing yet another tapestry of language in addition to structural dynamics, behavioral action, and verbal communication. The potential benefits of adding play allow clinicians to both assess and treat families in a manner that can decrease resistance, ignite excitement, allow family members to see each other in a new light, and encourage discharging of creativity, laughter, and communal pleasure.

The family illustration exemplifies the remarkable potential of play to be disarming and decrease resistance. But, more importantly, it demonstrates how revealing play can be and how it can bring forward metaphors for processing and discussing. The R. family was able to break the family secret about cross-generational agoraphobia. However, it was only when a safe enough distance was created that they felt liberated enough to allow these issues to surface. They found it much easier for them to talk about a nuclear threat, endangered species, an adventurer, a peaceful protester, a policeman, and a judge than the mother's cross-generational issues with agoraphobia and its impact on her family.

Tilly and her mother had clearly suffered with this paralyzing condition for years, and Michelle was exhibiting some of the signs of symptoms of adding another generation in which the condition would persist. Margie, likely the most outspoken family member, propelled herself to address this problem by expressing different expectations of her sister Michelle, demands that she could not make of her mother and grandmother.

The mother's therapy continued over two years and followed a traditional course of cognitive-behavioral therapy (desensitization and gradual exposure techniques). The mother became actively involved in teaching Michelle the lessons she learned, and Michelle turned around quickly, becoming much less anxious and more outgoing and developing a more authoritative voice. Tilly's mother remained in her trailer for years and was eventually moved to a senior care facility, where she lived happily in her room until she died at 105.

Both Michelle and Margie are divorced, remarried with five children between them, happy in stepfamilies in which stepfathers are more devoted to children than their birth fathers. Signs of agoraphobia are long gone, and all family members find their worlds safe and nurturing.

REFERENCES

Axline, V. M. (1947, 1969). *Play therapy*. New York, NY: Ballantine Books.

Bratton, S. C., Ray, D., & Rhine, T. (2005). The efficacy of play therapy with children: A meta-analytic review of treatment outcomes. *Professional Psychology: Research and Practice, 36*(4), 376–390.

Carter, E., & McGoldrick, M. (1989). *The changing family lifecycles: A framework for family therapy.* New York, NY: Allyn & Bacon.

Chasin, R. (1994). Interviewing families with children: Guidelines and suggestions. *Journal of Psychotherapy and the Family, 5*(3/4), 15–30.

Chasin, R., & White, T. B. (1989). Interviewing families with children: Guidelines and suggestions. In L. Combrinck-Graham (Ed.), *Children in family contexts: Perspectives on treatment* (pp. 5–25). New York, NY: Guilford Press.

Dermer, S., Olund, D., & Sori, C. (1994). Integrating play in family therapy theories. In C. F. Sori (Ed.), *Engaging children in family therapy: Creative approaches to integrating theory and research in clinical practice* (pp. 37–65). New York, NY: Routledge.

Eaker, B. (1986). Unlocking the family secret in family play therapy. *Child & Adolescent Social Work, 3*(4), 235–253.

Estrada, A. U., & Pinsof, W. M. (1995). The effectiveness of family therapies for selected behavioral disorders of childhood. *Journal of Marital and Family Therapy, 21,* 403–440.

Gil, E. (1994). *Play in family therapy.* New York, NY: Guilford Press.

Gil, E. (2006). *Helping abused and traumatized children: Integrating directive and nondirective approaches.* New York, NY: Guilford Press.

Gil, E. (Ed.). (2010). *Working with children to heal interpersonal trauma: The power of play.* New York, NY: Guilford Press.

Gil, E., & Shaw, J. (2009). Prescriptive play therapy. In K. J. O'Connor & L. D. Braverman (Eds.), *Play therapy theory and practice: Comparing theories & techniques* (2nd ed., pp. 451–487). Hoboken, NJ: Wiley.

Guerney, B. (1964). Filial therapy: Prescription and rationale. *Journal of Consulting Psychology, 28*(4), 304–310.

Irwin, E. C., & Malloy, E. S. (1975). Family puppet interview. *Family Process, 14,* 179–191.

Johnson, L. M. (1995). The inclusion of children in the process of family therapy. Unpublished doctoral dissertation, Purdue University, West Lafayette, IN.

Kaduson, H., Cangelosi, D., & Schaefer, C. E. (1997). *The playing cure: Individualized play therapy for specific childhood problems.* Northvale, NJ: Aronson.

Keith, D. V., & Whitaker, C. A. (1981). Play therapy: A paradigm for work with families. *Journal of Marital & Family Therapy, 7*(3), 243–254.

Landreth, G. L. (2002). *Play therapy: The art of the relationship.* New York, NY: Taylor & Francis.

Landreth, G. L., & Bratton, S. C. (2006). *Child–Parent Relationship Therapy (CPRT): A 10-session filial therapy model.* New York, NY: Routledge.

Miller, W. (1994). Family play therapy: History, theory, and convergence. In C. E Schaefer & L. J. Carey (Eds.), *Family play therapy* (pp. 3–19). Northvale, NJ: Aronson.

O'Connor, K. J. (1991). *The play therapy primer.* New York, NY: Wiley.

Orgun, I. N. (1973). Playroom setting for diagnostic family interviews. *American Journal of Psychiatry, 130*(5), 540–542.

Schaefer, C. E. (1994). Play therapy for psychic trauma in children. In K. J. O'Connor & C. E. Schaefer (Eds.), *Handbook of play therapy: Advances and innovations* (Vol. 2, pp. 297–318). New York, NY: Wiley.

Schaefer, C. E. (2003a). *Play therapy with adults.* Hoboken, NJ: Wiley.

Schaefer, C. E. (2003b). Prescriptive play therapy. In C. E. Schaefer (Ed.), *Foundations of play therapy* (pp. 306–320). Hoboken, NJ: Wiley.

Schaefer, C. E. (Ed.). (1992). *Therapeutic powers of play*. Northvale, NJ: Aronson.

Schaefer, C. E., & Carey, L. J. (1994). *Family play therapy*. Northvale, NJ: Aronson.

Stricker, G. (2010). *Psychotherapy integration: Theories of Psychotherapy Series.* Washington, DC: American Psychological Association.

Stricker, G., & Gold, J. R. (2002). An assimilative approach to integrative psychodynamic psychotherapy. In J. Lebow (Ed.), *Comprehensive handbook of psychotherapy: Integrative/Eclectic* (pp. 295–315). New York, NY: Wiley

Sori, C. F., & Sprenkle, D. H. (2004). Training family therapists to work with children and families: A modified Delphi study. *Journal of Marital and Family Therapy, 30*(4), 479–495.

Terr, L. (1990). *Too scared to cry: How trauma affects children and ultimately us all*. New York, NY: Basic Books.

Zilbach, J. J. (1989). The family life cycle: A framework for understanding children in family therapy. In L. Combrinck-Graham (Ed.), *Children in family contexts: Perspectives on treatment* (pp. 46–66). New York, NY: Guilford Press.

Zilbach, J. J. (1991). Children in family therapy: Treatment and training (introduction and overview). *Journal of Psychotherapy & the Family, 5*(3/4), 1–14.

Chapter 13

GROUP PLAY THERAPY

Daniel S. Sweeney

Within the context of community, group therapy has the potential to combat one of the greatest human pains—the loneliness of being alone. Play therapy clients, most often children, already struggle for autonomy and identity in this world and can be cruelly oppressed in the midst of trauma and chaos and left feeling unfairly isolated. In his discussion of loneliness, Clark Moustakas (1974) poignantly stated, "It is the terror of loneliness, not loneliness itself but loneliness anxiety, the fear of being left alone, of being left out, that represents a dominant crisis in the struggle to become a person" (p. 16).

Reflecting further words of Moustakas (1997), group play therapy is a unique way of "being in, being for, and being with" clients of all ages. While group play therapy cannot be classified as a specific technique or as a particular theoretical approach, it does create the opportunity for the loneliness of struggle to be addressed in a developmentally appropriate and expressive manner. Group play therapy is the recognition of children's medium of communication (play), combined with the natural benefit of human connection with other children, under the facilitation of a trained and caring adult.

While other chapters in this book discuss approaches to play therapy based on focused theoretical orientations, group play therapy is cross-theoretical and can be used by trained therapists from a wide variety of orientations. A wide variety of theories and techniques may be used in the development and process of play therapy groups. This chapter briefly comments on some of these variations but primarily focuses on the general structure and practice of group play therapy, with a brief review of the literature on the topic.

INTRODUCTION

Sweeney and Homeyer (1999) advocate for group play therapy in their book *Handbook of Group Play Therapy*, which is still considered the seminal and exhaustive resource on the subject:

> Group play therapy is a natural union of two effective therapeutic modalities. Play therapists and group therapists share several important traits. Both are committed to a therapeutic process that is creative and dynamic. Both are centered on the development and maintenance of safe and therapeutic relationships. Both are focused on facilitation

of an unfolding process, as opposed to the application of an immediate solution. Both are engaged in efforts requiring prerequisite training and supervision. The marriage of play therapy and group process is a natural and intuitive response to the needs of emotionally hurting children. (p. 3)

This partnership, however, is rarely exercised. It is posited that group play therapy is often a more powerful and expedient therapeutic intervention than individual work with children. A further discussion of the rationale for group play therapy occurs later in this chapter.

The following description of group play therapy is adapted from a classic definition of play therapy (Landreth, 2002, p. 17): Group play therapy is defined as a dynamic interpersonal relationship between two or more children and a therapist trained in both play therapy and group procedures, who provides selected play materials and facilitates the development of a safe relationship for children to fully express and explore themselves and others (including feelings, thoughts, experiences, and behaviors) through children's natural medium of communication, play.

A few elements of this definition require brief discussion. Any play therapy process should be characterized as a *dynamic interpersonal relationship*. When multiple children are in the therapy room, this fundamental element can and should be multiplied. This process should occur only when the therapist is *trained in both play therapy and group procedures*. In group play therapy, a skilled play therapist who lacks training and understanding of group dynamics is as potentially damaging as a skilled group therapist who lacks training and understanding of play therapy dynamics. The provision of *selected play materials* is also crucial. The group play therapist may choose to provide play media for a group different from media used in individual work, but it remains important to avoid a random collection of toys. Like any group therapist, the group play therapist should *facilitate*, which itself fosters the *development of safe relationships*. The safety that results from this facilitation also enables children to engage in *exploration of themselves and others*. This process is further facilitated by the recognition of *play as the natural medium of communication* for children.

Children can and do benefit from the relationships and interactions with other children within the context of a group play setting. In the same way that group counseling works with adults, group play therapy provides for children a psychosocial process through which they grow and learn about themselves and others. Berg, Landreth, and Fall (2006) suggest,

> In group counseling relationships, children experience the therapeutic releasing qualities of discovering that their peers have problems, too, and a diminishing of the barriers of feeling all alone. A feeling of belonging develops, and new interpersonal skills are attempted in a "real life" encounter where children learn more effective ways of relating to people through the process of trial and error. The group then is a microcosm of children's everyday world. In this setting children are afforded the opportunity for immediate reactions from peers as well as the opportunity for vicarious learning. Children also develop a sensitivity to others and receive a tremendous boost to their self-concept through being helpful to someone else. For abused children who have poor self-concepts and a life history of experiencing failure, discovering they can be helpful to someone

else may be the most profound therapeutic quality possible. In the counseling group, children also discover they are worthy of respect and that their worth is not dependent on what they do or what they produce but rather on who they are. (p. 254)

Children learn about others and themselves in group play therapy. They learn because they are permitted to communicate through play, and they learn as they hear and observe the perceptions of the therapist and the other children toward them. Children learn that being unique is not just acceptable—it is valued. Cooperation is valued in the group therapy process and, therefore, promoted. Compliance is expected only when limits need to be set or structured activities are implemented. At all times, creativity and originality are honored. Van der Kolk (1985) listed several elements of the play therapy group that contribute to these suppositions:

- Total acceptance of the child
- A simple invitation to play without explanations, goals, reasons, questions, or expectations
- Helping children learn to express themselves and enjoy respect
- Permitting but not encouraging regressive behavior early in therapy
- Permitting all "symbolic behavior" with limits on destructive behavior
- Prohibiting children from physically attacking each other
- Enforcing limits calmly, noncritically, and briefly mentioning limits only as necessary
- Feeling and expressing empathy

Although structure and process may vary according to therapeutic plan and theoretical approach, the group play therapy process should include most, if not all, of these elements.

It is possible that the therapeutic play group provides the closest thing to the structure and acceptance of a family as is available for some children. Landreth (1999) suggests that in group play therapy, "Children learn from each other, encourage one another, support each other, work out difficulties, share in pain and joy, discover what it is like to help each other, and discover that they are capable of giving as well as receiving help" (p. xii). These growth-producing qualities in families are all too often missing for children who are referred for play therapy. The vicarious learning, sharing, and processing that occur in group therapy are a natural blend with the expressive, projective, and freeing benefits of therapeutic play.

BASIC CONSTRUCTS, GOALS, AND TECHNIQUES

Rationale for Group Play Therapy

Before discussing some technical considerations of play group work with children, it is helpful to explore some of the benefits and rationale for group play therapy with children. Sweeney (1997) and Sweeney and Homeyer (1999) summarize the following basic advantages of therapeutic play groups:

1. Groups tend to promote spontaneity in children and may therefore increase their level of participation in the play therapy experience. The therapist's attempt to communicate permissiveness is also enhanced by the group dynamics, thus freeing children to risk engagement in various play and relational behaviors.

2. The affective life of children is dealt with at two levels. First, the *intrapsychic* issues of individual group members are given opportunity for exploration and expression. Second, the *interpersonal* issues between the therapist and child, as well as among the children themselves, are afforded the same opportunity.

3. Therapeutic groups provide opportunities for vicarious learning and cathar-sis. Children observe the emotional and behavior expressions of other group members and learn coping behaviors, problem-solving skills, and alternative avenues of self-expression. As children see other group members engage in activities that they may initially feel cautious or apprehensive about, they gain the courage to explore.

4. Children experience the opportunity for self-growth and self-exploration in group play therapy. This process is facilitated by the responses and reactions of group members to a child's emotional and behavioral expression. Children have the opportunity to reflect and achieve insight to self as they learn to evaluate and reevaluate themselves in light of peer feedback.

5. Groups provide significant opportunities to anchor children to the world of reality. While most expressions in the playroom should be acceptable, lim-its must be occasionally set and anchors to reality must exist. Limit setting and reality testing occur not only between the therapist and individual group members but also among the children themselves. The group serves as a tan-gible microcosm of society; thus, the group play therapy experience is tangi-bly tied to reality.

6. Since play therapy groups can serve as a microcosm of society, the therapist has the opportunity to gain substantial insight into children's everyday lives. This "real-life" perspective seen in the microcosm of the playroom can assist with treatment planning and work with parents and teachers.

7. The group play therapy setting may decrease a child's need or tendency to be repetitious and/or to retreat into fantasy play. While these behaviors may be necessary for some children in the processing of their issues, the group play therapy setting can bring those children "stuck" in repetition or fantasy into the here and now. This is again accomplished with therapist-initiated interactions and among children in the group.

8. Children have the opportunity to "practice" for everyday life in the group play therapy process. The group provides the opportunity for children to develop interpersonal skills, master new behaviors, offer and receive assistance, and experiment with alternative expressions of emotions and behavior.

9. The presence of more than multiple children in the play therapy setting may assist in the development of the therapeutic relationship for some children. As withdrawn or avoidant children observe the therapist building trust with other children, they are often drawn in. This helps reduce the anxiety of children unsure about the playroom and the person of the therapist.
10. Finally, as with therapeutic groups of any kind, group play therapy may provide a more expedient means of intervention in terms of time and expenditure for both children and parents.

Goals

The previous rationales also point to the goals of group play therapy because opportunities for growth and change that are provided for children in therapeutic play groups are so numerous. In the first of only two books focused on the topic, Haim Ginott (1961) suggested that group play therapy is based on the assumption that children modify their behavior in exchange for acceptance. This premise, combined with the capacity and tendency of children to seek out and establish relationships, underlies the therapeutic advantage for using group play therapy. Ginott also contended that the primary goal for group play therapy, like all therapy, is enduring personality change (a strengthened ego and enhanced self-image). To this end, Ginott proposes several questions from which we can summarize the primary therapeutic goals of group play therapy:

1. Does the method facilitate or hinder the establishment of a therapeutic relationship?
2. Does it accelerate or retard evocation of catharsis?
3. Does it aid or obstruct attainment of insight?
4. Does it augment or diminish opportunities for reality testing?
5. Does it open or block channels for sublimation? (p. 2)

The answers to these questions bring focus to the goals of therapeutic play groups. Group play therapy should facilitate the following:

1. The establishment of a therapeutic relationship
2. The expression of emotions
3. The development of insight
4. Opportunities for reality testing
5. Opportunities for expressing feelings and needs in more acceptable ways

These mirror the goals that G. Corey, Corey, Callanan, & Russell (2004) suggest are those shared by members of all group counseling experiences:

- To learn to trust oneself and others
- To increase awareness and self-knowledge; to develop a sense of one's unique identity

- To recognize the commonality of members' needs and problems and to develop a sense of universality
- To increase self-acceptance, self-confidence, and self-respect and to achieve a new view of oneself and others
- To develop concern and compassion for others
- To find alternative ways of dealing with normal developmental issues and resolving certain conflicts
- To increase self-direction, interdependence, and responsibility toward oneself and others
- To become aware of one's choices and to make choices wisely
- To make specific plans for changing certain behaviors and to commit oneself to follow through with these plans
- To learn more effective social skills
- To become more sensitive to the needs and feelings of others
- To learn how to challenge others with care, concern, honesty, and directness
- To clarify one's values and decide whether and how to modify them (pp. 4–5)

These should be expected goals in the group play therapy experience, regardless of theoretical orientation and specific group play therapy techniques.

Group Selection and Size

The success of a play therapy group may well be related to the selection of group members and the size of the group. Ginott (1975) asserts that the basic requirement for selection to a group is the presence of and capacity for "social hunger." This refers to children's need to be accepted by their peers and a desire to attain and maintain status in the group.

Some children simply do not respond well to group play therapy. These children can be seen on an individual basis, or they may be candidates for filial or family play therapy. Several issues may be considered in these cases—a child is simply not ready for a group experience, the presenting problem may lend itself to another intervention, or group work may be contraindicated for psychological or physiological safety concerns.

Participation in group play therapy is, therefore, generally a case-by-case clinical decision. Ginott (1961) offers several contraindications:

- Siblings who exhibit intense rivalry
- Extremely aggressive children
- Sexually acting-out children
- Children experiencing difficulty due to poor infant–mother attachment
- Sociopathic children (intending to inflict harm or revenge)
- Children with an extremely poor self-image

These suggested contraindications, however, are debatable. With the appropriate therapeutic conditions, these children may well benefit from the group play therapy experience. Ginott's purpose may be surmised as intending to protect children and therapists. Training and supervised experience can mitigate these safety concerns.

Using individual play therapy as part of the process of screening for potential group play therapy members is generally recommended. Even a single play session may reveal the indication or contraindication for inclusion in a group. Other screening methods may be appropriate, including parent and/or teacher report, behavioral assessment, and child interviews.

A crucial consideration in group play therapy is the size of the group. Initially, a good general rule to follow is that the younger the children, the smaller the group. Very young children are usually just beginning to learn how to function in groups of any kind outside their immediate family. A related issue is the level of structure necessary to be provided in the group and whether this should be related to the age of the children. Level of structure varies according to the group theory and the group population. It is challenging to attend to too many children, and most facilities cannot accommodate a large group. Structured activities and guidance counseling that involve play media may be given to larger groups, but these activities may not fit under the umbrella of group play therapy. Remember that two children make a group, and this may be the suitable size and the most beneficial.

It is always appropriate to keep these groups balanced. For example, whereas it is often helpful to run groups on particular topics and for particular populations, it may be appropriate to avoid composing a group of children who have experienced the same trauma to prevent an escalation of traumatic behaviors or emotions. This should be the judgment call of the play therapist.

Another balance issue may be gender. If a group has two girls, it may be helpful to balance it out with two boys. It is generally suggested that a group not have a majority of one gender. Additionally, if a group has two withdrawn children, it may be helpful to balance it with two outgoing or assertive children.

Although it varies with sibling group play therapy and some other cases, the age range of children in group play therapy should generally not exceed 12 months. The difference between a 3-year-old and a 5-year-old is simply too great. Unless developmental delays are an issue, this is an appropriate guideline to follow. In terms of gender, children generally do not need to be separated by gender until middle school or junior high school age. Also, consider the physical size of children. Given the variety of growth patterns of individual children, a single larger or smaller child is not recommended. For these and other group dynamics, balance is always important.

Group Setting and Materials

In the establishment and conduct of therapeutic play groups, it is crucial to consider the facility and materials available for use. A regular counseling office may not be appropriate because of the necessity to set too many limits. Although some group rooms are equipped with carpeting, chairs, and soft pillows, a therapeutic play group room often has different needs. Ideally, a group room that is particularly set aside for play therapy groups is best, floored with tile and equipped with sturdy toys and furniture. An adequately sized room that is not devoted to play therapy will work, while recognizing the need for adequate materials and the possible increased need for appropriate limits.

The room should obviously not be too small or too large—at least 12 by 15 feet is suggested. A playroom that is too small can lead to frustration and aggression among group members. The room that is too large not only creates the possibility of uncontrolled behavior but also enables the withdrawn child to avoid interaction. Because there is considerable potential for high levels of noise and messiness, the location of the group room in a counseling facility is an important consideration.

The play materials may vary according to theoretical approach and treatment purpose. Recognizing these variations, Landreth (2002) has helpful suggestions regarding the selection of play therapy media. He suggests that play materials should do the following:

1. Facilitate a wide range of creative expression
2. Facilitate a wide range of emotional expression
3. Engage children's interests
4. Facilitate expressive and exploratory play
5. Allow exploration and expression without verbalization
6. Allow success without prescribed structure
7. Allow for noncommittal play
8. Have sturdy construction for active use (p. 133)

Another consideration is that it may *not* be appropriate to provide enough toys of any one type so that each group member can have one. Whereas this may seem to promote fairness, children can lose the opportunity to learn to share and resolve conflict with limited play materials.

For older children and adolescents, an activity group setting of some kind is recommended (Bratton, Ceballos, & Ferebee, 2009). One of the primary benefits of activity groups is that group members enjoy the continued opportunity for non-verbal expression that play therapy provides, with the accompanying advantage of developmentally appropriate group activities and discussion.

Length and Frequency of Sessions

The length of each group play therapy session must be considered. A recommended guideline is to relate the length of the group session to the age of the members. The younger the child group members are, generally, the shorter the session. The group facilitator must consider the attention span of the children, considering psychological age over chronological age. For preschool children and early elementary–age children, a play therapy group may run for 20 to 40 minutes. For children approaching middle or junior high school, the groups may run well over an hour.

Another consideration is the stamina of the group play therapist. If there are several children in the group and the therapist is actively participating and communicating empathy and accepting to all group members, it is simply more tiresome than adult group therapy. A fatigued therapist will find it challenging to be an empathic one.

The duration of the group also varies. This may depend on play therapy groups meeting in different settings (schools, hospitals, etc.) and with different populations (sexually abused, grieving, etc.).

The frequency of therapeutic play groups correlates with the purpose of the group, the clinical setting, and the severity of the presenting problem. Intensive short-term groups, meeting two to five times per week, may be very effective. Tyndall-Lind, Landreth, and Giordano (2001) reported the significant efficacy of intensive group play therapy with children who have witnessed domestic violence, noting reductions in problem behaviors, depression, and anxiety, as well as increases in self-esteem.

Theory and Techniques

As noted, there are as many theoretical approaches to group play therapy as there are to individual play therapy. Accordingly, the variety of techniques varies considerably. For more techniques, see the *International Journal of Play Therapy* and Sweeney and Homeyer (1999). Four approaches are briefly discussed next.

1. Child-centered group play therapy

   is based on an abiding trust in the group's ability to develop its own potential through its movement in a positive and constructive direction. . . . This has significant implications for children, who are so often evaluated and so rarely given choices. The facilitator of a children's group should be very intentional to help each child to feel safe enough to grow (or not to grow) and make choices. (Landreth & Sweeney, 1999, p. 44)

2. Adlerian group play therapists consider group dynamics within the context of the essential phases of individual psychology. Kottman (1999) suggests,

   In some ways, a group approach is ideal for working with children using Adlerian play therapy—especially during the second (exploring the lifestyle), third (helping the child gain insight into the lifestyle), and fourth (reorientation/reeducation) phases. (p. 66)

3. Jungian group play therapy looks to the group as a container for both child members and the group itself. Bertoia (1999) summarizes,

   The general format in all Jungian group play therapy is to enter the work at a conscious level using clear rational language in the here-and-now. Within the session work deepens into the nonrational or metaphoric language of the unconscious. The sessions conclude by returning to external reality and firmly anchoring children in the present. (p. 93)

4. Gestalt group play therapy focuses on contact and awareness, as Oaklander (1999) states,

> The group is an ideal setting for children to enhance their contact skills. . . . It is natural for children, as well as an important developmental task, to seek out other children. . . . One's process in a group may be much different in a one-to-one therapy setting. When the behavior becomes foreground, we can examine it from all sides, play with it, change it. (pp. 166–167)

In these and other theories are a variety of techniques. These techniques may involve the structure of the groups, play media provided, specific games and activities, and directions from the therapist. An important reminder is necessary about therapeutic techniques. Theory is important, but theory without technique is merely philosophy. Techniques are valuable, but techniques without theory are reckless, and potentially damaging. Group play therapists as well as all therapists are encouraged to ponder some questions regarding employing techniques: (a) Is the technique developmentally appropriate? (which presupposes that developmental capabilities are a key therapeutic consideration); (b) What theory underlies the technique? (which presupposes that techniques should be theory-based); and (c) What is the therapeutic intent in employing a given technique? (which presupposes that having specific therapeutic intent is clinically and ethically important).

ROLE OF THE THERAPIST

Recognizing these variations, the primary role of the group play therapist is to remain a facilitator of the process. The therapeutic factors that Yalom and Leszcz (2005) advocate have become standard in the field of group therapy and certainly apply to group play therapy. While change is dependent on group members, it is important to remember that the therapist's role continues to include aspects such as the instillation of hope, promotion of altruism and universality, development of social skills, and promotion of imitative behavior and catharsis.

Therapeutic Responses

Across theoretical approaches, there are some fundamental considerations about therapeutically responding in the group play therapy process. The therapeutic role in group play therapy remains similar to that in individual play therapy. However, the group play therapist must have a high tolerance for messiness and noise and must be willing and adept at handling frequent chaos. It is crucial that therapists keep responses balanced among group members. This includes avoiding the tempting focus on children who are more active or needy. While this is an easy trap to fall into, it sends messages of nonacceptance to children who are less verbal and less active. Such messages generally reinforce an already present, and negative, view of self.

Although this may vary according to theoretical perspective, it is posited that with clients of any age and in any setting, therapeutic responses should not be intrusive—which may affect the flow of group process and affective expression. In addition, it is *imperative* in group play therapy to include the child's name. If a response is made without the child's name, group members may not know to whom the response is directed. A related issue involves the avoidance of using the third person when interacting with the children. For example, when simply tracking play behavior, it is best to avoid saying, "Anna is playing in the sand", but rather, "Anna, you're playing in the sand." Children, not unlike adults, are honored when talked *to* rather than talked *about*.

Limit Setting in Groups

One of the most curative and growth-promoting aspects of the group play therapy process is the appropriate setting of therapeutic limits. The pace of group play therapy is magnified considerably over that of individual sessions, thus the attending and responsive skills of the therapist may be greatly challenged. Fundamentally, the group play therapist must be an expert limit setter.

Sweeney and Landreth (2009) summarized the basic rationale for setting limits in the playroom:

(1) Limits define the boundaries of the therapeutic relationship; (2) limits provide security and safety for the child, both physically and emotionally; (3) limits demonstrate the therapist's intent to provide safety for the child; (4) limits anchor the session to reality; (5) limits allow the therapist to maintain a positive and accepting attitude toward the child; (6) limits allow the child to express negative feelings without causing harm, and the subsequent fear of retaliation; (7) limits offer stability and consistency; (8) limits promote and enhance the child's sense of self-responsibility and self-control; (9) limits protect the play therapy room; and (10) limits provide for the maintenance of legal, ethical, and professional standards.

Limits and limit setting are expected in the therapeutic play group. Group members experience limits set not only by the therapist but also by the other group members. The group play therapist should be keen in anticipating limits and firmly resolved to actually set limits. Conditional limits are counterproductive. Complete and unambiguous limits are therefore imperative when working with play therapy groups. However, because the activity level in these groups may be considerably high, it can be a temptation to constantly set limits to maintain control. The group play therapist should be patient and allow children to work things out for themselves while setting appropriate limits. A limit-setting model is briefly described in the case study later in the chapter.

ROLE OF THE PARENTS

The role of the parents in the group play therapy process is essentially similar to the role in the individual play therapy process. This role varies according to the theoretical orientation and personal style of the therapist. Many play therapists are inadequately trained to deal with parents, and many have chosen to exclusively work with children, which may compromise their ability or motivation to work with parents. These factors must be overcome for individual or group play therapy to work.

When parents bring their children to therapy, they are stressed. Often parents have tried everything they can think of to resolve the presenting issue. They are often sleep deprived (which naturally compromises their effectiveness as parents), and the very decision to bring their children in for therapy is stress inducing. If therapists can remain aware of this important dynamic and communicate empathy to parents for their situation, the therapy process is facilitated. This facilitation is then assisted or impeded by the therapist's attitude. Crane (2001) suggests,

> Given the parents' feelings and beliefs when they bring their child to therapy, the attitude the therapist has toward the parents can affect how therapy proceeds and whether or not the parents continue to bring the child to therapy. Overall, the therapist should convey an attitude of empathy, respect, acceptance, and hope toward the parents. These attitudes are not distinct from one another as they often overlap. It is important that the therapist not just have these attitudes, but that the parents perceive them from the therapist. The objective is to facilitate the parents' potential to learn, to explore themselves, and to grow. (p. 85)

All parents should be interviewed before any group play therapy sessions. Although not possible in some settings (e.g., school settings), this interview should be considered basic protocol. This initial assessment should not be considered an end to parental contact because ongoing evaluation is needed. Parents should be educated about the group play therapy process; in particular, the focus should be on the rationale for and benefits of play therapy and the group play therapy process. Ongoing involvement with parents may include having them join the group, providing family play therapy or Filial Therapy (both of which can be classified as group play therapy), and providing adjunctive therapeutic interventions apart from the therapeutic play group.

Legal and Ethical Considerations

Legal and ethical issues related to group play therapy are discussed briefly in this section because parents have the legal rights and are legally responsible for their children. Sweeney (2001) posits, "When working with children, it is imperative to remember that while the child may be the focus of treatment, the legal guardian is essentially the client from a legal and ethical perspective" (p. 65). Parents must be made aware of the purpose of the group and appropriate consent secured. Because child custody is frequently an issue, it is crucial for the therapist to ensure that the legal guardian provides the consent and that it be *informed* consent. Planned exercises should be explained to the parents and to the children.

As with any group, children cannot be given an absolute promise of confidentiality when in group play therapy. Confidentiality may need to be broken by the therapist in a "reportable" situation, whether reporting abuse to authorities or passing information on to school or agency administrators per policy.

Screening and preparation for the play groups are also ethical issues. Children are rarely self-referred, so it is the therapist's responsibility to ensure appropriate group placement. As with adult groups, children should have the opportunity to participate or leave the group.

A complete discussion of legal and ethical issues in the group play therapy process is beyond the scope of this chapter. Therapists must be familiar with the ethical codes of their own professional organizations, as well as the laws of the state in which they practice.

CASE ILLUSTRATION

In the following case example (adapted from Landreth & Sweeney, 1999) of child-centered group play therapy, three children (Rand, age 7; Lori, age 7; and Keith, age 8) are meeting for the first time in a play therapy group at an elementary school. They have all been referred because of "socialization problems." Rand has been described as an anxious child who does not have any friends; Lori, as an introverted child who relates more to adults than to children; and Keith, as a somewhat hyper child who tends to annoy his peers. The following is a brief transcript of some of the therapeutic interactions with the children in the playroom.

> **Therapist:** Rand, Lori, and Keith—this is our playroom, and you can play with the toys in a lot of the ways you would like to.

[The child-centered group play therapy approach is permission giving. The therapist uses each child's name, which honors each child, and establishes the egalitarian status of each group member.]

> **Keith:** (rushing into the room toward the sandbox) I want to play in the sand!

[It is not unusual to have children of varying levels of emotional and sociable levels.]

> **Therapist:** Keith, it looks like you've got something in mind. (Lori moves slowly into the room while looking at the toys.) Lori, it looks like you're checking out the toys on that shelf.

[In group play therapy, it becomes very important to use the child's name, so that each group member is aware of who is being addressed. Keith has an intentional plan, and the therapist needs to acknowledge this. At the same time, the other children need to be responded to. It can be a temptation to respond primarily to the most active and vocal children, but therapeutic responses should be spread out equally among the group members.]

> **Lori:** Yeah, I guess so. (Lori has reached out tentatively to touch the cash register but has pulled her hand back. Rand is still standing next to the door, furtively glancing around.)

[The initial session of group play therapy is often tentative and exploratory for the children. They are not just exploring the playroom but also checking out the therapist and the other children.]

> **Therapist:** Lori, it seems like you're wondering if it's OK to play with that. In here, you can choose what to play with. Rand, it looks like you're wondering about this place.

[The therapist's voice tone should match the voice tone and activity level of the child. The response to Lori is warm and empathic but places the responsibility for making the choices onto her. It might be tempting for the therapist to give Rand a specific invitation to play, because of his tentativeness. He should be allowed to make this choice himself.]

> **Keith:** (Grabs the rubber snake and runs across the room, poking the snake at Rand's face. Rand cringes and tries to fend off the snake.)
> **Therapist:** Keith, it looks like you would like to scare Rand with that snake, but he is trying to tell you he doesn't like what you are doing. He wants you to stop.

[Recognition of feelings is key to the child-centered approach. Verbalizing Rand's nonverbal message helps Keith to hear Rand's message and gives Rand needed support that he is understood.]

> **Keith:** (Leaves Rand and with great glee begins chasing Lori around the room as she screams, "Quit that!")
> **Therapist:** Keith, you're having lots of fun chasing Lori, but Lori, you are telling him you don't like what he is doing.

[Tracking of activity and responding to feelings is the same as in individual play therapy, just more so. It is important that both children be responded to equally. Both children need to know they have been heard and understood.]

(Keith drops the snake on the floor and goes back to the sandbox. Lori picks up some puppets and begins to make a puppet show. Rand plays with a toy in the corner behind the easel stand, out of sight.)

> **Therapist:** So, Keith, you decided to do something else, and Lori, you decided to play with the puppets.

[Recognizing that children have made a decision affirms their strength. No response is made to Rand because he seems to need to be left alone at the moment. The therapist is keenly sensitive to where he is and what he is doing but respects his choice to hide.]

> **Rand:** (Sits on the floor under the easel looking out at the group.)

Lori: (continues puppet story, saying to the therapist) Good morning. I'm the lion (gives a loud roar).
Therapist: Good morning, lion. That's a big roar.

[The therapist can interact without structuring.]

(Other interactions occur as Lori develops the puppet story.)

Therapist: Rand, looks like you decided to sit right there.

[Nonevaluative recognition communicates acceptance of his decision to sit and look.]

Keith: (has been digging in the sand, burying toy soldiers, and says to no one in particular) I'm going to bury all of these guys.
Therapist: (to Keith) Yep, looks like you've buried a bunch of them.

[Toys are not labeled until the child identifies the item.]

Rand: (emerges from under the easel, joins Keith, and begins digging in the sand)

(The activity of other children in group play therapy invites and entices shy, quiet children. Rand relaxes enough to begin playing.)

Keith: (to Rand) Hey! Neat! You can dig the holes, and I'll bury these guys.

[Keith's statement is encouraging to Rand and helps him feel included.]

Therapist: Rand, you've decided to play in the sand with Keith—and Keith, sounds like you like that!

[A simple tracking of the play activity provides affirmation of the choices made by the children, particularly Rand.]

Keith: (grabs the sand pail and yells) This is going to be a bomb! (holds bucket up high and drops it on the floor as Rand protests)
Therapist: Keith, I know that was fun for you, but the sand is for staying in the sandbox. You wanted the bucket—but Rand, you are telling Keith you want to play with it.

[The therapist shows understanding of each child's behavioral and emotional message and sets an appropriate limit. The limit setting follows the ACT model, proposed by Landreth (2002). This highly effective model includes **A**—Acknowledging the child's feelings (it is important to begin the setting of limits by continuing reflection and acceptance), **C**—Communicating the limit (in a neutral and nonpunitive manner), and **T**—Targeting an acceptable alternative (which recognizes that the child still has a need to express self and can do so within acceptable boundaries). A limit that is set objectively, with acceptance, and without disapproval is most often received and responded to by children with compliance.]

> **Rand:** (picks up bucket and begins to fill it with sand again) I'm going to build a castle.
> **Keith:** These soldiers can guard the castle.

[Keith's aggression has subsided because he has been allowed to act it out, and he joins in the play activity in a helpful way.]

> **Lori:** (stands watching the boys) There needs to be a family living in the castle. (She retrieves the doll family from the dollhouse and adds them to the castle scene.)
> **Therapist:** You're all making that castle just the way you want it to be.

[The therapist's comment empowers the children, recognizing their own decision making, effort, and creative ability. This comment also affirms their working together, while not providing praise and approval. The child-centered play therapist does not evaluate and focuses on the effort rather than the product. The difference between encouragement and praise is key in the child-centered group play therapy process. By focusing on the effort, the therapist can make self-esteem–building statements without creating the leading and approval-seeking dynamic that comes from statements of praise. It also models this important dynamic for the group members in their interaction with one another.]

> **Lori, Rand, and Keith:** (almost in unison) Yeah!

Each child in this case reacted differently to the therapist's attempts to establish basic rapport and promote therapeutic relationship. Although this was an initial session, some of the rationale for group play therapy noted previously is already evident. Rand demonstrated movement from being generally anxious in the group to interacting with the other children. His physical movement from distance to closer proximity to the therapist and the other children is one example of the benefit of placing shy, anxious children in play therapy groups. Keith's aggressive behavior was ameliorated by the group, particularly by the therapist's giving expression to the displeasure of the other children at some of his behaviors. He was given the opportunity to reevaluate his acting-out behaviors in the presence of Rand and Lori, as well as the therapist. Lori began by playing alone and seeking to engage the therapist, which is typical of her introverted behavior outside the playroom, where she attempts to relate primarily with adults. Like the others, she is drawn into the play process.

CLINICAL APPLICATIONS

While recognizing the need to appropriately screen group members as noted, group play therapy is considered widely applicable. All child ages and all childhood disorders respond to the benefits of play therapy combined with group process.

Many child populations have experienced the advantages of group play therapy. In addition to the research populations noted in the following section, the child groups and presenting issues include trauma victims (Hansen, 2006; Shen, 2002, 2010), sexual abuse (Gallo-Lopez, 2006; Homeyer, 1999; Jones, 2002; Klorer, 2003; Reichert, 1994; Van de Putte, 1994), witnesses of domestic violence (Huth-Bocks, Schettini, & Shebroe, 2001), anger issues (Badau & Esquivel, 2005; Fischetti, 2010), ADHD (Hansen, Meissler, & Ovens, 2000; Reddy, 2010), reading/speech difficulties (Danger, 2003; Kaplewicz, 2000), HIV/AIDS issues (Leavitt, Morrison, Gardner, & Gallagher, 1996; Willemsen & Anscombe, 2001), and troubled junior high students (Nicol & Parker, 1981; Zuchelli, 1993).

Additional applications of group play therapy include populations such as siblings (Oe, 1999), self-concept (DeMaria & Cowden, 1992), grief (LeVieux, 1999), conduct disorders (Kernberg & Rosenberg, 1991), selective mutism (Barlow, Strother, & Landreth, 1986), emotionally disturbed (Knudsen, 1985; Lockwood & Harr, 1973), preschool and kindergarten children (Ferrigno, 1979; Miller, 1999), elementary school children (Schiffer, 1957; White & Flynt, 1999), hospitalized children (Cooper & Blitz, 1985; Lingnell & Dunn, 1999), social skills problems (Blundon & Schaefer, 2006; Johnson, 1988; Schaefer, Jacobsen, & Ghahramanlou, 2000), hearing impaired (Troester, 1996), children with divorcing parents (Ludlow & Williams, 2006), and homeless children (Baggerly, 2004).

Specific Techniques

There are multiple group play therapy techniques, in addition to the many discussed in Sweeney and Homeyer (1999). Nicholas (2003) discusses the use of creative arts interventions within the context of "action therapy" for groups. Caldwell (2003) reviews various group play therapy techniques with adult clients, and Kendall (2003) explores the use of games with adults in a group play therapy setting.

One of the advantages of group play therapy is the ability to apply a wide variety of psychotherapeutic techniques. These do not even need to be established play therapy techniques. Because of the therapeutic milieu and the cross-theoretical nature of group play therapy, structured techniques that would not necessarily be considered to fit within the play therapy context can be adapted for use in the group play therapy process. Readers are encouraged to explore group therapy techniques for adaptation and application to group play therapy (see, e.g., Corey et al., 2004; Fehr, 2010; Jacobs, Masson, & Harvill, 2008; Sori & Hecker, 2003; Stoiber & Kratochwill, 1998; Viers, 2007).

Activity Group Play Therapy

Although group play is most often employed with young children, there are multiple examples of therapeutic play groups with preadolescents and adolescents, often called *activity therapy* or *activity group play therapy*. (Bratton & Ferebee, 1999; Smith & Smith, 1999). Bratton and colleagues (2009) detail the integration of structured expressive activities within group play therapy interventions with preadolescents, including rationale and specific techniques. Group activity therapy has been used with at-risk high school students (Paone, Packman, Maddux, & Rothman, 2008) and learning-disabled preadolescents with behavioral problems (Packman & Bratton, 2003).

Group Sandtray Therapy

There is increasing study and use of sandtray therapy within the context of groups. The basic process is comprehensively discussed in Homeyer and Sweeney (in press). Pearson and Wilson (2001) note a key benefit of group sandtray therapy in that it removes the focus of any one group member as being the problem. Hunter (2006) advocates for the use of group sandtray therapy:

> A group model that uses the expressive arts play therapy technique called sandtray play has been shown to be highly successful. . . . This approach combines client-centered attitudes and techniques of creating "free and protected space," witnessing the play, and facilitating the group, with a Jungian emphasis on the power of imaginative symbolic meanings and the dynamics and benefits of group therapy. This technique can successfully "travel" to schools, preschools, after-school programs, shelters, camps, and other locations where children spend most of their time. (p. 273)

In a case study of group sandtray therapy, Hughes (2004) suggests that the intervention engages the right hemisphere of the brain, leading to increased insight and relational dynamics. Flahive's (2005) research demonstrated positive results using group sandtray therapy at schools with acting-out preadolescents. Draper, Ritter, and Willingham (2003) detailed the use of group sandtray therapy with adolescents to address intrapersonal concerns, socialization skills, and community development. Kestly (2010) reviews group sandplay in elementary schools.

EMPIRICAL SUPPORT

Most of the literature on group play therapy focuses on case studies and specific techniques. However, because group play therapy has been used as an intervention with children, there has been continued empirical support for its efficacy. A representative sample is summarized.

Gibbs (1945) studied 63 children in three clinics and noted that, although not more successful than individual treatment, group play therapy is appropriate for educational problems, generalized anxiety, and behavior disorders. Fleming and Snyder (1947) reported measurable improvements in social adjustments in a study using nondirective group play therapy. Cowen and Cruickshank (1948) and Cruickshank and Cowen (1948) worked with five physically handicapped children and reported that four of the children experienced significant or slight improvements in home behavior.

Mehlman (1953) studied 32 institutionalized mentally retarded children using nondirective play therapy and reported statistically significant improvement on a behavior rating scale. In another early study with mentally retarded children, eight boys with comorbid behavior problems were treated with group play therapy. Leland, Walker, and Taboada (1959) reported that, although there were no significant changes in "social maturation," there is "good evidence to say that the experience did activate some of the intellectual potential which could not be tapped before the experiment" (p. 851).

Group play therapy was combined with behavioral reinforcements (tokens) in a study by Clement and Milne (1967). The three small groups in the study consisted of the play group, a verbal group, and a control group. The group play, accompanied by behavioral reinforcements, showed significant increases in social approach behavior and decrease in problem behavior. Schiffer (1967) discussed the effectiveness of group play therapy with children as demonstrated by increased peer relationship skills.

Myers (1970) studied the use of group puppet therapy with 48 mentally retarded children and found significant improvement in emotional adjustment in the treatment group. Studying 36 second-grade students, House (1970) found that following 20 sessions of child-centered play therapy, the experimental group showed significant increase in self-concept in comparison with the control group. Bouillion (1974) studied group play therapy with speech- or language-delayed children and found that group play therapy resulted in significantly higher positive changes in fluency and articulation in comparison with the control and another treatment group. Danger (2003) also studied children with speech difficulties, using child-centered group play therapy. Her study demonstrated significance in improving children's expressive and receptive language skills.

In a study of 80 elementary school children, Gould (1980) demonstrated the efficacy of group play therapy through significant improvements in self-concept in treatment group participants in comparison with the control group. In an investigation with 78 similarly aged school children, Amplo (1980) found that group play therapy resulted in significant increases in a willingness to try new tasks in comparison with another teaching intervention.

Tondow Smith (1988) investigated two play therapy approaches (directive and nondirective) in the treatment of social adjustment problems with children, reporting significant improvements in self-concept, social status, and social skills with the directive experimental group in comparison with the control and nondirective groups. Perez (1988) explored the effectiveness of individual and group play therapy with sexually abused children. Both interventions resulted in statistically significant improvement in self-concept and self-mastery. In a study of 66 third- through sixth-grade children, Utay (1991) found that following a group play therapy intervention, learning-disabled children performed significantly higher on teacher reports of social skills than the control group.

In a small study of six highly stressed children, Jackson, Rump, Ferguson, and Brown (1999) reported no statistically significant differences between the treatment and control groups but noted qualitative parental report of improvement in the children's psychosocial functioning. This is similar to Doubrava's (2005) study of the effect of child-centered group play therapy on emotional intelligence, behavior, and parenting stress. Tyndall-Lind, Landreth, and Giordano (2001) investigated the efficacy of intensive group play therapy with children who witnessed domestic violence. Children in the experimental group exhibited a significant reduction in behavior problems, aggression, anxiety, and depression, as well as significant improvement in self-esteem. In a study investigating the use of group play therapy with maladjusted children, McGuire (2001) found that although statistically significant results were not found on the measures used with the small sample, positive trends were reported by therapists and teachers.

Paone et al. (2008) studied the effect of group activity therapy with at-risk high school students and found significant positive effects in relation to moral reasoning. Baggerly (2004) demonstrated the positive effects of child-centered group play therapy on the self-concept and levels of anxiety and depression with homeless children. With a sample size of 42 children, Baggerly demonstrated statistical significance in reduction of anxiety and depression and increase of self-esteem.

Cross-Cultural Applications

Studies also support the use of group play therapy cross culturally. Wakaba (1983) studied the effects of group play therapy with Japanese children who stutter, reporting that stuttering and social adjustment had significantly improved. Group play therapy was researched with 48 bilingual Puerto Rican children by Trostle (1985). She reported that the experimental group demonstrated significantly greater self-control and increased positive perceptions of other children. Shen (2002) investigated the use of short-term, child-centered group play therapy with Chinese child victims of an earthquake and reported significantly lower levels of anxiety and suicide risk in the experimental group in comparison with the control group.

There is additional literature on the cross-cultural applications of group play therapy. Baggerly and Parker (2005) discussed child-centered group play therapy with African-American boys and provide therapeutic implications and research recommendations. Hopkins, Huici, and Bermudez (2005) review group play therapy with Hispanic clients, and Kao (2005) writes about the intervention with Asian children.

CONCLUSION

Group play therapy offers the opportunity for children, adolescents, and adults to connect with one another in reciprocal ways, which leads to a greater capacity to redirect behaviors into a more self-enhancing and interpersonally appropriate manner. Group members experience insight, which results in a greater degree of self-control and correspondingly helps to decrease externalizing (acting out or aggressive) and internalizing (acting-in and regressive) behaviors. Additionally, given the opportunity to communicate in their natural medium of communication, children also have greater opportunities to express feelings, desires, and needs in the group play therapy setting. This dynamic can also be true for adolescents and adults with verbal skills that are developmentally delayed or inhibited by the psychological and neurobiological effects of trauma.

Because this play therapy intervention actively merges the benefits of the group process with the advantages of the play therapy, therapeutic play groups promote safety and foster growth. This is a natural outcome, combining client's innate communication style and the usual course of interaction with other clients in the group experience. Children, adolescents, and adults learn about themselves, others, and life.

The play therapy literature demonstrates that therapeutic play groups have been successfully used with challenging clients for some time. The use and popularity of play therapy groups, however, seem to be somewhat limited in the play therapy world. This needs to change: "Group play therapy successfully blends the benefits of play therapy and group process, and may well serve to optimize the limited resources of both therapists and children. Children grow and heal in a process that helps them translate their learning into life outside the play setting. Group play therapy provides this setting" (Sweeney & Homeyer, 1999, p. 13).

REFERENCES

Amplo, J. (1980). Relative effects of group play therapy and Adlerian teacher training upon social maturity and school adjustment of primary grade students. *Dissertation Abstracts International, 41*(7A), 3001.

Badau, K., & Esquivel, G. (2005). Group therapy for adolescents with anger problems. In L. Gallo-Lopez & C. Schaefer (Eds.), *Play therapy for adolescents* (pp. 239–266). Lanham, MD: Rowman & Littlefield.

Baggerly, J. (2004). The effects of child-centered group play therapy on self-concept, depression, and anxiety of children who are homeless. *International Journal of Play Therapy, 13*(2), 31–51.

Baggerly, J., & Parker, M. (2005). Child-centered group play therapy with African American boys at the elementary school level. *Journal of Counseling & Development, 83,* 387–396.

Barlow, K., Strother, J., & Landreth, G. (1986). Sibling group play therapy: An effective alternative with an elective mute child. *School Counselor, 34*(1), 44–50.

Berg, R., Landreth, G., & Fall, K. (2006). *Group counseling: Concepts and procedures* (4th ed.). New York, NY: Routledge.

Bertoia, J. (1999). The invisible village: Jungian group play therapy. In D. Sweeney & L. Homeyer (Eds.), *Handbook of group play therapy* (pp. 86–104). San Francisco , CA: Jossey-Bass.

Blundon, J., & Schaefer, C. (2006). The use of group play therapy for children with social skills deficits. In H. Kaduson & C. Schaefer (Eds.), *Short-term play therapy for children* (2nd ed., pp. 336–376). New York, NY: Guilford Press.

Bouillion, K. (1974). The comparative efficacy of nondirective group play therapy with preschool, speech- or language-delayed children. *Dissertation Abstracts International, 35*(1B), 495.

Bratton, S., & Ferebee, K. (1999). The use of structured expressive art activities in group activity therapy with preadolescents. In D. Sweeney & L. Homeyer (Eds.), *Handbook of group play therapy* (pp. 192–214). San Francisco, CA: Jossey-Bass.

Bratton, S., Ceballos, P., & Ferebee, K. (2009). Integration of structured expressive activities within a humanistic group play therapy format for preadolescents. *Journal for Specialists in Group Work, 34*(3), 251–275.

Caldwell, C. (2003). Adult group play therapy. In C. Schaefer (Ed.), *Play therapy with adults* (pp. 301–316). New York, NY: Wiley.

Clement, P., & Milne, D. C. (1967). Group play therapy and tangible reinforcers used to modify the behavior of 8-year-old boys. *Behavior Research and Therapy, 5*(4), 301–312.

Cooper, S., & Blitz, J. (1985). A therapeutic play group for hospitalized children with cancer. *Journal of Psychosocial Oncology, 3*(2), 23–37.

Corey, G., Corey, M. S., Callanan, P., & Russell, J. M. (2004). *Group techniques* (3rd ed.). Florence, KY: Brooks/Cole.

Cowen, E., & Cruickshank, W. (1948). Group therapy with physically handicapped children. II: Evaluation. *Journal of Educational Psychology, 39*, 281–297.

Crane, J. (2001). The parents' part in the play therapy process. In G. Landreth (Ed.), *Innovations in play therapy: Issues, process, and special populations* (pp. 83–98). Philadelphia, PA: Brunner/Routledge.

Cruickshank, W., & Cowen, E. (1948). Group therapy with physically handicapped children. I: Report of study. *Journal of Educational Psychology, 39*, 193–215.

Danger, S. (2003). Child-centered group play therapy with children with speech difficulties. *Dissertation Abstracts International, 64*(09A), 3202.

DeMaria, M., & Cowden, S. (1992). The effects of client-centered group play therapy on self-concept. *International Journal of Play Therapy, 1*(1), 53–67.

Doubrava, D. (2005). The effects of child-centered group play therapy on emotional intelligence, behavior, and parenting stress. *Dissertation Abstracts International, 66*(3-B), 1714.

Draper, K., Ritter, K., & Willingham, E. (2003). Sand tray group counseling with adolescents. *Journal for Specialists in Group Work, 28*(3), 244–260.

Fehr, S. (2010). *101 Interventions in group therapy* (Rev. ed.). New York, NY: Routledge.

Ferrigno, J. (1979). The effects of group play therapy on preschool children when conducted by students functioning as therapists. *Dissertation Abstracts International, 39*(11A), 6524–6525.

Fischetti, B. (2010). Play therapy for anger management in the schools. In A. Drewes & C. Schaefer (Eds.), *School-based play therapy* (2nd ed., 283–306). Hoboken, NJ: Wiley.

Flahive, M. W. (2005). Group sandtray therapy at school with preadolescents identified with behavioral difficulties. *Dissertation Abstracts International, 66*(11A), 0158.

Fleming, L., & Snyder, W. (1947). Social and personal changes following nondirective group play therapy. *American Journal of Orthopsychiatry, 17*, 101–116.

Gallo-Lopez, L. (2006). A creative play therapy approach to the group treatment of young sexually abused children. In H. Kaduson & C. Schaefer (Eds.), *Short-term play therapy for children* (2nd ed., pp. 245–272). New York, NY: Guilford Press.

Gibbs, J. (1945). Group play therapy. *British Journal of Medical Psychology, 20*, 244–254.

Ginott, H. (1961). *Group psychotherapy with children: The theory and practice of play therapy.* New York, NY: McGraw-Hill.

Ginott, H. (1975). Group play therapy with children. In G. Gazda (Ed.), *Basic approaches to group psychotherapy and group counseling* (2nd ed., pp. 327–341). Springfield, IL: Thomas.

Gould, M. (1980). The effect of short-term intervention play therapy on the self-concept of selected elementary pupils. *Dissertation Abstracts International, 41*(3B), 1090.

Hansen, S. (2006). An expressive arts therapy model with groups for post-traumatic stress disorder. In L. Carey (Ed.), *Expressive and creative arts methods for trauma survivors* (pp. 73–91). London, UK: Kingsley.

Hansen, S., Meissler, K., & Ovens, R. (2000). Kids together: A group play therapy model for children with ADHD symptomology. *Journal of Child and Adolescent Group Therapy, 10*(4), 191–211.

Homeyer, L. (1999). Group play therapy with sexually abused children. In D. Sweeney & L. Homeyer (Eds.), *Handbook of group play therapy* (pp. 299–318). San Francisco, CA: Jossey-Bass.

Homeyer, L., & Sweeney, D. (in press). *Sandtray therapy: A practical manual* (Rev. ed.). New York, NY: Routledge.

Hopkins, S., Huici, V., & Bermudez, D. (2005). Therapeutic play with Hispanic clients. In E. Gil & A. Drewes (Eds.), *Cultural issues in play therapy* (pp. 148–167). New York, NY: Guilford Press.

House, R. (1970). The effects of nondirective group play therapy upon the sociometric status and self-concept of selected second grade children. *Dissertation Abstracts International, 31*(6A), 2684.

Hughes, S. (2004). The group sand tray: A case study. *Dissertation Abstracts International, 67*(02B), 1150.

Hunter, L. (2006). Group sandtray play therapy. In H. Kaduson & C. Schaefer (Eds.), *Short-term play therapy for children* (2nd ed., pp. 273–303). New York, NY: Guilford Press.

Huth-Bocks, A., Schettini, A., & Shebroe, V. (2001). Group play therapy for preschoolers exposed to domestic violence. *Journal of Child and Adolescent Group Therapy, 11*(1), 19–34.

Jackson, Y., Rump, B., Ferguson, K., & Brown, A. (1999). Group play therapy for young children exposed to major stressors: Comparison of quantitative and qualitative evaluation methods. *Journal of Child and Adolescent Group Therapy, 9*(1), 3–16.

Jacobs, E., Masson, R., & Harvill, R. (2008). *Group counseling: Strategies and skills* (6th ed.). Florence, KY: Brooks/Cole.

Johnson, M. (1988). Use of play group therapy in promoting social skills. *Issues in Mental Health Nursing, 9*(1), 105–112.

Jones, K. D. (2002). Group play therapy with sexually abused preschool children: Group behaviors and interventions. *Journal for Specialists in Group Work, 27*(4), 377–389.

Kao, S. (2005). Play therapy with Asian children. In E. Gil & A. Drewes (Eds.), *Cultural issues in play therapy* (pp. 195–206). New York, NY: Guilford Press.

Kaplewicz, N. (2000). Effects of group play therapy on reading achievement and emotional symptoms among remedial readers. *Dissertation Abstracts International, 61*(1B), 535.

Kendall, J. (2003). Using games with adults in a play therapy group setting. In C. Schaefer (Ed.), *Play therapy with adults* (pp. 317–323). Hoboken, NJ: Wiley & Sons.

Kernberg, P., & Rosenberg, J. (1991). Play group therapy for children with socialized conduct disorders. In S. Tittman (Ed.), *Psychoanalytic group theory and therapy: Essays in honor of Saul Scheidlinger* (pp. 195–210). Madison, CT: International Universities Press.

Kestly, T. (2010). Group sandplay in elementary schools. In A. Drewes & C. Schaefer (Eds.), *School-based play therapy* (2nd ed., 237–256). Hoboken, NJ: Wiley.

Klorer, P. G. (2003). Sexually abused children: Group approaches. In C. Malchiodi (Ed.), *Handbook of art therapy* (pp. 339–350). New York, NY: Guilford Press.

Knudsen, W. (1985). Psychopuppetry, nondirective group play therapy using puppets as the intermediary object: A comparison with traditional nondirective group counseling or no counseling in the treatment of emotionally handicapped elementary school children. *Dissertation Abstracts International, 45*(8A), 2452.

Kottman, T. (1999). Group applications of Adlerian play therapy. In D. Sweeney & L. Homeyer (Eds.), *Handbook of group play therapy* (pp. 65–85). San Francisco, CA: Jossey-Bass.

Landreth, G. (1999). Foreword. In D. Sweeney & L. Homeyer (Eds.), *Handbook of group play therapy* (pp. xi–xiii). San Francisco, CA: Jossey-Bass.

Landreth, G. (2002). *Play therapy: The art of the relationship* (2nd ed.). Philadelphia, PA: Brunner/Routledge.

Landreth, G., & Sweeney, D. (1999). The freedom to be: Child-centered group play therapy. In D. Sweeney & L. Homeyer (Eds.), *Handbook of group play therapy* (pp. 39–64). San Francisco, CA: Jossey-Bass.

Leavitt, K., Morrison, J., Gardner, S., & Gallagher, M. (1996). Group play therapy for cumulatively traumatized child survivors of familial AIDS. *International Journal of Play Therapy, 5*(1), 1–17.

Leland, H., Walker, J., & Taboada, A. (1959). Group play therapy with a group of postnursery male retardates. *American Journal of Mental Deficiency, 63*, 848–851.

LeVieux, J. (1999). Group play therapy with grieving children. In D. Sweeney & L. Homeyer (Eds.), *Handbook of group play therapy* (pp. 375–388). San Francisco, CA: Jossey-Bass.

Lingnell, L., & Dunn, L. (1999). Group play: Wholeness and healing for the hospitalized child. In D. Sweeney & L. Homeyer (Eds.), *Handbook of group play therapy* (pp. 359–374). San Francisco, CA: Jossey-Bass.

Lockwood, J., & Harr, B. (1973). Psychodrama: A therapeutic tool with children in group play therapy. *Group Psychotherapy and Psychodrama, 26*(3/4), 53–67.

Ludlow, W., & Williams, M. (2006). Short-term group play therapy for children whose parents are divorcing. In H. Kaduson & C. Schaefer (Eds.), *Short-term play therapy for children* (2nd ed., pp. 304–335). New York, NY: Guilford Press.

McGuire, D. (2001). Child-centered group play therapy with children experiencing adjustment difficulties. *Dissertation Abstracts International, 61*(10A), 3908.

Mehlman, B. (1953). Group play therapy with mentally retarded children. *Journal of Abnormal and Social Psychology, 48*(1), 53–60.

Miller, J. (1999). Effects of developmental group play on social competence of kindergartners. *Masters Abstracts International, 37*(05), 1187.

Moustakas, C. (1974). *Portraits of loneliness and love*. New York, NY: Prentice-Hall.

Moustakas, C. (1997). *Relationship play therapy*. Northvale, NJ: Aronson.

Myers, D. (1970). A comparison of the effects of group puppet therapy and activity group therapy with mentally retarded children. *Dissertation Abstracts International, 31*(10A), 5234.

Nicholas, M. (2003). Introduction: Action methods in group therapy. In D. Wiener & L. Oxford (Eds.), *Action therapy with families and groups: Using creative arts improvisation in clinical practice* (pp. 103–105). Washington, DC: American Psychological Association.

Nicol, A., & Parker, J. (1981). Playgroup therapy in the junior school: Method and general problems. *British Journal of Guidance and Counseling, 9*(1), 86–93.

Oaklander, V. (1999). Group play therapy from a Gestalt therapy perspective. In D. Sweeney & L. Homeyer (Eds.), *Handbook of group play therapy* (pp. 162–176). San Francisco, CA: Jossey-Bass.

Oe, E. (1999). Sibling group play therapy. In D. Sweeney & L. Homeyer (Eds.), *Handbook of group play therapy* (pp. 319–335). San Francisco, CA: Jossey-Bass.

Packman, J., & Bratton, S. (2003). A school-based group play/activity therapy intervention with learning disabled preadolescents exhibiting behavior problems. *International Journal of Play Therapy, 12*(2), 7–29.

Paone, T., Packman, J., Maddux, C., & Rothman, T. (2008). A school-based group activity therapy intervention with at-risk high school students as it relates to their moral reasoning. *International Journal of Play Therapy, 17*(2), 122–137.

Pearson, M., & Wilson, H. (2001). *Sandplay and symbol work: Emotional healing and personal development with children, adolescents and adults*. Melbourne, Australia: ACER Press.

Perez, C. (1988). A comparison of group play therapy and individual play therapy for sexually abused children. *Dissertation Abstracts International, 48*(12A), 3079.

Reddy, L. (2010). Group play therapy interventions for children with attention deficit/hyperactivity disorder. In A. Drewes & C. Schaefer (Eds.), *School-based play therapy* (2nd ed., pp. 307–332). Hoboken, NJ: Wiley.

Reichert, E. (1994). Play and animal-assisted therapy: A group-treatment model for sexually abused girls ages 9–13. *Family Therapy, 21*(1), 55–62.

Schaefer, C., Jacobsen, H., & Ghahramanlou, M. (2000). Play group therapy for social skills deficits in children. In H. Kaduson & C. Schaefer (Eds.), *Short-term play therapy for children* (pp. 296–344). New York, NY: Guilford Press.

Schiffer, A. (1967). The effectiveness of group play therapy as assessed by specific changes in a child's peer relations. *American Journal of Orthopsychiatry, 37*(2), 219–220.

Schiffer, M. (1957). A therapeutic play group in a public school. *Mental Hygiene, 41*, 185–193.

Shen, Y-J. (2002). Short-term play therapy with Chinese earthquake victims: Effects on anxiety, depression and adjustment. *International Journal of Play Therapy, 11*(1), 43–64.

Shen, Y-J. (2010). Trauma-focused group play therapy in the schools. In A. Drewes & C. Schaefer (Eds.), *School-based play therapy* (2nd ed., 237–256). Hoboken, NJ: Wiley.

Smith, D. M., & Smith, N. (1999). Relational activity play therapy group. In D. Sweeney & L. Homeyer (Eds.), *Handbook of group play therapy* (pp. 234–266). San Francisco, CA: Jossey-Bass.

Sori, C., & Hecker, L. (2003). *The therapist's notebook for children and adolescents: Homework, handouts, and activities for use in psychotherapy*. New York, NY: Haworth Press.

Stoiber, K., & Kratochwill, T. (Eds.). (1998). *Handbook of group interventions for children and families*. Boston: Allyn & Bacon.

Sweeney, D. (1997). *Counseling children through the world of play*. Eugene, OR: Wipf & Stock.

Sweeney, D. (2001). Legal and ethical issues in play therapy. In G. Landreth (Ed.), *Innovations in play therapy: Issues, process, and special populations* (pp. 65–81). Philadelphia, PA: Brunner/Routledge.

Sweeney, D., & Homeyer, D. (1999). *Handbook of group play therapy: How to do it, how it works, whom it's best for*. San Francisco, CA: Jossey-Bass.

Sweeney, D., & Landreth, G. (2009). Child-centered play therapy. In K. O'Connor & L. Braverman (Eds.), *Play therapy theory and technique: A comparative analysis* (2nd ed., pp. 123–162). Hoboken, NJ: Wiley.

Tondow Smith, L. (1988). The relative effectiveness of two group play therapy approaches in modifying the social adjustment of primary grade children. *Dissertation Abstracts International, 48*(7B), 2112.

Troester, J. (1996). A therapeutic play group for children with hearing impairments. *Journal of Child and Adolescent Group Therapy, 6*(2), 101–109.

Trostle, S. (1985). An investigation of the effects of child-centered group play therapy upon sociometric, self-control, and play behavior ratings of three- to six-year-old bilingual Puerto Rican children. *Dissertation Abstracts International, 46*(5A), 1198.

Tyndall-Lind, A., Landreth, G., & Giordano, M. (2001). Intensive group play therapy with child witnesses of domestic violence. *International Journal of Play Therapy, 10*(1), 53–83.

Utay, J. (1991). Effectiveness of a cognitive-behavioral group play therapy intervention on selected aspects of social skills of third through sixth-grade students with learning disabilities. *Dissertation Abstracts International, 52*(8A), 2826.

Van de Putte, S. (1994). A structured activities group for sexually abused children. In K. O'Connor & C. Schaefer (Eds.), *Handbook of play therapy: Advances and innovations* (Vol. 2, pp. 409–427). New York, NY: Wiley.

van der Kolk, C. (1985). *Introduction to group counseling and psychotherapy*. Columbus, OH: Merrill.

Viers, D. (2007). *The group therapist's notebook: Homework, handouts, and activities for use in psychotherapy*. New York, NY: Routledge.

Wakaba, Y. (1983). Group play therapy for Japanese children who stutter. *Journal of Fluency Disorders, 8*(2), 93–118.

White, J., & Flynt, J. (1999). Play groups in elementary school. In D. Sweeney & L. Homeyer (Eds.), *Handbook of group play therapy* (pp. 336–358). San Francisco, CA: Jossey-Bass.

Willemsen, H., & Anscombe, E. (2001). Art and play group therapy for preschool children infected and affected by HIV/AIDS. *Clinical Child Psychology and Psychiatry, 6*(3), 339–350.

Yalom, I., & Leszcz, M. (2005). *The theory and practice of group psychotherapy* (5th ed.). New York, NY: Basic Books.

Zuchelli, P. (1993). Group play therapy with junior high school students. *International Journal of Play Therapy, 2*(1), 15–32.

Chapter 14

ECOSYSTEMIC PLAY THERAPY
Kevin O'Connor[1]

INTRODUCTION

Ecosystemic theory and the model for applying it to the practice of play therapy were developed in the 1980s and integrate elements of many psychological, social work, and systems theories. The goal in creating an ecosystemic theory of play therapy was to encourage play therapists to take a very broadly systemic perspective in developing their case conceptualizations and treatment plans. The term *ecosystemic* as opposed to *systemic* was used to both differentiate it from family systems models and to convey the breadth of the approach. In ecosystemic theory, no system is excluded from consideration.

Ecosystemic theory shares some conceptual similarities to, and has adopted some terminology from, Urie Bronfenbrenner's (1979) ecological model. There are two significant similarities. One is the emphasis placed on the effects that the multiple systems in which children are embedded have on their day-to-day lives. The other is the terms used to cluster these systems into larger conceptual groupings: microsystems, mesosystems, exosystems (not used in ecosystemic theory), macrosystems, and chronosystems (changes produced by the passage of time). There are also some significant differences. First, Bronfenbrenner focused primarily on human development and the contribution of the ecological systems to the process and its outcome. Ecosystemic theory considers individual development to be a chronosystem both affected by and affecting other systems. Second, Bronfenbrenner put forth a nested systems model in which each system is embedded in other systems. He used the exosystem concept to link systems affecting one another without necessarily being embedded. In ecosystemic theory, the systems are viewed as hierarchically arranged, with systems closer to the top having broader and more powerful influence on the systems lower in the hierarchy. When governments make laws, the majority of the population is affected. However, a nonnested model allows for the possibility that some members of the society may somehow be insulated from those effects. Finally, Bronfenbrenner uses the term *microsystem* to group all of the systems with which the individual has the most consistent contact. Ecosystemic theory expands the microsystem to include individuals themselves as mind–body systems rather than just the basic units within other systems.

---

[1] Debra New was the second author on this chapter in the first edition of this text. Although she was not involved in writing this updated version, I am indebted to her for her original contribution and its continued importance in the current edition.

Ecosystemic theory goes on to recognize the unique way children are dependent on, and minimally able to influence, the many systems in which they are embedded. Because of this dependency, child therapists must often be open to intervening more directly in their clients' lives to affect a positive treatment outcome than would most therapists who work with adults. In fact, children are regularly brought to treatment not for internalized, neurotic sorts of problems but because they are negatively reacting to systemic problems such as crises experienced by their caregivers (medical, employment, marital, etc.), siblings (medical, school, legal, etc.), teachers, schools, communities, and so on. These interactions children have with other systems shape their worldview (O'Connor & Ammen, 1997). Their worldview, in turn, affects children's ability to enjoy their lives and to function optimally on a day-to-day basis. The overarching goal of ecosystemic play therapy becomes maximizing children's enjoyment of their lives so as to maximize their development and functioning in the present as well as the future.

BASIC CONCEPTS, GOALS, AND TECHNIQUES

One of the central assumptions underlying ecosystemic play therapy is the notion that therapists can be effective only when they consistently work from an organized theoretical frame. Ecosystemic play therapy does not presume that any one theoretical model is necessarily better than another. Therapists can be effective working from a psychodynamic, cognitive-behavioral, family system, or other theory as long as they use the theory consistently. Doing so allows therapists to present their child clients with clear and consistent interventions, both verbal and experiential. To be useful in shaping the therapist's thinking, any good theory must include certain key elements: an underlying philosophy, a way of conceptualizing personality, and a way of conceptualizing psychopathology.

Underlying Philosophy

Most of psychology is rooted in a Western, hard-sciences model. This model's primary assumption is that right and wrong answers to be found for every question. The answers may change as we come to know more, but eventually a final right answer can be uncovered. This philosophy tends to push a person into black-and-white thinking and into making value judgments based on perceptions of the rightness or wrongness of a given behavior or situation. For example, this philosophical position posits that a person could come to a definite and universal conclusion as to whether sexualized contact between an adult and a child is always harmful irrespective of variables such as the age of the child, the nature of the contact, the situation in which it occurred, or the larger cultural context. While ecosystemic play therapy acknowledges the potential value of treatment and research grounded in a hard-sciences philosophy, it is a theory grounded in phenomenology.

Phenomenology is a philosophy based on the notion that there are no absolute, right and wrong answers but, rather, all knowledge and its value are relative. All knowledge is based on how we perceive the "facts." For example, how do we know each of us sees the same color when we look at a cherry? All we really know is, whatever it is we see, we have been taught to call that color red. In fact, colorblind individuals say a cherry is red even though their perception of the color is known to be different from others' perceptions.

When phenomenology serves as the basis for a treatment model, it has two effects. The first is that the therapist consistently assumes the information provided by each of the people involved in a given case is accurate. When two people's stories differ significantly, the therapist does not assume one or the other is mistaken or lying. Instead, the therapist begins by assuming that each person perceives the situation very differently based on his or her experience and understanding. The other effect of working within a phenomenologic frame is that a person evaluates right and wrong only in context. In discussing the hard-sciences philosophy, the notion of being able to determine the universal impact of sexualized contact between adults and children was referenced. From a phenomenologic perspective, such a determination would be impossible. Each adult's and each child's experience of sexualized contact is unique and occurs in a unique context. The potential negative impact of the contact can only be evaluated in context.

Even when evaluating a relatively innocuous behavior, context can make all the difference. Generally, parents who kiss their children goodnight are doing the "right" thing. But most play therapists would agree that parents who kiss their child goodnight for the 20th time because the child has fussed and whined for hours about having to go to bed is probably reinforcing a problem behavior rather than giving appropriate nurturance.

Phenomenology is also subject dependent (Giorgi, 1983); we can never really know how another individual perceives the world, but we can attempt to come to such an understanding by considering the client's life and those experiences the client has had. When working with children, this also means trying to understand how their developmental level makes their experiences and worldviews radically different from those of adults. Subject dependency applies to us all. Therapists are not somehow magically excluded. Therapists' own experiences and worldviews affect how they understand children and their problems. This creates interplay between therapists' and children's subject-dependent perspectives. Therapy becomes a dance in which therapist and child learn to move between each other's worlds in search of ways to improve the child's quality of life.

Humanism (Herrick, 2005) is another philosophical perspective underlying ecosystemic theory. A significant aspect of humanism is the way in which it evaluates the "rightness" or "wrongness" of behavior. Unlike a fundamentalist or orthodox position, humanism does not maintain absolute standards of right and wrong across situations. Rather, all behavior must be evaluated in context. Behaviors with a positive or even neutral impact on the self and/or others are usually considered "right" while those with a negative impact are usually considered "wrong" or pathologic. An ecosystemic play therapist will examine the impact of children's behavior on the children themselves and those around them in order to determine if the behavior is problematic enough to warrant being the focus of therapy. To illustrate the

differences in fundamentalist and humanistic perspectives, let us consider hallucinations in children. From a fundamentalist perspective, hallucinations are seen as
inherently pathologic; a symptom requiring treatment. From a humanistic perspective, treatment would only be necessary if the hallucinations cause the child
distress or if they cause him or her to behave in ways that endanger others
(O'Connor, 2005).

Phenomenology and humanism give ecosystemic play therapy the flexibility
necessary to be effective across cultures. Phenomenology, by definition, takes into
consideration the many lenses through which people view their world and their
experiences in that world. These lenses are shaped by one's life experience and by
all of one's identities such as gender, race, ethnicity, and socioeconomic class, to name
but a few. For purposes of this discussion, all of these identities are loosely grouped
under the term *culture*. The way in which different cultures view something as
fundamental as time is a good example of the effect of such lenses. Anglo- and
Euro-Americans tend to place great value on time and expect others to share this
value by noting dates, following schedules, and being on time to appointments,
work, and school. Native Americans tend to minimize the importance of time and
place greater value on being in the moment and what one gains by allowing experiences to unfold naturally.

Phenomenology requires us to recognize both views as two different ways of
being in the world, both equally accurate and correct. Humanism complements this
aspect of phenomenology by also allowing both perspectives to be equally good
given that neither one causes harm to the self or others. At the same time, a humanistic philosophy recognizes the potential for harm when the two worldviews come
up against one another. In trying to navigate between the two, a child might have to
choose between staying on at a spontaneous yet important family event and being
on time for a test at school. Either choice has the potential to result in personal
distress or negative consequences. Finally, humanism can provide the framework
that a play therapist uses to minimize the negative impact in such situations by helping all concerned learn ways to balance the needs of the child and the various cultures and systems in which he or she is embedded (O'Connor, 2005).

Personality

In the ecosystemic model, personality is defined as the "sum of intra- and interpersonal characteristics, attributes, cognitions, beliefs, values, and so forth that
make a person unique" (O'Connor, 2000, p. 90). The basic motive driving personality is thought to be the desire to maximize the rewards obtained in daily life
while avoiding negative consequences (O'Connor, 1993). The egocentricity of this
motive is tempered by the early attachments motivating children to see rewards in
interpersonal and reciprocal relationships. Considerable emphasis is also placed on
the importance of developmental factors in conceptualizing children's personality.
An extensive discussion of various developmental models and the functioning of
children at different ages as incorporated in ecosystemic theory is presented elsewhere (O'Connor, 2000; O'Connor & Ammen, 1997). Here, we present additional

discussion of the particular importance of children's relationships with their primary caretaker(s).

It is the goal of all humans to attempt to have their basic biological needs met. As infants, these needs can be realized only through the relationship with the caregiver. As a result, this relationship is the most potent organizer of personality. In fact, we now know this relationship actually shapes the hard-wiring of the child's brain (Gerhardt, 2004), particularly with respect to how the child will expect the world to react to him or her (Siegel, 2002). As the relationship develops, the caregiver helps provide not only for the child's biological needs but also for the critical regulation of the child's affect. One of the primary responsibilities of the caregiver is to be attuned to infants' external cues as well as their emotional states (Schore, 2001). When infants are distressed, the caregivers respond and attempt to soothe them. In so doing, infants learn to count on others to get their basic needs met as well as to self-soothe. When infants become bored or withdrawn, the caregiver attempts to keep them engaged, thereby taking responsibility for maintaining the relationship. Beyond simple soothing and engaging, healthy caregivers encourage happiness and delight in the infant by engaging the child in fun and games such as peek-a-boo and tickling. These interactions help infants see others as a source of emotional satisfaction and pleasant stimulation (Jernberg & Booth, 2010).

Unfortunately, this reciprocal process of infant–caregiver attachment does not always go smoothly. Problems may arise because of individual, interactional, or systemic difficulties. On an individual level, either child or parent may present with problems, making both pragmatic and emotional transactions difficult. If a child is born with a medical condition, such as colic, the child is distressed more often than most and is more difficult to soothe. These children experience pain and, on some level, are aware of the caregiver's inability to soothe them. Unfortunately, young children do not have the cognitive sophistication needed to differentiate between the caregiver who is trying hard but is unable to find a way to soothe the infant from one who is being intentionally neglectful. In either case, unmediated distress on the part of the infant or child has significant potential to interfere with the attachment relationship. Alternatively, caregivers may also experience individual problems, making it more difficult for them to be attuned to their infants. Again, infants and young children are not able to grasp the reason for the caregiver's unavailability; they only know their basic pragmatic and/or emotional needs are not being met.

Sometimes the attachment relationships of otherwise healthy and functional children and caregivers are disrupted by problems in their interaction. A common example of such interactional problems is the caregiver's use of inappropriate discipline. Many caregivers still use spanking or other forms of physical aggression to control children's negative behavior. Spanking is not attuned to children's pragmatic or emotional needs, nor does it help the child learn strategies for either emotional or behavioral regulation. Rather, it simply teaches the child that aggression is a suitable means for getting others to suppress the expression of their needs. In ecosystemic play therapy, it is important to help caregivers manage children's behavior in ways that help them learn new behaviors rather than simply repress behavior. One of the best strategies for doing this is to use natural and logical consequences

(Dreikurs & Grey, 1970). Natural consequences are those the child would experience if allowed to engage in the behavior without interference. If you forget to take your lunch to school, you will go hungry. If you do not do your homework, you will get poor grades. Unfortunately, adults routinely interfere and prevent or soften natural consequences in the belief they are being "nice" to the child. Instead, they simply make it more difficult for children to learn to take responsibility for their own behavior.

Sometimes the natural consequence of a behavior is too severe to actually let it take place, such as letting children discover the dangers of failing to look both ways before crossing the street by allowing them to be hit by a car. In such instances, the caregiver needs to develop logical consequences to help contain the child's behavior. Logical consequences are clearly related to the targeted problem behavior. A child who runs toward the road might have the natural consequence of being unable to play outside for an hour or a day. An older child who values his or her independence but who fails to look both ways at a curb might have to spend the rest of a particular shopping trip holding the parent's hand. Logical consequences sometimes require some real ingenuity on the part of caregivers, but they typically avoid power struggles and facilitate children's learning the effects and consequences of their behavior.

Natural and logical consequences are most effective when caregivers simultaneously present children with acceptable alternative behaviors for which there is no consequence. The avoidance of power struggles and the presentation of acceptable alternatives make the use of natural and logical consequences valuable in preserving the attachment relationship. Behavior management becomes less about caregivers overriding children's desires or needs and more about facilitating children getting those needs met in acceptable ways. The dyad is working together toward an end rather than struggling against each other.

A popular alternative to spanking is the use of time-out. While the use of time-out can be a highly effective intervention, it is often overused and misused. Time-out should be used only as a logical consequence. Having to go to time-out because you refused to brush your teeth is not logical. Having to go to time-out (a form of social isolation) because you endangered someone or something makes perfect sense. If the child's behavior substantially interferes with the needs or rights of others, he or she needs to be separated for some period of time. Time-out as a consequence for hurting or threatening to hurt the bodies or feelings of others is perfectly logical. Besides overusing time-out, many caregivers misuse it by either failing to actually remove the child from a reinforcing environment or having the child spend longer in time-out than is age appropriate.

Sending children to their rooms is not usually a "real" time-out because most children have toys in their rooms with which to pass the time. It is highly preferable to have a chair or special location, removed from other stimulation, where the child can actually use time-out to calm down. It is also preferable to use frequent, short time-outs rather than longer time-outs. For toddlers, a time-out of even a minute can seem like an eternity. For preschoolers and older children, a time-out of 5 minutes plus 1 additional minute for each year of the child's age is usually suitable. In all cases, the time-out does not actually start until the child is sitting quietly—no matter how long this takes. Depending on the age and needs of the child, the caregiver may have to provide considerable assistance in helping the child calm down enough for the time-out to officially begin. When used appropriately, time-out teaches children the importance of behaving in socially appropriate ways and emphasizes their ability to manage their own behavior.

Finally, the attachment relationship may be disrupted by systemic factors. A sibling's medical crisis may require the caregiver to be away from the child more than is optimal. A job change may result in a highly disruptive change in residence. Or something as catastrophic as a natural disaster may interfere with the caregiver's ability to meet the child's pragmatic and emotional needs. Regardless of the source of the interference, these disruptions in the attachment relationship often lead the child to develop pathologic, that is, nonfunctional, behaviors.

Pathology

Consistent with the model of personality just presented, pathology, when viewed from an ecosystemic play therapy perspective, is conceptualized as involving one or more of three factors. First and foremost, pathology is defined as occurring in children who are "unable to get their needs met at a level they consider to be satisfactory, or those who are unable to get their needs met in ways that do not substantially interfere with the ability of others to get their needs met" (O'Connor, 1997, p. 241). Essentially, they have been thwarted in their attempts to satisfy their basic drives. This first factor is often inextricably linked to a second factor, the disruption of children's attachment relationships. By the time children are brought to therapy, it is often difficult to tell which came first—the failure to get basic needs met or the disruption of the attachment. Similarly, the first two factors are highly related to the last one. Consistent inability to get their needs met and/or disruption of important attachments can interfere with children's developmental progress. The disruption in children's behavior or pattern of reinforcement or the sheer energy required by children's attempts to cope with life can leave them without the resources necessary to continue to develop normally. Often these developmental disruptions are not obvious because they are confined to the child's inability to think in an age-appropriate way about the problem or things related to it. Many children who seem developmentally on target or even advanced suddenly manifest much more concrete thinking when their problems and associated affects come to the forefront. Temporary disruption in the ability to get needs met happens frequently and is not necessarily problematic—much less pathological. In ecosystemic play therapy, true pathology is conceptualized as occurring when a child "repeatedly engages in behavior that does not get his or her needs met and is unable to generate alternative behavior or to engage in effective problem solving" (O'Connor, 1997, p. 241).

Children may come to the point where they are manifesting pathology for several, often interconnected, reasons. These exactly parallel the factors previously discussed as contributing to disruptions in the attachment relationship. Individual factors children carry with them may make it difficult for them to get their needs met and/or to get them met appropriately, no matter the context. Children with neurologic, severe medical, developmental, or other conditions certainly fall into this category. These children's needs are simply not similar to those of other children, and, therefore, they demand more of those around them. Consequently, they are likely to experience more frustration, have more disrupted attachments, and experience more developmental problems.

Children may also come to manifest pathology because they are embedded in problematic interpersonal relationships. These children are basically able to function like those around them, but their interactions are not mutually satisfying. One or both parties would like to improve the quality of the interaction but are unable to find a way to do so. Finally, pathology may arise when children are embedded in pathogenic systems. The child has the capacity to function, but the system makes doing so difficult. No matter how well intentioned, systems such as medical hospitals, foster care, and schools may create an environment in which children's needs are simply not adequately met, usually resulting in frustration and pain on the part of both the system and the children. These causes of pathology are by no means orthogonal, and often any two or even all three are operating at the same time, significantly complicating treatment.

When developing a formulation to explain the child's current pathology and its source, ecosystemic play therapists are mindful of the major role of the child's current developmental level in shaping the nature of the problem. Always, developmental age is more important than chronological age, though significant differences between the two create problems of their own. A very good intervention plan can be designed for a child whose capacity for attachment is consistent with that of a 2-year-old, irrespective of the child's chronological age. However, if the child is chronologically only age 4, the caretakers and the environment are not likely to experience 2-year-old attachment behavior as particularly problematic. However, if the child is chronologically age 12, such behavior is far less likely to be tolerated by others. The 4-year-old is much more likely than the 12-year-old to get the kind of nurturance and support he or she needs to move on without heroic efforts to engage those around him or her.

One method for quickly assessing the child's current social–emotional developmental functioning is to use the Developmental Therapy Objective Rating Form (DTORF). It is a quick, semistructured interview in which the clinician gathers history from the caregiver and/or others who know the child well. Ratings are obtained in four domains: social, behavioral, academic, and communication. Additionally, because the items are worded as operationally defined objectives, the clinician has a list of six to eight specific therapy goals when the interview is completed. The DTORF can also be used to assess the child's progress as therapy proceeds. For direct access to the DTORF, the reader is referred to www.dtorf.com. The assessment method, as well as related intervention techniques, is detailed in *Teaching Responsible Behavior,* 4th edition (Wood, Quirk, & Swindle, 2007) and at www.fcs.uga.edu/dttp.

CONCEPTUALIZING GOAL/CURE

Just as the ecosystemic play therapy conceptualization of pathology flows from its definition of personality, its definition of the goal(s) of therapy flows from its definition of psychopathology. Specifically, the goal of ecosystemic play therapy is to "maximize the child's ability to get his (her) needs met effectively and in ways that do not interfere with the ability of others to get their needs met" (O'Connor, 2000, p. 135). Simultaneously, the ecosystemic play therapist works to develop or enhance children's attachment relationships to ensure they have the resources they need to achieve a positive outcome. Additionally, good attachment relationships ensure that the child does not become egocentrically or psychopathically invested in meeting his or her own needs at the expense of others. Finally, because children who are experiencing pathology have not made adequate developmental progress, ecosystemic play therapists work to ensure the child resumes normal developmental progress. The goal is to bring the child to a developmental level as close to age appropriate as possible and to even the child's development across domains. The therapist works to have the child function as well socially as behaviorally or as well socially and behaviorally as academically. This is important because children whose functioning is uneven across domains often garner less support from their environments than do those whose functioning is uniformly low. A child who is behind in all areas evokes sympathy from those who can see that the child is clearly in distress. In counterpoint, the child who does very well academically but is socially very immature is often seen by teachers as being excessively in need of adult attention and by peers as the "teacher's pet." Neither of these views is likely to gain the child much support on a day-to-day basis. Similarly, when a bright child is unable to perform academically due to emotional interference, the child is often criticized for not trying hard enough. More even developmental functioning will make it much easier for the child to get his or her needs met in daily life.

Once the therapist has formulated a case conceptualization consistent with ecosystemic theory, specific treatment goals are developed and a treatment plan is designed.

ROLE OF THE THERAPIST AND THE USE OF THE THERAPEUTIC POWERS OF PLAY

The ecosystemic play therapist has one primary task—to help the child "break set," thereby enabling the child to engage in new behavior, increasing the rate and intensity at which the child's needs are met. Here, *breaking set* is defined as helping children redefine their problems, thereby enabling creative problem solving. The very process of experiencing something differently or understanding different possibilities for getting their needs met can have a profound positive effect on clients (Elliott, 1984). Though this is the overarching goal, the therapist undertakes other highly related tasks as needed. First, because children do not usually seek out treatment on their own, the therapist must help the child understand the nature of treatment and do most of the work of establishing the initial therapeutic alliance. Second, the therapist actively helps the child engage in problem solving. The actual level of the therapist's guidance in this process will depend heavily on the child's developmental level and current capacities for problem solving. Therapist involvement in the problem-solving process may range from actively directing the session with developmentally younger children to simply providing support as developmentally older children work toward their own solutions.

The overt establishment of a very specific treatment contract with the child at the outset of play therapy may be one of the ways in which ecosystemic play therapy most differs from other play therapy models. By the end of the intake with the child, the therapist will present a potential treatment contract focusing on the child's unmet needs. From issues the child has discussed in the intake, the therapist selects the issues that seem most distressing to the child and defines the purpose of therapy as trying to minimize these distressing issues and maximize the child's enjoyment of life. The contract is never about creating change simply to satisfy others; rather, the contract emphasizes change that will concretely improve the child's quality of life. This contract/goal is frequently referenced in sessions with the child over the course of treatment and serves as the measure of treatment efficacy. After all, it would be difficult to say play therapy has been effective because the child changed in ways that satisfied others if the child is still unhappy. A parallel contract with the parents to help them focus on changing the child's problematic behaviors can also be made. When the contracts seem contradictory, which is not uncommon given a phenomenologic perspective, it is up to the therapist to help both sides see how mutual problem solving can result in both sides feeling happier and healthier and, best of all, having a better relationship.

Having established the treatment contract(s), the ecosystemic play therapist then engages the child and/or the caregivers and/or those in the child's environment in active problem solving to ensure qualitative change. In this context, the term *problem solving* does not simply refer to a cognitive, rational exercise. Instead, the term is used more loosely to refer to all efforts at getting the child's needs met consistently and appropriately. An ecosystemic play therapist might help one child to better express emotion so that others respond more appropriately while helping another child develop specific strategies for coping with a bully at school. The problem-solving process might be entirely covert. The therapist would actually do all of the problem solving and simply help the child follow along. Or the process might be overt, with the therapist training the child in basic problem-solving strategies.

Two therapeutic strategies are very much a part of this problem-solving process and bear special mention here. One is the therapist's role in helping children identify and express emotions in developmentally, socially, and culturally appropriate ways. The child stands little chance of getting his or her emotional/affectional needs met if no one knows what those needs are. One way of accomplishing this is through the use of fun, psychoeducational methods such as the Color-Your-Life Thermometer (O'Connor & New, 2002). This is a variation on the Color-Your-Life Technique in which children are taught to pair colors and affects so the colors become an indirect way of expressing and quantifying emotion (O'Connor, 1983). In this modification, children are given the outline of a thermometer at the beginning of the play session and asked to color in the feelings they have had since the last meeting. The therapist explains that just as medical personnel use body temperature to gauge the child's well-being, the play therapist uses feeling temperature to gauge emotional well-being. This method encourages the children to focus on their emotional experience between sessions and to understand the degree to which the therapist is interested in their emotions and in helping them feel better.

The other therapeutic strategy related to effective problem solving is limit setting. If the child is not experiencing negative consequences for engaging in behavior that substantially interferes with the ability of others to get their needs met, he or she has little motivation to change. To establish such motivation, the therapist ensures that proper limits are set in session and caregivers are setting appropriate limits as consistently as possible. When caregivers are able to successfully control their children's behavior, the children learn the extent and nature of the caregiver's and the environment's boundaries. In addition, they learn that the caregiver is able to keep them safely within those boundaries. This same principle applies in the playroom (Landreth, 2002).

In implementing all of these therapeutic strategies, ecosystemic play therapists draw on their knowledge of both the therapeutic powers of play and the research on therapeutic change processes to design specific activities or sessions to address the individual needs of their child clients. Table 14.1 is an attempt to delineate just some of the many ways in which the therapeutic powers of play (Schaefer & O'Connor, 1983) can be directly paired with known therapeutic change processes (Shirk & Russell, 1996).

Table 14.1   Implementing Change Processes in Play Therapy

	Specific Process	**How Change Is Produced**	**Related Therapeutic Power of Play**
Cognitive Processes	*Schema Transformation*	Through the modification of implicit assumptions/expectations embedded in the content (verbal or symbolic) the child brings to the session.	Intrapersonal*: Cognitive— acquire information, creativity, reality testing, symbolism, wish fulfillment
	Symbolic Exchange	Through recurrent participation in the structure of communicative exchanges. The process of communicating an experience to another person helps the child organize that experience and give meaning to it.	Interpersonal: Communication, metaphor
	Interpretation– Insight	Through the reorganization of the meaning of experiences or through expanded self-awareness.	Intrapersonal: Cognitive

*The underlined words reflect the major therapeutic power of play categories described by Schaefer and O'Connor (1983, p. 4).

(Continued)

Table 14.1   (Continued)

	Specific Process	How Change Is Produced	Related Therapeutic Power of Play
	Skill Development	Through learning adaptive or compensatory cognitive skills.	Biologic: Learn basic skills Intrapersonal: Self-control Interpersonal: Social skills
Emotional Processes	*Abreaction– Release*	Through the expression/discharge of feelings resulting in a sense of mastery or control.	Biologic: Tension release Intrapersonal: Catharsis, abreaction
	Emotional Experiencing	Through the integration of emotional experience with an understanding of its personal meaning.	Intrapersonal: Exploration
	Affective Education	Through teaching children to recognize, label, and talk about their own and others' feelings.	Interpersonal: Teaching, communication Sociocultural: Role-play
	Emotional Regulation	Through the development of coping strategies or the modification of psychological defenses.	Intrapersonal: Sublimation, mastery of conflicts
Interpersonal Process	*Interpersonal Validation and Support*	Through the provision of social-emotional support and validation of the child's worth.	Interpersonal: Attachment
	Supportive Scaffolding	Through coparticipation with the therapist in situations exceeding the child's functional capacity.	Interpersonal: Attachment, overcoming resistance Sociocultural: Role-play
	Corrective Relationship	Through modification of the repetitive relationship patterns through alternative or discrepant relationship experiences with the therapist. In other words, knowledge the child gains when the therapist does not repeat the behavior of the client's transference figures.	Biologic: Bonding Interpersonal: Attachment

As the child learns better problem-solving skills, the therapist must work to ensure those newfound skills and behaviors generalize to the child's life outside the playroom. This is most often done by gradually increasing the caretaker's involvement in the session while fading the therapist's involvement. However, because children are much more dependent on others in their day-to-day lives than are adult clients, ecosystemic play therapists may find themselves more involved with others in the child's environment. This may range from simple consultation or education with teachers to intense advocacy for the child in the legal arena. This ability to move between the world of the playroom and involvement in the child's real world characterizes ecosystemic play therapists and requires both great skill and the ability to maintain excellent boundaries.

ROLE OF THE CAREGIVERS

In the ecosystemic theory model, caregivers play a pivotal role in the therapeutic process. The therapist spends only one hour a week with the child, whereas the caregiver spends multiple hours with the child on a daily basis. The experiences the child has during the therapeutic hour must be generalized to the child's life. Without the participation of the caregiver, it is much more difficult to achieve generalization. For the therapist to be effective, rapport must be established with not only the child, but also the caregiver. This is accomplished in two ways. One is by actively involving the caregiver in the planning and execution of the child's treatment. The other is by ensuring that the parent does not feel blamed for the child's problems. This is usually facilitated by the therapist's identification of individual, interactional, and systemic factors contributing to the etiology and maintenance of the child's pathology. By focusing on the child's current needs and working to balance those against the caregiver's needs, the caregiver may be able to feel less guilty or defensive and, therefore, available to participate in the play therapy process.

Typically, ecosystemic play therapists conduct the initial intake session with the caregiver(s) alone. During this first session, the therapist gathers an intensive intake, including information on the child's developmental milestones, family system, the medical and legal history of the child and family members, and the caregiver's perception of the child's difficulties (O'Connor & Ammen, 1997). The intake is completed during the following session when the therapist meets with the child. It is during this phase that the therapist conducts a mental status exam and gets the child's opinions about how the problem is experienced and how it should be defined (O'Connor & Ammen, 1997).

After the intake is completed, the therapist might initially bring the caregiver and child into the session and play a game such as "Good Feeling/Bad Feeling Game" (Ammen, 1994). This allows the therapist to determine what has occurred during the past week and to observe how the dyad interacts. Dependent on the needs of the case, the caregiver might then leave the session while the therapist continues to work with the child. If the difficulty the child is experiencing is more dyadic, the caregiver would be involved in a greater portion of the session. If the child's problems have broader systemic roots, the caretakers would be involved to the extent they have a say in, or control of, the problem system. For example, parents might be engaged in asking the child's school to do some academic testing or in locating a different day care center for their child. Additionally, these collateral sessions are often used to help the caretaker address parenting-related issues to build parenting skills.

CLINICAL APPLICATIONS

While this chapter focuses on ecosystemic play therapy, the underlying ecosystemic theory can readily be used with clients of any age or with any presenting problem. Because the underlying model is both phenomenologic and systemic, it adapts to suit the individual and the context in which the individual lives. Because of its transactional aspects, it is also a model particularly suited to negotiating compromise between the needs of the individual and those of the various systems in which the individual is embedded. Finally, its incorporation of metasystems such as world community and historical time allows it to be radically adapted to suit the needs of persons from or living in very different cultural and systemic contexts. Ecosystemic play therapy is particularly adaptable for two reasons. First, its intense focus on child development in conceptualizing and treating children's difficulties allows the model to be flexible enough to be used with infants as easily as it can be used with adolescents. The other reason is related to the first: The developmental focus allows the therapist to vary the intervention style to match the client without having to vary the underlying theoretical model. The developmentally younger the child, the more the therapist will take responsibility for the content and structure of the sessions, and play will dominate. The developmentally older the child, the more the therapist will facilitate the child in doing his or her own problem solving and balancing play and verbal activity in the sessions.

EMPIRICAL SUPPORT

Ecosystemic play therapy is a relatively new model and, as such, has been the subject of very little research. The model has been widely adopted by play therapists who provide good anecdotal evidence to support its use. Further, acceptance of the model outside the Anglo-European cultural context of the United States suggests it is, in fact, a highly adaptable model. As previously noted, O'Connor has begun incorporating Shirk and Russell's (1996) notions of therapeutic processes into ecosystemic play therapy. These authors identify specific processes in therapy sessions and have linked these conceptually to specific conceptualizations of the dynamics of the child's presenting problem. Their ideas create a frame for quantifying and studying the impact of specific play therapist behaviors on the mental health of their child clients. Some preliminary research is beginning in this area. The author holds out considerable hope that this research strategy may begin to identify better and more focused interventions for play therapists to use in their work.

CASE ILLUSTRATION

The following example illustrates a sense of the potential depth and breadth of an ecosystemic intervention in which ecosystemic play therapy was a central component. More detailed examples of ecosystemic play therapy intakes, pretreatment assessments, treatment planning, and the course of treatment can be found elsewhere (O'Connor, 2000; O'Connor & Ammen, 1997; O'Connor & Braverman, 1997). The details of this case have been substantially altered, and, in fact, information from several cases has been combined both to protect the clients and to better illustrate the model.

Darren was 8 years old at the time he was brought for treatment. From his caretaker's perspective, there were several problems. At home, the caretaker was concerned about Darren's seemingly endless worries, most of which manifested in an inability to be physically separated from her for even a short time. He required her to leave the door open when she went to the bathroom and to be within earshot at all times. He also had trouble separating and going to bed. Unexpectedly, Darren was able to leave for school without protest, but he was constantly distracted once there and was often being mildly to moderately disciplined by his teachers. Darren also seemed to have trouble making and keeping peer friends. From Darren's perspective, the problem was that he was always worried and he often seemed to be getting in trouble for one thing or another. Because Darren so readily admitted to internal distress, the treatment contract made with the therapist was to help him worry less and to have more fun. The therapist also casually noted Darren would probably have more fun if they could figure out a way for him to get in trouble less.

Darren's history led the therapist to hypothesize that Darren's presenting problems were symptoms of underlying attachment deficits. Darren was the product of an unplanned teenage pregnancy. His mother did not have good prenatal care and may have abused substances during her pregnancy. The father disappeared before Darren was born. At birth, Darren was placed in foster care because he and his mother tested positive for drugs. Over the next few years, Darren lived with various members of his extended family and in several foster homes. Most caretakers found him too needy, and eventually he would be moved. He was in six different homes in five years. Finally, he was placed in a home with Beth, a potential adoptive mother. Here, he seemed to stabilize behaviorally. Unfortunately, he still had not been legally cleared for adoption because various relatives seemed reluctant to sign final papers. This left Darren in an ongoing unresolved situation, the nature of which he seemed to fully understand. While some could conceive of the ongoing involvement of extended family as a bonus, Darren saw it as a threat to his adoption, and it triggered perpetual vigilance in his relationship with Beth.

Based on this combination of history and presenting problems, a rather extensive list of treatment goals was developed. Some of these goals were to

1. Reduce Darren's overall anxiety, specifically, his separation anxiety.
2. Increase Darren's ability to enjoy his current relationship with his potential adoptive mother instead of focusing on his fear of losing it.

3. Increase Darren's attachment to other adults and children in his environment to increase his sense of interpersonal security and stability.

4. Work with Beth to develop strategies to decrease Darren's clingy, demanding behavior at home.

5. Work with Darren's teacher to see if the use of stress reduction strategies would reduce his distractibility in the classroom.

6. Work with Darren's court-appointed advocate to see if a more permanent placement plan could be developed.

Of these treatment goals, only the first three were to be addressed in the context of ecosystemic play therapy. Initially, only two types of intervention were planned—both of which targeted the core separation anxiety. Individual play sessions were to be used to address Darren's underlying separation anxiety and to provide him with a safe venue for expressing the concomitant anger he felt toward all those he saw as preventing him from having a permanent home. Collateral sessions were used with Beth to help her develop better insight as to the nature of Darren's anxieties and strategies for managing these on a day-to-day basis. It was hypothesized that Darren's symptoms were not the result of a less-than-adequate attachment to Beth but rather caused by his perpetual exposure to external threats to the relationship. Therefore, it was assumed that reducing the perceived external threat and reducing his anxiety would be sufficient to allow the pleasures of the attachment to come through. However, if this did not happen, the therapist planned to conduct dyadic sessions to help solidify the relationship between Darren and Beth. It was also hypothesized that a reduction in overall anxiety and greater security in his primary relationship would free Darren to develop better peer attachments. Again, should this have proven not to be the case, Darren would have been referred to an ecosystemic play therapy group to address his peer attachment and socialization issues.

Fortunately, the combination of advocacy and individual and collateral therapy proved so successful in reducing Darren's anxiety that his attachment relationships began to blossom spontaneously. All three interventions were conducted simultaneously. Darren's therapist worked closely with social services and the courts to advocate a permanent placement in spite of familial objections. The results of a variety of play assessments were used to reinforce the court's recognition of how critical permanency was to Darren's short- and long-term mental health. Through these assessments, the therapist was also able to demonstrate that the hypothesized bond between Darren and Beth was, indeed, very strong. As gradual legal advances were made, Darren began to shed his fear of being removed from Beth's care and to relax into the positive aspects of his relationship with her.

Darren's individual therapy focused on several issues. Initially, he enacted all of his attachment anxieties in his relationship with his therapist. Darren would act out in session as if to test how much the therapist would endure before abandoning him. When he finally decided the therapist could endure pretty much anything negative, he began to reveal an extremely needy and demanding part of himself. He insisted on nearly constant physical contact with the therapist and insisted that every minute of the session be focused on meeting his needs. Any attempts the therapist made to refer back to the underlying worries identified in their treatment contract were met with a certain amount of resistance. In spite of this, the therapist attempted to balance his efforts to meet Darren's current needs with reflections and interpretations of the underlying fears that made these needs so intense. At one point, the therapist began holding and feeding Darren while they talked. This proved to be the most effective way of demonstrating to Darren that he could address both what seemed to be overwhelming fears and still be safe and nurtured.

As Darren's need for nurturance began to abate, he started expressing more and more of the rage he harbored at having to live in perpetual fear of being moved. His individual sessions were divided into two parts. In one, he and his therapist would come up with ideas for simply venting Darren's anger. One of Darren's favorite activities during this period was to make Play-Doh representations of people he felt threatened him and to crush them. He would do this repeatedly. The other part of the session was geared toward helping Darren identify ways of managing his rage and underlying anxiety outside of the session. Initially, the therapist identified the anxiety as the source of the rage. He also noted that the rage, in turn, helped make Darren feel more powerful and less like a victim. As this interpretation was accepted, Darren turned to doing things to make himself feel powerful and safe. He began by inventing a fantasy protector whose picture he drew routinely. Later, he began to talk openly about his hope that both the therapist and Beth would keep him safe. During this part of the treatment, Darren became demanding and needy only in the face of the impending separation triggered by the end of the play sessions.

Toward the end of treatment, Darren began to rely less and less on the therapist to meet his intense needs for safety and attachment. He began to trust the legal system to keep him in his current home. As his anxiety abated, his need to control Beth's every move also abated. Although he continued to struggle in school, he seemed somewhat less impulsive and more easily redirected. It became more apparent there were underlying learning problems, and arrangements were made to have those assessed and appropriate interventions initiated. Most importantly, Darren began to make peer-age friends and to get some of his intense attachment needs met through these friendships. As these changes took place, therapy was terminated by very gradually increasing the length of time between sessions and by involving Beth more actively so Darren would generalize some of his play therapy experiences to his interactions with her. Together, they became proficient at identifying and resolving most difficulties that arose either in Darren's life or in their relationship.

CHALLENGES IN IMPLEMENTING THE MODEL

Play therapy in general is a challenging form of treatment to implement. Among other things, play therapists must be able to

1. Form therapeutic relationships with both their child clients and the adults who bring those children to therapy.

2. Be as skilled at communicating through action and play as they are at communicating through language.

3. Be comfortable moving between the role of therapist and advocate as the child's needs demand.

4. Be able to think, speak, and play all at the same time.

Play therapists face some additional challenges when implementing ecosystemic play therapy. They must be able to

1. Maintain an ecosystemic frame of reference at all times so as to develop both contextually based understandings of their client's problems as well as solutions to those problems.

2. Have an excellent understanding of the impact of a child's developmental level on both the nature of the problems he or she is experiencing and his or her response to therapy.

3. Be able to move between being very directive and very nondirective in sessions so as to match the child's developmental, emotional, behavioral, and interpersonal needs.

4. Be able to enter into concrete treatment contracts with children and to keep the goals of the contract at the forefront of every session.

In spite of these additional demands on the play therapist, ecosystemic play therapy need not be particularly difficult to implement. The primary challenge is for the play therapist to adopt a multisystemic, developmental, strength- and goal-oriented way of thinking. Having done so, the range of techniques he or she can incorporate into his or her work is virtually endless. Creativity and fun are emphasized, as are play and direct interaction between the child and therapist.

CONCLUSION

Psychology in general is going through a phase in its own development where the numerous, divergent theoretical models and techniques developed over the past century are being integrated, forming more comprehensive and, ultimately, useful theories. Ecosystemic play therapy is a manifestation of this general trend as it proceeds to attempt just such integration in the field of play therapy. Most ecosystemic play therapy concepts and practices are not new but exist within a wide variety of other psychology, medical, biological, social work, counseling, educational, and organizational theories, to name but a few of the models from which it draws. What makes ecosystemic play therapy unique is its integration of these into a solid theoretical framework. Anchored firmly by the theory, ecosystemic play therapists are free to employ numerous techniques, both in and out of their sessions, to help children live more fulfilling and happier lives. Simultaneously, ecosystemic play therapists recognize their role in balancing the needs of their child clients against those of the world in which they and we live. It is an awesome responsibility to be undertaken only with the greatest of care and respect.

REFERENCES

Ammen, S. (1994). The good feeling–bad feeling game. In K. O'Connor & C. Schaefer (Eds.), *Handbook of play therapy* (Vol. 2, pp. 283–294). New York, NY: Wiley.

Bronfenbrenner, U. (1979). *The ecology of human development: Experiments by nature and design.* Cambridge, MA: Harvard University Press.

Dreikurs, R., & Grey, L. (1970). *A parent's guide to child discipline.* Oxford, UK: Hawthorn.

Elliott, R. (1984). A discovery-oriented approach to significant change events in psychotherapy: Interpersonal process recall and comprehensive process analysis. In L. Rice & L. Greenberg (Eds.), *Patterns of change: Intensive analysis of psychotherapy process.* New York, NY: Guilford Press.

Gerhardt, S. (2004). *Why love matters: How affection shapes a baby's brain.* New York, NY: Brunner-Routledge.

Giorgi, A. (1983). Concerning the possibility of phenomenological psychological research. *Journal of Phenomenological Psychology, 14*(2), 129–169.

Herrick, J. (2005). *Humanism: An introduction.* Amherst, NY: Prometheus.

Jernberg, A., & Booth, P. (2010). *Theraplay: Helping parents and children build better relationships through attachment based play* (3rd ed.). San Francisco, CA: Jossey-Bass.

Landreth, G. (2002). Therapeutic limits setting in the play therapy relationship. *Professional Psychology: Research and Practice, 33*(6), 529–535.

O'Connor, K. J. (1983). The Color-Your-Life Technique. In K. O'Connor & C. Schaefer (Eds.), *Handbook of play therapy* (Vol. 2, pp. 251–258). New York, NY: Wiley.

O'Connor, K. J. (1993). Child, protector, confidant: Structured group ecosystemic play therapy. In T. Kottman & C. Schaefer (Eds.), *Play therapy in action: A casebook for practitioners* (pp. 245–280). Northvale, NJ: Aronson.

O'Connor, K. J. (1997). Ecosystemic play therapy. In K. O'Connor & L. Braverman (Eds.), *Play therapy theory and practice: A comparative presentation* (pp. 234–284). New York, NY: Wiley.

O'Connor, K. J. (2000). *The play therapy primer* (2nd ed.). New York, NY: Wiley.

O'Connor, K. J. (2005). Ecosystemic play therapy. *Japanese Journal of Psychiatry, 19*(3), 273–284.

O'Connor, K. J., & Ammen, S. (1997). *Play therapy treatment planning and interventions: The ecosystemic model and workbook.* San Diego, CA: Academic Press.

O'Connor, K. J., & Braverman, L. M. (1997). *Play therapy theory and practice: A comparative presentation.* New York, NY: Wiley.

O'Connor, K. J., & New, D. (2002). The Color-Your-Life Technique. In C. Schaefer & D. Cangelosi (Eds.), *Play therapy techniques* (2nd ed., pp. 245–256). Northvale, NJ: Aronson.

Schaefer, C., & O'Connor, K. (Eds.). (1983). *The handbook of play therapy.* New York, NY: Wiley.

Schore, A. (2001). Minds in the making: Attachment, the self-organizing brain, and developmentally-oriented psychoanalytic psychotherapy. *British Journal of Psychotherapy, 17,* 299–328.

Shirk, S., & Russell, R. (1996). *Change processes in child psychotherapy: Revitalizing treatment and research.* New York, NY: Guilford Press.

Siegel, D. J. (2002). *An interpersonal neurobiology of the developing mind: Contingent communication and the development of a coherent self.* Paper presented at the meeting of the UCLA Extension and Lifespan Learning Institute on Attachment: From Early Childhood through the Lifespan, Los Angeles, CA.

Wood, M., Quirk, C., & Swindle, F. (2007). *Teaching responsible behavior: Developmental therapy–developmental teaching for troubled children and adolescents* (4th ed.). Austin, TX: ProEd.

EMERGING MODELS

Chapter 15

THERAPLAY: ATTACHMENT-ENHANCING PLAY THERAPY

Evangeline Munns

Theraplay® is a structured form of play therapy that seeks to enhance parent–child attachments, self-esteem, and trust. It most often produces significant changes within a short period of time and is applicable across the whole age range and to a variety of emotional and social difficulties. It is based on attachment theory, which is well grounded in research regarding its impact on the developing brain, on emotions and behavior throughout one's life span (Gerhardt, 2004; Sunderland, 2006). Theraplay strives to replicate normal parent/child interactions, particularly those that occur when a child is first learning to connect with its primary caregiver.

Theraplay is not a verbal therapy. Interpretations are not made, but reflections of a child's feelings are given so the child feels the adult is attuned to him. Parents are guided to see that a child's behavior has underlying emotions and intentions. They are encouraged to verbally express this to the child through reflections of his feelings. Helping the parents become consistently attuned and responsive to their child's cues and needs is another major goal of Theraplay.

Children experience a range of emotions, from joyful exuberance to quiet, soothing calmness as the therapist and parents help the child to self-regulate. The adults join the child in sharing his excitement and delight, but not to the point of overstimulation. Being sensitive to the child's optimal arousal is very important as the child needs to feel peak experiences so he can develop spontaneity, optimism, motivation, wonder and joy (Sunderland, 2006). Aiding the child in regulating his emotions and impulses is considered to be one of the most important processes in strengthening the attachment bond. This also has an effect on the child's developing brain. Schore, a psychobiologist, believes that the processes of attunement, attachment, and emotional regulation have a direct impact on the development of the orbitofrontal cortex (Schore, 1994, 2005; J. Schore & Schore, 2008), which plays a central role in the development of empathy and emotional memory (Doidge, 2007; Gerhardt, 2004).

In Theraplay, no toys are used. The emphasis is on playful, positive, physical interactions first between the therapist and child, while the parents observe. Later, when parents enter the Theraplay activities, they are gradually guided to take over leading the activities. Bizarre behavior is ignored and there is an emphasis on noticing and promoting the positive aspects of the child, as well as the strengths of the parent. With this positive focus, the parents gradually develop a more positive perception of their child, and the child's self-image improves.

HISTORICAL BACKGROUND

Theraplay was founded in 1967 by Dr. Ann Jernberg (1979), a psychologist, who was given a federal grant to help mothers and their children increase their attachment bonds in the Head Start program in Chicago. She turned to the work of Austin Des Lauriers, who was working with schizophrenic and autistic children and was using unusual methods for his time. He was directive, ignored bizarre behavior, and was playfully intrusive and engaging through direct body and eye contact. She also incorporated some of the methods of Viola Brody, another psychologist, who used a lot of singing, rocking, cradling, and physical contact to engage her children. Ernestine Thomas's emphasis on the child's health and strengths was also included. Dr. Jernberg incorporated ideas from all three and added even more emphasis on physical touch and on meeting a child's younger needs. She tried to replicate normal activities that one might use with a young child in order to fill in gaps that might be missing in the child's emotional development.

Dr. Jernberg and Phyllis Booth taught Theraplay to many professionals and paraprofessionals with successful results. In 1971, the Theraplay Institute was established and continues to serve as the international headquarters for Theraplay. In the early 1980s, staff from the Institute started training professionals in other centers in the United States and Canada. One of those trained was Dr. Evangeline Munns (Munns, 2000), who became a certified Theraplay trainer and taught workshops across Canada. Similarly, Ulricke Franke established Theraplay in Germany, and Dr. Juka Makela and his staff created strong interest in the practice of Theraplay throughout Finland. Today, Theraplay is practiced in 29 countries around the world, including countries in Asia, Europe, South America, and North America, as well as in Australia and Russia (Booth & Jernberg, 2010).

BASIC CONSTRUCTS, GOALS AND TECHNIQUES

Theory

Theraplay is strongly based on attachment theory (Bowlby, 1988) and on the interpersonal theories of human development such as Self Psychology (Kohut, 1977) and Object Relations (Stern, 1995; Winnicott, 1965). All of these theories emphasize the importance of the infant–parent relationship since it is the first relationship or template for later relationships. Research has shown that if this relationship is not a secure one, problems in relating to others in the future are highly likely to occur and can be evident throughout the lifespan (Goldberg, 2000; Siegal & Hartzell, 2004). Theraplay advocates going back to that first relationship to make it a healthier one, through replicating what normal parents do with a young child, including activities such as cradling, rocking, feeding, powdering or lotioning the hands of the child, etc. In some cases in which a child experienced deprivation or abuse in his early history, he may be cradled and fed a lollipop or juice bottle while a special song would be sung about him. Through such activities, feelings and memories of an earlier time are evoked, but now the child is in a caring atmosphere receiving the attention and nurturing he might have missed when very young. The child revisits the roots of connecting to another person. The caregiver and child learn to attach with each other in a basic, healthy, and accepting way. This can have a powerful effect on their relationship. In later stages of treatment, there is more emphasis on activities suited to the chronological age of the child. Throughout, the parent is helped to be attuned and responsive, to reflect on the child's feelings, and to help him self-regulate within an atmosphere that is playful and joyful (Booth & Jernberg, 2010; Munns, 2000, 2009).

Theraplay's focus on building a positive self-image has similarities to positive psychology (Seligman, 2007) and to an important concept of attachment theory— the inner-working model. Theraplay tries to build an inner sense of a strong, competent self that is worthy of being loved and unconditionally accepted.

Theraplay is supported as well by the theory and research of neuroscientists such as Dr. Bruce Perry and his neurosequential programming (Perry & Salavitz, 2006). Dr. Perry has studied how extreme stress and trauma in early life can change the brain. His treatment method starts at the level of brain functioning of the client rather than at the chronological age of the child. It is well known that the brain develops sequentially, with its greatest spurt of growth in the first 3 years of life (Sunderland, 2006). The lower, more primitive part of the brain (brain stem and diencephalon) that controls our core regulatory functions such as body temperature, heart rate, respiration, blood pressure, and instinct to "freeze, fight, or flee" is the first to mature. The next to evolve is the middle or emotional brain (limbic system), which, along with the diencephalon, controls our emotions and responses such as fear, hatred, love, and joy. The last to mature is the cortex or higher part of the brain that regulates the most complex and highly evolved functions such as speech, language, abstract thinking, planning, and decision making (Perry & Salavitz, 2006). Each part is dependent on the maturation of the previous or lower part. If a child has not had the normal, healthy experiences it needs early in life, then the lower brain can be compromised, which in turn affects the development of the middle and, in turn, the upper brain regions. In neurosequential programming, treatment would begin with such a child (regardless of chronological age) by providing the kind of experiences that are needed at that level such as those involving touch, rhythm, and repetition. Dr. Perry uses massage (for physical contact), drumming, Theraplay activities, sensory motor activities, and so on. Later programming would include activities that would promote emotional expressiveness such as psychodrama, sandplay, play therapy, expressive arts, and the like. Later still, the more verbal and cognitive therapies would be included such as narrative therapy, cognitive–behavioral therapy, positive and self-psychology, and so on.

Another important aspect of brain development is that the right hemisphere is dominant in the first 3 years of life. The right hemisphere is preverbal and processes visual cues, and sensory data, and social emotional input. The right-brain limbic system, including its connections to the orbitofrontal cortex, controls our emotional response and helps to regulate the internal state of the body. It forms the biological basis for social interaction, empathy, and mind-set (Gerhardt, 2004;

J. Schore & Schore, 2008). Theraplay activities are geared for enhancing right-brain development.

Dimensions and Techniques

After observing hundreds of normal parent–child interactions, Jernberg categorized them into four main dimensions: structure, engagement, nurture, and challenge.

Structure

Structure, where the parents give clear directions, rules, and boundaries, can help to make the child's world safe and predictable. With a young child, the adult is usually in charge and makes major decisions. The child's daily routines around sleeping, eating, and bathing, along with rhymes and songs that have a pattern or rhythm to them, all contribute to giving the child a sense of regularity and security. This sense of regularity, first created by the parent, helps the child to develop an ability to self-regulate later on. In addition, in this process, the attachment bond is strengthened.

In Theraplay, structure is created by the therapist's or parent's leading the activities, which are preplanned according to the child's needs. Each session has a clear beginning and end. Activities are sequenced so that more exciting ones are followed by those that are calming so that the child does not get out of control. The child learns to follow rules and directions in simple games like "Mother May I" and "Simon Says." Structure is particularly emphasized with children who are dysregulated (Di Pasquale, 2009) or impulsive, have attention deficit/hyperactivity disorder (ADHD), or are unmanageable or uncooperative. Children who are tyrants, parentified, reactive attachment disordered, or conduct disordered need to learn that when their environment is structured and controlled by an adult, their world can become a safer, more secure place so they can relax and just be the child they were meant to be.

Examples of Structuring Activities

Mother May I. Child stands at starting point on the opposite side of the room where leader is standing and asks, "Mother may I—take three baby steps forward, etc." Leader responds, "Yes, you may" or "No, you may not" or changes it to "You may take two baby steps forward," etc. If the child omits saying, "Mother may I" first, then he misses his turn. Object of the game is to reach the leader, and the first person to do so becomes the next leader.

Simon Says. Played in the traditional way where the child responds to the directions of the leader such as "Simon says to put your hands on your head," etc. If the leader omits saying "Simon says" first, then no one should perform the action, but if he does, then he becomes the next leader. In Theraplay, directions such as "Simon says to say one nice thing you like about your neighbor" or "Simon says to give your neighbor a hug" are thrown in.

Red Light, Green Light. Children stand in a row at a starting line, while leader with his back turned shouts out "Green Light," which is a signal for everyone to move forward. "Red Light" means stop. Leader turns around and visually checks to see if anyone is moving. If so, then that child has to go back to the starting line. Whoever reaches the leader first is the next leader.

Follow the Leader. The leader moves in a variety of ways in a circle around the room followed by the child imitating the leader's movements. Person in front moves to the back of the line, and the next person becomes the leader.

Races. A signal is given such as the word *bananas,* and the race starts to the other side of the room, whether it is by hopping, crawling, running, etc., to the other side of the room.

Engagement

Through engagement, a child learns to connect with another person in an intimate way. Parents normally have many delightful ways of engaging their children where there is mutual enjoyment. There can be a sense of empathy with one another when both are attuned to each other. The adult hopefully meets the child in his enthusiasm but also knows how to modulate such feelings so the child does not escalate out of control. The child learns that surprises can be fun and that interacting with another person can be satisfying.

In Theraplay, engaging activities can sometimes seem intrusive, but they are guided by the therapist's sensitivity to the child's reactions and needs. This is especially true when working with children who have been traumatized or abused. If the child reacts with fear or high anxiety, the activity is stopped or modified in a way that becomes more comfortable for the child.

Engaging activities are used with all children but especially with withdrawn, rejecting, avoidant children who are afraid of intimacy, such as autistic children.

Examples of Engaging Activities

Mirroring. Therapist or parent stands facing the child. Therapist moves arms and body in various ways but slowly enough that the child can match the therapist's movements. The child is the "mirror" of the adult. Roles are then reversed. This activity is great for enhancing attunement between two people.

Clapping imitation. Adult claps hands in simple patterns while child copies the sequence of claps. Rhymes such as "Patty cake" or "Pease porridge hot" can be used. Claps can also include touching body parts of partner, such as shoulder, head, knees, etc., as part of the clap sequences.

Cotton ball guess, fight, and soothe. Partners face each other kneeling with a pile of cotton balls in front of them.

    a-Cotton ball guess. One partner closes his eyes while the other partner touches a spot on his face, ear, shoulder, etc., while the other partner guesses where he has been touched. Reverse roles. (A more challenging aspect is to have the partner guess if he has been touched with a cotton ball or a feather.)

    b-Cotton ball fight. Everyone takes one cotton ball, and when the leader shouts "go," everyone throws a cotton ball at someone but calls out the name of that person first. When the leader shouts, "Let her go," everyone throws as many cotton balls as they want at anyone without saying their name first. This is followed by seeing how quickly everyone can gather the balls and put them back into the bag. This is an excellent game for families and groups as well.

c-Cotton ball soothe. Partners face each other, and one closes her eyes while the other soothes her face with the cotton ball, commenting on the positive features such as, "You have healthy, rosy cheeks" or "nice straight nose," etc. Reverse roles.

Body part sounds. Therapist touches body parts of child making unique sounds such as "honk honk" for the child's nose or "eek, eek" as you touch his ears, and so on. Young children usually love this activity.

Nurture

Nurture is the most important dimension of Theraplay and is needed by all children. Every child needs caring, comforting, warm affection and the knowledge that their basic needs will be met. Normally, parents show their caring in countless ways: by feeding, bathing, powdering, soothing, caressing, cradling, rocking, hugging, and kissing their children and showing in numerous ways that they love and accept their children unconditionally. These interactions help children to feel valued, important, and safe in the knowledge that their parents will be responsive to their needs. This knowledge helps them to tolerate stress and to self-regulate. Nurturing is key in helping to build a secure attachment to the chief caregiver, which is usually the parent.

In Theraplay, all children are nurtured in every session through such activities as feeding (such as potato chips, pretzels, or favorite snack and/or drink). If the child's early history indicates that attachment difficulties started as an infant, then the child might be wrapped in a blanket, cradled, and rocked while being fed a lollipop or juice box or baby bottle while a song, using their name, is sung to them. When parents enter the session, they can gradually take over rocking and feeding their child, but this is guided by the child's reactions and is never forced. Other nurturing activities are lotioning or powdering of hurts on the child's hands or feet; combing the child's hair; giving a pedicure, manicure, or facial to older children; etc.

Children who have experienced deprivation or abuse are in special need of nurturing. Children who are pseudo-mature or those who are aggressive and acting out and receive constant criticism or rejection are also in need of a lot of nurturance.

Examples of Nurture

Lotioning or powdering of hurts. In every session, with every child, the therapist looks for hurts or "boo-boos" such as scratches, bruises, or even just freckles that are then soothed by powdering or lotioning them. Often, the child will soon start pointing out other "boo-boos" on arms, legs, etc. If a parent has also come from a deprived or abusive history, then sometimes the therapist will lotion the hurts of the parent first and then ask the parent to lotion the child.

Slippery-slip. This is a good substitute activity if at first the child resists lotioning of hurts. The therapist liberally smooths lotion on the child's hand and then asks the child to try to pull out his hand from the two-handed grasp of the therapist. When the child manages to pull out his hand, the therapist can exaggerate her reactions by falling over backwards, stating something like "you did it—you're so strong!"

Finding letters or numbers. The therapist generously powders the palms of the child and tries to find letters or numbers in the crevasses or lines of each palm made clearer by the powder.

Blanket swing and lollipop feed. Have the child lie face-up on a blanket that is gathered up at its corners by adults and gently swung from side to side while adults sing a lullabye with the child's name (e.g., "Rock-a-bye Johnny in the tree top"). At the end of the last line of the song, "and up will come Johnny, cradle and all," the child is heaved up into the parent's arms. Sometimes the parent is then guided to sit on pillows previously arranged against a wall and given a lollipop or bottle to feed the child who is still wrapped up in the blanket. More lullabies can be sung while the parent rocks and feeds the child. (Note that the blanket swing is one of the favorite activities of children of all ages.)

Challenge

This dimension helps a child to take age-appropriate risks and to master new skills leading to increased confidence. Being more open to new experiences, exploring the environment, and being less fearful are goals of this dimension, as well as increasing cooperation, since challenging activities in Theraplay are often done cooperatively with another person. It is important that the tasks are within the range of the child's abilities to perform them so the child does not fail.

Challenging activities are often exhilarating and tension releasing. They are used with children who are fearful, withdrawn, or timid or those who have been over-protected. Through challenging activities, the child learns his strengths and weaknesses. Aggressive children can benefit by releasing some of their inner tensions.

Examples of Challenging Activities

Bubble catch. Adult blows bubbles while child tries to catch them. For older children, this activity can be made more challenging by having the child touch a bubble only with a certain body part like thumb, elbow, knee, foot, etc.

Paper punch and basketball throw. Adult holds a sheet of newspaper tautly and gives the child a signal ("when I say 'cherries'") to punch his fist through the middle of the newspaper. Then the child punches through the half sheets and later quarter pieces of the newspaper (always in response to the adult's giving a signal first). The quarter sheets are then crumpled into balls, which the child throws into a basket hoop made by the adult gripping his arms in a circle formation. The adult can determine the difficulty of this activity by increasing or decreasing the distance between them. This is an excellent activity for releasing tension or aggression in a safe way.

Balloon tennis. Child and adult hit a balloon back and forth. For younger children, simply tossing the balloon in the air and keeping it in the air may be a sufficient challenge. Introducing more balloons is also fun.

Ping-pong blow. Adult(s) and child lie face-down on floor, facing each other while holding hands. Leader blows a ping-pong ball (or cotton ball) to someone else, who in turn blows it to the next person. Additional balls can be used to increase the fun. More challenge is introduced when everyone tries to keep the ball away from the area in front of themselves and into someone else's area.

Feather blow. Adult and child hold a pillow or large piece of construction paper in front of them. Each blows a feather back and forth, catching the feather on the paper or pillow. More than one feather can be used, depending on the skills of the child.

TREATMENT PLANNING AND PROCESS

Each session is planned according to the needs of the child and parents, which are assessed in several ways: by a careful, thorough family and developmental history (including parents' family and marital histories) and a family assessment called the Marschak Interaction Method (MIM) (Di Pasquale, 2000; Marschak, 1960). Rating scales such as Achenbach's Child Behavior Checklist (1991) and the Parenting Stress Index (short form) (Abidin, 1995), and so on are also sometimes given (these can be used for pre- and posttreatment measures).

The MIM is a method of assessing family relationships and dynamics using a series of standardized, simple tasks that are videotaped (with parents' written permission) and played back to the parents in a feedback session. Strengths are highlighted as well as problem areas from which goals are set. Often, a verbal contract of attending at least 12 sessions (sometimes more) is agreed upon.

In the first three or four sessions, parents observe through a one-way mirror or from a corner of the Theraplay room with an interpreting therapist (if a cotherapist is available) who answers parents' questions and helps them to become more attuned to their child's reactions. In the remaining sessions, parents participate directly with their child under the guidance of the therapist. Gradually, the leadership of the activities is turned over to the parents. The Theraplay session usually lasts about one-half hour and can be followed by a half hour of debriefing and parent counseling. The latter is optional but can be of enormous help in aiding the parents to have insights into their own reactions as well as their child's behavior. If this is not possible, then separate parent counseling sessions should be held. At the last session, a good-bye party is held where the family's favorite activities are included as well as favorite food and drink (which the parents usually provide). Mementos of the sessions are given to the child, sometimes with a small present. At least four checkups are planned for the coming year, starting with the first checkup occurring about a month later.

If warranted, sometimes it is recommended that the parents receive individual counseling or marital therapy. Further treatment such as nondirective play therapy, expressive arts, or trauma therapy (Hughes, 2006) also may be needed for the child.

Agenda for a Single Session

The following elements are included in a typical Theraplay session: a warm greeting; a fun entrance into the room; a welcome song (or special handshake with older children) while holding hands; a checkup or inventory; activities related to the dimensions of structure, engagement, nurture, and challenge; and a good-bye song. In every session, there are always some nurturing activities such as lotioning or powdering of hurts, as well as feeding. Activities may vary from fun and exciting ones to calm ones (to help with the child's self-regulation), from close, intimate activities to freely moving about the room, thus creating a balance of close physical contact with distance and space.

Example of Agenda for Fourth Session When Parents Enter

Greeting in hallway: "Hi, Johnny, I'm so glad you're here."

Entrance: "Stepping Stones"—child steps on sheets of construction paper (sometimes with a small candy underneath) leading to a pile of pillows on which he sits.

Hello song: "Hello Johnny, hello Johnny, hello Johnny, I'm glad you've come to play" (while holding hands).

Inventory or checkup: "Johnny, what have you brought today? I see you've brought your shiny hair, two sparkling brown eyes, rosy cheeks, and a big dimple right there—and two big shoulders—wow!"

Lotioning or powdering of hurts: "Let's see your strong hands—oh-oh—I see a little bruise right there—better take care of that—better put some lotion on that—and here's another red spot," etc.

Mirroring: Child and therapist face each other, with therapist leading movements slowly while child mirrors them. Switch roles.

Peanut butter–jelly: Therapist says "peanut butter" and child answers "jelly," imitating the loudness, softness, pace, and inflections of therapist's voice as he says "peanut butter."

Parents Come In

Child hide and find: Child hides under the blanket in preparation for parents to find him. Parents come in and pretend at first that they can't find him as they look everywhere in the room. When they find him, hugs are encouraged.

Balloon toss: Everyone tries to keep a balloon in the air, with more balloons tossed in as the fun increases.

Cheerios sit down: Everyone holds hands in a circle, and when leader says "cheerios," everyone sits down—"chips—cheesies—cheerios"!

Pass a gentle touch: Everyone sits in a circle facing inward. The therapist passes a gentle touch (could be a gentle pat on the shoulder) to her neighbor, who passes it on to the next person, and so on. (Each person adds on their new touch, or for younger children, just pass on one touch at a time.)

Silly bones: Everyone stands in a circle divided into pairs facing each other. The leader says, "Silly bones says—touch each other's hands, Silly bones says touch each other's elbows, knees, noses," etc.

Feeding: In a circle, sitting position, the therapist feeds everyone several rounds of a snack (potato chips, pieces of fruit, etc.). Each parent gets a turn feeding everyone as well.

Good-bye song: Holding hands in a circle, everyone sings, "Good-bye Johnny, good-bye Mom, good-bye Dad, good-bye (therapist's name), we're glad you came today." With adolescents, a rap song can be invented or a special hand-shake created with everyone.

The child is then taken by the interpreting therapist to a separate room, or the child goes alone to a corner of the room with books, puzzles, or quiet toys as the therapist and parents discuss the session, homework, and progress at home and school for about half an hour.

For homework, parents are given Theraplay activities of their choosing to prac-tice at home, at least once a week. They tell the therapist the specific day and time that the practice session is likely to be. It is very important that in the next session, the therapist check on how the homework progressed.

ROLE OF THE THERAPIST

After obtaining an in-depth family history and family assessment using the MIM, the therapist (in the feedback session) sets goals (such as enhancing parent–child attachment) with the parents. The therapist preplans the Theraplay session. The therapist tries to form an attuned, supportive relationship with both the child and parents. At first the therapist models healthy interactions with the child (while the parents observe) in an upbeat, engaging, playful atmosphere that is focused on the here and now, one involving physical and eye contact and sharing the child's excitement and joy, but also helping the child modulate his emotions so he learns to self-regulate. The therapist gives full attention and unconditional acceptance while helping the child to take appropriate risks and to meet challenges. The therapist also takes charge and leads the activities, modeling for the parents how to gain coop-eration from their child. If the child is impulsive and out of control, the therapist remains calm and firm and uses more structuring activities. If the child is timid and fearful, the therapist may use surprises and fun activities or paradox to engage the child. Throughout, the therapist tries to connect with the child in a way that raises his self-esteem and trust while helping to build the child's inner representation of himself as someone who is valued, loved, and cared for.

With parents, the therapist tries to strengthen the parent–child relationship by encouraging parents to be warm, affectionate, and accepting in their manner. However, they also need to be firm and consistent and set clear limits during mis-behavior of their child. They are guided to be attentive and responsive to the cues their child may be giving before the misbehavior occurs so that temper tantrums are prevented from occurring in the first place. Parents are guided to help their child self-regulate before the child is overwhelmed emotionally. The therapist helps the parents to self-reflect and to reflect on their child's underlying emotions and inten-tions. In parent counseling sessions, the therapist helps the parents gain insight into how their own attachment histories can be repeated and have an effect on their child. Finally, when needed, the therapist sometimes takes a nurturing role with the parents, giving them the care and attention they may have missed in their own child-hoods. Sometimes this is done by doing Theraplay with the parents alone for a few sessions. In Finland, a Theraplay session with parents is routinely done first, before Theraplay begins with their child (Booth & Jernberg, 2010).

ROLE OF THE PARENT

From the beginning, the parents are asked if they have the time to commit to at least 12 (or more) sessions, since Theraplay is a short-term therapy and all sessions are important. The nature of Theraplay is explained so that parents have an idea of what might happen. After parents observe the therapist interacting with their child for the first three or four sessions, their perception of their child often changes. Upon referral, their focus is on all of the child's problems, but the therapist does the opposite—he or she focuses on the child's positive attributes. The child most often responds in a pleasant way and often becomes cooperative and motivated to please the therapist. Parents, who might be skeptical at first about how playing with their child will bring meaningful results, slowly realize that a transformation is taking place. Their child can be fun and a source of delight—not a source of constant worry and even shame. The parents learn how to work through their child's resist-ance appropriately, when it arises, without any shouting or anger.

As the sessions progress, parents are asked to lead some of the activities so the managing of their child falls more and more to them. If their child resists, the therapist helps the child to be more cooperative. Practicing the activities at home is very impor-tant, and homework sessions are strongly encouraged and supported. Often, the children are excited about their "Theraplay night" at home and remind their parents about it.

After the last session (which is a party session), another Marschak is given (this is optional), followed by a feedback session where pre- and post-progress is dis-cussed. Have goals been met? What else needs to be done? Is further treatment required for the child or parents? Recommendations are made and the date set for the first of four checkups during the year. The first checkup is made in about four to six weeks' time, giving the family some comfort in knowing that they will see the therapist again.

CASE ILLUSTRATION

Carol was a 9½-year-old girl diagnosed as severely autistic and moderately mentally handicapped, but she had higher functioning in some areas. Her additional refer-ral problems were behavior management difficulties, resistive, self-abusive, moody, cyclic behavior, low frustration tolerance, sleep problems, picky eater, and severe communication problems. She had some use of sign language and when younger, had been able to verbalize single words, but at 4 years of age this stopped.

Carol's parents were "burnt out" and had considered placing Carol in an insti-tution. Both parents looked tired, and her mother appeared depressed. Dad often worked late at a senior executive position. Mother was at home full time. Both parents were university educated and truly wanted the best for their child. Their marital relationship was described as excellent.

Carol had two siblings who were described as normal. The 13-year-old sister did not want to associate with Carol in any way. The 4-year-old brother was described as functioning on a higher level than Carol, in spite of being considerably younger.

Carol's early history indicated normal development (including being affectionate) until 2 years of age, except for language, which was delayed. At 2 years of age, she started spinning and tantruming, became cyclic in her moods, would mouth and smell new objects, and so on. At 5 years of age, she would hit peers and adults. (At present, she stomps her feet and hits her forehead with a fist when she gets angry or does not want to do something.)

Parents sought treatment from a number of agencies, including some specializing in the treatment of autistic children, which she attended for many years.

At the time of referral, Carol had been transferred from a multiple handicapped class to a regular class split between grades 3 and 4 with a teacher assistant. She was also attending an autistic center for life skills training and swimming lessons. She also had begun a facilitative communication program at school.

After obtaining the family history, a Marschak assessment took place, was videoed, and feedback given and goals set. The MIM revealed that both parents tried very hard to obtain Carol's cooperation and were gentle, loving parents with a good deal of patience and a sense of humor. Carol controlled her parents by stomping her foot (a warning) or progressed to hitting her forehead with her fist while making loud, bizarre noises if she really wanted an activity to end. Carol appeared to be anxious, tense, and hyperactive. No words were heard, but she used some sign language.

First Theraplay Session

Carol came into the Theraplay room looking highly anxious and fearful. She kept bringing her fist to her mouth while looking apprehensively around the room. She was able to separate from her parents, who observed from a one-way mirror. The agenda was preplanned, with an emphasis on structure, engagement, and nurture.

The therapist held her hands and, while walking around in a circle, sang a welcoming song. She did a quick inventory, noticing her brown eyes, lovely braids, and the like. She lotioned her "boo-boos" on her hands and then changed to an activity where Carol could move around—"tossing a balloon in the air." It was important to keep the activities short and to move quickly from one activity to another in order to keep her attention. Soon, Carol's cooperation faded, and she started to stomp her feet and then escalated to hitting her forehead with her fist as she made loud, bizarre noises. It did not matter what activities were offered—Carol resisted. In desperation, the therapist started to mirror Carol's behavior, including the stomping, hitting, and strange sounds. This stopped Carol in her tracks—momentarily. She looked shocked that someone was imitating her! However, her resistance soon returned, and the therapist's mirroring continued. The session ended with the therapist trying to feed Carol chips. Carol resisted and roamed about the room but spontaneously came back to the therapist when she realized that was the only way she was going to get more potato chips. Throughout the session, the therapist tried to be attuned to Carol and would reflect her feelings—"I know this is all strange for you"—"I know that you are afraid"—"This will not hurt you."

In debriefing this session, the parents gained insight into how controlling Carol was with her self-abusive and bizarre behavior. The therapist suggested that Carol needed to be taught to perhaps simply shake her head for a "no" and to nod her head for a "yes," instead of the elaborate and bizarre pattern she had developed for refusing to do something. It was important to ignore her bizarre behavior and not to cave in to her demands, or this would continue to reinforce her negative behavior.

Second Session

Surprisingly, Carol came running to the therapist's room ahead of her parents with a big smile on her face. She seemed genuinely happy to see the therapist. The agenda included the welcome song, inventory, lotioning of hurts, catching bubbles, making powder handprints, singing "Ring around the Rosie" and "Patty Cake," drawing her body outline, and feeding. The activities were kept simple and short, with little transition time in between. A very important component was to ignore Carol's bizarre behavior when she did not want to do something and to cheerfully carry on with the agenda.

Third Session

Carol came running to the therapist's room again with a beaming smile. She was amazingly cooperative and seemed happy and even eager to do some of the activities. There was little evidence of her bizarre behavior, although she lifted her foot a few times as if to stomp, but then stopped. She started to express simple words like *chips.* There was a gradual increase of physical contact for longer periods between therapist and child. Activities became slower paced and more relaxed. Activities included the usual beginning ones, and later a manicure was given, which she attended to fully and seemed to enjoy.

Carol's mother reported that she had tried hard to ignore Carol's bizarre behavior at home, and this had resulted in a decrease in such behavior. (Dad was having a harder time ignoring this behavior.) Following the therapist's suggestions, her mother was also trying to teach Carol to be useful in the kitchen, such as having her set the table. (Before therapy, she was afraid to have Carol in the kitchen because of her potentially dangerous, impulsive behavior around the stove.)

Fourth Session

Carol was cheerful and cooperative during the first part of the Theraplay session. However, when her parents joined her, she gradually reverted to some of her original habits, particularly targeting her father, who had difficulty ignoring her bizarre behavior. Activities chosen were simple and mostly enjoyable, such as balloon toss; pass a gentle touch; one potato, two potato; hug; and the like, as well as feeding.

Fifth Through Eighth Sessions

Carol became more cooperative again, with less targeting of her father. She seemed to be able to learn and understand new activities quickly. Her expressive language increased to two-word phrases, although no attempt was made to teach her any language. Her gross motor skills were good, so the therapist taught her how to dance, which she tolerated well, in spite of the close physical proximity. The therapist suggested to the parents that Carol might do very well in sports because of her good coordination and agility.

A significant event occurred at home. Neighboring girls started to take Carol out to cycle with them.

The therapist asked Carol's mother to invite Carol's teaching assistant to observe a Theraplay session. She came, and the therapist encouraged her to ignore Carol's bizarre behavior at school and to teach her simple signals for "no" and "yes."

Ninth Session

This was the last session, and a party was held that included the family's favorite activities and food.

This session went well. Parents reported that they felt Carol had made many significant gains. She was more cooperative at home and school, her bizarre behavior had dramatically decreased, she used more sign language and spoken words, she was happier and smiled and laughed more often, and she was more spontaneous emotionally and could receive and give affection more often. She was calmer, less anxious and tense, and more aware of others. Her parents felt she had increased her attachment to them.

Checkups

The first of two checkups was planned and carried out. Carol was eager to see the therapist and cooperated fully even after not seeing her for a year.

Follow-up

Two years after treatment had ended, the therapist phoned Carol's mother to check on Carol's progress. Carol was now 12 years of age and doing very well. She had been integrated into the sixth-grade level, was reading beyond her grade (with facilitative communication), and was at grade level in math. Her printing and writing skills were still poor but improving. Socially, she was doing well with her peers at school and with her siblings at home.

Her mother felt that the biggest improvement was that she could now occupy herself. She was more easily controlled, more obedient, and was now speaking in three-word phrases. At last she could say "no" without having to stomp her foot or hit herself.

Summary

This child, although initially presenting as a severely autistic girl with multiple delays, progressed remarkably well in a short period of time. After only nine Theraplay sessions, her bizarre behavior had practically disappeared, and her true potential became more evident, especially in the gross motor area, cognition, and oral language. Her social skills improved significantly, as did her academic progress. She became more open to learning and was more motivated to please adults, which increased her cooperation. Best of all, the attachment relationship with her parents and with her siblings had significantly improved. Key factors that contributed to her progress were having healthy, loving parents and flexible teachers and using Theraplay with a skilled therapist.

CLINICAL APPLICATIONS

Theraplay has been used for a very wide range of emotional, behavioral, and social difficulties with clients ranging from infants and toddlers (Berndt, 2000) to the elderly and ages in between (Booth & Jernberg, 2010; Munns, 2000, 2009). It has been used in a variety of formats such as individual, family, marital, group (Munns, 2009; Rubin, 2010; Rubin & Tregay, 1989; Zanetti, Matthews, & Hollingsworth, 2000), and multifamily groups (Rubin, 1995, 2000; Sherman, 2000. Theraplay has been conducted in a variety of settings, including clinics, mental health settings, schools (Chaloner, 2006; Martin, 2000), day cares, primary health centers (Talen, 2000), and residential (Buckwalter & Findlay, 2009; Finnell, 2000) and group homes. Theraplay groups have included peers (adolescent groups; see Gardiner & Spickelmier, 2009), mother–child, father–son (Sherman, 2009), and family groups. Family Theraplay has been especially applicable to situations where there have been relationship and/or attachment issues, such as those found with stepchildren, foster and adopted children (Booth & Lindaman, 2000; Finnell, 2000; Lindaman & Lender, 2009; Miller-Mroz, Lender, Rubin, & Lindaman, 2010), and autistic children (Bundy-Myrow, 2000; Lindaman & Booth, 2010; Schlanger, 2010).

Theraplay has been used with children who have a wide range of physical and cognitive functioning (Azoulay, 2000). Children who are impulsive, dysregulated (Booth & Jernberg, 2010; Di Pasquale, 2000), aggressive, and resistant (DiPasquale, 2009; Eyles, Boada, & Munns, 2009) have responded well to the structuring and nurturing aspects of Theraplay. At the opposite end of the spectrum, children who are withdrawn, timid, and even mute have become more expressive emotionally and verbally (Manery, 2000).

Children who have come from deprived, abusive backgrounds or those who have witnessed domestic violence (Blanchard & Breuer, 2000) have been helped through Theraplay. However, traumatized children need a modified approach and usually need additional treatment. Hughes's (2006, 2007) Dyadic Developmental Therapy is increasingly used along with Theraplay for this population (Rubin, Lender, & Mroz, 2009). This reflects a trend for integrating Theraplay with other treatment methods such as multisensory approaches (Chaloner, 2006; Johanson-Maddox & Bettendorf, 2009), Circle of Security (Smillie, 2009), and equine-assisted therapy (Weiss, 2009). There is also an increased awareness of cultural differences and modifications of Theraplay to harmonize with different ethnic values and traditions—that is, with aboriginal people (Perry & Sutherland, 2009), with the Chinese (Siu, 2009b), with the Japanese (Manery, 2000), with the Germans (Franke, 2009), and with multiple cultures (Atkinson, 2009).

EMPIRICAL SUPPORT

Theraplay is well supported in its theoretical foundation, which lies in attachment theory that has a great deal of research behind it in terms of the impact of secure and insecure attachment patterns throughout the life span (Goldberg, 2000; Rutter, 1994; van Ijzendoorn & Sagi, 1999; Waters, Weinfield, & Hamilton, 2000) and between generations (van Ijzendoorn, 1995; Zeanah & Zeanah, 1989).

Theraplay is also supported in its emphasis on physical contact (Field, 2001). Nurturing touch is crucial for the normal development of infants, stimulating growth, enhancing digestion and immunoglobulin, aiding in regulation, and in improving intellectual and motor development. A lack of touch is related not only to a failure to thrive but also to increased violence in later life (Field, 2001; Nickelson & Parker, 2009; Thayer, 1998). When babies are cradled, rocked, and cuddled, this tactile stimulation promotes the release of hormones called oxytocins and opioids, which strengthen the mother–infant bond (Nickelson & Parker2009; Sunderland, 2006).

Theraplay promotes sensory-motor development and uses a preverbal approach, which are all factors involved in the organization and maturation of the right hemisphere as well as the maturation of the lower and middle (emotional) parts of the brain (J. Schore & Schore, 2008). The importance of parental attunement and responsiveness, which Theraplay encourages, is well documented (Gerhardt, 2004; Sunderland, 2006). The research involving Theraplay directly will now be reviewed.

Theraplay Research

Overall, in research studies using Theraplay, the majority use pre- and post-comparisons without control groups, but the number of studies with control groups, including randomly assigned groups, is steadily increasing. The research studies have shown significant results mainly in three areas: Theraplay increases self-esteem, lowers aggression, and increases parent–child attachment.

Morgan (1989) found that clinical children receiving Theraplay over a five-month period showed significant improvement in ratings of self-esteem, self-confidence, trust, and self-control. Limitations of this study included not only a lack of a control group but also a lack of blind, third-party ratings. This was overcome by Siu (2007a), who randomly assigned her children to a wait list control group and a Theraplay group. Those receiving Theraplay showed significantly higher self-esteem scores and fewer internalizing symptoms. Self-esteem improvements were also significant compared with a control group in a research study of Korean children (Hong, 2004).

A decrease in aggressive scores was found in two separate studies by Munns, Jensen, and Berger (1997) using Achenbach's Child Behavior Checklist (Achenbach, 1991) in behavior-disordered children. This finding was replicated by Makela and Vierikko (2004) using the same checklist with a group of foster children in Finland. Both Munns and Makela's research did not include control groups. However, a large study by Wettig, Franke, and Fjordbak (2006) using randomly assigned control and treatment groups found a significant reduction in oppositional and defiant behaviors in 60 children, as well as receptive language improvements. In a follow-up evaluation two years later, the behavioral and language improvements still remained. A second, larger study by the same authors drawing children from 9 different clinics and using 14 different therapists, including behavior-disordered children and matched controls, again found significant improvements for oppositionality, inattention, hyperactivity, impulsivity, and receptive language after receiving Theraplay.

A number of studies have focused on using Theraplay for children with attachment disorders: Mahon (1999) used fraternal twins who showed significant symptom reduction of over 50% on the Randolph Attachment Disorder questionnaire (Randolph, 1999). Meyer and Wardrop (2009) found that 9 out of 10 children showed significant improvement on attachment scores of the Kinship Questionnaire after receiving Theraplay. Ammen (2000) found a significant improvement in empathy scores in her high-risk teenage mothers compared with a control group after receiving Theraplay and giving infant massage to their babies. Lassenius-Panula and Makela (2007) found positive, significant results regarding behavior symptoms, parent–child relationships, and stress hormone levels of children referred for psychiatric care (for behavior and attachment problems) in three locations in Finland. Positive results were still evident at a six-month follow-up. Bojanowski (2005) found significant, positive Theraplay treatment effects using the Marschak and Child Behavior Checklist in a pre/post study of 11 parent–child dyads. Kim (2007) found significant positive results using a group Theraplay program designed to enhance the attachment of infants and their mothers compared with a control group.

Although clinicians often report on Theraplay making significant changes to autistic children, there have been few research studies to test this out. Cross and Howard (2007) applied intensive Theraplay (every day for a two-week period) on eight autistic children and found that there were no significant changes on autistic scale scores or the Parenting Stress Index (Abidin, 1995), but there were significant improvements across Marschak dimensions (Marschak, 1960) and normalization of epinephrine levels (stress indicators) for both children and parents. This study was limited in having a small number of subjects, too short a period of treatment and no control group.

An earlier study (Ritterfeld, 1990) using three groups—Theraplay (treatment 1), speech therapy (treatment 2), and arts and crafts (control), all having children with language problems—achieved surprising results. The group receiving Theraplay not only significantly improved in social emotional scores compared with the other groups but also increased significantly in expressive language scores (in spite of the fact that the speech therapy group was treated by professional speech therapists).

Kwon (2004) included nonclinical preschoolers in a treatment group (Theraplay) and control group. On posttesting, the Theraplay group showed greater capacity

‌

for self-awareness, self-control, awareness of others, and overall emotional intelligence.

Six additional studies using control groups focusing on Theraplay's effectiveness have been conducted at Sookmyung Women's University in Seoul, Korea (cited in Lender & Lindaman, 2007).

The efficacy of Theraplay has a growing body of research to support it. It is hoped that in the future, there will be more use of randomized control groups, besides the ones described here. In addition, control groups that involve face-to-face interactions, in order to control for placebo effects, are needed. Finally, more research studies need to be published in peer-reviewed journals.

CONCLUSION

Theraplay is a play therapy method that now has an increasing amount of empirical evidence to support it. It is structured, relationship based, cost effective, and short term. It replicates normal parent–child interactions, so it is easy to understand and learn. It uses physical contact and engaging, playful interactions to enhance attachments/relationships between parent–child and siblings. Increasing self-esteem, trust, the capacity to self-regulate, attunement and responsiveness, and self-reflective capacity are all goals of Theraplay. It is oriented to the development of the right hemisphere. Attachment and brain research studies showing the importance of touch and right-brain maturation give further credence to the tenets of Theraplay.

Theraplay can be applied to all ages and has significantly alleviated a wide range of emotional, social, and behavioral problems, particularly those stemming from attachment and/or relationship difficulties such as those found in adoptive, foster care, and divorced families and in autistic and behavior-disordered children.

REFERENCES

Abidin, R. (1995). *Parenting Stress Index: Professional manual* (3rd ed.). Odessa, FL: Psychological Assessment Resources.

Achenbach, T. (1991). *Manual for the Child Behavior Checklist/4-18 and 1991 profiles*. Burlington, VT: University of Vermont.

Ammen, S. (2000). A play-based teen parenting program to facilitate parent/child attachment. In H. Kaduson & C. Schaefer (Eds.), *Short-term play therapy for children* (pp. 345–369). New York, NY: Guilford Press.

Atkinson, N. (2009). Theraplay used in a multi-cultural environment. In E. Munns (Ed.), *Applications of family and group theraplay* (pp. 137–160). Northvale, NJ: Aronson.

Azoulay, D. (2000). Theraplay with physically handicapped and developmentally delayed children. In E. Munns (Ed.), *Theraplay: Innovations in attachment enhancing play therapy* (pp. 279–300). Northvale, NJ: Aronson.

Berndt, C. (2000). Theraplay with failure-to-thrive infants and mothers. In E. Munns (Ed.) *Theraplay: Innovations in attachment enhancing play therapy* (pp. 117–138). Northvale, NJ: Aronson.

Blanchard, S., & Breuer, J. (2000). Treating family violence through Theraplay. In E. Munns (Ed.), *Theraplay: Innovations in attachment enhancing play therapy* (pp. 103–116). Northvale, NJ: Aronson.

Bojanowski, J. (2005). *Discriminating between pre- versus post-Theraplay treatment Marschak Interaction Methods using the Marschak Interaction Method rating system.* Psy.D. diss., Alliant International University, Fresno, CA.

Booth, P., & Jernberg, A. (2010). *Theraplay: Helping parents and children build better relationships through attachment-based play.* San Francisco, CA: Jossey-Bass.

Booth, P., & Lindaman, S. (2000). Theraplay for enhancing attachment in adopted Children. In H. Kaduson and C. Schaefer (Eds.), *Short-term play therapy for children* (pp. 194–227). New York, NY: Guilford Press.

Bowlby, J. (1988). *A secure base: Clinical applications of attachment theory.* New York, NY: Brunner-Routledge.

Buckwalter, K., & Findlay, A. (2009). Theraplay: The powerful catalyst in residential treatment. In E. Munns (Ed.), *Applications of family and group Theraplay* (pp. 81–93). New York, NY: Aronson.

Bundy-Myrow, S. (2000). Group Theraplay for children with autism and pervasive developmental disorder. In E. Munns (Ed.), *Theraplay: Innovations in attachment enhancing play therapy.* Northvale, NJ: Aronson.

Chaloner, W. B. (2006, Fall). One therapist's journey as a Head Start mental health consultant integrating child-centered with sensory/Theraplay-based approaches to play therapy with at-risk children. *The Theraplay Institute Newsletter.*

Cross, D., & Howard, A. (2007). *An evaluation of Theraplay with children diagnosed with PDD or mild to moderate autism.* Paper presented at the Third International Theraplay Conference, Chicago, IL.

Di Pasquale, L. (2000). The Marschak Interaction Method. In E. Munns (Ed.), *Theraplay: Innovations in attachment enhancing play therapy* (pp. 27–51). Northvale, NJ: Aronson.

Di Pasquale, L. (2009). The dysregulated child in Theraplay. In E. Munns (Ed.), *Applications of family and group Theraplay* (pp. 27–44). Northvale, NJ: Aronson.

Doidge, N. (2007). *The brain that changes itself.* Toronto, Canada: Penguin Books.

Eyles, S., Boada, M., & Munns, C. (2009). Theraplay with overtly and passively resistant children. In E. Munns (Ed.), *Applications of family and group Theraplay* (pp. 45–55). Northvale, NJ: Aronson.

Field, T. (2001). *Touch.* Cambridge, MA: Massachusetts Institute of Technology.

Finnell, N. (2000). Theraplay innovations with adoptive families. In E. Munns (Ed.), *Theraplay: Innovations in attachment enhancing play therapy* (pp. 235–256). Northvale, NJ: Aronson.

Franke, U. (2009). Theraplay in Germany. In E. Munns (Ed.), *Applications of family and group Theraplay* (pp. 127–136). Northvale, NJ: Aronson.

Gardiner, B., & Spickelmier, M. (2009). Working with adolescents. In E. Munns (Ed.), *Applications of family and group Theraplay* (pp. 249–264). Northvale, NJ: Aronson.

Gerhardt, S. (2004). *Why love matters: How affection shapes a baby's brain.* New York, NY: Brunner-Routledge.

Goldberg, S. (2000). *Attachment and development.* New York, NY: Oxford University Press.

Hong, J. (2004). *Effects of group Theraplay on self-esteem and interpersonal relations for abused children.* Presentation at Sookmyurg Women's University, Seoul, South Korea.

Hughes, D. (2006). *Building the bonds of attachment: Awakening love in deeply troubled children.* Northvale, NJ: Aronson.

Hughes, D. (2007). Attachment-focused family therapy. New York, NY: Norton.

Jernberg, A. (1979). *Theraplay: A new treatment using structured play for problem children and their families.* San Francisco, CA: Jossey-Bass.

Johanson-Maddox, A., & Bettendorf, C. (2009). Theraplay in combination with sensory and handling techniques: The body/mind connection in pediatrics. In E. Munns (Ed.), *Applications of family and group therapy* (pp. 197–209). Northvale, NJ: Aronson.

Kim, Y. (2007). *Development and evaluation of a group Theraplay program to enhance attachment of infants.* Unpublished manuscript (cited in Lender & Lindaman).

Kohut, H. (1977). *The restoration of the self.* New York, NY: International Universities Press.

Kwon, E. (2004). The effect of group Theraplay on the development of preschoolers' emotional intelligence quotient. In D. Lender & S. Lindaman, *Research supporting the effectiveness of Theraplay and Marschak Interaction Method.* Chicago, IL: The Theraplay Institute.

Lassenius-Panula, L., & Makela, J. (2007). *Effectiveness of Theraplay with symptomatic children ages 2–6: Changes in symptoms, parent-child relationships and stress hormone levels of children referred for psychiatric care in three university hospital districts in Finland.* Paper presented at the Third International Theraplay Conference, Chicago, IL.

Lender, D., & Lindaman, S. (2007). *Research supporting the effectiveness of Theraplay and Marschak Interaction Method.* Paper presented at the Third International Theraplay Conference, Chicago, IL.

Lindaman, S., & Booth, P. (2010). Theraplay for children with autism spectrum disorders. In P. Booth & A. Jernberg (Eds.), *Theraplay: Helping parents and children build better relationships through attachment-based play* (pp. 301–358). San Francisco, CA: Jossey-Bass.

Lindaman, S., & Lender, D. (2009). Theraplay with adopted children. In E. Munns (Ed.), *Applications of family and group Theraplay.* Northvale, NJ: Aronson.

Mahon, M. (1999). *Theraplay as an intervention with previously institutionalized twins having attachment difficulties.* Unpublished doctoral dissertation, Chicago School of Professional Psychology, Chicago, IL.

Makela, J., & Vierikko, I. (2004). *From heart to heart: Interactive therapy for children in care. Report on the Theraplay project in SOS children's villages in Finland 2001–2004.* Published by the SOS children's villages in Finland.

Manery, G. (2000). Dual family Theraplay with withdrawn children in a cross-cultural content. In E. Munns (Ed.), *Theraplay: Innovations in attachment enhancing play therapy* (pp. 151–194). Northvale, NJ: Aronson.

Marschak, M. (1960). A method for evaluating child–parent interaction under controlled conditions. *Journal of Genetic Psychology, 97,* 3–22.

Martin, D. (2000). Teacher-led Theraplay in early childhood classrooms. In E. Munns (Ed.), *Theraplay: Innovations in attachment enhancing play therapy* (pp. 321–337). Northvale, NJ: Aronson.

Meyer, L., & Wardrop, J. (2009). Research on Theraplay effectiveness. In E. Munns (Ed.), *Applications of family and group Theraplay* (pp. 17–24). Northvale, NJ: Aronson.

Miller-Mroz, J., Lender, D., Rubin, P., & Lindaman, S. (2010). Theraplay for children who are adopted or in foster care. In P. Booth & A. Jernburg (Eds.), *Theraplay: Helping parents and children build better relationships through attachment-based play* (pp. 405–493). San Francisco, CA: Jossey-Bass.

Morgan, C. (1989). *Theraplay: An evaluation of the effect of short-term, structured play on self-confidence, self-esteem, trust and self-control.* Unpublished research, York Center for Children, Youth and Families, Richmond Hill, Ontario, Canada.

Munns, E. (2000). *Theraplay: Innovations in attachment enhancing play therapy.* Northvale, NJ: Aronson.

Munns, E. (2009). *Applications of family and group Theraplay.* Northvale, NJ: Aronson.

Munns, E., Jensen, D., & Berger, L. (1997). *Theraplay and the reduction of aggression.* Unpublished manuscript, Blue Hills Child & Family Services, Aurora, Ontario, Canada.

Nickelson, B., & Parker, L. (2009). *Attached at the heart.* New York, NY: Universe.

Perry, B., & Salavitz, M. (2006). *The boy that was raised as a dog.* New York, NY: Basic Books.

Perry, L., & Sutherland, P. (2009). Theraplay and aboriginal peoples. In E. Munns (Ed.), *Applications of family and group Theraplay* (pp. 97–114). Northvale, NJ: Aronson.

Randolph, E. (1999). *Randolph Attachment Disorder Questionnaire.* Evergreen, CO: Attachment Center Press.

Ritterfield, U. (1990). Theraplay auf dem prufstand. Bewertung des Therapieerfolgs am Beispiel sprachauffalliger Vorschulkender (Putting Theraplay to the test: Evaluation of therapeutic outcome with language delayed preschool children). *Theraplay Journal, 2,* 22–25.

Rubin, P. (1995, Fall). Multi-family Theraplay in a shelter for the homeless. *Theraplay Institute Newsletter,* 5.

Rubin, P. (2000). Multi-family Theraplay groups with homeless mothers and children. In E. Munns (Ed.), *Theraplay: Innovations in attachment enhancing play therapy* (pp. 211–234). Northvale, NJ: Aronson.

Rubin, P. (2010). Group Theraplay. In P. Booth & A. Jernberg (Eds.), *Theraplay: Helping parents and children build better relationships through attachment-based play* (pp. 495–519). San Franscisco, CA: Jossey-Bass.

Rubin, P., & Tregay, J. (1989). *Play with them—Theraplay groups in the classroom: A technique for professionals who work with children.* Springfield, IL: Thomas.

Rubin, P., Lender, D., & Mroz, P. (2009). Theraplay and dyadic developmental psychotherapy. In E. Munns (Ed.), *Applications of family and group Theraplay* (pp. 171–182). Northvale, NJ: Aronson.

Rutter, M. (1994). *Clinical implications of attachment concepts: Retrospect and prospect.* Paper presented at the International Conference on Attachment and Psychopathology. Toronto, Ontario, Canada.

Schlanger, R. (2010). *For the love of Melissa.* Bloomington, IN: AuthorHouse.

Schore, A. (1994). *Affect regulation and origins of self. The neurobiology of emotional development.* Hillsdale, NJ: Erlbaum.

Schore, A. (2005). Attachment, affect and the developing right brain: Linking developmental neuroscience to pediatrics. *Pediatrics Review, 26,* 204–217.

Schore, J., & Schore, A. (2008). Modern attachment theory: The central role of affect regulation in development and treatment. *Clinical Social Work Journal, 36,* 9–20.

Seligman, M. (2007). *The optimistic child.* New York, NY: Houghton Mifflin.

Sherman, J. (2000). Multi-family Theraplay. In E. Munns (Ed.), *Theraplay: Innovations in attachment enhancing play therapy* (pp. 195–210). Northvale, NJ: Aronson.

Sherman, J. (2009). Father–son group Theraplay. In E. Munns (Ed.), *Applications in family and group Theraplay* (pp. 237–248). Northvale, NJ: Aronson.

Siegel, D. (1999). *The developing mind: How relationships and the brain interact to shape who we are.* New York, NY: Guilford Press.

Siegel, D., & Hartzell, M. (2004). *Parenting from the inside out.* New York: Tarcher/Putman.

Siu, A. (2009a). Theraplay in the Chinese World: An intervention program for Hong Kong children with internalizing problems. *International Journal of Play Therapy, 18*(1), 1–12.

Siu, A. (2009b). Theraplay for Chinese children. In E. Munns (Ed.), *Applications of family and group Theraplay* (pp. 115–125). Northvale, NJ: Aronson.

Smillie, G. (2009). In sync. In E. Munns (Ed.), *Applications of family and group Theraplay* (pp. 161–169). Northvale, NJ: Aronson.

Stern, D. (1995). *The motherhood constellation: A unified view of parent–infant psychotherapy.* New York, NY: Basic Books.

Sunderland, M. (2006). *The science of parenting.* New York, NY: DK Publishing.

Talen, M. (2000). Using Theraplay in primary health care centers: A model for pediatric care. In E. Munns (Ed.), *Theraplay: Innovations in attachment enhancing play therapy* (pp. 339–361). Northvale, NJ: Aronson.

Thayer, T. (1998). March encounters. *Psychology Today*, 31–36.

van Ijzendoorn, M. (1995). Adult attachment representations, parental responsiveness and infant attachment: A meta-analysis on the predictive validity of the adult attachment interview. *Psycholgical Bulletin, 117,* 387–403.

van Ijzendoorn, M., & Sagi, A. (1999). Cross-cultural patterns of attachment. In J. Cassiday & P. Shaver (Eds.), *Handbook of attachment* (pp. 713–734). New York, NY: Guilford Press.

Waters, E., Weinfield, N., & Hamilton, C. (2000, May/June). The stability of attachment security from infancy to adolescence and early adulthood: General discussion. *Child Development*, 71(3), 703–706.

Weiss, D. (2009). Equine-assisted therapy and Theraplay. In E. Munns (Ed.), *Applications of family and group Theraplay.* (pp. 225–233). Northvale, NJ: Aronson.

Wettig, H., Franke, U., & Fjordbak, B. (2006) Evaluating the effectiveness of Theraplay. In C. E. Schaefer & H. G. Kaduson (Eds.), *Contemporary play therapy: Theory, research and practice* (pp. 103–235). New York, NY: Guilford Press.

Winnicott, D. (1965). *The maturational process and the facilitating environment: Studies in the theory of emotional development.* London, UK: Hogarth Press.

Zanetti, J., Matthews, C., & Hollingsworth, R. (2000). Adults and children together (ACT): A prevention model. In E. Munns (Ed.), *Theraplay: Innovations in attachment enhancing play therapy* (pp. 257–275). Northvale, NJ: Aronson.

Zeanah, C., & Zeanah, P. (1989). Intergenerational transmission of maltreatment: Insights from attachment theory and research. *Psychiatry, 52,* 171–196.

Chapter 16

SOLUTION-FOCUSED PLAY THERAPY: HELPING CHILDREN AND FAMILIES FIND SOLUTIONS

Donald R. Nims

INTRODUCTION

Language is powerful. Equally powerful is the manner in which language is spoken. One has only to watch the interaction between a parent and child to witness this "magical dance" of words and presence that results in positive childhood development. Unfortunately, circumstances of life such as abuse, neglect, and physical and emotional deprivation negatively impact this parent–child relationship. This creates distress and inhibits normal development. These children are often the ones who struggle in school, engage in high-risk behaviors, and become involved in the mental health system. Play therapy provides the therapeutic presence when working with these children. The solution-focused model provides the language through which children can find their own solutions. Leggett (2009) wrote that it is necessary to consider a therapeutic approach designed particularly for children that combines the use of language and play. A study by Bonsi (2006) supported the power of language in the solution-focused approach. He recognized that clients are the experts regarding their own lives and that language shapes and molds the perception of reality and constructs solutions.

Solution-focused play therapy (SFPT) is different from other forms of play therapy (Elliott, 2009). Chief among these differences is that the therapeutic process of SFPT is driven not by mechanistic external forces but by the dialogue between child and therapist (McKergow, 2009). These are the principles of "solution thought" and "solution talk." The therapist believes that children know what they want and need. Therefore, the therapist is always thinking of how to frame the therapeutic experience so that children can begin to see for themselves their own solutions. The use of play therapy techniques in SFPT facilitates the "solution talk," which is designed to help children articulate their goals.

The experiential activities inherent in play therapy such as art, sand tray, and the use of puppets serve as the medium for this dialogue (Nims, 2007; Taylor, 2009). The solution-focused approach is a new way of thinking for therapists to use with their clients (Metcalf, 2009). According to Berg and Steiner (2003), this approach begins with an assessment of possible solutions, that is, the outcome that the client expects and desires. The key is to discover children's own talents and skills and appreciate how they came to develop them. "From this the therapist learns how to use those abilities to arrive at solutions" (Berg & Steiner, p. 7). The solutions are already present in the child's history. SFPT provides a clear, concrete framework for rediscovering and reusing these solutions.

The solution-building approach was pioneered with the work of Steve de Shazer (1985, 1988, 1991, 1994), who was greatly influenced by Milton Erickson's use of language (Erickson & Rossi, 1979; Hogan, 2009). Erickson wrote that individuals have a reservoir of wisdom learned and forgotten but still available (Minuchin & Fishman, 1981) and that a successful intervention must focus on solutions rather than problems. In Solution-Focused Brief Therapy (SFBT), the client is seen as competent and in charge, able to visualize the changes he or she desires, and build on the positive aspects of what the client is already doing (DeJong & Berg, 1998). Trebing (2000) described two reasons why a solution-focused approach was relevant: "There are so many children to reach and so few child therapists to go around . . . because children's character structure is more flexible, their personalities are more resilient, and their outlook is more positive" (p. 144). Shapiro (1994) observed that the goal of short-term therapy is to enable children to use their internal resources for growth and development within their own environment.

BASIC CONCEPTS

In SFBT, the therapist uses a variety of techniques to help the client experience positive behaviors or solutions that establish the foundation for their new thinking. The structure of SFBT has several important elements that are designed to elicit these positive behaviors. SFBT calls for creating hypothetical goals that include desired behaviors as a way to help clients see what is possible for them (Sklare, 2005). These goals need to be concrete and focused on the positive expression of a behavior rather than the absence of a negative behavior and on some specific behavior that the client has a desire to experience.

Establishing and articulating goals is vitally important because this provides the foundation for the entire solution-focused process. According to Sklare (2005), identification of a clear goal is the best predictor of effective counseling outcomes. Problems with succeeding steps in the process are usually traced to an ill-defined goal. A child's goal might be the desire for parents to come back together after a divorce. The therapist has to redirect the child by asking the child what has happened since the divorce and elicit how the divorce has affected the child. Then the therapist turns the child's answer into a positive behavioral goal: "If you weren't so sad, what would you be doing differently?"

In SFBT, the miracle question is used to help the child visualize a picture of his or her reaching these goals. The child is asked to imagine that while sleeping, a miracle takes place and the problem that he or she is experiencing has disappeared. The therapist asks relationship questions to help clarify what the miracle looks like, what is different, and what others would notice that indicates a miracle has occurred. Children often wish for a miracle that is impossible to obtain such as the return of a loved one who has died. While it is important to affirm and validate the child's wish, the miracle question is related to the goal of what the child would be doing differently when he or she is feeling better or less sad. Relationship questions help the child to express how other people might respond to these positive changes in behavior. The purpose is to affirm the child's visualization of these new behaviors.

Another important element in SFBT is the idea of an exception. Exceptions are past occasions in the child's life when he or she experienced even a "little bit" of the miracle. It is important to explore at least two or three exceptions in order to subtly remind the child that past success can be repeated in the present and into the future.

The SFBT technique of scaling is an attempt to objectively demonstrate the achievement of goals in order to provide clients with a measure of their success. The child is asked to rate success on a scale of 1 to 10, with 1 meaning "no success" and 10 meaning "complete success" in achieving one's goal. The therapist affirms the response and asks why the number is what it is and why it is not any lower. Again, this process subtly challenges the child to view life in more positive terms.

The final step in SFBT is to reinforce the child's efforts to this point, remind the child of any past success, and look for ways to move up to the next higher number on his or her scale. The therapist prepares a "solution message" to give to the child to take as a reminder of the session and provide opportunity for growth. This message is important as a visual representation of the SFBT process and becomes the basis for the next session.

THERAPEUTIC POWERS OF PLAY UNDERLYING THE MODEL

Goal Setting

The first and most important step in the SFBT process is establishing clear and concrete goals that fit the individual need of the child or adolescent. The child's goals are simply stated as getting along better with a peer, doing homework, or feeling better about being with a stepparent. The goal must be concrete, positive in nature, and clearly behavioral. The important thing is that the child wants this goal to happen. The therapist and child work together to set goals and to find ways to achieve them (Haley, 2000).

It is crucial that goals are relevant, meaningful, and specific to the child's situation. The more concrete, behavioral, and measurable the goal, the more potential there is for making progress toward solutions (DeJong & Berg, 2002). For example, a child who has a history of abuse may have feelings of guilt and worthlessness. The goal becomes specific things the child would be doing that are a sign that life is better and more hopeful. A child with a disability might wish to cope a little better. The goal then is what the child might be doing that was evidence that he or she was coping more effectively. If a child is angry, the goal is what the child would be doing differently if the anger were not present. An adolescent wanting to be respected is asked what would be a sign to an observer that he or she was feeling respected. Other questions asked in this important stage are, "What brings you here today?" "What has to happen so you won't have to come and see me anymore?" "What would you like to be doing that would be a sign that things for you were better?" "If there were something we could work on together that would help you feel different, what would that be?" "If you were not _____, what would you be doing instead?" Expressive play therapy techniques enable children to display their goals through their play.

Seth, 9 years old, had a problem with anger. First, he drew a picture of a red thunderbolt to describe his anger. When asked what would be different if he wasn't angry, he answered that he would be calm. He then drew a picture of a blue stream of water to describe being calm. What he would be doing as a sign he was calm became the goal for the session.

The author's technique of the "wows and hows" (Nims, 2007) uses statements that begin with the words *wow* and *how*. They are designed to affirm children's positive conclusions about their lives in spite of what has happened to them, the "wow," and of asking them how they knew their behavior was the right thing to do under these circumstances, the "how." This helps them to discover their own capabilities and feel encouraged to use these skills in the future. Examples of this technique are "Wow, you were able to control your anger that time and stay calm. I wonder how you knew to do that" "Wow, you did your homework that day. I wonder how you did that? There have been so many times you didn't do your homework. What was different that time?"

The Miracle Question

The miracle question helps children transition to experiencing what life would be like if the problem that brought them to therapy were magically solved. This step is not intended to minimize the multiple and complicated problems that children can experience. The child has identified a goal; the miracle question helps the child to visualize how life would be different if the goal were achieved, "even a little." The therapist engages the child: "If a miracle happened tonight while you were asleep and you woke up tomorrow and the problem that brought you here today was solved by magic, what would be the first small thing you would notice that told you this miracle has happened?"

Andy is 8 years old. He lives with his biological mother and older sister. He comes to play therapy because of aggression and severe mood swings. In his miracle, he describes waking up and being greeted by his mother with a smile and a hug. As a consequence of his mother's greeting, he would look forward to having a "great day" both at home and at school. He then described what he would be doing differently during his "great day." He would go to school with a smile on his face and look forward to seeing his friends and being in his literature class since he likes his teacher. After a great day at school, he would come home and be happy to see his mom.

Relationship questions help to clarify and expand the miracle: "What would you be doing differently now that the miracle has taken place?" "How would your mother or teacher respond differently to you?" "Picture yourself next week, next month; how will you recognize the signs that a miracle has indeed taken place, that things are different, even better?" It is important to provide as much detail as possible to the miracle. Again, the more one can visualize what these positive feelings and new behaviors look like, the more likely the change can take place. Berg (2005) observed that it is important to experience the state of the miracle as well as the usefulness of the relationship questions.

Exceptions

Exceptions, the third step in the SFBT process, are little pieces of the miracle or times in the past when the problem that brought the child to therapy did not occur. Exceptions are also used to describe past occasions when the child experienced some of the goal. As clients recall the instances in their lives when the problem did not exist, they discover the details of how they avoided the problem, which provides a road map for solutions, success, and empowerment (Sklare, 2005). Children very often do not know how to appreciate the success they have had in the past. Individuals tend to minimize or dismiss the importance of their perceptions where a measure of success was achieved (DeJong & Berg, 2002). Whatever previous success children have in achieving some of their goal, they will often insist on giving someone else the credit. "My mother made me." "The teacher told me I had to do it." An effective response is to remind them that they do not always do what their mother or teacher says. "What was different about those times?" With this positive self-awareness, children begin to identify and access an internal locus of control, enabling them to take responsibility for their own behavior in the future.

Chris is 13 years old. His miracle is waking up knowing he no longer has to be in day treatment but back in regular school. Chris and the therapist talked about those times before day treatment when he was in regular school and enjoyed it. They looked for pieces of the miracle. Chris eventually told the therapist he did not want to have to talk to him anymore. "What has to happen so that we don't have to talk anymore?" The therapist told Chris they both knew what had to happen. Therapy ended the week after Chris was back in regular school.

Scaling

As part of scaling, clients are shown a strip of paper with 10 faces with numbers from 1 to 10. This is a pictorial technique adapted by the author to elicit levels of feeling in children (see Appendix C). The faces range from one that looks extremely angry to one that looks extremely happy. This exercise is a visual representation of the scaling question: "On a scale of 1 to 10, with 1 being the worst and 10 the best, where are you on the way to your miracle?" Scaling is an activity that sets the tone for the client's new learning process that is active, spontaneous, relaxed, participatory, and fun (Zalter, 2005). Once the child has identified a number on the scale, the therapist might ask, "Wow! How is it a (the number identified by the child on the scale) and not a (one number lower on the scale)?" "Wow, how did you know that (the number the child circled) was better?" "Now, what do you have to do to get to a (one number higher)?"

Sarah is 13 years old. She is defiant at home and school. She tells the therapist she feels ugly. When asked what she would be doing differently when she didn't feel ugly, she said she would speak out in class. This became the goal. When asked to scale how she was working toward her goal, she indicated a "6." It was a "6" and not a "5" because she did speak out successfully in one of her classes a few days earlier.

Solution Message

The solution message is the final step in the SFBT process. This is a concrete written summary of the session that the child can take home as a visual representation of the child's efforts toward finding his or her own solution. This message is written in the presence of the child with the child's participation. The solution message has three parts: the credits, the bridge, and the solution task. The credits are a series of compliments and affirmations about the child and the efforts the child has expressed in participating in the play therapy session. The child is given "credit" for taking part in the process, for being vulnerable in sharing what is happening in his or her life, and for achieving past success as expressed in the exceptions. The therapist provides a written list of all these positive attributes for the child. The bridge is the connection between the credits and the solution task. The therapist indicates in the bridge the commitment and willingness of the child to work on his or her goal. The solution task is simply asking the child to aim for the next number on the scale. The solution task can also be to pick a "miracle day" and remember what is different about that day. The child is asked to report on the task in the next session.

Charlie is 6 years old. His parents are newly divorced. Charlie was experiencing episodes of rage when it was time to spend the weekend with his dad. When asked what he likes to do, Charlie drew a picture of his mother and him playing a favorite board game together. The therapist and Charlie each put on a puppet. The therapist's puppet told Charlie's puppet how much he enjoyed their being together in the session and reinforced the goal for Charlie to tell his mother when he feels frustrated about having to visit his dad. He and his mother would then plan what they would do when he came home on Sunday afternoon. Together, the therapist and Charlie composed the solution message for Charlie to take home with him. The therapist wrote Charlie's name at the top of a piece of drawing paper and listed several of his attributes (the credits): Charlie was a courageous little boy who was trying very hard to do well at school; it is difficult when parents get divorced, but Charlie was doing his best even when he got frustrated. Charlie liked to draw and play with puppets. He also liked to play board games with his mother. Because Charlie was willing to talk to his mom when he got frustrated about going to his dad's house on the weekends (the bridge), the therapist asked Charlie to pick a time every day when he would talk to his mom about his feelings (the solution task). With Charlie's permission, the therapist shared the solution message with Charlie's mother.

Follow-up Sessions

Subsequent sessions begin with remembering the goal as stated previously. The key is to ascertain what is different or better for the child since the last session. Relationship questions that describe who noticed this change help to provide detail about what is different or better for the child. Scaling is used to establish a baseline of progress and what needs to happen to move to the next higher number on the scale. The miracle question is repeated if the therapist determines this step will be helpful. Using art enables the child to draw what is better or different. The sand tray is used for the same purpose. Puppets enable the child and therapist to role-play what has happened since the last session and what the child can do to move up the scale. As described earlier, a solution message is given to the child that establishes the groundwork for the next session.

ROLE OF THE THERAPIST

The role of the therapist is one that involves a process of discovering what it is that the child wants as a realistic goal for the session. The SFBT model is one of solution thinking and solution talking that frames the therapeutic direction. In SFBT, the therapist uses a variety of techniques to help the client experience positive behaviors or solutions that establish the basis for this new thinking. The structure of SFBT has several important elements that are designed to elicit positive behaviors. (Refer to Appendix A for a list of the steps in the solution-focused process that are described in this model.) SFBT calls for creating hypothetical goals that include desired behaviors as a way to help clients see what is possible for them (Sklare, 2005). Sometimes children are able to articulate their goals; at other times, the use of play techniques such as art, sand tray, and puppets reveal these potential goals. When children are unable to communicate their goals, the therapist can make a "therapeutic assumption" of what the child wants as a solution.

Consider the example of Joey, a 5-year-old boy with aggressive behaviors at home and at school. Joey was unable to articulate wants and desires in words, but in drawing activities, he consistently drew a tight edge around the perimeter of the board. The therapist made the assumption that Joey wanted some consistency in his life. This was supported by the knowledge that Joey's parents were divorced with shared custody. On Monday mornings, Joey's teacher knew by his behavior with which parent he had spent the weekend. The therapist then instituted play therapy activities that focused on Joey's "solution," the need for consistency. Joey responded very well to a routine in his therapy sessions. They began with Joey's helping the therapist put masking tape on the floor around the perimeter of the playroom. Joey enjoyed playing in the sand tray in a certain way and talking with his puppets.

ROLE OF THE PARENT

The role of the parent is vital in SFBT. The therapist must keep in mind the expectations of the parent and caregivers while understanding what the child wants to see happen. SFPT is more than merely an expectation of a change in behavior; it helps the child and family see what is different when these changes in behavior take place—even a little change.

Parents are collaborators in identifying clear behavioral goals that fit the needs of both the parents and their children. Often, parents view therapeutic success in more abstract terms, such as "I want my child to behave" or "I want my child to be more responsible." In school, success might be to "pay attention" or "be more cooperative." It is absolutely necessary that the therapist work with the parents and caregivers to articulate clearly and concretely what their goals are for the child. With the child's permission, the therapist shares the child's goals and miracle with his or her parents. They need to appreciate what their child's goals are; how they, as parents, can participate in the solution; and what they, as parents and caregivers, can do differently to facilitate this process. The children's miracles give the parents insight into their children's dreams for themselves as well as their place in the family. The steps in solution-focused therapy are equally valid in working with the parents to help them see solutions in clear and concrete terms. For goals to have a chance for successful accomplishment, both children and parents must work together. Appendix B provides a description of how to identify goals that meet both children's and parent's needs. The collaboration of parents and children in the therapeutic process is certainly desirable and appropriate as the therapist, child, and parents work together in finding solutions that benefit the entire family.

CLINICAL APPLICATIONS

SFPT is used with children and adolescents with a variety of mental health diagnoses from attention deficit/hyperactivity disorder, reactive attachment disorder, obsessive-compulsive disorder, and posttraumatic stress disorder to bipolar disorder. The issue is not so much the nature of what brings a child or adolescent into therapy but what the child and therapist together discover is a working behavioral goal. As mentioned earlier, it is the solution-focused thinking of the therapist that makes this process relevant regardless of the clinical situation. It is an effort to help the child find some order in the midst of chaos. Through play, the child presents what he or she wants to have happen; how things can be different; and what this difference will look like. The therapist uses these same techniques to play out the child's miracle and look ahead to success by looking back at the exceptions or pieces of the miracle. Scaling is a tool that has clinical application by providing clear evidence of progress.

SFPT is also used in family therapy. Each family member is involved in a family picture, family sand tray, or family puppet show. The family picture shows the way parents and children see things now and what they would like to see happen that would be better. The use of the sand tray can provide similar information for the therapist. In the puppet show, each family member is asked to describe what the family would be doing when things are going well or what the family would be doing when the miracle takes place and things are better.

EMPIRICAL SUPPORT

SFBT is relevant for working with children whose cognitive ability is sufficient to comprehend and appreciate the concepts integral to the solution-focused process. In a study by DeJong and Berg (1998), it was reported that 78% of children 12 years old and younger and 89% of children 13 to 18 years of age made progress toward achieving their goals through this process. DeJong and Berg (2002) described success with children as young as 5 years old when making language adjustments for the developmental age of the children. Considering the cognitive requirements for this model, the solution-focused approach is probably not appropriate for children younger than kindergarten age.

Berg and Steiner (2003) noted that the nonverbal, playful, and creative habits of children support successful therapy based on the SFBT model. Selekman (2005) presented a model that combined the best elements of modified traditional play and art therapy techniques with a solution-oriented approach when working with children. In a study by Perkins (2006) of clients receiving treatment in an urban child and adolescent mental health clinic over 14 months, the therapeutic success with children was statistically significant using a solution-focused approach. She affirmed that the high satisfaction level among children and parents using this approach was "not surprising given its emphasis on early treatment, encouragement, and increasing the sense of hopefulness in the client" (Perkins, 2006, p. 223). Corcoran and Stephenson (2000) found a significant improvement between pretest and posttest scores on the Conners' Parent Rating Scale and positive improvements on the Feelings, Attitudes, and Behavior Scale for Children when using the solution-focused approach. Working with adolescents using the SFBT approach, Paylo (2005) found that this process empowered families to find solutions in the future while drawing on their own expertise and strengths to promote the desired change. Myers (2009) found the solution-focused approach in a school setting to be successful, respectful, and thoughtful when working with children and adolescents who were having behavioral difficulties. In addition, Kim (2008) found positive treatment effects in a meta-analysis of solution-focused brief therapy versus a control group of children with behavioral disorders.

CASE ILLUSTRATION

Kim is 5 years old. She was sexually abused by an older neighbor child. There has been no further contact with this other child. Kim comes to therapy because of aggressive behavior in her kindergarten class. Her behavior toward her peers was provocative and resulted in emotional isolation from others in the classroom who did not want to be around her. At home, she was also aggressive toward a younger brother. The therapist used the play therapy techniques of sand tray and puppets to build a relationship with her.

Kim used the sand tray at first as an opportunity for free expression. Play therapy activities are always used to develop rapport and trust with the child as well as provide additional insight to the therapist regarding the child's underlying level of emotional distress. The therapist then asked Kim to use the sand tray to make a tray of school. It became evident that what was causing Kim the most distress was not having friends at school. Making friends became the focus of the therapy. Using the wizard puppet who waved his magic wand, the therapist proceeded to the miracle question. Kim wished for a friend at school. The therapist asked, "What would you and your friend do together? What games would you play? What else would you do with your friend? What would friend do?" The result of this process is to paint a vivid picture of Kim playing with her friend. At this point, the therapist and Kim each chose a puppet and played various imaginary games together. They described some times in the immediate past when Kim did get to play successfully with another child at school. On the scaling sheet, Kim selected the "7" picture face as the measure of where she thought her miracle was.

The therapist and Kim used their puppets to practice how Kim would play when she went back to school. The solution message was a picture that the therapist and Kim drew together. The therapist divided a piece of drawing paper in half. On their half of the paper, the therapist and Kim each drew a picture of Kim playing with a friend. On the back, the therapist listed several attributes for Kim: "You really like to play. You are willing to talk to me about your feelings. You would really like to have a friend with whom to play, and you are willing to learn how to be a friend." The therapist then wrote a big "8" on the paper. The solution task was to aim for an 8 in the coming week when playing with her friend in kindergarten. With Kim's permission, the therapist shared the solution task with both Kim's mother and her teacher in order to help facilitate an opportunity for Kim to play with another child at school. Follow-up sessions showed that Kim's aggressive behavior decreased, and she was able to play more appropriately with her peers.

Billy is 15 years old. He was sexually abused by a friend of his father when Billy was 11. Billy lives with his mother and stepfather. Billy's older sister was also abused during the same time period. She is currently in a long-term residential care facility. Billy is in an alternative school setting because of behavioral issues and a history of substance abuse. Although Billy is 15 years old, he responded to experiential play therapy techniques, particularly art and modeling clay. The therapist became involved with Billy when the school reported that Billy had threatened to hurt himself. After the suicide threat was resolved, weekly therapy sessions were instituted. At first, Billy was not open to communication. The therapist gave Billy some modeling clay and asked him to make what he wanted with it. This activity opened up discussion. Billy was asked to use the modeling clay to describe how he was feeling. Next, he was asked to use the clay to describe how it might look if he felt differently and what he would be doing as a sign that he was feeling better. This led to a discussion of the relationship between Billy and his mother.

The goal Billy decided for his therapy was to have a better relationship with his mother. The therapist asked, "What would this look like? What would you be doing when this relationship is better?" The miracle question was directed toward this goal of how Billy and his mother's relationship would look following the miracle. Billy drew a picture of this miracle. Exceptions described some times when Billy and his mother experienced some of the miracle "even a little bit." Scaling provided an opportunity to reinforce Billy's efforts to this point. He chose a "6" on his scale because he and his mother had talked that morning without arguing. The solution message was a joint statement in the form of a picture drawn by the therapist and Billy, with each using half of a piece of drawing paper. The therapist and Billy each drew Billy and his mother doing something together in a positive way. After sharing their pictures, the therapist listed Billy's attributes on the other side of the paper: "You are a young man who knows what he wants, and you are willing to work toward achieving your goal. You really want to have a good relationship with your mother. You know when things are not working well, and you will stop and take a breath and start over talking to your mom. I am confident in you and look forward to hearing how things go this next week." The therapist added a big "7" and told Billy to aim for that 7 when talking with his mother. Again, with permission, the therapist shared the solution message with Billy's mother.

CHALLENGES IN IMPLEMENTING THE MODEL

The biggest challenge in implementing this model is recognizing the maturity level of the child. Younger children do not have the developmental skills to grasp the concepts inherent in this model. Also, effort is required to develop a therapeutic relationship with the child before proceeding with the steps in the model. Without the necessary level of involvement between the child and therapist, therapeutic assumptions are often incorrect; consequently, solutions are difficult to ascertain and accomplish. It is important that children's goals and miracles be understood by the parents. Sometimes parents see the child's goal as an excuse not to work on what the parent identifies as the problem. The whole emphasis of SFPT is recognizing that previous success is the foundation for solutions in the future.

CONCLUSION

Solution-focused play therapy is a model of play therapy founded on the principles of "solution thought" and "solution talk." The therapist believes that children know what they want and that together they can devise a solution to the issues they bring to therapy. It is a process of talk through play in order to articulate clearly what these goals look like and what the child would be doing when the goal is achieved. The therapist and the child together paint this picture of success with layers of evidence from when some of the goal has already been achieved. Experiential play therapy techniques of art, sand tray, and puppets are the medium for this therapeutic process. The positive reinforcement technique of the "wows" and "hows" is designed to help children take credit for their efforts. SFPT is a clear systematic process with a strong theoretical and practical foundation. Research supports the efficacy of the solution-focused approach. While this method is not appropriate for every child, it is an approach that is worthy of consideration and further study.

REFERENCES

Berg, I. K. (2005). The state of miracles in relationships. *Journal of Family Psychology, 16,* 115–118.

Berg, I. K., & Steiner, T. (2003). *Children's solution work.* New York, NY: Norton.

Bonsi, E. (2006). An empirical investigation of the usefulness of solution talk in solution-focused therapy. *Dissertation Abstracts International Section A: Humanities and Social Sciences, 66,* 3924.

Cocoran, J., & Stephenson, M. (2000). The effectiveness of solution-focused therapy with children with child behavior problems: A preliminary report. *Families in Society, 81,* 468–474.

DeJong, P., & Berg, I. K. (1998). *Interviewing for solutions.* Pacific Grove, CA: Brooks/Cole.

DeJong, P., & Berg, I. K. (2002). *Interviewing for solutions* (2nd ed.). Pacific Grove, CA: Brooks/Cole.

de Shazer, S. (1985). *Keys to solution in brief therapy.* New York, NY: Norton.

de Shazer, S. (1988). *Clues: Investigating solutions in brief therapy.* New York, NY: Norton.

de Shazer, S. (1991). *Putting difference to work.* New York, NY: Norton.

de Shazer, S. (1994). *Words were originally magic.* New York, NY: Norton.

Elliott, C. (2009). Overview of solution-focused therapy. In C. Elliott & L. Metcalf (Eds.), *The art of solution focused therapy* (pp. 1–19). New York, NY: Springer.

Erickson, M., & Rossi, E. (1979). *Hypnotherapy: An exploratory casebook.* New York, NY: Irvington.

Haley, T. (2000). Solution-focused counseling with a sexual abuse survivor. *Guidance and Counseling, 15,* 1–7.

Hogan, D. (2009). My encounter with the solution focused therapy model. In C. Elliott & L. Metcalf (Eds.), *The art of solution focused therapy* (pp. 175–188). New York, NY: Springer.

Kim, J. S. (2008). Examining the effectiveness of solution-focused brief therapy: A meta-analysis. *Research on Social Work Practice, 18,* 107–116.

Leggett, E. S. (2009). A creative application of solution-focused counseling: An integration with children's literature and visual arts. *Journal of Creativity in Mental Health, 4,* 191–200.

McKergow, M. (2009). In between—neither inside nor outside: The radical simplicity of solution-focused brief therapy. *Journal of Systemic Therapies, 28,* 34–49.

Metcalf, L. (2009). Solution focused therapy: Its applications and opportunities. In C. Elliott & L. Metcalf (Eds.), *The art of solution focused therapy* (pp. 21–43). New York, NY: Springer.

Minuchin, S., & Fishman, C. (1981). *Family therapy techniques.* Cambridge, MA: Harvard University Press.

Myers, S. (2009). Review of solution-focused counseling in schools, second edition. *Child and Family Social Work, 14,* 386–387.

Nims, D. R. (2007). Integrating play therapy techniques into solution-focused brief therapy. *International Journal of Play Therapy, 16,* 54–68.

Paylo, M. (2005). Helping families search for solutions: Working with adolescents. *Family Journal, 13,* 456–458.

Perkins, R. (2006). The effectiveness of one session of therapy using a single-session therapy approach for children and adolescents with mental health disorders. *Psychology and Psychotherapy: Theory, Research and Practice, 79,* 215–227.

Selekman, M. D. (2005). *Children in therapy: Using the family as a resource.* New York, NY: Norton.

Shapiro, L. (1994). *Short-term therapy with children: A multi-modal approach to helping children with their problems.* King of Prussia, PA: Center for Applied Psychology.

Sklare, G. (2005). *Brief counseling that works: A solution-focused approach for school counselors and administrations* (2nd ed.). Thousand Oaks, CA: Corwin Press.

Taylor, E. R. (2009). Sandtray and solution-focused therapy. *International Journal of Play Therapy, 18,* 56–68.

Trebing, J. (2000). Short-term solution-oriented play therapy for children of divorced parents. In H. G. Kaduson & C. E. Schaefer (Eds.), *Short-term play therapy for children.* New York: Guilford Press.

Zalter, B. (2005). The state of miracles in relationships. *Journal of Family Psychology, 16,* 115–118.

Appendix A

Solution-Focused Play Therapy Note Taking

Client: _____   Date: _____

Client Goal:

- What brings you here today?
- What could we talk about that would make you happier?
- If things were better, what would you be doing?

Miracle Question:

- If a miracle happened tonight and you woke up tomorrow and your problem was solved, what would be the first sign that the miracle has occurred?
- What would you be doing differently?
- What else would be different after the miracle?

Relationship Question:

- Who would notice the change in you?
- What would they notice?
- How would they respond to you?
- How would you then respond to them?

  (Repeat entire sequence three or four times.)

Exceptions/Pieces of the Miracle:

- When has this miracle already happened, even a little?
- How were you able to make this happen?
- (Remember the "wows" and " hows.")

Scaling: 1 2 3 4 5 6 7 8 9 10

- On a scale of "1" to "10," with "1" being the worst and "10" being the best, where would you rate yourself today?
- How did you get to a "#" day? (Insert the number from the scale here.)
- When you move one number higher, what will you see yourself doing?

Mark the Obstacles:

- Discuss any potential obstacles to aiming toward your goal.

Unfinished Business:

- Is there anything else we need to discuss?

Solution Message:

- Credits (3): To exhibit current success
- Bridge: To connect their goal and your task
- Task: Notice the actions and observations in moving up the scale 10%.

Appendix B

Child-Specific Solution-Focused Play Therapy Goals

(x): scaling now   (0): scaling goal*

Name: _____ Evaluation: Initial: __ 3-mo: __
6-mo: __ 9-mo: __ Other: __ Exit: __

A. Home: If your goal identified in this area were achieved, what would you be doing? Be specific about positive behaviors and actions involving the child and the parent.

   1. (Child): I would be:

   _____
   _____
   _____
   _____

   _____

1   2   3   4   5   6   7   8   9   10
Total absence of goal   Total success of goal

   2. (Parent): I would like the child:

   _____
   _____
   _____
   _____

   _____

1   2   3   4   5   6   7   8   9   10
Total absence of goal   Total success of goal

B. School: If your goal identified in this area were achieved, what would you be doing? Be specific about positive behaviors and actions involving the child and the teacher.

   3. (Child): I would be:

   _____
   _____
   _____
   _____

   _____

1   2   3   4   5   6   7   8   9   10
Total absence of goal   Total success of goal

* On the scale, put an X on the number where you are now. Circle the number where you would like to be.

(Continued)

Appendix B (*Continued*)

4. (Teacher): I would like the child to:

_____

_____

_____

_____

_____

1	2	3	4	5	6	7	8	9	10

Total absence of goal   Total success of goal

Appendix C

How Are You Feeling Today?

1	2	3	4	5	6	7	8	9	10

Chapter 17

COGNITIVE-BEHAVIORAL PLAY THERAPY

Susan M. Knell

Cognitive-behavioral play therapy (CBPT) is an offspring of cognitive therapy (CT) as conceptualized by Aaron Beck (1964, 1976). The cognitive model of emotional disorders involves the interplay among cognition, behavior, and physiology (Beck & Emery, 1985) and contends that behavior is mediated through verbal processes; the way individuals construe the world in large measure determines how they behave and feel and how they understand life situations (Beck, 1967, 1972, 1976). In cognitive theory, emotional experiences are determined by cognitions that have developed in part from earlier life experiences. Over the past 40 years, CT has been applied to an increasingly broad range of populations. Included are psychiatric populations, such as individuals with depression, anxiety, and personality disorders, as well as nonpsychiatric populations such as prison inmates and medical patients (Beck, 1995).

CT as practiced with adults is inappropriate for use with adolescents and children without modification, as a more developmentally appropriate approach is necessary. Over time, adaptations of CT for use with increasingly younger populations have emerged, (e.g., adolescent—Emery, Bedrosian, & Garber, 1983; school-age children—Kendall & Braswell, 1985). However, many believed that CT could not be adapted for preschool and very young school-age children. Clinical lore suggests that therapy with preschoolers must involve some level of play therapy in order to engage the child in what is traditionally a more verbal endeavor. The developmental literature might suggest that preoperational-stage children do not have the cognitive sophistication and flexibility to benefit from CT. CT with adults requires the ability to follow a rational, logical sequence. It assumes that the individual has the capacity to differentiate between rational and irrational/logical and illogical thinking. An adult may need some guidance in identifying and labeling irrational, illogical thoughts. However, once identified, the individual can understand the inconsistencies. Young children, however, may not understand the differences and may not be able to distinguish between irrational, illogical thinking and more rational, logical thought. The application of CT with young children is thus fraught with difficulties, which largely explains why most of the work with youth and CT has focused on adolescents and older school-age children. The preoperational-stage child's egocentrism, concrete thought processes, and seemingly irrational thinking would seem to preclude the kind of cognitive abilities necessary to participate in CT.

CT, with its emphasis on verbal interventions, and play therapy (PT), with its focus on play, appeared to many as incompatible. Nonetheless, by the mid-1980s, Phillips (1985), himself a developmentalist, not a clinician, hypothesized that incorporating cognitive-behavioral techniques into play interventions offered a promising direction in the field of PT. By the late 1980s, others, such as Berg (1982), had begun to incorporate CT and play interventions, although Berg's target population was slightly older, school-age children. Knell & Moore (1990), writing about a 5-year-old boy with encopresis, published the first case report of the integration of cognitive interventions and PT with a preschool-age child.

Adapting CT for preschoolers has received increasing attention over the past 10 years. CBPT, as conceptualized by Knell (Knell, 1993a, 1993b, 1994, 1997, 1998, 1999, 2000, 2003; Knell & Beck, 2000; Knell & Dasari, 2006, 2009; Knell & Moore, 1990; Knell & Ruma, 1996, 2003), was developed for use with children between 2½ and 6 years and incorporates cognitive, behavioral, and traditional play therapies. CBPT is based on the cognitive theory of emotional disorders and cognitive principles of therapy and adapts these in a developmentally appropriate way. CBPT is sensitive to the developmental issues of children and emphasizes the empirical validation of effectiveness of interventions.

Cognitive distortions in very young children may be developmentally appropriate yet maladaptive. For example, a child whose parents separate shortly after he misbehaves may believe that he was the cause of the separation. In most cases, children incorporate life experience into their thinking, and with the help of everyday parent–child discourse are able to integrate this learning into a more adaptive thought ("My parents weren't getting along. Dad didn't move out because of my behavior. He moved out because he and mom fight too much."). Given that maladaptive thoughts may be developmentally appropriate, the concept of cognitive distortions is problematic with young children. For this reason, it is more appropriate to label these thoughts as maladaptive rather than distorted.

Sometimes, children do not attach any set of beliefs or meanings to an event. In these instances, maladaptive cognitions may not be present. However, there may be an absence of adaptive beliefs that would facilitate coping, if present. In these instances, the child might need some assistance in creating functional, adaptive self-statements as a coping device, not to replace the maladaptive ones but to boost more adaptive thinking and behavior. For example, a young child may have difficulty coping with the birth of a sibling. Maladaptive beliefs (e.g., "I'm not the baby anymore"; "No one loves me") may not be present, or they may not be expressed verbally. Helping the child cope with the new sibling by providing adaptive, positive coping statements can facilitate the child's functioning. Statements such as "We have a new baby, but Mom and Dad still love me" can provide the child with a positive outlook on the experience.

Thus, facilitating adaptive cognitive change is not only possible but quite common with young children. Often, as mentioned, inducing such change takes place in the normal, everyday life of parent–child interactions. When situations are brought to a therapist, evidence supports the use of developmentally appropriate adaptations of CT to facilitate such changes. Bierman (1983) wrote about interviewing techniques, including the use of concrete examples and less open-ended questions, as a means of facilitating the young child's understanding of complex problems. Through the use of play, cognitive change can be communicated indirectly (Knell, 1998; Shirk & Russell, 1996). Additionally, the therapist's ability to be flexible, reduce focus on verbalizations, and increase use of experiential approaches can contribute to the successful adaptation of CT with young children.

BASIC CONSTRUCTS, GOALS, AND TECHNIQUES

CBPT is based on behavioral and cognitive theories of emotional development and psychopathology and on the interventions derived from these theories. These theoretical roots are considered with regard to their influence on CBPT.

Behavior Therapy

Behavior therapies (BTs) for youth were developed, in part, to help children and parents translate knowledge gained in therapy to the natural environment. Behavioral approaches to child management are often taught directly to parents or significant others. Such approaches have proven extremely effective with problems such as child noncompliance. However, BT can be implemented directly with a child. A direct approach may be necessary for some problems of preschoolers. This may be particularly true if the child's problem is aversive to the parent (e.g., Knell & Moore, 1990), if the parent–child relationship has inhibited development of the child's self-mastery (Klonoff, Knell, & Janata, 1984; Klonoff & Moore, 1986), or if issues of control are prominent. Whether the therapy is direct or delivered through a significant other, the therapist tries to identify factors that reinforce and maintain problematic behaviors so that they can be altered. Many interventions are based on classical conditioning (e.g., systematic desensitization) and operant conditioning (e.g., contingency management). Interventions from social learning theory also emphasized observational learning and more cognitive aspects of behavior, which provided much of the impetus for the development of cognitive therapy.

Cognitive Therapy

CT was developed as a structured, focused approach to help individuals make changes in their behavior by changing the thinking and perceptions that underlie behavior. Originally developed as a short-term, present-oriented therapy for depressed adults, the treatment was directed toward changing dysfunctional thinking and behavior. Adaptations to younger populations have changed the methods through which CT is delivered but not the theoretical underpinnings of the approach. Finding ways to deliver CT without an emphasis on language that might be too complex for a young child represents one of the challenges faced in the development of CBPT.

Cognitive-Behavioral Play Therapy

Knell (1993a, 1993b, 1994, 1997, 1998) argued that CT could be modified for use with young children if presented in a way that was highly accessible for children. For example, puppets, stuffed animals, books, and other toys could be used to model cognitive strategies. With a coping model approach, the model (e.g., puppet) might verbalize problem-solving skills or solutions to problems that parallel the child's own difficulties.

Principles of CBPT

Some of the principles of CBT (as adapted from work with adults—Beck & Emery, 1985) apply to young children as well. CBPT is based on the cognitive model of emotional disorder and is brief, time limited, structured, directive, problem oriented, and psychoeducational in nature. A sound therapeutic relationship is a necessary condition for effective CBPT. Though a collaborative relationship is important, and a more Socratic/inductive approach fundamental in CBT, its implementation with young children must be modified for use with children.

Setting

CBPT is usually conducted in a playroom or office equipped with appropriate play materials. Ideally, the room is stocked with toys, art supplies, puppets, dolls, and other materials. Although an array of toys is usually sufficient, there are times when a specific toy may be needed to treat a particular child. At times, play materials that are available can be adapted to meet these specific needs. At other times, a specific toy may need to be brought into the playroom, because the child cannot "pretend" or be flexible in the use of already existing toys. An example of this would be a child who was having a difficult time wearing prescription glasses. She might be able to cut out glasses on paper and use these with a doll. Or the child might have difficulty with this flexible use of the paper-cut glasses and might respond better to actual plastic glasses that fit the doll.

Treatment sometimes takes place outside the playroom/office setting. This is particularly true for children with specific anxieties, such as phobias, which are best treated *in vivo*. For these children, treatment may take place in a setting that more closely resembles the feared situation. For example, systematic desensitization of elevator-phobic children can take place in and around an elevator (Knell, 1993a, 2000). Similarly, a child with obsessive-compulsive disorder may be treated in a setting that elicits obsessions and compulsions (March & Mulle, 1998).

Similarities/Differences

CBPT is different from more traditional forms of play therapies, although it incorporates several of the assumptions underlying traditional play therapies. CBPT is similar to other types of play therapy in its reliance on a positive therapeutic relationship, use of play as a means of communication between therapist and child, and the message to the child that therapy is a safe place. Despite these similarities, there are assumptions inherent in CBPT that run counter to the premises on which traditional play therapies are based. Several important areas of difference involve the focus on CBPT on directions and goals, choice of play materials and activities, play as educational, and the importance of making connections between the child's behavior and thoughts. Whereas the therapist in nondirective play therapy is a more neutral observer, the CBP therapist provides direction, establishes goals, and develops interventions that are suited to facilitate these goals. Similarly, the CBP therapist, along with the child, selects play materials and activities and provides a psycho-educational component to the treatment. Finally, the CBPT brings conflicts and problems into verbal expression for the child, using the therapeutic time and relationship to help the child make connections between words and behavior. (See Knell, 1993a, for more details regarding the similarities and differences among various types of play therapies).

Goals

Establishing goals is an important part of CBPT. The CBP therapist works with the child and family to set goals and help the child work toward these goals. The therapist assesses movement toward goals on an ongoing basis. Whereas goals and movement toward goals are counter to the basic philosophy of client-entered play therapy (see Axline, 1947), they are an integral part of CBPT. The CBP therapist's selection of a direction may be based on the child's lead or on knowledge of the child's situation as understood from the parent interview or other source. In CBPT, the therapist may introduce themes and provide direction based on knowledge obtained from a parent or teacher and not necessarily from the child him- or herself. For example, the CBP therapist may purposefully and systematically have a puppet behave in a certain way and verbalize issues that the child reportedly exhibits.

Methods

Most cognitive behavioral interventions with children include some form of modeling. This is particularly true of CBPT, where modeling is a critical component. Modeling is an efficient and effective way to learn, as well as to acquire, strengthen, or weaken behaviors (Bandura, 1977). Modeling designed to enhance skills often involves a coping model. Coping models display less-than-ideal skills and then gradually become more proficient. The efficacy of modeling is improved by the use of coping models (Bandura & Menlove, 1968; Meichenbaum, 1971).

In CBPT, modeling is used to demonstrate adaptive coping skills to the child. The model may behave in a way that demonstrates use of a positive coping skill. This can involve the model talking out loud as well as acting in a way compatible with adaptive behavior. In CBPT, the model is usually a toy (stuffed animal, puppet, or other toy) that demonstrates the behavior that the therapist wants the child to learn. Modeling can also be presented in other forms, such as through books, movies, or television shows.

Less often used in CBPT, but still an important method of intervention, is role-playing, where the child practices skills with the therapist and receives ongoing feedback. Role-playing is usually more effective with school-age children, although it is possible to deliver role-playing through a modeling technique. In this way, models are actually role-playing, and the child is observing and learning from watching the models practice particular skills. For example, a child with separation fears may watch an equally fearful puppet as it "practices" leaving the parent and interacting with others.

Interventions

Empirically supported CBT techniques are incorporated into play and adapted to the child's developmental level. In general, research suggests that it is the combination of cognitive and behavioral interventions that is effective in helping children cope (Compton et al., 2004; Velting, Setzer, & Albano, 2004). There is a wide array of interventions from both the behavioral and cognitive literature. The more common techniques are described in the following sections and summarized, with examples of how these techniques are integrated into play therapy, in Table 17.1 (Behavioral Interventions) and Table 17.2 (Cognitive Interventions).

Table 17.1   Examples of Behavioral Interventions in CBPT

Positive reinforcement	Puppet who is fearful of talking receives stickers for each attempt to talk to another puppet.
Shaping/Positive reinforcement	Puppet who is fearful of talking begins to make utterances, speech sounds, words, and gradually begins to talk (shaping). The puppet receives encouragement and positive feedback (positive reinforcement) from the therapist as it makes closer and closer approaches to speaking.
Systematic desensitization	Puppet who is afraid to ride on an elevator systematically goes through a hierarchy (from situations least to most feared) while simultaneously engaging in relaxation (mutually exclusive with anxiety).
Stimulus fading	Puppet who is clingy and unable to go to bed when its mother says goodnight, is able to appropriately go to sleep when father does the good-night routine. The dad puppet takes care of the goodnights while gradually fading the mom back into the nighttime routine.
Extinction/DRO	Puppet who is acting aggressively toward other puppets does not receive any positive attention (extinction), while more adaptive behaviors, such as playing nicely, keeping hands to oneself, and using words rather than action (DRO) are rewarded.
Time-out	Puppet who is throwing toys in the playroom is put in time-out, away from his puppet friends.
Self-monitoring	Child marks feelings on a scale with frowning and smiley faces.
Activity scheduling	Events and activities are scheduled for a child who tends to withdraw from others.

Table 17.2   Examples of Cognitive Interventions in CBPT

Recording dysfunctional thoughts	Child draws pictures in a notebook or records into a tape recorder, trying to capture thoughts about particular situations.
Cognitive change strategies/ countering irrational beliefs	Puppet thinks that no one likes him because another puppet teased him. The therapist "walks" the puppet through the process of examining this by talking about his friends, exploring other reasons why he was teased, and trying out his friendships with other puppets.
Coping self-statements	Puppet who is afraid to put his head underwater in the swimming pool says, "I can put my head in"; "I will like getting my face wet."
Bibliotherapy	Child whose parents are divorcing is read a book about another child in the same situation.

Behavioral Interventions. A variety of techniques based on the three models of behavior therapy (classical conditioning, operant conditioning, social learning) can be incorporated into play therapy. Techniques from classical (e.g., systematic desensitization) and operant (e.g., contingency management, shaping, differential reinforcement of other behavior [DRO]) conditioning are typically used to help a child incorporate more adaptive behaviors. Techniques from social learning theory (e.g., modeling) are used extensively in CBPT, utilizing observational learning as a tool for learning new behaviors.

Systematic desensitization (SD) is the process of reducing anxiety by replacing a maladaptive response with an adaptive one (Ollendick & King, 1998; Wolpe, 1958, 1982). This is accomplished by breaking the association between a particular stimulus and the anxiety or fear response that it usually elicits. The stimulus is presented, but the anxiety is prevented from occurring. This is usually done by teaching muscle relaxation to elicit a state of calm that is incompatible with anxiety (Jacobson, 1938). With children, SD may be used in a different way. Older children can be taught a modified relaxation technique (e.g., Cautela & Groden, 1978), whereas relaxation in younger children may be induced through calming play activities or visualization of calming scenes (Knell, 2000). Both imaginal and *in vivo* desensitization are used with children, though the latter, where anxiety-provoking stimuli are presented in real life, may be superior (Emmelkamp, 1982; King & Ollendick, 1997; Ultee, Griffioen, & Schellekens, 1982).

Contingency management is a general term that refers to techniques that modify a behavior by controlling its consequences. Forms of contingency management are positive reinforcement, shaping, stimulus fading, extinction, and DRO. These interventions can all be used in the CBPT setting and are described briefly here:

- *Positive reinforcement.* In this important component of much of CBPT, a specific target behavior is identified, reinforcers determined, and the reinforcement is made contingent on the occurrence of the targeted behavior. Social reinforcers (e.g., praise) or material reinforcers (e.g., stickers) can be used. Reinforcement can be direct (e.g., praising a child for specific behaviors) or more subtle (e.g., in a child with separation anxiety, reinforcing a behavior, such as independent play, which ultimately would lead to the desired behavior, separation from parent figure). Reinforcement can be part of the actual CBPT, and the therapist may also instruct parents and significant others in the appropriate use of reinforcers in the natural environment.

- *Shaping*. Shaping is a means of helping a child get closer and closer to a targeted goal. Positive reinforcement is offered for closer and closer approximations or steps toward the desired response. For example, the child who is fearful of sleeping in her own room can be shaped through reinforcement of small steps toward the eventual goal of sleeping in her own room (e.g., sleeping on the floor next to the parents' bed, sleeping on the floor in the hall near her room, sleeping on the floor in her room, sleeping in her own bed).

- *Stimulus fading*. If a child has some of the skills for a behavior but only exhibits them in certain circumstances or with certain people, stimulus fading may be used. The therapist will help the child transfer these skills to different settings or with different people by gradually fading out the situation or person so that the child is currently able to perform the skill. For example, a child who separates from his father to go to school but is clingy and unable to separate from his mother may initially be dropped off at school by Dad, with Mom gradually faded back into the drop-off routine.

- *Extinction and DRO*. Some children exhibit maladaptive behaviors because they have been or are being reinforced for performing them. In order for the maladaptive behaviors to drop out, the reinforcement must be removed. A common reinforcer is parental attention. Often, it is the contributing or causal factor in the child's behavior. If reinforcement is withheld (extinction), behaviors will decrease or disappear. However, extinction does not teach new behaviors, so it is often used in conjunction with reinforcement, where a new, more adaptive behavior is reinforced (DRO), while the maladaptive behavior is extinguished.

When a child needs to be removed from reinforcers that are maintaining maladaptive responses, time-out is often used. Technically, time-out means time out from reinforcement, though it has come to mean removing the child from a desirable environment to a less attractive one. Though used more frequently in the natural environment, time-out can be used in play therapy when a child is not following rules (e.g., violates a "no breaking toys" rule) and needs to be removed from the play therapy situation to a neutral place devoid of toys. During the time-out period, the child would not have access to the reinforcing aspects of the therapy (e.g., the therapist's positive attention, the play therapy materials).

Self-monitoring (SM) refers to an individual's observations and recording of information. This can involve the monitoring of activity or mood and can provide important information. However, SM can be used with young children only if it is offered in a simple form, usually with visual cues (such as smiley faces).

In *activity scheduling*, specific tasks are planned for, then implemented. Although originally designed for work with depressed adults, activity scheduling can be used with young children, usually with some level of parental involvement. Planned activities may reduce time spent in ruminative or passive activities and can be useful for depressed, anxious, or withdrawn children.

Cognitive Interventions.   Behavioral methods in CBPT usually involve an alteration in activity, whereas cognitive methods deal with changes in thinking. Since maladaptive thoughts are hypothesized to lead to maladaptive behavior, changes in thinking should produce changes in behavior. The therapist helps children identify, modify, and/or build cognitions. Through this work, children learn to identify maladaptive thoughts and replace them with more adaptive ones.

Recording dysfunctional thoughts can help adults self-monitor thoughts. Young children can be encouraged to use simple recording devices (e.g., drawing pictures in a notebook or recording in a tape recorder). Often, monitoring is done by the parent rather than the child him-/herself.

With adults, a three-pronged approach is used for *cognitive change strategies* and *countering irrational beliefs* (maladaptive beliefs): look at the evidence, explore the alternatives, and examine the consequences (maladaptive beliefs). Many strategies to counter irrational thoughts are used, including examining the evidence to support the belief, considering multiple scenarios (e.g., "What if?"), and examining alternatives (Beck, Rush, Shaw, & Emery, 1979). The hypothesis testing inherent in these approaches makes them difficult to use with children. Especially with young children, the therapist needs to guide the child in generating alternative explanations, testing them, and changing beliefs (Emery, Bedrosian, & Garber, 1983).

Individuals of all ages can use *coping (positive) self-statements* to facilitate positive coping. Many children have more neutral thoughts—they lack positive self-statements rather than having negative thoughts. For some children who have negative thoughts, replacing these with more neutral statements can be an intermediate step (Kendall & Treadwell, 2007). Individuals of all ages can use positive self-statements to facilitate positive coping. Turning praise from parents and significant adults into self-statements is not automatic. Children often need help in developing positive self-affirming statements (Velting et al., 2004). Young children need to learn how to have clear, self-affirming positive statements that are linguistically and conceptually simple (e.g., "I am strong"; "I can do this"). These statements are in part self-rewarding ("I am doing a good job") and can involve an element of coping strategies ("I can walk past that bully with a smile on my face"). Further, they can help reduce aversive feelings ("I can sleep in my own room when I'm ready") and enhance reality testing ("There really are no ghosts in the attic") (Schroeder & Gordon, 1991).

Though technically not a cognitive intervention, *bibliotherapy* is used increasingly as an adjunct to therapy. It contains strong cognitive interventions, usually through modeling. In most stories used with young children, a model copes with a similar situation, shows reactions, and problem solves the situation. Children often respond to such stories with increased understanding that others have faced the situations they confront and with ideas about how to approach the problem.

In summary, cognitive interventions are utilized with young children to help them modify their thoughts and learn more adaptive coping skills. For cognitive interventions to be useful for young children, they must be relatively simple, concrete, and not verbally complex. Particularly useful with this age group are coping self-statement and bibliotherapy.

THERAPEUTIC POWERS OF PLAY UNDERLYING THE MODEL

Much has been written about the therapeutic powers of play (e.g., Schaefer & Drewes, 2009), and recently there has been increasing interest in the characteristics of play that make it a change agent (e.g., Russ, 2004). Schaefer (1999) identified 25 factors culled from a review of the literature, which he believed contributed to the role of play in change. Most of these appear to play a role in CBPT. Factors such as self-expression and abreaction are important in the nonstructured, spontaneous components of the therapy. Particularly relevant for the more structured components are those factors that are inherent in the psychoeducational component of CBPT: direct/indirect teaching, stress inoculation, creative problem solving, and behavioral rehearsal.

Role of the Therapist

The role of the CBP therapist is to involve the child in treatment through play. The child's issues can be dealt with directly rather than through a parent. The therapist's task is to listen, with both ears and eyes, to hear and see what the child is communicating through his/her play. In addition, the CBPT therapist provides, in a developmentally appropriate way, strategies for developing more adaptive thoughts and behaviors. Such coping skills are modeled through toys and puppets, which necessitates that the therapist be comfortable playing with toys.

Role of the Parents

Inclusion of parents/significant adults in the child's treatment is an important consideration and should be determined on a case-by-case basis. The initial assessment is usually completed with the parent in order to gain the most complete understanding possible about the child and his/her difficulties. After the parents are interviewed, the child is seen for an evaluation, and upon its completion, the therapist will usually meet with the parents to present evaluation findings and work on a specific treatment plan. The treatment plan may primarily involve CBPT with the child, work with the parents, or a combination of CBPT and parent work. Such decisions are usually made based on an assessment of the nature of the problem and the best method by which to intervene. Considerations include whether the parent will need help in modifying interactions with the child and whether the child will need assistance in implementing a treatment program outside of therapy.

Even when the primary work is with the child through CBPT, it is still important to periodically meet with the parents. During these parent sessions, the therapist will obtain information about the child, continue to monitor the parents' interaction with the child, work on areas of concern, and assist the parent in implementing appropriate child management strategies at home. The therapist may provide support for the parents, which may include information related to specific topics (e.g., developmental issues, appropriate expectations at various ages, diagnostic-specific information).

CASE ILLUSTRATIONS

Case 1: Kelly

Kelly was a 4-year-old girl who had been home with her mother and three siblings when their home burned down. An electric fire in the walls was the cause of the fire, which emitted various noises from the walls before the family realized what was happening. Mom and children were able to leave the house without getting hurt, but the house was burnt to the ground before the fire could be put out. The family watched the house burn, and the fire department's attempts to save it, from a neighbor's home. They also spent many hours at the home in the months ahead as it was rebuilt. Kelly refused to speak and would not enter the house as it was being repaired. She also refused to separate from her parents, feared various noises, and wouldn't sleep by herself at night. During play therapy, her play revolved around characters in a home, firemen, and animals that made strange noises that no one could figure out. When characters tried to find the source of the noises, the animals would hide. Additionally, random frightening things would happen in her play (e.g., bathtubs would fall from the sky). She would replay this repeatedly. During the play, the therapist took on the characters who made the connection between the animal noises and the noise before the fire at her home. At the therapist's request, mom brought in pictures of the burnt home as well as the rebuilt home, and they were used in the play sessions to help the child talk through what had happened and how it turned out (e.g., "We have sprinklers in all the rooms now"; "Our new house is safer than our old house"). The characters also received stickers for their efforts to sleep in their own beds (as Kelly's parents were giving her at home), and during the sessions, the therapist, mom, and Kelly would practice the skills of separating from mom and feeling safe by using positive self-statements and other coping techniques.

Case 2: Isabella

Isabella was a 6-year-old girl who had recently moved to a new community with her family. Parents described her as shy and clingy. She had difficulty making friends. Recently, another child had become her friend, but the other girl, Ann, was extremely bossy, often telling Isabella, "If you don't do this, I won't be your friend." CBPT with Isabella began with the therapist organizing a friendship group. The therapist modeled a group of friends who played with each other and talked about being friends and what that entailed. As they interacted, the therapist had one puppet (a bossy donkey) try to dictate what they would all do and who would take the next turn. The therapist had another puppet tell the donkey that it wasn't fair to be that bossy. Various puppets modeled assertive behavior, both verbally and nonverbally. Isabella engaged in the play readily. However, in the early stages of therapy, she would never take on a character who "stood up" to the bossy donkey. The therapist modeled assertive behavior via various puppets, with Isabella watching and listening intently. As therapy progressed, Isabella would request that the therapist (via a puppet) "talk back to the bossy donkey."

CLINICAL APPLICATIONS

CBPT has been used successfully with a wide variety of patient populations, including children with diagnoses such as selective mutism (Knell, 1993a, 1993b), encopresis (Knell, 1993a; Knell & Moore, 1990); separation anxiety (Knell, 1998, 1999), and phobias (Knell, 1993a, 2000). Additionally, CBPT has been used with children who have experienced traumatic life events, such as divorce (Knell, 1993a) and sexual abuse (Knell & Ruma, 1996; Ruma, 1993). Populations that might benefit from CBPT include children with control issues, anxious and depressed children, and children who have experienced a traumatic event, such as maltreatment. Additionally, CBPT might be useful for children who need to learn more adaptive coping skills or those whose direct involvement in treatment is important.

Other children may best be treated indirectly through the parents. In such cases, the parent is taught child management skills that will provide parenting that is better suited for that particular child. Children who are more like to benefit from a parent-implemented approach are those whose parents clearly exhibit deficits in parenting or children presenting with noncompliant behavior or habit disorders, such as sleep difficulties. Also, children from families with significant psychopathology might benefit from CBPT in combination with family therapy or individual therapy for either or both of the parents.

EMPIRICAL SUPPORT

CBPT is a developmentally based, integrated model of psychotherapy. It incorporates empirically supported techniques, such as modeling. Research suggests that learning through modeling is an effective way to acquire, strengthen, or weaken behaviors and thus is an efficient and effective way to acquire behaviors and skills (Bandura, 1977). Other well-documented interventions, such as systematic desensitization, are utilized in CBPT (Wolpe, 1958, 1982).

CT with adults is a well-established, empirically supported treatment with a range of presenting diagnoses. Controlled studies have demonstrated its efficacy in the treatment of major depression (see Dobson, 1989, for a meta-analysis), generalized anxiety disorder (Barlow, Craske, Cerney, & Klosko, 1989; Beck, Sokol, Clark, Berchick, & Wright, 1992; Clark, Salkovskis, Hackmann, Middleton, & Gelder, 1992), and social phobia (Gelernter et al., 1991; Heimberg et al, 1990), to name a few. CBPT adapts empirically supported techniques for use with young children using developmentally appropriate play. The efficacy of such adaptations of CBT have yet to be demonstrated. Empirical validation of CBT with adults does not necessarily mean that such treatment is most effective with children. Recently, the question of efficacy of CBPT has been subjected to empirical study.

A 2007 study by Pearson found that teachers reported significantly higher hope, higher social competence, and fewer anxiety–withdrawal symptoms in a CBP intervention group than a matched control group of preschool children without play. The children in the CBP intervention group were seen individually for three sessions incorporating CB interventions, though this was not technically CBPT. However, this study represents the first to empirically support CBPT interventions. More such studies are needed in order to establish the efficacy of CBPT.

CHALLENGES IN IMPLEMENTING THE MODEL

There are a number of challenges facing the CBP therapist. Balancing the structured versus unstructured aspects of CBPT is likely the most difficult of these challenges. The process of change takes place in both the structured and unstructured components of the session (Knell, 1993a, 1999), and the balance between the two is considered critical. (See Knell, 2009; Knell & Dasari, 2009, for a discussion of structured versus unstructured play in CBPT.) Given the importance of both, the CBP therapist is faced with the challenge of balancing the session, attempting to obtain the spontaneous material that comes from the unstructured play, as well as the more goal-directed modeling of more adaptive skills that are inherent in the structured play.

CONCLUSION

CBPT is appropriate for preschool and early school-age children. It emphasizes the child's involvement in therapy and addresses issues of control, mastery, and responsibility for changing one's own behavior. The child is helped to become an active participant in change (Knell, 1993a). The therapist facilitates the child's involvement in therapy by presenting developmentally appropriate interventions. Many behavioral and cognitive interventions can be incorporated into CBPT.

CBPT provides structured, goal-directed activities while allowing the child to bring spontaneous material to the session. The balance of spontaneously generated and more structured activities is a delicate one, though both are critical to the success of CBPT. Without the spontaneous material, a rich source of clinical information would be lost. Similarly, if the structure and direction of CBPT were not present, it would be impossible to help the child develop more adaptive coping skills.

REFERENCES

Axline, V. (1947) *Play therapy.* New York, NY: Houghton Mifflin.

Bandura, A. (1977). *Social learning theory.* Englewood Cliffs, NJ: Prentice Hall.

Bandura, A., & Menlove, F. L. (1968). Factors determining vicarious extinction of avoidance behavior through symbolic modeling. *Journal of Personality and Social Psychology, 8,* 99–108.

Barlow, D., Craske, M., Cerney, J. A., & Klosko, J. S. (1989). Behavioral treatment of panic disorder. *Behavior Therapy, 20,* 261–268.

Beck, A. T. (1964). Thinking and depression. Part 2: Theory and therapy. *Archives of General Psychiatry, 10,* 561–571.

Beck, A. T. (1967). *Depression: Clinical, experimental, and theoretical aspects.* New York, NY: Harper & Row.

Beck, A. T. (1972). *Depression: Causes and treatment.* Philadelphia, PA: University of Pennsylvania Press.

Beck, A. T. (1976). *Cognitive therapy and the emotional disorders.* New York, NY: International Universities Press.

Beck, A. T., & Emery, G. (1985). *Anxiety disorders and phobias: A cognitive perspective.* New York, NY: Basic Books.

Beck, A. T., Rush, A. J., Shaw, B. F., & Emery, G. (1979). *Cognitive therapy of depression.* New York, NY: Guilford Press.

Beck, A. T., Sokol, L., Clark, D. A., Berchick., R. J., & Wright, F. D. (1992). A crossover study of focused cognitive therapy for panic disorder. *American Journal of Psychiatry, 149,* 778–783.

Beck, J. (1995). *Cognitive therapy: Basics and beyond.* New York, NY: Guilford Press.

Berg, B. (1982). *The changing family game: A problem-solving program for children of divorce.* Dayton, OH: Cognitive-Behavioral Resources.

Bierman, K. L. (1983). Cognitive development and clinical interviews with children. In B. B. Lahey & A. Kazdin (Eds.), *Advances in clinical child psychology* (Vol. 6, pp. 217–250). New York, NY: Plenum Press.

Cautela, J. R., & Groden, J. (1978). *Relaxation: A comprehensive manual for adults, children, and children with special needs.* Champaign, IL: Research Press.

Clark, D. M, Salkovskis, P. M., Hackmann, A., Middleton, H., & Gelder, M. (1992). A comparison of cognitive therapy, applied relaxation, and imipramine in the treatment of panic disorder. *British Journal of Psychiatry, 164,* 759–769.

Compton, S. N., March, J. S., Brent, D., Albano, A. M., Weersing, V. R., & Curry, J. (2004). Cognitive-behavioral psychotherapy for anxiety and depressive disorders in children and adolescents: An evidence-based medicine review. *Journal of the American Academy of Child and Adolescent Psychiatry, 43,* 930–959.

Dobson, K. S. (1989). A meta-analysis of the efficacy of cognitive therapy for depression. *Journal of Consulting and Clinical Psychology, 57,* 414–419.

Emery, G., Bedrosian, R., & Garber, J. (1983). Cognitive therapy with depressed children and adolescents. In D. P. Cantwell & G. A. Carlson (Eds.), *Affective disorders in childhood and adolescence—an update* (pp. 445–471). New York, NY: Spectrum.

Emmelkamp, P. M. G. (1982). Anxiety and fear. In A. S. Bellack, M. Herzen, & A. E. Kazdin (Eds.), *International handbook of behavior modification and therapy* (pp. 349–395). New York, NY: Plenum Press.

Gelernter, C. S., Uhde, T. W., Cimbolic, P., Arnkoff, D. B., Vittone, B. J., Tancer, M. E., & Bartko, J. J. (1991). Cognitive-behavioral and pharmacological treatment of social phobia: A controlled study. *Archives of General Psychiatry, 48,* 938–945.

Heimberg, R. G., Dodge, C. S., Hope, D. A., Kennedy, C. R., Zollo, L. J., & Becker, R. E. (1990). Cognitive behavioral group treatment for social phobia: Comparison with a credible placebo control. *Cognitive Therapy and Research, 14,* 1–23.

Jacobson, E. (1938). *Progressive relaxation.* Chicago, IL: University of Chicago Press.

Kendall, P. C., & Braswell, L. (1985). *Cognitive-behavioral therapy for impulsive children.* New York, NY: Guilford Press.

Kendall, P. C., & Treadwell, K. R. H. (2007). The role of self-statements as a mediator in treatment for youth with anxiety disorders. *Journal of Consulting and Clinical Psychology, 75*(3), 380–389.

King, N. J., & Ollendick, T. H. (1997). Annotation: Treatment of childhood phobias. *Journal of Child Psychology and Psychiatry and Allied Disciplines, 38,* 389–400.

Klonoff, E. A., Knell, S. M., & Janata, J. W. (1984). Fear of nausea and vomiting: The interaction among psychosocial stressors, developmental transitions, and adventitious reinforcement. *Journal of Clinical Child Psychology, 13,* 263–267.

Klonoff, E. A., & Moore, D. J. (1986). "Conversion reactions" in adolescents: A biofeedback-based operant approach. *Journal of Behavior Therapy and Experimental Psychiatry, 19,* 305–310.

Knell, S. M. (1993a). *Cognitive-behavioral play therapy.* Northvale, NJ: Aronson.

Knell, S. M. (1993b). To show and not tell: Cognitive-behavioral play therapy in the treatment of elective mutism. In T. Kottman & C. Schaefer (Eds.), *Play therapy in action: A casebook for practitioners* (pp. 169–208). Northvale, NJ: Aronson.

Knell, S. M. (1994). Cognitive-behavioral play therapy. In K. O'Connor & C. Schaefer (Eds.), *Handbook of play therapy: Vol. 2. Advances and innovations* (pp. 111–142). New York, NY: Wiley.

Knell, S. M. (1997). Cognitive-behavioral play therapy. In K. O'Connor & L. Mages (Eds.), *Play therapy theory and practice: A comparative presentation* (pp. 79–99). New York, NY: Wiley.

Knell, S. M. (1998). Cognitive-behavioral play therapy. *Journal of Clinical Child Psychology, 27,* 28–33.

Knell, S. M. (1999). Cognitive-behavioral play therapy. In S. W. Russ & T. Ollendick (Eds.), *Handbook of psychotherapies with children and families* (pp. 385–404). New York, NY: Plenum Press.

Knell, S. M. (2000). Cognitive-behavioral play therapy with children with fears and phobias. In H. G. Kaduson & C. E. Schaefer (Eds.), *Short term therapies with children* (pp. 3–27). New York, NY: Guilford Press.

Knell, S. M. (2003). Cognitive-behavioral play therapy. In C. E. Schaefer (Ed.), *Foundations of play therapy* (pp. 175–191). Hoboken, NJ: Wiley.

Knell, S. M. (2009). Cognitive-behavioral play therapy: Theory and applications. In A. A. Drewes (Ed.), *Blending play therapy with cognitive behavioral therapy: Evidence-based and other effective treatments and techniques* (pp. 117–133). Hoboken, NJ: Wiley.

Knell, S. M., & Beck, K.W. (2000). Puppet sentence completion task. In C. E. Schaefer, K. Gitlin-Weiner, & A. Sandgrund (Eds.), *Play diagnosis and assessment* (Vol. 2, pp. 704–721). New York, NY: Wiley.

Knell, S. M., & Dasari, M. (2006). Cognitive-behavioral play therapy for children with anxiety and phobias. In H. G. Kaduson & C. E. Schaefer (Eds.), *Short-term therapies with children* (2nd ed., pp. 22–50). New York, NY: Guilford Press.

Knell, S. M., & Dasari, M. (2009). CBPT: Implementing and integrating CBPT into clinical practice. In A. A. Drewes (Ed.), *Blending play therapy with cognitive behavioral therapy: Evidence-based and other effective treatments and techniques* (pp. 321–352). Hoboken, NJ: Wiley.

Knell, S. M., & Moore, D. J. (1990). Cognitive-behavioral play therapy in the treatment of encopresis. *Journal of Clinical Child Psychology, 19,* 55–60.

Knell, S. M., & Ruma, C. D. (1996). Play therapy with a sexually abused child. In M. Reinecke, F. M. Dattilio, & A. Freeman (Eds.), *Casebook on cognitive-behavior therapy with children and adolescents* (pp. 367–393). New York, NY: Guilford Press.

March, J. S., & Mulle, K. (1998). *OCD in children and adolescents: A cognitive-behavioral treatment manual.* New York, NY: Guilford Press.

Meichenbaum, D. (1971). Examination of model characteristics in reducing avoidance behavior. *Journal of Personality and Social Psychology, 17,* 298–307.

Ollendick, T. H., & King, N. J. (1998). Empirically supported treatments for children with phobic and anxiety disorders. *Journal of Clinical Child Psychology, 27,* 156–167.

Pearson, B. (2007). *Effects of a cognitive behavioral play intervention on children's hope and school adjustment.* Unpublished doctoral dissertation, Case Western Reserve University.

Phillips, R. D. (1985). Whistling in the dark? A review of play therapy research. *Psychotherapy, 22,* 752–760.

Ruma, C. (1993). Cognitive-behavioral play therapy with sexually abused children. In S. M. Knell (Ed.), *Cognitive-behavioral play therapy* (pp. 199–230). Hillsdale, NJ: Jason Aronson.

Russ, S. W. (2004). *Play in child development and psychotherapy. Toward empirically supported practice.* Mahwah, NJ: Erlbaum.

Schaefer, C. E. (1999). Curative factors in play therapy. *Journal for the Professional Counselor, 14*(1), 7–16.

Schaefer, C. E., & Drewes, A. A. (2009). The therapeutic powers of play and play therapy. In A. A. Drewes (Ed.), *Blending play therapy with cognitive behavioral therapy: Evidence-based and other effective treatments and techniques* (pp. 3–15). Hoboken, NJ: Wiley.

Schroeder, C. S., & Gordon, B. N. (1991). *Assessment and treatment of childhood problems.* New York, NY: Guilford Press.

Shirk, S. R., & Russell, R. L. (1996). *Change processes in child psychotherapy: Revitalizing treatment and research.* New York, NY: Guilford Press.

Ultee, C. A., Griffioen, D., & Schellekens, J. (1982). The reduction of anxiety in children: A comparison of the effects of systematic desensitisation in vitro and systematic desensitisation in vivo. *Behaviour Research and Therapy, 20,* 61–67.

Velting, O., Setzer, J., & Albano, A. M. (2004). Update on and advances in assessment and cognitive-behavioral treatment of anxiety disorders in children and adolescents. *Professional Psychology Research and Practice, 35,* 42–54.

Wolpe, J. (1958). *Psychotherapy by reciprocal inhibition.* Stanford, CA: Stanford University Press.

Wolpe, J. (1982). *The practice of behavior therapy* (3rd ed.). New York, NY: Pergamon Press.

Chapter 18

NARRATIVE PLAY THERAPY

Aideen Taylor de Faoite

INTRODUCTION

As children, we are often told bedtime stories. In our family, there was a chant that signaled bedtime and preceded story time. These stories were "told" stories. They were made up at the time and included themes of the day. As we participated in Brownies (the junior Guides), the Brownies were often included as the heroes of the day. The stories incorporated all the elements of story, the hero(es), the obstacle to be conquered or the problem to be solved, and the eventual successful outcome once the hero(es) faced or conquered their greatest fears. These stories were requested and retold repeatedly. The main ingredients remained constant, with seasonal variations. Similar themes often appeared in our play, whether it was befriending the dragon or reenacting the Three Billy Goats Gruff.

As an early childhood educator and a trainee play therapist, I was drawn back into the world of story, narrative, and children's play. As a term project in the early education environment, the children were introduced to and became fascinated with traditional fairy tales. They requested that these stories be retold. Different versions were presented, and each child developed an interest in a version of the tale. Different fairy tales evoked different responses. A group of children became fascinated by Little Red Riding Hood. They developed a Little Red Riding Hood game, which was primarily a chasing game. The wolf ran after Little Red Riding Hood, and the woodcutter ran after the wolf. Some children became frightened by the chase but wanted to remain in the game. A safe place or "den" was identified, and its whereabouts kept secret from the wolf. This allowed the children who were at risk of being overcome by their fears to temporarily opt out of the game and thus regulate their emotional responses. It was interesting to reflect that the core group of children involved in developing this game were children who were due to transfer to the primary school system (rising 5-year-olds) at the end of term. It was also noted that the children who were most frightened by the game were younger children.

At this time, I was also struck by two children's fascination with the Three Little Pigs. They made regular requests for this story to be reread and they always chose the version of the story where the three pigs survive, each moving on to the next pig's house until the three pigs end up in the house of brick and escape the big bad wolf. Both children were enthralled by the story. The children struggled with the mother pig's role, and their questions suggested their struggle with understanding her motives in sending the little pigs off to find a home of their own. At the time, both children were involved with social services and were spending time away from home in respite care or in the care of neighbors.

Children can also create stories to support their understanding of stressful situations or transitions in life. Mai was 30 months old when she first visited the emergency room. Mai was a curious and inquisitive little girl. When the physician came to take blood, her parents were requested to distract her so that she wouldn't notice the needle. Mai's curiosity was explained to the physician, and he was requested to explain to Mai what he would be doing "as if" it were a scientific experiment. Cream was applied to numb the site, and the physician explained that it might "sting a bit." Mai then constructed the following story:

The bee is coming.

He is going to sting.

Then he is going to collect the honey.

"Look, Mom, there goes the honey up the tube."

The bee got a little bit of honey.

Four attempts were made to draw enough blood for testing. Each time the physician arrived, Mai began the narrative of the bee coming to collect the honey and wondered if he would have enough honey this time.

This chapter presents an outline of the development of narrative and play in children, the interplay between play and narrative, and the role both play and narrative have in the child's development. The theoretical contribution of concepts from social constructionism and narrative therapy to the development of narrative play therapy will be considered. A model of narrative play therapy is then identified to include the therapeutic role of play and narrative, the role of the therapist, and the support offered to parents/caretakers in facilitating change. A number of composite case studies are presented to illustrate the practice of narrative play therapy.

BASIC CONCEPTS, GOALS, AND TECHNIQUES

The Development of Play and Narrative in Children

The sequence of play development can be constructed in a number of ways. The developmental model of play identified within Narrative Play Therapy is the EPR model (Embodiment, Projection, and Role Play). This has been proposed by Sue Jennings (1999) and Ann Cattanach (1994) and is presented as a useful construct in thinking about play and play development in play therapy.

Embodiment play is identified as exploration through the senses (Cattanach, 1994). Developmentally, in the first year of life, the young infant begins to explore the world through the senses, particularly through taste, then touch and sight. The child finds his or her find their own feet and hands, and the play with these parts of the physical self becomes a source of pleasure for many hours. Embodiment play reinforces the development of the body self and is a stimulus for sensory awareness and discrimination (Jennings, 1993). The social games of peek-a-boo and hide-and-seek emerge and offer the infant opportunities to explore "there" and "not there" in the context of a safe and predictable structured interaction. The older child explores embodiment play as he or she plays with clay, sand, Play-Doh, and other sensory materials. This embodiment play can include the use of the body in dramatic and role-play, for example, as a log rolling down the hill or an airplane buzzing around in the playground.

Projective play emerges at the beginning of the second year. As the toddler begins to play with toys, materials, and objects, she begins to project experiences, feelings, thoughts, and wishes onto the toys, objects, or materials (Cattanach, 1994; Jennings, 1999). For example, the 18-month-old might hug the doll or give it a drink (Stagnitti, 1998). In this projective play, the child can explore different worlds, what it is like for the sand to be wet, for the doll to be invited to the bear's tea party, for the tree that she painted to take on a life of its own. Projective play provides the child with a means to "make sense" of images, thoughts, and feelings in nonverbal media such as finger paints, clay, and sand play (Jennings, 1993). Projective play also enhances the imagination and encourages the development of symbols, symbolic language, and metaphor (Jennings, 1999).

Role-play or dramatic play provides the child with opportunities to try out roles, whether real (the mother) or imagined (the witch), and practice appropriate behaviors necessary for his or her social universe. Behaviors include the social skills required to negotiate roles, the sharing and turn taking necessary for each role within the enactment to develop, and the negotiation and organization of the enactment. Character work enables the child to encounter a whole range of experience, real and imagined, positive and negative (Cattanach, 1994; Jennings, 1993, 1999).

The development of pretend play can be traced across this model of play. Stagnitti and Jellie (2006) define pretend play as having four observable behaviors. These behaviors include

1. The use of symbolic thinking in play (e.g., the block becomes the cell phone)
2. The attribution of properties to an object (e.g., the brown Play-Doh is a delicious chocolate cake)
3. The reference to absent objects in play (e.g., pretend that there is a river here)
4. Ordering play actions, logically and sequentially to form a story

Projective play, role-play, and dramatic play contain the significant elements of pretend play. Children's dramatic play provides opportunities to order and sequence action to enact a story. Social role-play allows for the negotiation of attributions of properties to objects, and motives and actions to characters. Meaning, motive, actions, and properties can be projected onto objects and toys, and in this projection absent objects can be referred to. Embodiment play supports the exploration of roles and the development of sensory language such as feeling, sensations, and actions.

The development of pretend play can be seen over the first 6 years of the child's life (Stagnitti, 2009). At 24 months, children can reenact life events in a logical, sequential manner. By 3 years old, children begin to introduce fictional characters and begin to preplan play by thinking about their ideas for action and then finding materials to carry out their ideas. The 4-year-old can engage in role-play by himself or with others. This includes preplanned play ideas and what objects will be needed in the play and negotiating with others how the dramatic events will unfold. Five-year-olds can create imagined worlds using both fictional and nonfictional characters and events and can use symbolic language to mediate ideas and negotiate a shared meaning in their play. Six- and 7-year-olds can infer character motives from the story and within the story enacted. A detailed account of the developmental sequences of pretend play is presented by Karen Stagnitti in her book, *Learn to Play* (Stagnitti, 1998).

Narrative skills are acquired in play and are supported by the parents and other adults who interpret children's play behavior and either respond "as if" or construct a story around their action. Take the 12-month-old who first lifts an object to her ear and says "hiya." The adult may support the play by holding her hand to her ear and replying, "Hi, how are you?" by commenting "Oh, you're on the phone" or questioning, "Who are you calling?" thus responding "as if" the toddler had just phoned her. Alternatively, the adult may respond by generating a story: "You're calling Grandma, you are just checking if she is coming to see us tonight." Trevarthen (1995) has noted that the acquisition of narrative skills is facilitated by the mother–infant interaction when using music and traditional rhymes. These help to build a capacity to use the basic structure of storytelling. The infant learns introductions, buildup, climax, and resolution. Simple rhymes such as "round and round the garden" offer an example of this structure with a buildup to the climax of "one step, two step, and a tickly under there." Bruner and Lucariello (1989), in their research on narratives in the crib, identified the emergence of story between 22 months and 36 months. The taped monologues revealed clearly identifiable stories, stories that became more structured and more complex over time, and that narratives were used to re-create the child's world or to solve problems.

As children's play skills and pretend play develop, so too do their narrative skills. Nicolopoulou (2006) has proposed that play and storytelling are "complementary expressions of children's symbolic imagination, that draws from and reflect back on the interrelated domains of emotional, intellectual and social life" (p. 249). Engel (2005) has identified three broad levels of narrative language, suggesting that these develop first in play and later in narrative. The three broad levels are as follows:

1. *Play episodes that hang on a narrative framework.* This emerges sometime during the second year. An example of this is when the young child plays in the home corner. The use of the narrative framework of moms and dads and babies can be observed. If there is an adult present, the young child will use the narrative of making a refreshment (tea) for the guest (the adult).
2. *Play episodes where the child narrates her play, and language guides and permeates the play.* This emerges at the end of the second year and

progresses into the third year. Children can be observed negotiating roles, characters, and sequences of action. "You be the mom and pretend that I hurt my leg and I come home and you put the bandage on." The child uses language to guide the play but then needs to act on this before being able to progress the narrative.

3. *The child presents purely verbal narratives or stories.* This emerges at 4 years of age. The child can tell a story of real or imaged events that has an order and a sequence of action.

Nicolopoulou (2006) proposed that play and narrative initially develop independently and that over time the interplay between play and narrative develops through the themes that emerge, allowing for continuity and a cross-fertilization of ideas. In early pretend play, the focus of the child's attention is on increasing the richness and depth of the character representation while in storytelling and narrative, increasing complexity, coherence, and sophistication of plot construction is observed (Nicolopoulou, 2006).

Play provides the opportunities for understanding and coordinating multiple mental perspectives (Kavanaugh & Engel, 1998), and for the construction of relatively consistent perspectives for the characters while coordinating different characters within the play. Play promotes the ability to understand characters' actions in terms of mental states such as motives, desires, and beliefs. The child begins to see the world from the characters' point of view. In John's pretend play, his character used the pretense of "running out of credit" to end an undesired telephone conversation, thus demonstrating his awareness of how the other character might feel about being cut off and yet portraying his own character's lack of interest in continuing the conversation.

The focus of storytelling and narrative is on plot development. This includes the construction, elaboration, and extension of coherent plots. In this focus on plot, the child begins by creating lists of characters, describing explicitly the characters' actions, and then beginning to construct a sequence of actions and events. These become more complex and sophisticated. However, the representation of the character remains generic (e.g., the mom, with little description of motivation or psychological depth) (Nicolopoulou, 2006).

The interplay between narrative, play, and themes in play begins to enter the child's storytelling and vice versa. Each then begins to influence and change the other, thus allowing for flexible coordination and cross-fertilization of themes (Nicolopoulou, 2005). The richness of the interplay between play and narrative would suggest that, combined, they are greater than each element individually in facilitating the development of complex plots with character representations who had a depth to their being. This allows the child to describe and delineate a range of alternative worlds through narrative play, expanding exponentially the child's ability to create and explore alternative domains (Engel, 2005).

In a clinical setting, 3-year-old Sam began by taking the cars and placing them in different places on the mat. The action of placing the cars appeared very intentional, and different cars were placed beside each other. The therapist began to support the development of a narrative around the actions of the cars.

Therapist: The red car is parking beside the blue car.
Sam: "Yes, that's my aunt's car beside Jim's car."
Therapist: "Are they parked outside your aunt's house?"
Sam: "Yes, they are going to drive to the beach, and this is Nanny and Granddad's car (pointing to a jeep), and they are going to the beach, too."

A long narrative about the different pairings of cars, which had taken on the characteristics and actions of their owners' experiences at the beach, ensued, as Sam played with the cars in the sand tray.

This pretend play, as a precursor to narrative story, acted as the starting point for the movement between "what is" and "what if." Engel (2005) described "what is" as that which "mirrors everyday lived consensual reality," while "what if" explores alternatives to such reality (p. 515). The play narrative previously described supported Sam in exploring different "spheres of reality," such as the "what is" reality of going to the beach with the family, and "what if" spheres of reality, such as the imagined unpredictable event of getting stuck in the quicksand and the implausible event of the other cars being able to shunt the "stuck car" out of the quicksand. In play, the development of the characters, actions, setting, and problem allowed Sam to consider alternative versions of reality. The addition of language allowed for new levels of complexity and power to create and explore different "spheres of experience" (Engel, 2005).

Narrative Therapy, Social Constructionism, and the "Not Knowing" Stance

Social constructionists assume that knowledge is socially constructed and that there are many and diverse ways of understanding ourselves and others. They assume that all knowledge, including "scientific knowledge," is "perspectival" (Smith, 1997). Gergen (1991) suggests in perspectival knowing, people make interpretations and conclusions based on "a particular community of interpretation" (p. 104). Within therapy, attention is focused on the social world of the person, with an emphasis on intersubjectivity and therapeutic curiosity. The narratively oriented therapist assumes that people's actions are guided by culturally diverse meanings and stories that they continuously construct about themselves (Smith, 1997).

From the constructionist perspective, the view of "self" differs from that of other orientations. The "self" is not perceived as an entity but as a social construction. The "person" is identified as an active agent engaged in intentional activity, a relational being who is constituted by his or her mutual relations with one another (Macmurray, 1961). The person is situated within a culture and a social setting and in relation to other persons. Stories are the means by which we can express ourselves and our relationship. Spence (1982, as cited in McLeod, 1997) proposed that part of my sense of self depends on my being able to go backwards and forwards in time and weave a story about who I am, how I got that way and where I am going, a story that is continuously nourishing and self-sustaining. Take that away from me and I am significantly less. (p. 458)

The "problem" is identified as a problem and is differentiated from the person so that the person is not seen as the problem. It is seen as socially constructed and defined (McLeod, 1997). The client comes to therapy with a problem-saturated story. This story has often become stuck, resulting in the client's being blind to alternative stories.

Stories take a central role in constructionist narrative therapies. The goal of therapy is "not to replace a story with another" but to "enable the client to participate in the continuous process of creating and transforming meaning" (Gergen, 1996, p. 215). The therapist aims to develop "local" knowledge of the client, his social and cultural history, and the stock of stories the client brings with him. McLeod (1997) proposes that "it is through stories that we best express our sense of ourselves as active, relational beings" (p. 92). The person is the author of the story, and therapy is an opportunity to reauthor stories. This happens in the safe space that is opened up between the therapist and the person, as the therapist listens to the story and the person tells his story to the therapist as a listener. It is in this space that the relationship developed that allows for the coconstruction of new or alternative selves. McLeod identifies four elements of narrative therapy:

1. *The ambiguity of stories.* The therapist does not know where the story will lead or what alternative stories will emerge.
2. *The coconstruction of the therapy narrative.* Through skillful listening and questioning on the part of the therapist, therapy narratives are coconstructed.
3. *The story is a purposeful act.* The structure of a story with a beginning, middle, and end supports the engagement in the purposeful act of reauthoring stories.
4. *The existence of a cultural stock of stories is acknowledged, and exploring these is seen as part of the therapy process.*

The not-knowing stance is also identified as a significant change from traditional therapeutic stances. It is a move away from the interpretation of the person's story within a theoretical framework. Not-knowing aims to communicate to the person an abundant genuine curiosity about what the person has to say and to listen in a way that supports the unfolding of his or her story. It aims to elicit the person's interpretation of his story, giving primary importance to the person's worldview, meaning, and understanding. The therapist relies on the person's own continuing analysis of his or her experiences as these occur and in the context in which the experiences occur. The therapist's task is to attempt to understand from the changing perspective of the person. Open conversational spaces are created for the person, thus increasing the likelihood of narrative development that includes new agency and personal freedom (Anderson & Goolishian, 1992).

THERAPEUTIC POWERS OF PLAY UNDERLYING THE MODEL

> In play a child always behaves beyond his average age, above his daily behavior: in play it is as though he were a head taller than himself. As in the focus of a magnifying glass, play contains all the developmental tendencies in a condensed form and is itself a major source of development. (Vygotsky, 1978, p. 102)

Play offers the child a symbolic system by which to communicate his or her ideas, thoughts, beliefs, and actions. Play allows the child to explore a variety of real and imagined worlds within the safety of knowing that it is "just pretend." It offers the child a greater range of possibilities, and thus the child is not limited by the reality of the objects or what can be seen. Play allows for the exploration of different perspectives and opportunities to problem solve. It offers a context for relationships and social and emotional understanding to develop. The creative nature of play allows for the development and exploration of characters and worlds that may be beyond the child's lived world. Play is also motivating for children. Children are naturally curious when presented with a fear-free environment. They are motivated to explore, discover, and create. Pretend play supports the emergence of narrative, and narrative and storytelling in turn support the development of more complex, comprehensive, and pretend play.

It is the developmental, creative, exploratory, and symbolic potential of play that is utilized as a therapeutic tool in play therapy.

A developmental range of material is made available for the child. Materials and toys are chosen to address the EPR developmental model of play (Cattanach, 1997). A range of sensory materials can include slime, Play-Doh, finger paints, clay, "gloop" (cornstarch and water), sand and water, materials of different textures, shells, stones, shiny gemstones and marbles, sensory balls, stress balls, a soft blanket, and bean bags. The range is limited only by the amount of space available. Children are often drawn to explore these materials at the beginning of therapy and later to include these materials in imaginative play. Children may also return to embodiment play at times of stress and to self-soothe.

When working in a hospital play area, I was curious about a group of children's extended interest in playing with gloop. The children spent time moving it around, lifting and dropping it, and squeezing it through their fingers. This gloop was requested on several consecutive days. In conversation with parents, it was reported that this group of children was undergoing medical tests for ongoing problems with encopresis.

Other children are drawn to the pieces of material such as Lycra and blankets, which they then use for making nests, cocoons, and swings. Julie was a 4-year-old who was having some difficulties attaching to her adoptive mother, following an international adoption at 20 months. Julie played with the sand for a number of weeks, moving it around, piling it up, making it wet, and flattening it out. One day she noticed the blankets and questioned if the therapist slept in the playroom. When it was explained that the blanket was there for the children who came to therapy,

Julie became curious, asking what others did with the blanket. Suggestions of how children can play with the blanket were given. Julie requested that she try the swing idea. Her mother was invited into the play to help the therapist swing the blanket. Songs and rhymes were sung to Julie. This then became a game between Julie and her mother and created the beginning threads of a successful attachment.

A range of small-world characters; dolls; real animals and people; imaginary animal-like creatures and characters from children's programs; furniture; vehicles; and architectural structures such as gates, fences, miniature towers, castles, houses, trees, and stones are made available to the child to support projective play and the creation of the predictable and unpredictable, plausible and implausible worlds from his or her imagination. Some children choose embodiment material such as the slime or Play-Doh to create spaces for the story to unfold. Others use the sandbox as the container for their world, some use the mat, and some create several worlds in different spaces around the room. Bridget was 2½ years old when she came to therapy following the death of her father in a road traffic accident. Bridget spent time creating different rooms in the house, using the dollhouse furniture and the tiled mats of the room as the boundaries for each room. She created, ordered, and organized rooms that were plausible and predictable. The sand tray became outside with roads and traffic lights, houses, cars, dogs, and cats. This changed from week to week, but the organized house with a place for everything and everything in its place remained the same throughout the therapy.

Role-play and dramatic play are supported by the presence of some props such as phones, microphones, hats, glasses, shoes, and the different lengths of materials. Some equipment such as syringes, breathing masks, foam swords, home corner equipment and hand and finger puppets are also made available. In role-play, the child takes on the role of actor–director, while the therapist acts as an actor, looking for direction from the child. Children will often use the furniture in the room to create the space for the event to happen. Jennifer was 8 years old when she first came to therapy. She and her sibling had been adopted when she was 3 following neglect. She was being looked after by her sibling, who was only a year older. Jennifer set up many role-play scenes. These included the "cross mother" and the "lazy sister." A large armchair in the room became like a throne for the cross mother to sit in and shout orders from. The lazy sister was not, in fact, lazy; she just couldn't keep up with the demands made of her. A silver tea set was added as a prop by Jennifer. The role of cross mother changed to the "queen," who had every right to be ordering her servants around and expecting them to work doubly quickly.

The toys and materials provided within this developmental framework support exploration and creative and symbolic expression. They allow for the exploration of real and imagined worlds. Narratives and stories are generated with complex plots and action and characters that portray thoughts motives and beliefs. The facilitation of a fear-free environment allows for the developmental potential of play and narrative to emerge in relationship with the therapist. By participating and coconstructing the pretend play with the child, the therapist enters the child's world and the child feels safe. In this therapeutic space and through the relationship with the therapist, the child can begin to test out and define his or her possible selves (Cattanach, 1999). The therapeutic power of the play and narrative is to act as a container for the child to explore a range of stories and narratives, thus expanding the range the child has access to in his or her lived world outside the play therapy room.

ROLE OF THE THERAPIST

The role of the therapist is to create a safe and fear-free open space in which the child can play and create stories in relationship with another person. The play and narratives allow the child to explore a range of stories, to explain the range of stories available to him or her, and to try out possible stories and possible selves. The story doesn't have to be true, but it needs to be believable, and the role of the therapist is to nurture the storyteller so that the story line can flow (Cattanach, 1997). This is achieved through the not-knowing but curious stance adopted by the therapist while entering the child's world of play and story. In this world, play and stories are coconstructed through careful listening and questioning to gain an understanding of the child's understanding and interpretation of the stories he or she is creating.

The process begins with listening to the stories that parents, caregivers, referrers, and others are telling about the child, by identifying what their "local" interpretation of the "problem" is in relation to the child and in the context of the systems in which the child functions. It is explained to the relevant people in the child's life why and how the therapist and child might play together. At this time, it is important for the therapist to identify if there is sufficient support for the child as he or she explores and expands his or her stories. Sometimes there isn't enough support or a sufficiently fear-free environment available to the child to progress with the intervention. The role of the therapist in this instance is to identify what needs to happen in the environment before therapy can commence.

Introducing the child to narrative play therapy is another key element in creating the open space required. The therapist may speak to the child about her knowledge that something has happened to the child or her family. These might be the scary or sad (and happy things), and the child might have all sorts of feelings about what has happened. The therapist invites the child to play and make stories to sort out some of these things. The child is introduced to the idea that the play and stories do not have to be about the child but that the themes might end up being similar. "The stories and play we do together are 'not about you but I bet you that the same things have happened to the people in the stories as have happened to you'" (Cattanach, 1997, p. 36). The child-led nature of the session is introduced to children by letting them know that they can choose the toys and how they want to play and that if it's a story, the therapist can write it down. General rules and boundaries may also be introduced to the child at this point. These include respect for each other and the toys and the limitations that the toys need to stay in the room and that if the child leaves the room (without good reason), the session will end. It is through the communication of these rules and boundaries, roles, and responsibilities that the therapist communicates to the child that the therapist can enter the child's play world and help him or her make sense of confusions (Cattanach, 1999).

During sessions, the role of the therapist is to play with the child and to write stories. The therapist mediates the cultural and social world that the child inhabits by asking questions about the stories and narratives brought into the therapeutic space (see Sam's story earlier). When children first begin to play and tell stories, these are often confusing. The therapist is left unclear, for example, as to who is the "goodie" and who is the "baddie" or how one got to be the other. The therapist listens for stories. Through questioning and talking about the story, the therapist and the child negotiate meanings and coconstruct the story and the storyteller's and listener's understanding of the story. The therapist doesn't interpret the stories or play, but together with the child, the therapist mediates some satisfactory meanings which are congruent with the child's lived-in world (Cattanach, 1999). The therapist facilitates an exchange of ideas and thoughts about the story. The therapist is a listener to stories and a scribe for stories. The child is given permission to explore and experiment with different stories, real and imagined worlds, and possible selves. He or she is free to experiment with alternative stories and alternative endings. Cattanach (2006) recounts the story 4-year-old Mary told about the wicked witch and the wicked dragon. In the first version, the witch died. In discussing with Mary what it meant to be dead, Mary generated four more endings for the story, namely, that the witch could die forever, die and come back, go to prison, or become a good witch. Elements of the story can be played around with, such as time and space, characters, and roles.

The therapist can also take the role of storyteller. This can be in the retelling of the child's dictated story and in the identification and telling of stories that may be supportive and helpful to the child. In the case study of Louise (discussed later), the *Bye Bye Baby* story by Janet and Allan Ahlberg became a story that was requested regularly. Other published stories are available to children in the play therapy space. These include traditional fairy tales such as the Three Little Pigs and alternative versions of the story, such as "The True Story of the Three Little Pigs." One published story, *Not Now, Bernard* by David McKee (1980), became a fascination for twins who were both seen for play therapy. This is about a boy who interrupts his busy parents and is always told that the time is not right. He eventually tries to tell them of the monster in the garden, but even this doesn't get their attention. The story ends with the mother bringing cookies and milk to Bernard in bed, but she doesn't even notice that what is in the bed is not her child but the monster that has eaten Bernard. Both children requested that this story be read at some time during each play therapy session. They looked closely at the pictures, and they asked questions to try and understand why the parents didn't have time for Bernard. Different understandings were coconstructed around the story and reflected the social world the children lived in, including meanings around both parents working and finding it difficult to juggle the demands of work and the demands of children and family life. However, the children remained fascinated by and struggled with the fact that the mother hadn't noticed that Bernard was not there and that supper was left for a monster.

The therapist has a role in supporting endings. In the same way that the stories generated and told in therapy have a beginning, middle, and end, the end of therapy has to be signaled and an agreed ending coconstructed. The therapy may be ended naturally, or it may be the end of an agreed number of sessions. The therapist uses similar questioning techniques to coconstruct with the child how he or she would like the therapy to end. Some ritual or celebrating can be a part of this. Children can be asked about what they would like to do with their stories. Some children wish to create these as their own storybook. Others request that the therapist hold the stories for the child. When deciding what to do with the stories, consideration is given to the readiness of the people in the child's lived world to hear these stories. If the child decides to make a book of stories, the therapist and child identify the stories to be included, if pictures or drawings are to be included with the story, and where the storybook will live when it moves into the child's lived world. Maryann made a beautiful cover for her book with leaves of gold and red paper. She only included the series of stories about trees, and she said that it would live under her bed and she could take it out at night and read it to herself if she had a "bad day" at school.

ROLE OF THE PARENT

The role of the parent before therapy begins is to share stories of the child that identify the "problem" as it has been constructed in the family and by the parents. This helps the therapist to understand the social and cultural community that the child comes from and begin to build the therapist's bank of "local" knowledge. Thus, the parent's role is to begin the story.

Once the parents have been introduced to play therapy and how and why the child and therapist might play together, the parents' role is to be there to support the child. If this support is not available, "the intervention will not be held emotionally and the child could be further defeated instead of uplifted" (Cattanach, 1997, p. 31). Parents may also need their own support at this time; otherwise, the attention being received by the child in therapy may become a source of jealousy or anger for the parents, thus reducing their ability to be supportive.

Parents also have a role in exploring alternative stories about their child. Parents are very familiar with the problem-saturated story of their child. They may be getting reports from school, from the child care services, from neighbors or friends. Parents may therefore need to share these stories as they can become overpowering and thus reduce their ability to support the child. Opportunities to share stories of success and the ordinary things in the child and family's life are invaluable in supporting parents.

As therapy comes to an end, the parent's role is to prepare a space for the child to try out new stories. The parents have shared the journey with the child, bringing him or her to therapy each week, meeting regularly with the therapist, managing behaviors as they escalated during therapy, and beginning to notice that things are changing, that the child moves between different environments more easily, and that he or she can accept the parents' leaving and be happy at their coming back. The story may not be replaced by a different story. The child may continue to have difficulties from time to time, but there are more stories and more ways of seeing the child and his or her behavior. The parents begin to prepare a place for their child's new and varied stories and possible selves to emerge. Initially, this will be within the family and then can begin to extend into the wider community as stories of success are shared about and with their child.

CASE STUDIES

For children who have experienced significant neglect and abuse in early childhood, the developmentally unfolding nature of play and narrative as means of symbolically exploring alternative worlds and personal experiences are not as available to them as to the children described in the introduction. Once such children are familiar with the role and purpose of narrative play therapy and they have had opportunities to explore the materials available in the therapy role, the child may then look for support in beginning the narrative play therapy process. One approach to supporting the developing relationship between the child and the therapist and process of therapy is to invite the child to draw.

Mark is a 7-year-old who came to therapy following significant neglect as an infant and current concern about his behavior and emotional well-being. He had been in foster care since he was 2 years old, with an experienced caregiver. On commencing therapy, he explored the materials, taking out and naming every toy or object in the play therapy room. He appeared unable to move beyond exploration. Following a number of such exploratory sessions and when the therapist felt that the relationship between the therapist and the child was such that the child felt able to accept or reject an invitation to engage in an activity, Mark was invited to draw a picture of a tree. When the drawing was completed, Mark was invited to tell a story about the tree. Questioning was used to support the construction of the story. This included demographic details such as the age of the tree, where it was located, and if others lived around it; action questions, such as how it got there; and motivation questions, such as how the tree felt about being there and its likes and dislikes. Mark dictated the following story about his tree:

The Tree

It was sown in 1969 by a lady called Jane Smith. People used to use some of the branches for fire in the old days.

It was duggen up and put in a safer place, because people wanted to build a road.

It preferred the new place because the roots were kind of dying in the old place.

As Mark had also drawn a house in the picture, he was invited to tell a story of the house. This is Mark's dictated story:

The House

The house was built in 1649. The person who built it was called Malachy Browne, the worst and silliest builder in the world. Nobody wanted to live in it because they knew who built it.

At last, someone dared to live in it. But they were killed because the house fell in.

The house was near an Old Norman Castle called O'Grady Castle. It (the house) was very happy to be built but was sad to be built by such a maniac.

Mark continued to explore materials in play therapy and spend large parts of his time setting up play scenarios but running out of time to actually play them. The setup scenes included baking and preparing food and cleaning and organizing the environment. His self-esteem was reported to have significantly improved, though he continued to have behavioral difficulties.

Children, when invited to play, may initially explore the toys and then begin to create story scenes with the toys. The toys take on roles, and the child then narrates a plot with character representations, an event, obstacle, or struggle. The child may present different scenarios to overcome the struggle. At this time, children are invited to dictate their story.

Jack was a 6-year-old who was diagnosed with cancer. Play therapy was requested to support him through this stressful time. A portable play kit with a limited number of toys was provided at the child's bedside. These included a play mat; soft toys such as snakes and miniature teddies; small-world toys, including a bear, a shark, a crocodile, and a dolphin who had mouths that could be opened to reveal big empty tummies; puppets of these animals; and objects such as a box with a lid, a spoon, and shiny marbles. The toys were presented to the child in an open basket. After exploring the materials that were available, Jack chose a number of soft toys, including the snakes and teddy bear and the shark and dolphin puppets. The characters swam around playing and eating objects in the water (e.g., the shiny marbles). The therapist was invited to be one of the puppets. As the play unfolded, it was difficult to identify the "good" characters from the "bad" characters, as roles changed frequently. "Bad" characters attached and bit the other characters. "Good" characters appeared to help the "victim" escape by either attacking the "bad" character or providing a secret passage that was too small for the "bad" character to enter. The following story was dictated following the enactment of this story in Jack's play:

Once upon a time, there was a sea and there's these four snakes and the dolphin were friends and a bad shark wasn't their friend. He ate all the snakes and the dolphin wanted to save them but he couldn't. So he nearly got eaten and a bear came along and tried to save the dolphin. The dolphin got eaten fully and the bear got eaten. They put the snake and dolphin and bear in the grave.

The End

Similar pretend play sequences emerged over the next few sessions. Jack did not wish to dictate any further stories but asked for the first story to be read to him on a number of occasions. On one occasion, he indicated that he wanted to draw a picture to go with the story already dictated. This was a line drawing of a snake with its head facing to the left of the page and "Sad dolphin" underneath, with its head facing the right of the page. Treatment was unsuccessful, and Jack returned home.

Maryann was 11 years old when she first came to therapy. Parents described her as a child who had moved from being an outgoing, "happy-go-lucky" child to a "sad and withdrawn child." They indicated that this appeared to have coincided with a change of grade. Mary was introduced to narrative play therapy. She became enthralled with storytelling, story making, and dictating stories. While all play materials were available to her, she often chose drawing. She interspersed drawing with conversations about her difficulties in school and her sense of unfairness and injustice observed in how different children were treated in the classroom. She also talked about her loss of friends as they moved out of the area or to different schools. Sometimes Maryann would dictate a story in relation to the drawing she had completed. This is one such dictated story:

The Tree

One day Jane and Maggie were playing in the park. They saw a bare space and planted an apple tree. They grew up with the tree and often went there with groups of children. They would feed some of the apples to the birds.

Then one day they found out that one of the trees was to be cut down. They protested. That was the bird's habitat. They couldn't cut down the trees.

After Jane and Maggie died, their grandchildren and families came and fed the birds. Birds still come and people still feed the birds.

On the next-to-last session of a short play therapy intervention, Maryann returned to this story. She came to therapy with a picture she had drawn and said she wanted to dictate the following story:

The Very Special Tree

There was this tree in the corner of the park. It was an apple tree. It was there since Jane and Maggie saved it a long time ago. People were beginning to think that they should save a lot more trees than usual.

They went to the council meeting that night to see what they could do about the shortage of trees because the birds were losing their natural habitat. Some birds might even die. They said that if nothing was done they would go on a protest until something was done about the shortage of trees. The council were afraid that they would lose their jobs so they immediately wrote down what they could do, to see if they could do something about the shortage of trees.

People were wondering if they were lying or trying to do something to save their jobs. Very soon people had lost faith and they tried to do something about it themselves. And they gathered seeds from the apple trees and plants. They brought the seeds to a big open space in the city, to what was going to be their wild life habitat.

Very soon an election came around the corner. Some of the people who planted the local habitat ran for council. Very soon they had a new council who was ready to listen to the people and their problems with the plans and the wildlife.

Things got better for the town. Very soon a park was built in the town for the children for during the summer.

The End

While Maryann had little power over her school environment, the alternative worlds she created in drawing and narrative posed problems and offered opportunities to develop solutions to the problems, with solutions created that empowered the characters in the story. The child-led nature of the play therapy environment offered Maryann opportunities to control her environment. This was contained within the structure of the narrative. Maryann was able to play around with time, moving forward to the next generation, while keeping the theme of saving the trees as the consistent thread.

Other children use the structure of already written narratives to grapple with understanding their life experiences. Louise was one such child. She was 3½ years old when she first came to play therapy. Louise was identified as being at risk of neglect, after her mother abandoned her to her father on a Christmas visit, when she was 2 years old.

Louise became fascinated with *Bye Bye Baby*, by Janet and Allen Ahlberg (1989), which tells the story of a little baby who has to look after himself, feed himself, and change his own diaper. The baby then decides that this is too much for a baby to be expected to do. He sets off on a journey to find a mother. Along the way, he meets a range of characters that can't be his mother but will help him find a mother, with certain conditions attached. Eventually, he finds a mother who was looking for a baby, and the story appears to end until there is mention of a father in a story read by the old uncle (a character met along the way). The baby then sets out to find a father, and the story ends happily ever after.

Louise was familiar with this story from her nursery school environment. During play therapy, Louise set up a series of enacted plays based on the themes of this book. "You be the mom. I have no mom. You have to go over there. Don't talk to me. I have to find the mom." This was often the direction given by Louise to set up the enacted story. A number of obstacle courses were arranged and often included struggling through tight spaces and quicksand to get to a place where there was a mother waiting and looking for a baby. The baby was then nurtured, told stories, and tucked safely in bed. Occasionally, the mom and baby would have to swim back through the obstacle course together before reaching the safety of home. The baby would get hurt on this journey. The mom then had to take the baby to the hospital, where she had several bandages applied. Sometimes this enacted play was followed by a search for a father. The enactment of this search tended to be more straightforward, such as going to the shopping mall and finding him. The role of the mother was initially assigned to the therapist, and the scenarios for the story were directed by the child. Following a number of repetitions with variations of these enacted scenarios, Louise began to explore other roles within the story, primarily the mother, and a doll became the baby. At these times, the therapist became like the old uncle, helping the mother in creating a supportive environment for the care of the baby. Other roles assigned to the therapist were observer and narrator. Initially, Louise was reluctant to try out different roles. This became coconstructed, and the narrative structure provided by the story appeared to support changes of roles within the enactment of the story.

At a therapy review meeting, Louise's father, who was her primary guardian, talked about his recent marriage and birth of a half-sibling to Louise. He expressed the hope that his new wife would become a mother to Louise over time. His own narrative around Louise had been about his search for a mother for her over the previous year and a half.

CHALLENGES IN IMPLEMENTING THE MODEL

Practice in this model presents a number of challenges for the therapist, the child, and the systems in which the child and therapist work. The therapist is challenged to think about, and acknowledge his or her own assumptions about, the "self," the "problem," and the role of therapy. Many therapies assume an "objective" and "expert knowledge" stance, both of which are challenged by this model of working. Instead, the therapist is asked to adopt a "not-knowing" and curious stance and to use the "local" knowledge of the child and his or her family and the relationship between the therapist, the child, and caregivers in order to understand. From a position of not knowing, the therapist is challenged to find questions, and to allow questions to emerge, that support the development or flow of the story while not interrupting the flow of the story or the child's play. This requires the therapist to maintain a position of openness and uncertainty. Interpretation is also based on this "local" knowledge rather than a theoretical framework. The process is to access the child or caregiver's interpretation with the aim of enriching their understanding rather than imposing an expert opinion and closing down understanding (Cattanach, 2006).

The challenge for the child is to explore possible stories, possible worlds, and possible selves and to enter into the relationship with the therapist through his or her play and stories. In this open, safe, and fear-free space, children are challenged to begin to think about beginnings, middles, and endings and to begin to expand the range of options for themes, stories, and endings that they can then access and explore in their lived world.

A challenge for the systems around the child, whether for the parents/caregivers, families, teachers, or the wider community, is to be open to hearing new stories and to be open to the impact that the new stories might have on how the child is seen.

This model of working challenges the systems to be open to allowing the child to try out new stories and new possible selves. These systems are also challenged to become increasingly aware of the language chosen to tell a story and the limiting impact this may have on the child.

This model also poses a challenge for academics, scholars, and policy makers in considering the scientific tools that are used to identify the effectiveness of interventions. For this model of working, the challenge is to identify research models that will be able to identify the effectiveness of narrative play therapy, while still remaining faithful to the centrality of the individual in relationship with others, and acknowledging that concepts such as "scientific knowledge" and "effectiveness" are constructs and not "truths."

CONCLUSION

Narrative play therapy is a branch of play therapy that uses the developmental potential of both play and narrative to support the child in understanding events that have happened in his or her life and how they have impacted the child. It is child led in that the child chooses the toys and materials that he or she wishes to play with. The child's lived world and imagined world(s) come together in his or her play in play therapy. Real objects can be used in imagination, and the imagination can be used to create real worlds. Starting points for coconstructed narratives come from children, their play, and the stories they create. The narratives that children present in their play are explored, and the therapist facilitates an exchange of ideas and thoughts about the story. It is in the context of the relationship between the therapist and the child, as listener and storyteller, that the story is coconstructed and created. The curious and not-knowing stance of the therapist facilitates the creation of an open, safe, and fear-free space for the child to explore, play, and make stories. Narrative play therapy is about supporting the child to generate alternative endings to stories and to generate a range of different stories within his or her play, creating both a cognitive and emotional flexibility, which can then be utilized and accessed by the child in his or her lived world.

REFERENCES

Ahlberg, J., & Ahlberg, A. (1991). *Bye bye baby: A sad story with a happy ending.* London, UK: Mammoth.

Anderson, H., & Goolishian, H. (1992). The client is the expert: A not-knowing approach to therapy. In S. McNamee & K. J. Gergen (Eds.), *Therapy as social construction.* London, UK: SAGA.

Bruner. J. S., & Lucariello, J. (1989). Monologue as narrative recreation of the world. In K. Nelson (Ed.), *Narratives from the crib* (pp. 73–97). Cambridge, MA: Harvard University Press.

Cattanach, A. (1994). *Play therapy: Where the sky meets the underworld.* London, UK: Kingsley.

Cattanach, A. (1997). *Children's stories in play therapy.* London, UK: Kingsley.

Cattanach, A. (1999). Co-construction in play therapy. In A. Cattanach (Ed.), *Process in the arts therapies* (pp. 79–102). London, UK: Kingsley.

Cattanach, A. (2006). Narrative play therapy. In C. E. Schaefer & H. G Kaduson (Eds.), *Contemporary play therapy: Theory, research and practice.* New York, NY: Guilford Press.

Engel, S. (2005). The narrative worlds of *what is* and *what if. Cognitive Psychology, 20,* 514–525.

Gergen, K. J. (1991). *The saturated self: Dilemmas of identity in a contemporary life.* New York, NY: Basic Books.

Gergen, K. J. (1996). Beyond life narratives in the therapeutic encounter. In J. E. Birren, G. M. Keyton, J-K. Ruth, J. J. F. Schroots, & T. Svensson (Eds.), *Aging and biography: Explorations in adult development* (pp. 205–230). New York, NY: Springer.

Jennings, S. (1993). *Playtherapy with children: A practitioner's guide.* Oxford, UK: Blackwell Scientific.

Jennings, S. (1999). *Introduction to developmental playtherapy.* London, UK: Kingsley.

Kavanaugh, R. D., & Engel, S. (1998). The development of pretense and narrative in early childhood. In O. N. Saracho & B. Spodek (Eds.), *Multiple perspectives on play in early childhood education.* Albany: State University of New York Press.

Macmurray, J. (1961). *Persons in relation.* London, UK: Faber.

McKee, D. (1980). *Not now, Bernard.* London, UK: Random House Children's Books.

McLeod, J. (1997). *Narrative and psychotherapy.* London, UK: Sage.

Nicolopoulou, A. (2005). Play and narrative in the process of development: Commonalities, differences and interrelations. *Cognitive Psychology, 20,* 495–502.

Nicolopoulou, A. (2006). The interplay of play and narrative in children's development: Theoretical reflections and concrete examples. In A. Goncu & S. Gaskins (Eds.), *Play and development: Evolutionary, sociocultural and functional perspectives.* Mahwah, NJ: Erlbaum.

Smith, C. (1997). Comparing traditional therapies with narrative approaches. In C. Smith & D. Nylund (Eds.), *Narrative therapies with children and adolescents.* New York, NY: Guilford Press.

Stagnitti, K. (1998). *Learn to play: A programme to develop the imaginative play skills of children.* Melbourne, Australia: Co-ordinates.

Stagnitti, K. (2009). Children and pretend play. In K. Stagnitti & R. Cooper (Eds.), *Play as therapy: Assessment and intervention* (pp. 59–69). London, UK: Kingsley.

Stagnitti, K., & Jellie, L. (2006). *Play to learn: Building literacy in the early years.* Melbourne, Australia: Curriculum.

Trevarthen, C. (1995). The child's need to learn a culture. *Children and Society, 9,* 5–19.

Vygotsky, L. S. (1978). *Mind in society: The development of higher psychological processes.* Cambridge, MA: Harvard University Press.

Chapter 19

INTEGRATIVE PLAY THERAPY
Athena A. Drewes

INTRODUCTION

The integration of theory, technique, and common factors in psychotherapy has gained prominence since the 1990s. Previously called e*clecticism, integration* has now become the more preferred term in the blending together of theory, technique, and common factors (Norcross, 2005). Previously, *eclectic* "simply means that you select from different theories and techniques a therapeutic strategy that appears best for a particular client" (Schaefer, 2003, p. 308). However, Norcross (1987) takes eclecticism further into *integration* whereby various theories are applied to one interactive and coordinated means of treatment.

Because psychological disorders, especially for children and adolescents, are multilayered, complex, and multidetermined, a multifaceted treatment approach is needed (Schaefer, 2003). Indeed, many clients come with not one clearly defined diagnosis, but rather several overlapping problems due to the comorbidity of issues (such as in the case of complex trauma resulting in overlapping anxiety and attention problems, along with phobias and sexualized behaviors). Clinicians trained in one theoretical and treatment approach are finding that "one size" cannot fit all of the presenting problems they are being faced with today. In addition, there is no clear research evidence that shows that one single theoretical approach (such as cognitive-behavioral, Jungian, Rogerian, etc.) is able to create therapeutic change across all of the various different and multidimensional psychological disorders that exist (Schaefer, 2003; Smith, Glass, & Miller, 1980). Because of this multidimensional aspect, child/play therapy calls for the unique demand that the therapist wear many different hats and be skillful in changing from one therapeutic stance to another in order to meet the needs of the child and the various members in the child's life (Coonerty, 1993). One moment the play therapist is intensely involved in deeply evocative, often very conflicted, play therapy with the child client. At that moment, the therapist needs to deal with the child's internal struggles, setting limits and being an educator or mediator with the child, while in the next moment the therapist needs to engage with a parent or school psychologist or classroom teacher to assess the child's functioning. These often conflicting and rapidly changing roles lead many child/play therapists to adopt an eclectic prescriptive style in which therapeutic interventions are chosen and then changed according to the most pressing external demand (Coonerty, 1993).

In addition, in direct contrast to linear models of psychopathology, integrative theories of psychopathology assume a weaving of various aspects of the client's personal experience, thereby conceptualizing psychopathology from the viewpoint of multicausation. Thus, equal weight is given to various aspects of personal functioning, and they are seen in a blended and unified whole (Coonerty, 1993). Such blending implies a circularity as well as the containment of multiple relationships that are seen between cognitive, dynamic, interpersonal, and behavioral aspects of the individual (Coonerty, 1993). Rather than just jumping from one type of treatment to another, the child/play therapist can develop an integrative approach to treatment that broadens the therapist's concept of what is appropriate from the various theoretical points of view and can offer a wider array of tools with which to work. In addition, the prospect of change in one sphere of functioning can potentially lead to broad reverberations and changes throughout all aspects of the client's maladaptive functioning (Coonerty, 1993).

Further adding to the push toward and benefits of an integrative treatment approach is that funding sources (state, federal, and insurance companies) are mandating that clinicians and agencies utilize evidence-based treatment approaches in order to receive continued funding. Consequently, they want to be sure clients are receiving the best treatment as well as the most effective treatment available. So the selection of treatment interventions should be ruled not by a subjective personal preference or the staying within a comfort zone in the way one always works, but rather by evidence-based practices over personal opinion (Schaefer, 2003).

Finally, the extensive research being done with regard to child sexual abuse and trauma has resulted in evidence-based practices that push for an integrative treatment approach. For example, Stien and Kendall (2004) recommend a three-pronged integrated approach:

> Although cognitive/behavioral interventions address problematic behaviors and help the child build new skills, psychodynamic interventions are needed to help integrate traumatic memories and emotions along with buried parts of the self. At the same time, the therapist must pay close attention to family interactions—sequences of action and reaction—to root out any that maintain and reinforce symptoms. (p. 139)

Gil (2006) states,

> Evidence also suggests that trauma memories are imbedded in the right hemisphere of the brain, and thus that interventions facilitating access to and activity in the right side of the brain may be indicated. The right hemisphere of the brain is most receptive to nonverbal strategies that utilize symbolic language, creativity and pretend play. (p. 68)

Thus, the need for the use of expressive arts, play, and pleasurable activities within therapy has been found to be helpful and needed in helping traumatized and abused children create their trauma narratives (Cohen, Deblinger, Mannarino, & Steer, 2004; Gil, 2006; van der Kolk, 2005).

Therefore, it is not surprising, then, that therapists, and notably play therapists, need to become more flexible in their treatment approaches. The need for flexibility results in changing one's style of working, expanding one's orientation, and seeking out approaches that can best address a particular client's needs or concerns.

Within the past 20 years, integration of theory and treatment has developed into a clearly delineated area of interest for clinicians (Norcross, 2005). Jensen, Bergin, and Greaves (1990) found in a survey of 423 mental health professionals that a majority use an eclectic form of therapy. A recent survey by Norcross, Hedges, and Castle (2002) found that 36% of psychologists responding claim to be eclectic/ integrative. Among play therapists, Phillips and Landreth (1995) found that the most common approach reported was an eclectic and multitheoretical orientation by respondents. Such a shift may be due to the growing dissatisfaction with a single-school or "one-size-fits-all" treatment approach. There is no one approach that appears to be clinically effective for all clients and situations. Also, there has been a growing desire in the psychotherapy field to find out what can be learned from other theories. All these factors have made an integrative approach necessary. Finally, Norcross (2005) highlights eight possible reasons for the rapid increase in integrative psychotherapies. Among them are

1. A large increase in therapies
2. The lack of a single theory or treatment that is adequate
3. A rise in short-term, problem-focused treatment
4. The rise in evidence-based treatments resulting from the identification of specific therapy effects
5. The recognition that there are therapeutic commonalities that heavily contribute to outcome

BASIC CONCEPTS, GOALS, AND TECHNIQUES

There are several different avenues toward creating an integrative treatment approach. Norcross (2005) lists them as technical eclecticism, theoretical integration, common factors, and assimilative integration.

Technical eclecticism is a prescriptive approach in that it selects the best treatment for the person and the problem. This decision is guided by research on what has worked best for others in the past with similar problems and having similar characteristics (Norcross, 2005).

Theoretical integration takes the best elements of two or more approaches to therapy and blends them with the expectation that the result will be more than the sum of the two separate therapies. The emphasis is on integrating the underlying theories along with integration of therapy techniques. The results lead to a new direction for both practice and research (Norcross, 2005).

The *common factors* approach ascertains the underlying core ingredients that the different therapies share in common. The goal is to come up with the simplest and most effective treatment based on those commonalities. Grencavage and Norcross (1990) reviewed 50 publications to discern commonalities among the proposed therapeutic common factors. Factors per publication ranged in number from 1 to 20, with a total of 89 different commonalities noted. Their analyses revealed that 41% of the proposed commonalities had to do with change processes, while only 6% were attributed to client characteristics. Consensus across categories were the development of a therapeutic alliance, opportunity for catharsis, acquisition and practice of new behaviors, and the clients' positive expectancies (Grencavage & Norcross).

With *assimilative integration,* the clinician is required to have a strong grounding in one theoretical system but a willingness to selectively incorporate or assimilate practices and views from other systems (Messer, 1992; Norcross, 2005). Assimilative integration thereby "combines the advantages of a single, coherent theoretical system with the flexibility of a broader range of technical interventions from multiple systems" (Norcross, 2005, p. 10). Most clinicians have been and continue to be trained in a single approach. Rather than throw away that foundation as they discover the limitations of their original approach, many rework their approach by gradually incorporating parts and methods from other approaches and molding it into a new form (Norcross, 2005).

Play therapists lag behind mainstream psychotherapy with regard to an integrative treatment approach. While there have been some play therapy articles and chapters written regarding an integrative play therapy approach, mostly through case studies, to date there has been little empirical research conducted. There has been some promising work done in coming up with various new approaches and conceptualizations for an integrative approach to treatment that fall under several of Norcross's categories.

Technical eclecticism, utilizing a prescriptive approach, is reported by Kenny and Winick (2000) in a case study of working with an 11-year-old autistic girl with behavioral difficulties. Using a sequential approach, Kenny and Winick chose treatment approaches that would build on one another over time, rather than a blending together within one session. This case is also particularly unique in that fewer than 20% of surveyed play therapists (Phillips & Landreth, 1998) believe that play therapy would help in treating the problems associated with pervasive developmental disorders. The reasoning is that the child's limited cognitive or play skills would inhibit the therapy. Usually, treatment for autistic children has included medications for lessening aggressive and self-injurious behaviors; increasing attention span, along with controlling seizures; decreasing agitation; and reducing stereotyped and other maladaptive behaviors (Dawson & Castelloe, 1992). Often, behavioral techniques are utilized to lessen self-stimulatory behaviors, and nondirective, child-centered treatment is not utilized at all.

Kenny and Winick utilized the rapport-building component of nondirective play therapy with directive techniques in targeting maladaptive behavior and offering parent education. The rationale for using a flexible integrative approach was due to the multidimensional aspects of the child's behaviors along with her developmental delays. They combined different treatment approaches into a coherent intervention sequence (Shirk, 1999). They blended nondirective play therapy and directive interventions focused on personal hygiene and social skills and parent education and support.

During the initial stages (sessions 1–7), child-centered play therapy was utilized as the sole treatment approach to build rapport and establish minimal limit setting. This sequence involved nondirective sessions that allowed for the child to be able to begin to express feelings and offered a needed sense of constancy of the therapist and room. Midway through treatment, the sessions stopped being nondirective and became directive, with the therapist focusing on specific behavioral issues that were presented, such as refusal to brush her teeth and lack of personal hygiene. Although a play-based approach was utilized, the sessions were strictly directive and skill based. As treatment progressed, the therapist brought in parent education and training to help the mother carry over the skill-building components into the home while also working to lower the mother's frustration level and parent–child conflict.

Utilizing this integrative, sequential, and prescriptive approach, brief therapy successfully lessened the autistic child's noncompliant behaviors at home and lessened irritable mood while it increased basic living skills, social behavior, and compliance at home.

An example of *theoretical integration* in play therapy is Ecosystemic Play Therapy (EPT) developed by Kevin O'Connor. The clinician is required to consider the child, his or her problems, and the therapy process within the framework of the child's ecosystem (O'Connor, 2001). EPT is heavily grounded in theory and emphasizes the flexibility of the theory, allowing the play therapist to work with children at any developmental level using a variety of contexts. O'Connor (2001) states,

> EPT is an integrative model of play therapy incorporating key elements of the analytic (Freud, 1928; Klein, 1932), child-centered (Axline, 1947; Landreth, 1991), and cognitive-behavioral models (Knell, 1993) of play therapy, as well as elements of Theraplay (Jernberg, 1979; Jernberg & Booth, 2010) and reality therapy (Glasser, 1975). (p. 33)

Ecosystemic Play Therapy is theory dependent (rather than technique dependent). The theory is used to match a wide array of techniques and creative activities and interventions and utilize them with specific clients and their problems following a well-developed treatment plan. EPT focuses primarily on helping the child client function optimally in the contexts in which he or she lives. EPT was first formally described in 1994 by O'Connor (O'Connor, 1997). Concepts of personality, psychopathology, nested environments that the client is in, treatment goals, and the role of play and techniques are combined into the ecosystemic integrative approach (O'Connor, 1997). These multiple interacting systems are taken into account by the play therapist in conceptualizing the child's presenting problems and formulating the best treatment approach (O'Connor, 1997). EPT is seen as a treatment modality that can be "readily adapted to work with any child or problem because of its developmental and broad systemic approach to the conceptualization of problems" (O'Connor, 1997, p. 245). Consequently, the various components are combined, resulting in an approach and theoretical framework whose sum is far greater than its parts. The play therapist utilizing EPT can develop well-defined treatment goals and design creative interventions geared toward achieving those goals (O'Connor, 2001).

Another example is that of Paris Goodyear-Brown (2010), who has recently developed the Flexibly Sequential Play Therapy (FSPT) model of treatment for traumatized children. She initially takes a variety of treatment techniques to give the child the space to disclose and adjust his or her exposure to the sharing of the trauma content (continuum of disclosure) as well as restore the child's lost sense of empowerment that occurs due to abuse (experiential mastery plan, or EMP). These two intertwined processes are grounded in play and expressive mediums and woven in with skill-based work. "The FSPT model delineates specific treatment goals, delivered through a variety of specific play-based technologies and supported by an understanding of the facilitative powers of play and the therapist's use of self in the play space" (Goodyear-Brown, p. 3). This model requires the therapist to be flexible in order to integrate directive and nondirective approaches.

In order to utilize FSPT, the therapist must have a breadth of knowledge along with the finesse to utilize a variety of treatment technologies. Coping, emotional literacy, and cognitive restructuring require knowledge of cognitive-behavioral theory and therapy for children and teens. In order to soothe the traumatized child's physiology, knowledge of trauma, physiological stress responses, and theoretical components of somatic therapies and mindfulness practices are required as well. In order to work effectively with the parents, the play therapist must also have a good understanding of family systems theory and attachment theory, along with being familiar with the latest dyadic interventions, such as parent–child interaction therapy, Theraplay, child–parent psychotherapy, Child–Parent Relationship Therapy, and the Circle of Security Project (Goodyear-Brown, 2010).

The therapist is not required to be expert in each and every one of the models. However, a working knowledge of their approach and how to conduct dyadic interventions and psychoeducational components in working with the parent is needed.

Goodyear-Brown (2010) states that FSPT relies heavily on the therapeutic and facilitative powers of play in order to deliver the developmentally sensitive treatment plan. She delineates how each of the curative factors of play facilitates the treatment process. In particular, she notes that counterconditioning of negative affect and the reestablishment of the child's sense of power and control work together in lessening the toxic impact that trauma content and events have on the child. She states that "play becomes the digestive enzyme through which the child is fully able to ingest the therapeutic content that is being conveyed. Play ensures the most potent absorption of conceptual information for children" (Goodyear-Brown, p. 11).

Common factors as seen in play therapy were utilized by Weir (2008) in working with an adoptive family and their child with reactive attachment disorder (RAD). The essential components of structural family therapy, Theraplay, and other selected family play therapy models were utilized to target the needs of the families and adoptive children with RAD. Numerous treatment approaches exist in order to deal with attachment disorders. Filial therapy (Van Fleet, 1994), Theraplay (Booth & Lindaman, 2000), as well as structural family therapy and the work of Daniel Hughes (1997) encourage the use of an integrative model that utilizes a play therapy–based approach within family work with adoptive children when attachment disorders are present. The commonalities across each of these treatments are the use of play therapy techniques that are utilized within sessions and at home with the parent and child, along with psychoeducational principles of parenting. Consequently, key components of family therapy theories and models and play therapy modalities were extrapolated and utilized to treat a family in which an adopted child was diagnosed with RAD. The simplest components of each theory and technique were utilized, rather than using any one treatment approach in its purest form (Weir, 2008). An amalgam of play, stories, drawings, puppet work, homework assignments, and techniques fostering a balance of structure, engagement, nurture, and challenge dimensions were utilized within the therapeutic context of playfulness that fostered relationship building between child and family. Homework assignments of "special time" allowed for the practicing of what was learned in the session at home and gave an opportunity for the parents and child to have designated unconditional play time together to further enhance positive interactions. Weir reported success in his case study using this integrated attachment-based model.

A good example of *assimilative integration* is seen in a case study within a school setting by Fall (2001), who utilized integrative play therapy as the blending of two or more theoretical foundations into a cohesive treatment approach driven by the child's or family's needs and problems. In a prescriptive way, the child's needs and problems helped to direct which theory to use and assist the play therapist in addressing academic, personal, and social issues at any particular time (Fall, 2001). Each theory came with corresponding techniques. There is some play therapy research that corroborates that differing play therapy interventions are useful in meeting the treatment needs of children and families (Landreth, Homeyer, Glover, & Sweeney, 1996).

Fall (2001) stressed that the integrative approach in a school counseling setting should be guided by the child's problem, a prescriptive approach (Baker, 2000). In addition, she states how the "integrative play therapy approach is both proactive and reactive, two components of a school counselor's job description" (p. 325). As a result, the core theory and approach of child-centered play therapy was blended with Adlerian and cognitive-behavioral play therapy approaches and theory. Fall found that such an integration works well in addressing the variety of problems a school counselor faces.

For example, in helping a child deal with angry feelings, the play therapist may utilize directive cognitive-behavioral techniques to address behaviors and offer alternative strategies that impact on peer interactions (reactive) while also allowing the child the opportunity to master his intense affect through an Adlerian or child-centered approach, which is child-led play and nondirective. Treatment approaches may be blended within one treatment session or independently presented sequentially over a series of sessions.

Another good example of assimilative integration is object relations play therapy, originated and utilized by Helen Benedict (2006). Object relations play therapy relies primarily on child-responsive, invitational, and highly attuned therapy techniques with specific goals and techniques easily tailored prescriptively to meet each child's specific needs and interpersonal relatedness (Benedict, 2006). This treatment approach is grounded in attachment-based object relations theory, which is a collection of loosely organized models held together by three basic ideas. The first and most important is the prevailing belief that interpersonal relationships are the central driving and motivational force in human development (Benedict, 2006). This is backed by neuroscience research that has been able to show that early brain development requires attuned and interactive events that are experience dependent (Schore, 2003). The second component is that through relating to others over one's initial 2 to 3 years of life, a cognitive-affective structure develops, which is not only about the self but also about others, thus forming into object relations. These templates serve as an internal guide to understanding and responding to oneself and others in relationships (Benedict, 2006; Bowlby, 1988). The third assumption is that object relations begin to develop from infancy through the initial relationships between the infant and primary attachment figure. These object relations, which have a neurological and experiential basis, significantly influence the child's (and later adult's) interpersonal relationships. But these templates can be impacted by ongoing relationships.

As a result, the therapist–child relationship becomes the crucible whereby the child's maladaptive internal working models can be modified into a more adaptive object relation.

The core component of object relations play therapy is the therapist and child relationship (Benedict, 2006). A lengthy part of treatment is the development of a secure base relationship with the child, who is slow to trust, has negative internal models of self and others, and resists interpersonal connections due to past relational trauma. Therapy with these children is often difficult and time consuming. In order to do this, the therapist is prescriptive in choosing his or her own activity level and degree of being directive in direct response to cues from the child (Benedict, 2006; Gil, 1991). It is child initiated, rather than directive or nondirective, whereby the therapist creates a safe and protected space (both emotionally and physically) and demonstrates attunement, warmth, acceptance, constancy, developmental appropriateness, and child responsiveness (Benedict, 2006). An "invitational" approach is taken by the therapist in watching the child's cues and being attuned before moving into any directive work, which the child can freely either accept or reject.

The goal of the therapy is to modify the child's internal working models or object relations. Thematic play becomes pivotal in the healing of traumatic experiences and in turn challenging the child's object relations (Benedict, 2006):

> Play, especially thematic play, is an important avenue to correcting distorted cognitive understandings and resolving both affective reactions and traumatic memories. . . .
> Thematic play is where the child imagines roles, relationships, and events and enacts

these through playful use of objects, role play, and actions. . . . Thematic play serves as a communicative medium to convey their concerns, feelings and ideas. . . . It is often the therapist's understanding of and response to the child's play that facilitates therapeutic change. (pp. 7–8)

THERAPEUTIC POWERS OF PLAY UNDERLYING THE MODEL

As noted previously, the common factors aspect of integrative psychotherapy were assessed by Grencavage and Norcross (1990). In their review, they found that almost half of the proposed commonalities had to do specifically with change processes over client characteristics. Consensus across categories were in the development of a therapeutic alliance, opportunity for catharsis, acquisition and practice of new behaviors, and the clients' positive expectancies (Grencavage & Norcross, 1990).

Looking at the variety of integrative approaches in play therapy, the curative powers of play become the change mechanism within play that can help child and adolescent clients overcome psychosocial, behavioral, and emotional difficulties (Drewes, 2009). Consequently, the integrative and prescriptive approach pulls for the play therapist to become skilled in numerous therapeutic powers and differentially apply them to meet the individual needs of the clients. "This approach is based on the individualized, differential, and focused matching of curative powers to the specific causative forces underlying the client's problem" (Drewes, 2009, p. 1).

Depending on which theoretical frameworks are utilized within the integrative approach, the therapeutic powers of play underlying the models can vary. Aside from those noted earlier (using Schaefer's [1999] terms: catharsis, rapport building, behavioral rehearsal, and sense of self), any number of the following factors may also be seen as change agents: self-expression, access to the unconscious, direct/indirect teaching, abreaction, stress inoculation, counterconditioning of negative affect, positive affect, sublimation, attachment and relationship enhancement, moral judgment, empathy, power/control, competence and self-control, accelerated development, creative problem solving, fantasy compensation, and reality testing (Schaefer & Drewes, 2009).

Further research is needed to illuminate which specific therapeutic powers of play are most effective with specific presenting problems and within the blending of different models and treatment approaches. It will be most important for play therapists to understand what "invisible powerful forces resulting from the therapist-client play interactions are successful in helping the client overcome and heal psychosocial difficulties" (Schaefer & Drewes, 2009, pp. 4–5). The greater our understanding of these curative factors and change mechanisms, the more effective the play therapist is in being able to apply them to meet the particular needs of his or her clients (Schaefer, 1999).

ROLE OF THE THERAPIST/ROLE OF THE PARENT

Because each treatment model can vary, the role of the play therapist will vary accordingly. There will be times when the play therapist will need to be nondirective, or child initiated, allowing the child or adolescent to lead. Other times, the therapist will need to take a much more directive and involved stance, offering parent training or introducing treatment components and tasks. Such shifts in approach may happen within the same session or might occur sequentially over the treatment. Consequently, the play therapist needs to be flexible both in thinking and in treatment approach.

The same can be said of the role of the parent. This can vary, depending on which theories are utilized and style of treatment. Some integrative play therapy approaches (e.g., Filial Therapy or Child–Parent Relationship Therapy) require the parent to observe the therapist conducting the sessions with the child, thereby learning and rehearsing approaches prior to actually working with the child together in a dyad. Other approaches may not include the parent in the session at all until the end, when the child "teaches" the parent what she learned, allowing for solidifying and the generalizing of skill development. Still other approaches may work exclusively with the client and have contact with the parent only to obtain information regarding treatment progress and systemic changes.

CLINICAL APPLICATIONS

The integrative play therapy model can be utilized across all disorders and developmental levels. Because it pulls together various theories, along with treatment approaches, the best "fit" can occur. By its nature, integrative play therapy is also a prescriptive approach in that it seeks out the best treatment for this child's presenting problems at this time and is flexible within and across sessions in achieving the treatment plan. As a result, an integrative play therapy model allows for a broad application in its use over single fixed theoretical and treatment approaches.

CASE ILLUSTRATION

The following is a case illustration that fits assimiliative integration in that several theoretical approaches were utilized along with a variety of related techniques.

JT was an 8-year-old boy in foster care who presented with behavioral difficulties in school due to mood dysregulation and struggled with issues related to his father's death, three years before, along with his mother's current wish to surrender parental rights so he could be adopted due to the reemergence of her cancer. Treatment goals were to work on helping JT utilize (a) child-led play therapy to help build rapport and a therapeutic alliance, along with offering control in selection of materials and tasks and a release from traumatic and stressful material; (b) the use of directive cognitive-behavioral therapy techniques to manage and reduce his strong emotional affect (anger, depression), become aware of the emotional triggers, and develop alternative coping skills; and (c) bereavement work to focus on helping JT deal with unresolved grief and loss of his father and pending loss of his mother. Parent–child dyadic therapy was also utilized to help JT and his mother talk about the past events of his father's death and to better understand his mother's wishes to have him adopted. In addition, this author maintained contact with his school setting and foster home parents for information regarding progress and systemic issues. The various theoretical frameworks used and concomitant techniques included psychodynamic play therapy, sandtray therapy, cognitive-behavioral play therapy, family therapy, and systems theory.

JT was seen in individual weekly play therapy sessions over the course of two years for 75 sessions. Our 45-minute sessions were structured and divided into components that allowed for the integrative use of several treatment approaches. Prior to having JT enter the therapy room, I would meet for 5 to 10 minutes with the foster parent(s) regarding how JT was doing in their home, school, and on visits with his mother. Then, after the foster parent(s) left, JT came into the session. The first 10 to 15 minutes was a "check-in," which facilitated time to talk about how his week was, relaying any information I received from his foster parents that needed to be shared; following up on any "homework" assignments he might have had. The check-in also allowed us to work on specific directive techniques. The next 25 to 30 minutes were child led, which allowed JT to select what he wished to play with and how, and what emotional material he wished to convey. The last 5 to 10 minutes were for cleanup and a closing ritual of using bubbles or deep breathing for affect regulation and transitioning from the session.

In the initial session, I shared with JT what I knew of his history and why he was seeing me as well as what our time together would be like. Using a balloon to blow in all his angry and upset feelings, JT was helped to see how the big balloon was like his head and heart, containing so many upset feelings that he felt as though he would "pop." By letting out some of the air at a time and seeing how much smaller the balloon was getting, JT better understood that this was like our time together in letting out his angry feelings in a safe, slow way with my help. We then looked at what difficulties he felt he needed to work on, and we created a treatment plan together. Using strips of paper to write on, we worked together on selecting three issues/problems each about home, school, and his family, for a total of nine items we would work on in therapy. We left one paper blank, which would allow him to spontaneously address something not covered. JT wrote on each strip the goal we selected and decorated an envelope in which the paper strips were placed. Each session when he entered, the envelope would be put out, and he would get to pick one of the pieces of paper for us to focus on. He could put back the paper and select a different one only once before we had to work on it. Then, after we talked about the issue or used a directive technique, he would rip off a small piece of the paper and put it back. This way, he saw we were making progress on the goal but still not finished with it.

In this first session, JT then used his child-led, nondirective time to create a sand tray showing me what his world was like. During other sessions, JT often used the play therapy toys, art materials, and clay to express feelings. But he often preferred to use the sand tray when there were deep issues he was facing around the death of his father and worries about his mother.

Over the first four sessions, I was able to obtain a good sense of JT's developmental level and emotional issues as well as build rapport and facilitate the creation of a therapeutic relationship.

Over the course of treatment, JT began to delve more deeply into his feelings and memories regarding his father's death when he was only 4½ years old. There were missing details to the narrative of his father's death, as well as information lacking as to what happens when someone dies, and even where his father was buried. At this point, once a month the mother joined JT for dyadic family therapy. His mother was able to discuss with him where his father was buried and details surrounding his illness and death. The foster parents were willing to take JT to the grave, where he was able to leave a letter to his father (that we worked on in sessions) telling him his feelings and that he missed him. Sessions with JT's mother continued and allowed for discussion about why she wanted him adopted, how she had only one relative available who was not mentally stable, and she wanted to know he was in a good adoptive home. This was her second bout with cancer, and his mother was unsure, even if she went into remission again, that she would not ultimately die from cancer in the near future, leaving him an orphan with no place to go. His mother also was able to share the unknown fact that she had been in foster care as a child and adopted as well. This was a good experience for her, and she wanted to have JT in a loving home. We were able to work out an "open" adoption in New York, which allowed for JT and his mother to maintain contact around birthdays and holidays with the consent of the adoptive family.

Through the healing powers of play and the integrative treatment approach, JT was able to learn and apply better coping strategies; gain access to his unconscious issues around his father's death previously unexplored; allow for catharsis in getting out his anger and rage over feeling abandoned; gain power and control, along with competence, self-control, and a greater sense of himself; and, through CBT techniques, apply creative problem solving, behavioral rehearsal, and counterconditioning of negative affect.

By the end of treatment, an adoptive family was found, and we were able to work toward his successful adoption. He still remains with his adoptive family and has periodic contact with his biological mother. His acting-out behaviors in school significantly diminished, and he is better able to manage his sadness and anger.

CHALLENGES IN IMPLEMENTING THE MODEL

While integration is gaining hold in psychotherapy, there are obstacles to its growth in the treatment arena. The most severe obstacle comes from territoriality of the "purists," who hold their single-theory views as being the best. As a result, there is inadequate training in eclectic/integrative therapy in university settings (Norcross, 2005). Graduate students may occasionally be taught to look at treatment through the lens of one or two theoretical frameworks. So students graduating will call themselves *eclectic,* but what they are really saying is that they have been taught two different approaches (usually cognitive-behavioral and Rogerian). Consequently, they are not fluid in thinking between the two theories and approaches and do not feel well grounded in either approach, resulting in an inability to truly integrate them. Thus, the push toward a truly integrative treatment approach is lacking.

In the field of play therapy, limited coursework, articles, books, and workshops are available to help play therapists in becoming more flexible and integrative. There are still some "purists" who feel that being well grounded in one treatment approach and theoretical framework is satisfactory for the treatment of most clients. However, in recent years, there has been a surge in interest, books, and training in blending play therapy with cognitive-behavioral therapy, which has helped to move play therapists toward a more integrative direction.

Finally, a lack of a common language and contradictory assumptions about personality development, human nature, and origins of psychopathology (Messer, 1992) add further roadblocks to the progress of integrative play therapy (Norcross, 2005). In spite of the hurdles, in recent years empirical outcome literature in mainstream psychotherapy has grown considerably (Schottenbauer, Glass, & Arnkoff, 2005). There is little research being conducted by play therapists specifically looking at the benefits of an integrative treatment approach. It is now time for play therapists to also add to the body of research in studying the effectiveness of integrative treatment approaches. More process research is needed in order to identify which mediators or therapeutic factors produce the desired change in the client's behaviors and presenting problems. Research needs to address which specific change agents in play can be combined to optimize treatment effectiveness (Schaefer & Drewes, 2009). Such knowledge not only would allow the therapist to be able to borrow flexibly from available theoretical positions to tailor treatment to a particular child based on his or her treatment plan but also would result in the most cost-effective play interventions.

CONCLUSION

Integrative play therapy is a relatively newly developing approach to working with children and adolescents. It offers promise in its flexible use of integrating theory and techniques in order to offer the client the best treatment for his or her presenting problems. Much work is needed in creating training within university settings on this approach as well as within the play therapy field through workshops, conference presentations, and publications to help play therapists become flexible in their thinking and approach.

REFERENCES

Axline, V. (1947). *Play therapy.* Boston, MA: Houghton Mifflin.

Baker, S. (2000). *School counseling for the twenty-first century* (3rd ed.). Upper Saddle River, NJ: Merrill.

Benedict, H. (2006). Object relations play therapy. Applications to attachment problems and relational trauma. In C. E. Schaefer & H. G. Kaduson (Eds.), *Contemporary play therapy: Theory, research, and practice* (pp. 3–27). New York, NY: Guilford Press.

Booth, P. B., & Lindaman, S. (2000). Theraplay for enhancing attachment in adopted children. In C. E. Schaefer & H. G. Kaduson (Eds.), *Short-term play therapy for children* (pp. 194–227). New York, NY: Guilford Press.

Bowlby, J. (1988). *A secure-base: Parent–child attachment and healthy human development.* New York, NY: Basic Books.

Cohen, J. A., Deblinger, E., Mannarino, A. P., & Steer, R. A. (2004). A multi-site, randomized controlled trial for sexually abused children with PTSD symptoms. *Journal of the American Academy of Child and Adolescent Psychiatry, 43*, 393–402.

Coonerty, S. (1993). Integrative child therapy. In G. Stricker & J. Gold (Eds.), *Comprehensive handbook of psychotherapy integration* (pp. 413–426). New York, NY: Plenum Press.

Dawson, G., & Castelloe, P. (1992). Autism. In C. E. Walker & M. Roberts (Eds.), *Handbook of clinical child psychology* (2nd ed., pp. 375–398). New York, NY: Wiley.

Drewes, A. A. (2009). Rationale for integrating play therapy and CBT. In A. A. Drewes (Ed.), *Blending play therapy with cognitive behavioral therapy: Evidence-based and other effective treatments and techniques* (pp. 1–2). Hoboken, NJ: Wiley.

Fall, M. (2001). An integrative play therapy approach to working with children. In A. A. Drewes, L. J. Carey, & C. E. Schaefer (Eds.), *School-based play therapy* (pp. 315–328). New York, NY: Wiley.

Freud, A. (1928). *Introduction to the technique of child analysis* (L. P. Clark, Trans.). New York, NY: Nervous and Mental Disease Publishing.

Gil, E. (1991). *The healing power of play.* New York, NY: Guilford Press.

Gil, E. (2006). *Helping abused and traumatized children: Integrating directive and nondirective approaches.* New York, NY: Guilford Press.

Glasser, W. (1975). *Reality therapy.* New York, NY: Harper & Row.

Goodyear-Brown, P. (2010). *Play therapy with traumatized children: A prescriptive approach.* Hoboken, NJ: Wiley.

Grencavage, L. M., & Norcross, J. C. (1990). Where are the commonalities among the therapeutic common factors? *Professional Psychology: Research and Practice, 21*(5), 372–378.

Hughes, D. (1997). *Facilitating developmental attachment: The road to emotional recovery and behavioral change in foster and adopted children.* Northvale, NJ: Aronson.

Jensen, J. P., Bergin, A. E., & Greaves, D. W. (1990). The meaning of eclecticism: New survey and analysis of components. *Professional Psychology: Research and Practice, 21*(2), 124–130.

Jernberg, A. (1979). *Theraplay.* San Francisco, CA: Jossey-Bass.

Jernberg, A., & Booth, P. (2010). *Theraplay: Helping parents and children build better relationships through attachment based play* (3rd ed.). San Francisco, CA: Jossey-Bass.

Kenny, M. C., & Winick, C. B. (2000). An integrative approach to play therapy with an autistic girl. *International Journal of Play Therapy, 9*(1), 11–33.

Klein, M. (1932). *The psycho-analysis of children*. London, UK: Hogarth Press.

Knell, S. (1993). *Cognitive behavioral play therapy*. Northvale, NJ: Aronson.

Landreth, G. (1991). *Play therapy: The art of the relationship*. Muncie, IN: Accelerated Development.

Landreth, G., Homeyer, L., Glover, G., & Sweeney, D. (1996). *Play therapy interventions with children's problems*. Northvale, NJ: Aronson.

Messer, S. B. (1992). A critical examination of belief structures in integrative and eclectic psychotherapy. In J. C. Norcross & M. R. Goldfried (Eds.), *Handbook of psychotherapy integration* (pp. 130–168). New York, NY: Oxford University Press.

Norcross, J. (2005). A primer on psychotherapy integration. In J. C. Norcross & M. R. Goldfried (Eds.), *Handbook of psychotherapy integration* (2nd ed., pp. 10–23). New York, NY: Oxford University Press.

Norcross, J. C. (1987). *Casebook of eclectic psychotherapy*. New York, NY: Brunner/Mazel.

Norcross, J. C., Hedges, M., & Castle, P. H. (2002). Psychologists conducting psychotherapy in 2001: A study of the Division 29 membership. *Psychotherapy, 39,* 97–102.

O'Connor, K. (1997). Ecosystemic play therapy. In K. O'Connor & M. K. Braverman (Eds.), *Play therapy theory and practice: A comparative presentation* (pp. 234–284). New York, NY: Wiley.

O'Connor, K. (2001). Ecosystemic play therapy. *International Journal of Play Therapy, 10*(2), 33–44.

Phillips, R. D., & Landreth, G. (1995). Play therapists on play therapy: A report of methods, demographics, and professional/practice issues. *International Journal of Play Therapy, 4,* 1–26.

Phillips, R. D., & Landreth, G. (1998). Play therapists on play therapy: II. Clinical issues in play therapy. *International Journal of Play Therapy, 7*(1), 1–20.

Schaefer, C. E. (1999). Curative factors in play therapy. *Journal for the Professional Counselor, 14*(1), 7–16.

Schaefer, C. E. (2003). Prescriptive play therapy. In C. E. Schaefer (Ed.), *Foundations of play therapy* (pp. 306–320). Hoboken, NJ: Wiley.

Schaefer, C. E., & Drewes, A. A. (2009). The therapeutic powers of play. In A. A. Drewes (Ed.), *Blending play therapy with cognitive behavioral therapy: Evidence-based and other effective treatments and techniques* (pp. 3–15). Hoboken, NJ: Wiley.

Schore, A. N. (2003). Early relational trauma, disorganized attachment, and the development of a predisposition to violence. In M. F. Solomon & D. J. Siegel (Eds.), *Healing trauma: Attachment, mind, body, and brain* (pp. 107–167). New York, NY: Norton.

Scottenbauer, M. A., Glass, C. R., & Arnkoff, D. B. (2005). Outcome research on psychotherapy integration. In J. C. Norcross & M. R. Goldfried (Eds.), *Handbook of psychotherapy integration* (pp. 459–493). New York, NY: Oxford University Press.

Shirk, S. (1999). Integrated child psychotherapy: Treatment ingredients in search of a receipe. In S. Russ & T. Ollendick (Eds.), *Handbook of psychotherapies with children and families* (pp. 369–384). New York, NY: Kluwer Academic/Plenum.

Smith, M. L., Glass, G. V., & Miller, T. I. (1980). *The benefits of psychotherapy*. Baltimore, MD: Johns Hopkins University Press.

Stien, P. T., & Kendall, J. (2004). *Psychological trauma and the developing brain: Neurologically based interventions for troubled children.* New York, NY: Haworth Press.

van der Kolk, B. A. (2005). Developmental trauma disorder: Towards a rational diagnosis for children with complex trauma histories. *Psychiatric Annals, 35*(5), 401–408.

Van Fleet, R. (1994). Filial therapy for adoptive children and parents. In K. J. O'Connor & C. E. Schaefer (Eds.), *Handbook of play therapy, Volume 2: Advances and innovations.* New York, NY: Wiley.

Weir, K. N. (2008). Using integrative play therapy with adoptive families to treat reactive attachment disorder: A case study. *Journal of Family Psychotherapy, 18*(4), 1–16.

Chapter 20

PRESCRIPTIVE PLAY THERAPY

Charles E. Schaefer

Prescriptive psychotherapy is the term used for approaches that attempt to tailor the application of psychological interventions to individual clients (Beutler, 1979; Beutler & Clarkin, 1990). Prescriptive psychotherapists seek to answer the age-old question: What treatment procedures administered by which therapist to which client with which specific problems are predicted to yield the best outcomes (Paul, 1967)? This client × therapist × treatment interaction view of effective psychotherapy is at the heart of the prescriptive approach.

The task of the prescriptive therapist is to codevelop with the client a set of achievable goals, a coherent problem formulation (an explanation for why the presenting problem exists or what is causing it), and a treatment plan tailored to the individual client's specific problem and situation.

The prescriptive psychotherapy approach is not new (Dimond, Havens, & Jones, 1978; Goldstein & Stein, 1976). However, the popularity of this approach has mushroomed over the past 30 years (Beutler & Harwood, 1995) and is likely to continue to expand in the years ahead.

FUNDAMENTAL BELIEFS

Every school of psychotherapy is founded on a set of core propositions or beliefs that serve as fundamental cornerstones of the approach. The four basic tenets of prescriptive play therapy are described in the following sections.

Tenet 1: Differential Therapeutics

Play therapy has been developing over most of its 100-year history based on the "one true light" assumption. This is basically a nonprescriptive position that holds, in the absence of supportive evidence, that one's preferred treatment approach is equally and widely applicable to most or all types of client problems. From this perspective, treatment is instituted essentially independent of diagnostic information. The difficulty with this "one-size-fits-all" assumption is that no one theoretical school (e.g., Rogerian, Adlerian, Jungian) has proven strong enough to produce optimal change across the many different and complex psychological disorders that have been identified (Smith, Glass, & Miller, 1980).

The prescriptive approach to play therapy (Kaduson, Cangelosi, & Schaefer, 1997) is based on the core premise of *differential therapeutics* (Francis, Clarkin, & Perry, 1984), which holds that some play interventions were more effective than others for certain disorders and that a client who does poorly with one type of play therapy may do well with another (Beutler, 1979; Beutler & Clarkin, 1990). It rejects the dodo bird verdict that all major forms of psychotherapy are equally effective for specific disorders (Beutler, 1991; Luborsky, Singer, & Luborsky, 1975; Norcross, 1995). Rather than forcing clients to adapt to one therapeutic modality, prescriptive therapists vary their remedies to meet the different treatment needs of individual clients.

Notwithstanding the "common" or "nonspecific" elements that characterize effective therapies of all types, increasing evidence has shown that specific interventions work better for specific disorders or syndromes (Chambless & Ollendick, 2001). Support for the strength of specific treatment effects is seen in the findings of psychotherapy outcome meta-analytic studies, which indicate that mean effect sizes of specific factors consistently surpass those of common factors (Lambert & Bergin, 1994; Stevens, Hyman, & Allen, 2000).

Tenet 2: Eclecticism

In order to effectively tailor one's intervention to the individual needs of a client, one must be eclectic. Eclectic psychotherapists select from different theories and techniques a therapeutic intervention that they consider best for a particular client (Norcross, 1986). They reject strict adherence to any one school or system and instead select what is most valid or useful from a wide therapeutic spectrum. Prescriptive therapists assert that the more remedies you have in your repertoire, coupled with the knowledge about how to differentially apply them, the more effective you'll be across the multitude of presenting problems one encounters in clinical practice (Goldstein & Stein, 1976). Using more than one modality in therapy helps therapists avoid the trap that Abraham Maslow is quoted as saying, "If the only tool you have is a hammer, every problem starts to look like a nail."

According to Norcross (1987), "synthetic eclecticism" involves combining various theories into one coordinated treatment intervention. This differs from "kitchen-sink eclecticism" which, Norcross states, is an atheoretical treatment approach. In the latter, practitioners apply techniques from various schools of thought in a manner that ignores the theory that underlies them. Such an approach, Norcross warns, is haphazard and ineffective at best and may, in fact, be harmful to some clients.

Surveys of clinicians have indicated that many identify themselves as eclectic, making the eclectic, "meta-theory" approach the modal theoretical orientation across disciplines (Brabeck & Welfel, 1985; Norcross, 2005; Prochaska & Norcross, 1983). A poll of play therapists (Phillips & Landreth, 1995) found that an eclectic, multitheoretical orientation was, by far, the most common approach reported by the respondents. Although eclectic psychotherapy is still not widely taught in graduate schools, it is likely to remain the treatment of choice by most practitioners in this country (Norcross, 2005).

As Goldfried (2001) observed,

> Most of us as therapists eventually learn that we cannot function effectively without moving outside of the theoretical model which we had originally been trained, recognizing that the strength of another orientation may at times synergistically complement the limitations of our own approach. (p. 45)

The widespread eclectic movement reflects a decisive departure from the aforementioned "purist," one-size-fits-all orthodoxy, together with a much greater openness by psyhotherapists to adapt to differing contexts of the client's life and thus tailor their strategies to the circumstances and needs of individual clients.

Tenet 3: Integrative Psychotherapy

Since prescriptive play therapists are not confined by single-school theories, they often combine different theories and techniques to strengthen an intervention and broaden the scope of their practice. The term *integrative psychotherapy* is used to describe any multimodal approach that combines theories. Thus, individual, group, and family play strategies may be integrated to treat a particular case or psychodynamic and humanistic play theories. An integrated, multicomponent intervention reflects the fact that most psychological disorders are complex and multidimensional, that is, they are caused by an interaction of biological, psychological, and social factors. Because most disorders are multidetermined, they need an integrated, multifaceted remedy. The fact that there is high comorbidity among many psychological disorders, such as conduct disorder and attention deficit/hyperactivity disorder, also points to the need for an integrative treatment approach.

Clearly, prescriptive therapists need to be both integrative and eclectic; however, most prefer to call themselves integrative rather than eclectic (Norcross & Prochaska, 1988). The type of integrative psychotherapy practiced by most prescriptive play therapists is "assimilative integrative." This means they begin their training with a firm grounding in one primary orientation, typically child centered, and then gradually incorporate or assimilate during their career a number of practices from other schools (Messer, 1992).

Tenet 4: Prescriptive Matching

Since differential rates of improvement are being found among different treatment procedures, prescriptive play therapists seek to "match" the most effective play intervention to a specific disorder (Norcross, 1991). On the face of it, practically every therapist endorses the premise that treatment should be tailored or matched to the needs of the individual case. It makes intuitive sense. However, prescriptive matching at the optimum level goes beyond this simple acknowledgment. It differs from the typical basis in the following way.

The typical basis of matching is a theory of psychotherapy rather than—at the highest level—direct matching of a change agent to the cause of the disorder.

Optimally, in formulating a treatment plan, the clinician selects a therapeutic change agent that is designed to reduce or eliminate the cause of the problem. Thus, by treating not only the symptoms but the underlying cause(s), the problem will be less likely to reoccur in the future. For example, Theraplay, an attachment-oriented play intervention, would be a logical match for a child presenting with an attachment disorder. Similarly, abreaction/reenactment play therapy is a trauma-focused intervention intended for children who have experienced a recent trauma or stressor. Cognitive play therapy is geared toward changing the dysfunctional thoughts triggering anxiety and depression in children.

One of the goals of a comprehensive assessment prior to treatment selection is to pinpoint the underlying cause of the disorder so that the therapist can then select a change agent (a therapeutic power of play) that is most likely to remedy the determinant or causal factor.

While "causal therapy" (i.e., therapy that eliminates the cause of the problem) would be the highest form of prescriptive matching, it is not always possible to identify the pathological process underlying the problem, or the precipitating cause may no longer be operative. In such cases, the prescriptive play therapist turns to other bases for matching treatment to the client, such as "evidence-informed" matching and "client–therapist" matching.

Evidence-informed matching (Bohart, 2005) is one that tailors an intervention to a client by considering three main factors: empirically supported treatments for a specific disorder, client needs and preferences, and therapist variables, such as clinical expertise and practical experience.

"Client–therapist" matching involves matching the personal qualities of clients to the personal qualities of therapists (e.g., similar personalities, values, backgrounds, genders, conceptual levels).

In the event a prescriptive play therapist is not comfortable in implementing an intervention that is clearly the best match for a client's problem, the therapist will then recommend referral to professionals who are able to provide such treatment.

Thus, treatment selection for a prescriptive play therapist is a systematic, reflective, and client-centered procedure rather than one that is haphazard, intuitive, or therapist centered.

CORE PRACTICES

In light of the basic beliefs described earlier, prescriptive play therapists attempt to implement the following core practices.

Empirically Supported Treatments

In the past, the field of psychotherapy has relied too heavily on practices that have little supporting evidence or, at worst, poor outcomes. Therapy has been provided based on "that's what we've always done" rather than on an emerging evidence base for "what works." Research on the effectiveness of play therapy interventions for children continues to grow at a rapid rate (Reddy, Files-Hall, & Schaefer, 2005), but there remains a large gap between evidence-supported treatments and what is practiced in the field. One of the primary criteria employed by prescriptive play therapists to match an intervention to a disorder is *scientific evidence* of what works best for that disorder. This is a "bottom-up" approach in that interventions with empirically supported efficacy are applied and subjected to further scientific validation.

If empirically supported treatments have not been reported for a particular disorder, prescriptive therapists look to the clinical experiences of self and/or other therapists as to what has worked best in actual practice for the dysfunction. If both research and practice are uninformative, therapists turn to the most compelling theory linking change mechanisms to the disorder.

Therapeutic Change Mechanisms

In recent years, there has been a shift away from the development of elaborate, formal theories of psychotherapy to a focus on identifying the basic mechanisms of therapeutic change, that is, healing forces that are not tied to any specific theory or model (Beutler & Harwood, 2000). Change mechanisms are not theories—they are descriptions of observed relationships. They are more general than techniques, and they are more specific than theories.

Perhaps the most basic question faced by play therapists today relates to the mechanisms of change in play therapy; that is, what are the therapeutic forces that actually produce the desired change in a client's behavior (Schaefer, 1993)? Once the active ingredients in a play intervention have been identified, the inert factors can be eliminated and a more time-efficient and cost-effective intervention can be developed (Goldfried, 1980).

Therefore, in addition to outcome research, prescriptive play therapists look to process or *component analysis* research (Hunsley & Rumstein-McKean, 1999) to identify the therapeutic change mechanisms underlying effective outcomes. Furthermore, they continually search for the mediator and moderator variables that can help them understand the relationships between a specific play treatment and outcome (Shadish & Sweeney, 1991).

The major therapeutic powers of play (Schaefer, 1993) are listed in Table 20.1. The most well-known powers of play are its communication powers (e.g., young children express themselves better through play activities than with words), its teaching power (e.g., children learn and remember better when instruction is made fun and enjoyable), its ego-boosting powers (e.g., children gain a sense of power, control, and competency through play), and its self-actualization power (e.g., children, adolescents, and adults have the freedom to be completely themselves in play).

Prescriptive play therapists continually seek to acquire a deeper understanding of all the therapeutic powers of play and try to determine for which disorders each of these change mechanisms is best applied. Based upon their understanding of the therapeutic powers of play, they seek a prescriptive matching of these therapeutic

Table 20.1   Therapeutic Powers of Play

I. Communication
    Self-expression/Self-understanding
        1. Conscious thoughts and feelings
        2. Access to the unconscious
        3. Direct teaching
        4. Indirect teaching

II. Emotional Regulation
        5. Counterconditioning of negative affect
        6. Abreaction
        7. Catharsis
        8. Sublimation

III. Relationship Enhancement
        9. Alliance
        10. Attachment
        11. Friendship—peers
        12. Friendship—adults

IV. 13. Moral Judgment

V. Coping with Stress
        14. Stress inoculation
        15. Stress management

VI. Ego-Boosting
        16. Power
        17. Competence
        18. Self-control
        19. Creative problem solving
        20. Fantasy compensation
        21. Reality testing

VII. Preparation for Life
        22. Role-playing
        23. Behavioral rehearsal
        24. Accelerated development

VIII. 25. Self-Actualization

remedies to the causes or determinants of a disorder. For example, attachment-oriented play therapy would likely be the treatment of choice for a child exhibiting signs of an insecure attachment (Benedict & Mongoven, 1997). Based on a functional analysis, Kearney & Silverman (1999) identified four main causes of school refusal in childhood: (1) avoidance of stimuli that provoke a general sense of negative affect, (2) escape from aversive social and evaluative situations, (3) attention-seeking, (4) and/or positive reinforcement. They found that children who received prescriptive treatment (matching specific remedy to the specific cause of the disorder) showed substantial improvement. However, those who were given nonprescriptive treatment exhibited a worsening of their symptoms. By incorporating most or all of these curative powers of play into their repertoire, prescriptive play therapists are able to offer specific treatment for a wide range of psychological disorders.

PRAGMATIC

An overarching principle that guides prescriptive play therapists is if it works, use it. This pragmatic attitude is based on the philosophical writings of William James, John Dewey, and Charles Pierce. The central idea is that the truth of a theory or the value of a technique is demonstrated by its practical consequences, that is, its *usefulness* (Fishman, 1998). The best therapeutic intervention is one that gets the job done with an individual case in the most cost-effective manner. Pragmatists do not let theoretical alliance, elegance, or biases blind them to what works and what doesn't work for a disorder in the real world.

They encourage continued experimentation to improve the knowledge base.

COMPREHENSIVE ASSESSMENT

The prescriptive approach to treatment planning begins with a comprehensive assessment of the symptoms and determinants (internal and external) of a client's problem. Multiple sources and methods of assessment (interviews, rating scales, projective techniques) are often used to gather data. Based on this information, an individualized case formulation is conducted before initiation of therapy. A case formulation is a descriptive and explanatory summary of the client's most important issues/problems (as well as strengths) and of the probable causal or contributory factors. The case formulation also includes the treatment goals and strategies, predicted obstacles, and a means for evaluating progress.

An individualized, tailored intervention is the object of this assessment and case formulation. As the treatment proceeds, the prescriptive play therapist collects more assessment data to evaluate treatment progress and to revise the intervention as needed.

PRACTICE GUIDELINES

The basic premise behind best practice guidelines is that research evidence has accumulated enough to provide guidance as to the interventions that have the best outcomes with specific disorders. Treatment guidelines help practitioners update their training to include the latest findings, which should not only improve treatment efficacy but also give clients confidence that practitioners are relying on cutting-edge science. This, in turn, will encourage clients to seek and continue in treatment.

Table 20.2   Practice Guidelines

Childhood Disorder/Condition	Play Intervention with Research
Adjustment reaction	Release therapy (Brown, Curry, & Tittnich, 1971; Burstein & Meichenbaum, 1979; Rae, Werchel, & Sanner, 1989)
ADHD	Cognitive-behavioral play group therapy (Kaduson & Finnerty, 1995; Hansen, Meissler, & Ovens, 2000)
	Child-centered play therapy (Ray, Scholekorb, & Tsai, 2007)
Aggression	Play group therapy (Bay-Hinitz, Peterson, & Qualitch, 1994; Dubow, Huesmann, & Eron, 1987; Orlick, 1981)
Anger	Cognitive-behavioral (Lochman, Fitzgerald, & Whidby, 1999)
Anxiety	Cognitive-behavioral play therapy (Barrett, 1999; Barrett & Sonderegger, 2001
Autism	Behavioral play therapy (Rogers, 1991); integrated play group (Wolfberg & Schuler, 1993)
Bereaved	Play group therapy (Netel-Gilman, Siegner, & Gilman, 2000; Zambelli & DeRosa, 1992)
Children of divorce	Play group therapy (Netel-Gilman, Siegner, & Gilman, 2000; Zambelli & DeRosa, 1992)
Chronic illness	Filial/family play therapy (Van Fleet, 2000)
Conduct disorder	Incredible years program (Webster-Stratton & Reid, 2003, 2009)
Fears and phobias	Systematic desensitization (Knell, 2000; Mendez & Garcia, 1996); emotive imagery (King, Molloy, & Ollendick, 1998)
Foster/adoptive	Filial/family therapy (Van Fleet, 1994)
Obesity	Play group therapy (White & Gauvin, 1999)
OCD	Cognitive-behavioral play therapy (March & Mulle, 1995)
Oppositional/defiant	Parent-child interaction therapy (Eyberg et al., 2001)
Peer relationship problems	Play group therapy (Schaefer, Jacobson, & Ghahramanlou, 2000)
Posttraumatic stress disorder	Release therapy (Galante & Foa, 1986)
Reactive attachment disorder	Theraplay (Booth & Koller, 1998)
Sexually abused	Abuse-specific play therapy (Fenkelhor & Berliner, 1995; Corder, 2000)

Treatment guidelines prepared by this author listing play therapy interventions with the strongest empirical support for a number of childhood disorders can be found in Table 20.2. Typically, best practice guidelines such as these are promulgated by a task force convened by a professional organization. The task force compiles the best practice list based on a review of the current outcome research. This is an important way to link clinical practice with scientific research (Hayes & Gregg, 2001).

The American Psychological Association's Division of Clinical Psychology created a special task force whose expresse purpose was to promote the dissemination of empirically validated psychological treatments (Chambless, 1995). The task force initially identified and published 22 "well-established" treatments for 21 different syndromes. Hopefully, the Association for Play Therapy will soon establish such an interdisciplinary task force to develop and publish a consensus list of evidence-based play interventions.

ROLE OF THE THERAPIST

The therapist who wishes to practice prescriptive play therapy must become familiar with the major theories of play and play therapy. The therapist should develop a clear understanding of play and the way it has been integrated into play therapy, the way play behavior changes with development, the many play materials and techniques now available, and the diverse ways in which these materials and techniques need to be modified to deal with specific client populations.

The therapist's role in the prescriptive approach varies depending on the particular play approach that is tailored to a case. For example, the therapist is directive and structured when implementing a behavioral strategy but nondirective when following a child-centered orientation. The degree to which support, insight, or instruction is offered depends on the approach chosen. At times, the therapist trains a child's parents to be partners in treatment, while such parent training may be contraindicated in other cases. The prescriptive play therapy approach is best suited to therapists who are open, flexible, and skillful in adapting a particular treatment protocol to their own personal style.

CHALLENGES

It has been suggested that a weakness of prescriptive psychotherapy is its lack of investment in theory generation. Indeed, the main interest of prescriptive therapists is not in the development of single theories but, rather, in the identification of change mechanisms underlying successful psychotherapy of all types and in the development of a prescriptive matching of change mechanisms to underlying determinants of a disorder. In essence, it is a mega-theory that transcends single theories of therapeutic change while utilizing the healing forces within multiple theories.

Since prescriptive therapists need to be competent in more than one therapeutic orientation, a second challenge for them is the expanded training needs implicit in this approach. As part of their graduate training, prescriptive therapists receive in-depth instruction and supervision in one or two major schools of psychotherapy. Then they gradually expand their areas of competence by supervision and enrolling in continuing education workshops and institutes. Believing that learning is a lifelong process, they gradually acquire knowledge and skills in several schools of play therapy, such as humanistic, psychodynamic, and cognitive-behavioral, as well as in the three main modalities—individual, group, and family play therapy.

A third challenge of the prescriptive approach is that flexibility can deteriorate into mindless fluidity of approaches. According to Hans Eysenck (1981), "Eclecticism can become little more than a mish-mash of theory, a hugger-mugger of procedures, and a hodge-podge of therapies" (p. 2). However, when you follow a rational, systematic procedure for prescriptive matching of remedy to disorder, this criticism can be avoided.

SUMMARY AND CONCLUSION

This chapter contains an overview of basic premises and core practices of the prescriptive approach to play therapy. Prescriptive play therapists draw from a number of therapeutic approaches so as to have a wealth of change agents at their disposal. They then tailor their therapeutic interventions to the needs of the individual client by utilizing four sources of information: underlying causes of the presenting problem, empirical evidence, clinical experience/expertise, and client preferences/context.

Most play therapists today are more (big P) or less (small P) prescriptive in their practice. This means that there are few, if any, "purists" who strictly and dogmatically adhere to a single theoretical orientation (Kazdin, Siegel, & Bass, 1990). If the impressive growth and development that the field of play therapy experienced in the 20th century is to continue throughout the 21st century, it will likely be because the prescriptive (eclectic, integrative, evidenced-informed) approach becomes more fully and widely implemented by practitioners across the world.

REFERENCES

Bay-Hinitz, A., Peterson, R. F., & Quqlitch, H. R., (1994). Cooperative games: A way to modify aggressive and cooperative behaviors in young children. *Journal of Applied Behavior Analysis, 27,* 435–446.

Barrett, P. M. (1999). Child anxiety disorders. In C. E. Schaefer (Ed.), *Short-term psychotherapy groups for children* (pp. 249–276). Northvale, NJ: Aronson.

Barrett, P.M., & Sonderegger, R. (2001). Evaluation of an anxiety-prevention and positive-coping program (Friends) for children and adolescents. *Behavior Change, 18*(2), 78–91.

Benedict, H. E., & Mongoven, L. (1997). Thematic play therapy: An approach to treatment of attachment disorders in young children. In H. D. Kaduson, D. Cangelosi, & C. E. Schaefer (Eds.), *The playing cure: Individualized play therapy for specific childhood problems* (pp. 277–315). Northvale, NJ: Aronson.

Beutler, L. E. (1979). Toward specific psychological therapies for specific conditions. *Journal of Consulting and Clinical Psychology, 47,* 882–897.

Beutler, L. E. (1991). Have we all won and must all have prizes? *Journal of Consulting and Clinical Psychology, 59,* 226–232.

Beutler, L. E., & Clarkin, J. (1990). *Systematic treatment selection. Toward targeted therapeutic intervention.* New York, NY: Brunner/Mazel.

Beutler, L. E., & Harwood, T. M. (1995). Prescriptive psychotherapies. *Applied and Preventive Psychology, 4,* 89–100.

Beutler, L. E., & Harwood, T. M. (2000). *Prescriptive psychotherapy: A practical guide to systematic treatment selection.* New York, NY: Oxford University Press.

Bohart, H. C. (2005). Evidence-based psychotherapy means evidence informed, not evidence-driven. *Journal of Contemporary Psychotherapy, 35*(1), 39–53.

Booth, P. B., & Koller, T. J. (1998). Training parents of failure-to-attach children. In J. M. Briesmeister & C. E. Schaefer (Eds.), *Handbook of parent training* (2nd ed.). New York, N Y: Wiley.

Brabeck, M. M., & Welfel, E.R. (1985). Counseling theory: Understanding the trend toward eclecticism from a developmental perspective. *Journal of Counseling and Development, 63,* 343–349.

Bratton, S. E. (1998). Training parents to facilitate their child's adjustment to divorce using the filial/family play therapy approach. In J. M. Briesmeister, & C. E. Schaefer (Eds.), *Handbook of parent training* (2nd ed., pp. 549–572). New York, NY: Wiley.

Brown, N. S., Curry, N. E., & Tittnich, E. (1971). How groups of children deal with common stress through play. In N. E. Curry & S. Arnaud (Eds.), *Play: The child strives toward self-realization.* Washington, DC: National Association for the Education of Young Children.

Burstein, S., & Meichenbaum, D. (1979). The work of worrying in children undergoing surgery. *Journal of Abnormal Child Psychology, 7,* 121–132.

Chambless, D. L. (1995). Training and dissemination of empirically-validated psychological treatments: Report and recommendations. *The Clinical Psychologist, 48*(1), 3–24.

Chambless, D. L., & Ollendick, T. H. (2001). Empirically supported psychological intervention: Controversies and evidence. *Annual Review of Psychology, 52,* 685–716.

Corder, B. F. (2000). Using games and game play in group therapy with sexually abused children and adolescents. In C. E. Schaefer & S. E. Reid (Eds.), *Game play* (2nd ed., pp. 263–280). New York, NY: Wiley.

Dimond, R., Havens, R., & Jones, A. (1978). A conceptual framework for the practice of prescriptive eclecticism in psychotherapy. *American Psychologist, 33,* 239–248.

Dubow, E. J., Huesmann, L. R., & Eron, L. D. (1987). Mitigating aggression and promoting prosocial behavior in aggressive elementary school boys. *Behavior Research and Therapy, 25,* 525–531.

Eyberg, S. M., Funderbuck, B. W., Hembree-Kigin, T. L., McNeil, C., Querido, J. G., & Hood, K. (2001). Parent–child interaction therapy with behavior problem children: One and two year maintenance of treatment effects in the family. *Child & Family Behavior Therapy, 23,* 1–20.

Eysenck, H. J. (Ed.). (1981). *A model for personality.* Berlin, Germany: Springer.

Fenkelhor, D., & Berliner, L. (1995). Research on the treatment of sexually abused children. A review and recommendations. *Journal of the American Academy of Child & Adolescent Psychiatry, 34,* 1408–1420.

Fishman, D. B. (1998). *The case for a pragmatic psychology.* New York, NY: New York University Press.

Francis, A., Clarkin, J., & Perry, S. (1984). *Differential therapeutics in psychiatry.* New York, NY: Brunner/Mazel.

Galante, R., & Foa, E. (1986). An epidemiological study of psychic trauma and treatment effectiveness of children after a natural disaster. *Journal of the American Academy of Child Psychiatry, 25,* 357–363.

Goldfried, M. R. (1980). Toward a delineation of therapeutic change principles. *American Psychologist, 35,* 991–999.

Goldfried, M. R. (2001). *How therapists change: Personal and professional reflections.* Washington, DC: American Psychological Association.

Goldstein, A. P., & Stein, N. (1976). *Prescriptive psychotherapies.* New York, NY: Pergamon Press.

Hansen, S., Meissler, K., & Ovens, R. (2000). Kids together: A group play therapy model for children with ADHD symptomatology. *Journal of Child and Adolescent Group Therapy, 10*(4), 191–211.

Hayes, S. C., & Gregg, J. (2001). Factors promoting and inhibiting the development and use of clinical practice guidelines. *Behavior Therapy, 32,* 211–217.

Hunsley, J., & Rumstein-McKean, O. (1999). Improving psychotherapeutic services via a randomized clinical trial. *Journal of Clinical Psychology, 55,* 507–517.

Kaduson, H. G., Cangelosi, D., & Schaefer, C. E. (Eds.). (1997). *The playing cure: Individualized play therapy for specific childhood problems.* Northvale, NJ: Aronson.

Kaduson, H. G., & Finnerty, K. (1995). Self-control game interventions for attention-deficit-hyperactivity disorder. *International Journal of Play Therapy, 4,* 15–29.

Kazdin, A. A., Siegel, T. C., & Bass, D. (1990). Drawing on clinical practice to inform research on child and adolescent psychotherapy: Survey of practitioners. *Professional Psychology: Research and Practice, 21*(3), 189–198.

Kearney, C., & Silverman, W. (1999). Functionally based prescriptive and nonprescriptive treatment for children and adolescents with school refusal behavior. *Behavior Therapy, 30,* 673–695.

King, N. J., Mallory, G., & Ollendick, T. M. (1998). Emotive imagery treatment for children's phobias: A credible and empirically validated intervention. *Behavioral and Cognitive Psychotherapy, 26,* 103–115.

Knell, S. M. (2000). Cognitive-behavioral play therapy for childhood fears and phobias. In H. Kaduson, & C. Schaefer (Eds.), *Short-term play therapy for children* (pp. 3–27). New York, NY: Guilford Press.

Lambert, M. J., & Bergin, A. (1994). The effectiveness of psychotherapy. In S. L. Garfield & A. E. Bergin (Eds.), *Handbook of psychotherapy and behavior change* (4th ed., pp. 143–189). New York, NY: Wiley.

Lochman, J. E., Fitzgerald, D. R., & Whidby, J. M. (1999). Anger-management with aggressive children. In C. E. Schaefer, (Ed.), *Short-term psychotherapy groups for children* (pp. 301–350). Northvale, NJ: Aronson.

Luborsky, L., Singer, B., & Luborsky, E. (1975). Comparative studies of psychotherapies: Is it true that "everyone has won and all must have prizes?" *Archives of Abnormal Psychiatry, 32,* 995–1008.

March, J. S., & Mulle, K. (1995). Manualized cognitive-behavioral psycho-therapy for obsessive-compulsive disorder in childhood. *Journal of Anxiety Disorders, 9,* 175–184.

Mendez, F. J., & Garcia, M. J. (1996). Emotional performances: A treatment package for childhood phobias. *Child and Family Behavior Therapy, 18,* 19–34.

Messer, S. B. (1992). A critical examination of belief structures in integrative and eclectic psychotherapy. In J. C. Norcross & M. R. Goldfried (Eds.), *Handbook of psychotherapy integration.* New York, NY: Basic Books.

Netel-Gilman, E., Siegner, S., & Gilman, R. (2000). The use of the "goodbye game" with bereaved children. In C. E. Schaefer & S. E. Reid (Eds.), *Game play* (2nd ed., pp. 213–232). New York, NY: Wiley.

Norcross, J. C. (Ed.). (1986). *Handbook of eclectic psychotherapy.* New York, NY: Brunner/Mazel.

Norcross, J. C. (1987). *Casebook of eclectic psychotherapy.* New York, NY: Brunner/Mazel.

Norcross, J. C. (1991). Prescriptive matching in psychotherapy: An introduction. *Psychology, 28,* 439–443.

Norcross, J. C. (1995). Dispelling the dodo bird verdict and the exclusivity myth in psychotherapy. *Psychotherapy, 32,* 500–504.

Norcross, J. C. (2005). A primer on psychotherapy integration. In J. C. Norcross & M. R. Goldfried (Eds.), *Handbook of psychotherapy integration* (2nd ed.). New York, NY: Oxford University Press.

Norcross, J. C., & Prochaska, J. O. (1988). A study of eclectic (and integrative) views revisited. *Professional Psychology: Research and Practice, 19*(2), 170–174.

Orlick, T. (1981). Positive socialization via cooperative games. *Developmental Psychology, 17,* 426–429.

Paul, G. (1967). Strategy of outcome research in psychotherapy. *Journal of Consulting Psychology, 31,* 109–119.

Pedro-Carroll, J. L., & Cowen, E. (1985). The children of divorce intervention project. *Journal of Consulting and Clinical Psychology, 53,* 603–611.

Phillips, R. D., & Landreth, G. L. (1995). Play therapists on play therapy: A report of methods, demographics and professional practice issues. *International Journal of Play Therapy, 4,* 1–26.

Prochaska, J. O., & Norcross, J. C. (1983). Contemporary psychotherapists: A national survey of characteristics, practices, orientations, and attitudes. *Psychotherapy: Theory, Research, and Practice, 20,* 161–173.

Rae, W. A., Werchel, F., & Sanner, J. H. (1989). The psychosocial impact of play on hospitalized children. *Journal of Pediatric Psychology, 14,* 611–627.

Ray, D. C., Schollelkorb, A., & Tsai, M. (2007). Play therapy with children exhibiting symptoms of attention deficit hyperactivity disorder. *International Journal of Play Therapy, 16*(2), 95–111.

Reddy, L. A., Files-Hall, T. M., & Schaefer, C. E. (2005). *Empirically based play interventions for children.* Washington, DC: American Psychological Association.

Rogers, S. J. (1991). A psychotherapeutic approach for young children with pervasive developmental disorders. *Comprehensive Mental Health Care, 1,* 91–108.

Schaefer, C. E. (1993). *The therapeutic powers of play.* Northvale, NJ: Aronson.

Schaefer, C. E., Jacobson, A. E., & Ghahramanlou, M. (2000). Play group therapy for social skills deficits in children. In H. G. Kaduson & C. E. Schaefer (Eds.), *Short-term play therapy for children* (pp. 296–334). New York, NY: Guilford Press.

Shadish, W. R., & Sweeney, R. B. (1991). Mediators and moderators in meta-analysis: There's a reason we don't let dodo birds tell us what psychotherapies should have prizes. *Journal of Consulting and Clinical Psychology, 59,* 883–893.

Smith, M. L., Glass, G. V., & Miller, T. I. (1980). *The benefits of psychotherapy.* Baltimore, MD: Johns Hopkins University Press.

Stevens, S. E., Hyman, M. T., & Allen, M. (2000). A meta-analysis of common and specific treatment effects across the outcome domain of the phase model of psychotherapy. *Clinical Psychology: Science and Practice, 7,* 275–290.

Van Fleet, R. (1994). Filial therapy for adoptive children and parents. In K. O'Connor & C. Schaefer (Eds.), *Handbook of play therapy* (Vol. 2, pp. 371–387). New York, NY: Wiley.

Van Fleet, R. (2000). Short-term play therapy for families with chronic illness. In H. Kaduson & C. Schaefer (Eds.), *Short-term play therapy for children.* New York, NY: Wiley.

Webster-Stratton, C., & Reid, M. (2003). Treating conduct problems and strengthening social and emotional competence in young children. The Dina Dinosaur Treatment Program. *Journal of Emotional and Behavioral Disorders, 11*(3), 130–143.

Webster-Stratton, C., & Reid, M. J. (2009). Parents, teachers, and therapists using child-centered play therapy and coaching skills to promote children's social and emotional competence and build positive relationships. In C. E. Schaefer (Ed.), *Play therapy for preschool children* (pp. 245–273). Washington, DC: American Psychological Association.

White, D. R., & Gauvin, L. (1999). Mildly to moderately overweight children and adolescents. In C. E. Schaefer (Ed.), *Short term psychotherapy groups for children.* (pp. 351–378). Northvale, NJ: Aronson.

Wolfberg, P. J., & Schuler, A. L. (1993). Integrated play groups: A model for promoting the social and cognitive dimensions of play in children with autism. *Journal of Autism and Developmental Disorders, 23,* 467–489.

Zambelli, G., & DeRosa, A. (1992). Bereavement support groups for school-age children: Theory, intervention and case example. *American Journal of Orthopsychiatry, 62,* 484–493.

Author Index

Subject Index —————————————

psychoanalytic approaches to, 43–56

therapeutic powers of. *See* Therapeutic powers of play

Play-Doh, 67, 137. *See also* Clay

Playing cards, 7, 137

Playrooms

cognitive-behavioral play therapy (CBPT), 316

group play therapy, 233, 234

Jungian analytical play therapy, 70, 72

overview, 6, 7

Positive affect, 18, 19, 97, 357

Positive emotion, 97

Posttraumatic stress disorder (PTSD)

death in play, 191

Release Play Therapy (RPT), 107, 110–111, 116–118, 120, 125

release therapy, 372

Power/control

Experiential Play Therapy (EPT), 187–191

Gestalt play therapy, 179, 180

therapeutic powers of play, 97, 357

Preschool children, 6, 20, 148, 234, 243, 244, 258, 291, 313–315, 325

Prescriptive play therapy

clinical applications, 371–373

comprehensive assessment, 371

concepts, 365–368

core practices, 368–371

differential therapeutics, 365, 366

eclecticism, 22, 366, 367, 374

empirically supported treatments, 368, 369, 371–373

goals, 365

implementation challenges, 373, 374

in integrative play therapy, 355

integrative psychotherapy, 367

overview, 22, 365, 374

practice guidelines, 371–373

pragmatic approach, 371

prescriptive matching, 367, 368

therapeutic change mechanisms, 369–371

therapeutic powers of play, 369–371

therapist, role of, 211, 365, 373

therapist, training and competence of, 373

Problem solving, creative. *See* Creative problem solving

Projection, use of in Gestalt play therapy, 175, 179

Psychoanalytic approaches to play therapy

case example, 53–56

contemporary approaches, 47, 48

historical background, 43–47

overview, 56

play, conceptions of, 48–52

spoken language and, 49–52

therapeutic relationship, 47, 48, 52, 53

Psychoeducational intervention, 154, 155. *See also* Filial Therapy (FT)

Psychopathology

cognitive-behavioral play therapy, 315, 324

ecosystemic play therapy, 254, 353, 361

Gestalt therapy, 171

integrative theories, 350, 353, 361

Jungian analysis, 61, 64, 65, 69

Psychosis, 74

Puppets

Adlerian play therapy, 87, 94, 97, 101, 102

basic play materials, 7

child-centered play therapy, 137

cognitive-behavioral play therapy (CBPT), 316–319, 322–324

family play therapy, 211–223

Gestalt play therapy, 175, 178, 180, 185

Jungian analytical play therapy, 70, 72

solution-focused play therapy, 297, 302–307

Rapport building

stage of play therapy, 9

therapeutic powers of play, 21, 22, 97, 357

Reactive attachment disorder, 278, 304, 354, 372

Reality testing, 21, 97, 357, 370

Regression, in Experiential Play Therapy (EPT), 190, 195, 196, 198, 199

Relationship enhancement

adults, friendship with, 370

alliance, 370

attachment, 370

Filial Therapy, 161

peers, friendship with, 370

therapeutic powers of play, 4, 19, 97, 210, 357

Release Play Therapy (RPT)

case example, 120–123

clinical applications, 119, 120